WOMEN OF LIBERTY

Studies in Critical Social Sciences Book Series

Haymarket Books is proud to be working with Brill Academic Publishers (www.brill.nl) to republish the *Studies in Critical Social Sciences* book series in paperback editions. This peer-reviewed book series offers insights into our current reality by exploring the content and consequences of power relationships under capitalism, and by considering the spaces of opposition and resistance to these changes that have been defining our new age. Our full catalog of *SCSS* volumes can be viewed at https://www.haymarketbooks .org/series_collections/4-studies-in-critical-social-sciences.

WOMEN OF LIBERTY

STEVE J. SHONE

Haymarket Books
Chicago, IL

First published in 2019 by Brill Academic Publishers, The Netherlands.
© 2019 Koninklijke Brill NV, Leiden, The Netherlands

Published in paperback in 2020 by
Haymarket Books
P.O. Box 180165
Chicago, IL 60618
773-583-7884
www.haymarketbooks.org

ISBN: 978-1-64259-351-8

Distributed to the trade in the US through Consortium Book Sales and
Distribution (www.cbsd.com) and internationally through Ingram Publisher
Services International (www.ingramcontent.com).

This book was published with the generous support of Lannan Foundation and
Wallace Action Fund.

Special discounts are available for bulk purchases by organizations and
institutions. Please call 773-583-7884 or email info@haymarketbooks.org for
more information.

Cover design by Jamie Kerry and Ragina Johnson.

Printed in United States.

10 9 8 7 6 5 4 3 2 1

Library of Congress Cataloging-in-Publication Data is available.

Contents

         1   The Bible as a Weapon Used against
             Women   220
         2   Marriage and Divorce   227
         3   Self-Sovereignty and the Solitude of Self   230

8   Margaret Sanger: The Scientist of Human Salvation   239

         1   Sanger's Anarchist Influences   246
         2   Not a Marxist   253
         3   Not a Racist   255
         4   Birth Control and a New Morality   258

9   Forever an Anarchist: Mollie Steimer   265

         1   Russia Attacked: Two Leaflets   265
         2   Deported   275

Illustrations

Introduction

The intention of this work is to show the many overlaps between (mostly American) anarchist, libertarian, feminist, free love, and Anti-Federalist writings, while at the same time restricting the subject matter to women in order to emphasize the lack of attention given to many of these thinkers and their ideas in the past. Following a pattern used in an earlier book, *American Anarchism*, the goal in *Women of Liberty* is again to engage with and sometimes challenge the scholarly literature about each of the theorists.

Among the ideas of the ten women discussed here, there are voluminous overlaps. The book includes the first two women to run for Congress: Elizabeth Cady Stanton, who ran in New York City's Eighth US House of Representatives District in 1866, and Tennie C. Claflin, who stood for the same constituency a few years later. All ten nourished a strong belief in liberty, which as Mercy Otis Warren argued convincingly, was the only reason that the Patriots fighting for what would become the United States had been able to defeat the British. Thus it is unsurprising that both Louise Michel (on trial for many crimes associated with her role in the Paris Commune, including murder) and Mollie Steimer (accused of hurling seditious leaflets out of a window in New York City) refused to ask for leniency. Both Otis Warren and Cady Stanton sympathized with the plight of Ireland and criticized British oppression there. Victoria C. Woodhull, Claflin, Stanton, and Margaret Sanger were all admirers of John Stuart Mill. Both Woodhull and Steimer had their presses destroyed by authorities when they were charged, regardless of the fact they had not yet been convicted of a crime.

However, the thinkers described here also viewed freedom in a different way, in terms of the associations between women and men, and the many ways that a gendered society like the United States might be improved using a radical reinterpretation of what liberty meant. Woodhull, Claflin, Lois Waisbrooker, and Itō Noe each at some point in their lives advocated free love; Cady Stanton defended the position of Woodhull and its other supporters, and Itō was herself part of a four-way free love experiment. Woodhull, Claflin, Waisbrooker, and Sanger were committed to planned pregnancy and limiting how many children would be born, wanting them to be guaranteed a quality, healthy life, not just to exist as the result of an accident. Both Sanger and Rose Pesotta were attacked and demonized by the Catholic Church for their beliefs. The influence of Cady Stanton on the history of feminist thought was toned down and is less well known because she skillfully pointed out what she identified as the Bible's sexist preconceptions.

Waisbrooker was twice persuaded by her father to marry, relationships that both quickly failed; Pesotta emigrated to avoid a marriage set up by her parents; Itō agreed to a brief and immediately unsuccessful arranged marriage in order to be allowed to continue her education; Michel rejected two suitors while still a child. Cady Stanton had to persuade her own father to allow her to wed her husband, Henry Stanton. Accordingly, Michel, Woodhull, Claflin, and Waisbrooker compared marriage or marriage without love to prostitution.

Itō, Sanger, Pesotta, and Steimer each viewed Emma Goldman as a role model, while for Goldman herself, Michel was an inspirational hero. Itō, Pesotta, and Steimer were also influenced by the ideas of another anarchist, Peter Kropotkin. Pesotta was a friend of Steimer, and met both her (after she had been deported) and Goldman (who had also been deported) when she visited France. Sanger was involved with the League for the Amnesty of Political Prisoners, which complained about the conviction of Steimer for leafleting, and she also published an article about Michel (Mann 1914a, 1914b) in her periodical, *Woman Rebel*.

Today, the existence of the subfield of political theory is frequently questioned, as political science departments heavily influenced by admiration for statistical methods take the view that theory is incompatible, out-of-date, or not empirical or rigorous enough, or lacks "results," with some tenured political theorists retiring only to be replaced by someone who does a completely different type of research. This situation has not been helped by the subfield's persistence in presenting the history of ideas largely through the prism of a very small selection of white men chiefly from Athens, Rome, the United Kingdom, or the United States, a cast of characters that was mainly compiled in the distant past, with the particular reasons for the choices being hardly self-explanatory, and seldom clarified for students or even understood by those appointed to teach them. Fortunately, recent years have seen some interest in mixing in a few classical Confucian and Islamic thinkers as part of the canon, though in the absence of a more substantial and reflective revision, the newcomers will likely always linger on the periphery. A serious omission remains the contributions of women for, while they are often discussed in Women's Studies classes, teaching devoted to political philosophy within the traditionally mainstream areas of the academic world remains largely men-only, a place where the rather ignorant and unscientific views of Aristotle and Thomas Aquinas concerning females are given more than adequate space. As Offen pointed out, some time ago:

> We need critical editions of the complete works of feminist political writers in various languages – Stanton, Antoinette Brown Blackwell, Maria

Deraismes, Louise Otto-Peters, Ellen Key, and many others. Then – and only then – we can analyze and critique a full range of texts with the same attention and respect that have been given to the political writings of Rousseau, Kant, Marx, or Mill.

OFFEN 1989, 201

Additionally, while much time is devoted by political theorists in classrooms and scholarly journals alike to explicating the ideas of Machiavelli and the social contract theorists and their far from convincing arguments supporting the eventual eternal authority of governments; as well as to Marx, whose writings lie at the root of the slavery, imprisonment, genocide, inefficiency, and gobble-dygook that has characterized most communist systems; little attention, in an age of permanent conflict and the suffering of endless numbers of refugees, elected dictatorships, and widespread global poverty and discontent, is given to anarchist ideas or to their creators. Much as the present author is inclined to regard the more vulgar "number-crunching" sort of study that has come to dominate most of the other areas of political science skeptically as a species of anti-intellectualism that has the effect, intended or unintended, of glorifying the *status quo*, the fact remains that its potential rival, so-called (by its methodological opponents) "normative" political theory, remains relatively stagnant too, no longer addressing the serious problems faced by contemporary humankind; in that respect, it mirrors the inappropriate lack of relevance displayed by much of the rest of political science. One of the purposes of *Women of Liberty*, therefore, is to contribute an appreciation of both feminism and anarchism, and in particular, of the areas where they intersect, to a subfield (political theory) that many consider to have atrophied and to a discipline (political science) that increasingly has little to add to the actual study of politics. All ten of the women whose philosophies are described herein were admirers and exponents of liberty in one way or another, not just with respect to the characteristic anarchistic defense of individual freedom to live life as each person pleases, but also in the feminist sense that societal rules and conventions, and particularly those that regulate marriage and sexuality, oppress women, trapping them in relationships, subordinating and tying them to men, and thus eliminating any meaningful opportunity to be free.

A word about anarchism, a belief system that was embraced by eight of the ten thinkers included in this work – either fully, throughout their lives (Lois Waisbrooker, Itō Noe, Mollie Steimer, Rose Pesotta) or for a particularly significant and productive section of their lives (Louise Michel, Victoria C. Woodhull, Tennie C. Claflin, Margaret Sanger). Anarchism is *not* anarchy. Unfortunately, understandings of original or literal meanings of words can lead to gross misconstructions of what ideas generally mean in practice. Regardless of curt dictionary and police department-type definitions of what anarchism might denote, no anarchist intellectual has ever argued for zero government. The original classical Greek word, *anarkhiā*, does not mean "no government at all," just the absence of a leader. Rather, the commitment – if it is appropriate to speak of a commitment when describing a theory that is surprisingly wide-ranging and not at all constraining – is to allowing the individual, each person, the maximum ability to make their own decisions, unfettered by the power of others, uncoerced, though quite possibly in agreement with others under circumstances by which a compact could legitimately be negotiated, to exercise self-government in the absence of any other kind of authority, whose tendency is ever to restrict the liberty of the individual, and must always be oppressive, even if its intentions are good, which usually they are not.

Of course, throughout history, "anarchy" has been used denote anarchism, which adds to the confusion. Thus Louise Michel uses "anarchy" to describe the belief system to which she subscribes, and Victoria C. Woodhull, in her anarchist phase, denounces it. "Libertarian" is also a word that has been used to describe anarchist ideas. Today, despite the frequent application of the term to the philosophy of the Libertarian Party of the USA and similar "right-libertarian" perspectives, it is possible to consider anarchism as a form of "left-libertarian" thinking; certainly, there are many overlaps between anarchist perspectives and scholars who describe themselves as left-libertarian, who, for instance, advocate universal basic income (UBI), just as anarchists tend to follow Kropotkin in believing that every person should be guaranteed their most fundamental needs of housing, food, and access to education and healthcare.

The author is grateful to Nolan Bennett, Nicholas Buccola, Jenny B. Clark, Andrius Gališanka, Michael Gibbons, Nathan Jun, and Allison Rank for their helpful comments and valuable suggestions for improvement that have allowed him to refine many of the arguments presented in this volume. All errors should, of course, be blamed on the writer himself. An earlier version of Chapter Three was presented in San Francisco, California at the 2018 annual meeting of the Western Political Science Association. An alternate version of Chapter Five was presented in San Diego, California at the 2016 annual meeting of the Western Political Science Association.

Mercy Otis Warren (1728–1814), the subject of Chapter One, is chiefly respected for her work, *History of the Rise, Progress and Termination of the American Revolution*. A gifted historical writer, poet, playwright, and polemicist, she was a prominent Anti-Federalist critic of the US Constitution and of the second president, her friend and correspondent, John Adams. Under the influence of J.G.A. Pocock and other controversial revisionist interpreters of political history, Otis Warren is often presented as a "republican," even in recently published research. However, in the light of contemporary retreat from Pocockian formulations, this chapter asks whether it is still appropriate to consider her as a "republican," rather than as what she more clearly was, an unvarnished promoter of liberty.

The ideas and life of Louise Michel (1830–1905), one of the leaders of the highly inspirational Paris Commune, are discussed in Chapter Two. Following the crushing of the Commune by the national government, she was transported to New Caledonia, but eventually pardoned, returning to live in France, where she remained the object of much police surveillance. Scholars have quarreled about her romantic attachments or the lack of them, and the motivation for her views while she remains, atypically for a radical in the eyes of ordinary people, much admired as a symbol of freedom, a defender of the rights of poor people and animals alike, and in the second half of her life, an unabashed anarchist.

In her day, Victoria Claflin Woodhull (1838–1927), the first woman to run for US president and the theme of Chapter Three, was widely reported to be the person who "outed" an adulterous preacher, and she and her sister, Tennie C. Claflin, were celebrated as the first two women to work as stockbrokers. Notwithstanding her interest in anarchist ideas and her involvement with the First International, from which she was expelled by Karl Marx, Victoria's political ideas have received only limited attention. Consequently, much of the focus of this chapter is on Woodhull as a feminist political theorist, an aspect of her many accomplishments that is surely deserving of more scrutiny.

Chapter Four looks at Tennie C. Claflin (c. 1845–1923), whose life and contributions to political thought have long lain submerged in accounts of the much more widely known exploits of her sister. As with Victoria, Tennie's activities during her life, including her probable affair with Cornelius Vanderbilt and eventual marriage to wealthy Lord Cook, were often considered scandalous and they attracted more attention than her ideas, as did her appearance, which writers in newspapers and memoirs often went to great trouble to describe. The consideration of Claflin's beliefs presented in this chapter reveals her original analysis of the way women dress and of the nature of seduction, and her opinions about marriage, illegitimacy, prudery, and prostitution.

Today, few scholars are familiar with the thought of Lois Waisbrooker (1826–1909), the topic of Chapter Five, a prolific writer and radical activist whose ideas have been credited to the influences of spiritualism, anarchism, and feminism. Here it is argued that the key to Waisbrooker's political philosophy, from the perspective of which she came to regard voting as being a pointless activity, is her rejection of marriage as a failed institution that of necessity will always oppress women, while, in reality, Nature demands that women should be the ones who take charge of raising the next generation.

Itō, Noe (1895–1923), obliged to endure a brief marriage arranged by her parents from which she quickly escaped, was an ardent anarchist, much-influenced by Emma Goldman, who like her idol criticized conventional societal rules that condemned women to lives of gender inequality. In her fictional writing, and as the editor of *Seitō*, Itō, the focus of Chapter Six, championed more modern insights, questioning Taishō era norms regarding marriage and celibacy, before being murdered along with her lover, directly or indirectly at the hands of the Japanese government.

Chapter Seven attempts to explain why the contributions of Elizabeth Cady Stanton (1815–1902), who seems today generally to be remembered just as a person who organized a conference on women's rights in Seneca Falls, New York's Wesleyan Chapel and produced a document there, the Declaration of Sentiments, are so questionably absent from the mainstream history of political thought. In reality, she was a major, multi-faceted, and intellectual contributor to feminist consciousness. Correspondingly, some of the emphasis here is upon her more radical and most important, but rarely discussed writings, *The Woman's Bible* and "The Solitude of Self."

Often attacked by conservative thinkers for promoting contraceptive use, smaller families, and the view that sex should no longer be considered mainly as a means for becoming pregnant, but rather as a way to achieve happiness, dignity, and autonomy, and also vilified by false charges that she was somehow a racist, Margaret Sanger (1879–1966), the topic of Chapter Eight, was a champion of women's rights around the globe who was in many respects substantially influenced by anarchist thought, which from time to time she praised.

Mollie Steimer (1897–1980) is the subject of Chapter Nine. She was one of the defendants in the important First Amendment case, *Abrams v. United States* (1919), which resulted in her deportation for distributing printed materials that criticized the US government's deployment of troops to Siberia. Steimer was a lifelong activist in favor of anarchism and the rights of poor people throughout the world, who was just as scathing about the excesses she found under V.I. Lenin's new and increasingly reactionary Soviet political system as she had been in New York. Finally, she was able to find a home in Mexico.

Chapter Ten looks at the life and ideas of Rose Pesotta (1896–1965), who like Steimer was an immigrant to the United States from Ukraine, and who, though an active defender of other anarchists subject to deportation on the basis of their radical activities, expressed her own anarchist and feminist beliefs differently, through the medium of labor activism, often representing poor, minority seamstresses in hard-fought strikes. Despite her considerable tactical ingenuity and frequent success in this role, she remained limited in what she could achieve within her own union due to constant gender-based discrimination against her on the part of many of her male colleagues.

ILLUSTRATION 1   Mercy Otis Warren, by John Singleton Copley. Painting, oil on canvas, circa 1763
PHOTO: WIKIMEDIA COMMONS. CURRENT LOCATION OF ARTWORK: MUSEUM OF FINE ARTS, BOSTON, USA.

Mercy Otis Warren, the So-Called "Republican" Patriot

Born at Otis Farm on Cape Cod, in Barnstable, Massachusetts in 1728, in an area now known as West Barnstable, Mercy Otis Warren was one of thirteen children, the most famous of whom is James Otis, Jr., a lawyer who made one of the first intellectual contributions to what would become the American Revolution with his argument, in 1761, before the Massachusetts Supreme Judicial Court (which was known at the time of the case and until 1780 as the Superior Court of Judicature), against "taxation without representation." Mercy's mother, Mary Allyne (or Allyn), lived for a while in Wethersfield, Connecticut, home to a prison that Tocqueville would visit[1]; she was born in Plymouth in 1702, a decade after the merger of the Plymouth and Massachusetts Bay colonies. Mercy's father, James Otis, Sr., who married Mary in Wethersfield in 1724, was born in Barnstable and was the same age as his wife; although educated informally, he worked as a lawyer, frequently appearing in the Barnstable Court, becoming a member of the colony's legislature in 1745, advancing rapidly, and serving as lower house Speaker (Brown 1896, 10, 11, 12; Davies 2005, 3; Hutcheson 1953, 379; Roberts 2008, 134; Stuart 2008, 5; Waters 1975, 63, 68–76; Zagarri 1995, 5). For Davies (2005, 2, 22, 189), life in Cape Cod at the time – or even, as she argues, citing the perspective of Otis Warren's correspondent, Hannah Winthrop, who herself lived only a few miles away from Boston in Cambridge, life in Cambridge – was to reside outside of the metropolitan mainstream and to be isolated from its most recent cultural developments. Nonetheless, the Otis family had an important role to play in the life and history of the colony. Growing up, Mercy was very close to her brother, James Jr., the eldest of the children, whom she and other associates called Jemmy. In fact, the nickname became widely known, with political opponents even publishing a critical song about him that was called "Jemmibullero" (Richards 1995, 9; Waters 1975, 63).

James Otis, Jr. (1725–1783) benefited from a childhood education from his uncle, the Rev. Jonathan Russell, the pastor of West Barnstable church, a very well-educated tutor, who introduced him to classical languages and authors,

---

1   When Tocqueville and Gustave de Beaumont visited Boston, they were welcomed at the home of Harrison Gray Otis, the nephew of Mary Otis Warren; she had died almost two decades before.

preparing him for his later legal studies at Harvard. Informally, Mercy derived
great benefit from being present with her brother in Russell's house, being able
to access the minister's library, and from her many conversations with Jemmy.
Despite the significant disadvantage that accrued from being female, she was
able to grow up reading Shakespeare, Milton, Sir Walter Raleigh, and other
prominent writers. Later, when Jemmy became an undergraduate, his discussions with Mercy continued, partly through their correspondence, and, in
consequence, so did her familiarity with high culture, including many works
by Greek and Roman authors (Brown 1896, 27–28; Davies 2005, 5; Hutcheson
1953, 379; Stuart 2008, 4, 13; Waters 1975, 74; Zagarri 1995, 13–15).

1   The Legacy of Mercy's Brother

James Otis, Jr. was regarded by many of his contemporaries, including John
Adams, as one of the most influential political thinkers of the time, and even
as the original cerebral instigator of the American Revolution. Mercy comments in her *History of the Rise, Progress and Termination of the American
Revolution, Interspersed with Biographical, Political and Moral Observations*
[hereafter referred to as her *History*] that her brother "may justly claim the
honor of laying the foundation of a revolution, which has been productive of
the happiest effects to the civil and political interests of mankind" (Warren
1805a, 46). Between 1762 and 1765, Jemmy produced five significant political
treatises, including *The Rights of the British Colonies Asserted and Proved* (1765),
in which he asked, for example, "Are not women born as free as men? Would it
not be infamous to assert that the ladies are all slaves by nature?" (Otis 1765, 5).
Thus Otis' subsequent mental decline was a significant loss for the community
at large, for few of his contemporaries were able, at the time, to articulate what
would come to be viewed as fundamental libertarian and feminist concerns, or
to match what many of them, including John Adams, saw as his eloquence, a
style that Adams tried to copy. Jemmy's influence and importance quickly
faded (Farrell 2006, 536; Ferguson 1979, 195, 213–214; Kerber 1986, 30–31;
McCullough 2001, 49; McIlwain 1931, 540; Samuelson 1999, 522–523).

The deterioration in James Otis, Jr.'s mental capacity appears to have been
the consequence of a chance assault. He had published an article criticizing
the excessive power of the four locally based British commissioners of the customs to conduct searches of buildings for contraband at any time they wished,
and without specific court sanction, using warrants known as writs of assistance; this was a practice that angered business owners. "Assistance" referred
to the fact that, to participate in these activities, the customs agents could

request the help of nearby law enforcement. Jemmy's venting led, shortly afterwards, to a violent response by some of the royal customs officers in question, an act that took place in the British Coffee House in Boston where he was meeting with a friend. Believing Jemmy, who was wounded in the head, to be dead, his attackers left the area on a ship. Although he survived, James Otis, Jr. was never the same again, the assault having apparently damaged his brain (Breen 1998, 378; Brown 1896, 39, 45–46; Farrell 2006, 535; Hutcheson 1953, 381; McCullough 2001, 61–62; Warren 1805a, 63). Later, Mercy Otis Warren (1805a, 62) would refer to this attack on her brother as "the attempted assassination of the celebrated Mr. Otis, justly deemed the first martyr to American freedom." Jemmy's supporters considered implementing their own fierce response to the beating, but decided to forgo this option, which may have proved counterproductive to their cause (Maier 1991, 124). In her book about Mercy Otis Warren, Stuart (2008, 27) writes that "[o]mitted from Mercy's *History*, which extolled Jemmy as James "the Patriot" Otis and "the first champion, of American freedom," was his increasingly erratic behavior." However, this point is hard to reconcile with Otis Warren's account of the attack on her brother – for example, with the following comment:

> Mr. Otis lived to see the independence of America, though in a state of mind incapable of enjoying fully the glorious event which his own exertions had precipitated. After several years of mental derangement, as if in consequence of his own prayers, his great soul was instantly set free by a flash of lightning, from the evils in which the love of his country had involved him.
>
> WARREN 1805a, 64

On a single day in February 1761, the case of the merchants against the royal customs collectors was heard, with Otis giving a four-hour speech against the practice of employing general (rather than specific) writs of assistance. The oratory took place before five judges of the Superior Court of Judicature, one of whom, the presiding judge, was Chief Justice (former Lieutenant Governor and future Royal Governor) Thomas Hutchinson. It was an argument that was at once both breathtakingly radical and yet arguably already out of date, a presentation either of tremendous significance or one largely irrelevant to the subsequent unfolding of history. Although general writs of assistance had been used in Massachusetts in the past, the death of King George II provided a tactical opportunity to review and criticize the practice, because a 1702 statute required that all writs be reissued under the authority of the new monarch, George III. In order to be able to represent the interests of Massachusetts businesses (a duty he shared with Oxenbridge Thacher, who, in his speech, questioned the authority of the court to hear the case), Jemmy gave up his current position as acting advocate general. The government was represented by Jeremiah (or Jeremy) Gridley, in whose Boston legal office Jemmy had in the mid-1840s studied the law (Brown 1896, 30, 40–41; Farrell 2006, 535–536; Frese 1957, 496–497; Waters 1975, 113; Zagarri 1995, 32–33).

The court proceedings were not recorded, and today some of what is known of the specifics of the deliberations derives from a recreation of Jemmy's comments that John Adams made from the notes that he took while sitting among the substantial audience who were in attendance. Later, Adams would complain to Mercy Otis Warren that her discussion of her brother's trial performance in her *History* made no mention of his efforts to reconstruct its content (Farrell 2006, 534, 537–538). Arguing forcibly against slavery, and for equal rights for slaves and women, and invoking a particularly libertarian interpretation of the unwritten British Constitution, Otis distinguished between special and general writs of assistance, claiming that general writs were unconstitutional. Moreover, he argued, they violated people's basic liberties that were sanctioned by natural law. Here, Otis advanced the view that if a government practice violated the Constitution, it must be stopped (McCullough 2001, 132–133; Zagarri 1995, 32–33). As Breen (1998, 379) points out, the notion that every individual, regardless of race or gender, possesses a number of basic rights that can never be usurped by government, is to apply the arguments of John Locke to the circumstances of the American colonies. In *The Rights of the British Colonies Asserted and Proved*, Otis (1765, 33–34) quotes Locke's argument that the people retain the right to remove a government that strays from representation of its needs, and later (98–99) restates this Lockean perspective, continuing that, if the fiduciary character of the citizenry's delegation of powers is violated, as it appears to have been by the imposition on the American colonies of taxation without representation, then the constitutional set-up itself, the permission of all the people to the governing institutions to rule, comes to an end (Brennan 1939, 697). Otis writes:

> The sum of my argument is, That civil government is of God: that the administrators of it were originally the whole people: that they might have devolved it on whom they pleased: that this devolution is fiduciary, for the good of the whole: that by the British constitution, this devolution is on the King, lords and commons.
>
> OTIS 1765, 98

Otis went beyond Locke, and indeed beyond the Levellers, who had advanced an argument for near-unanimous adult male suffrage, with his contention that inquired, "had not apple-women and orange-girls as good a right to give their respectable suffrages for a new king as" men? (Breen 1998, 387; Kerber 1992, 353; Otis 1765, 8). If today, we returned to the state of nature, would we not, Otis wonders, include women among those allowed to participate in political decisions? Within the bounds of the existing social contract, he asks, "Who acted for infants and women, or who appointed guardians for them? Had these guardians power to bind both infants and women during life and their posterity after them?" (Otis 1765, 4, 8). His attention to gender exclusion represents a significant moment in the history of political thought.

In his speech, Jemmy quoted Sir Edward Coke, who, as the Chief Justice of the Court of Common Pleas in *Thomas Bonham v. College of Physicians* (1610) (often referred to as "Bonham's Case"), had maintained that, in order to eliminate conflict, courts should interpret laws that were "against common right or reason, or repugnant, or impossible to be performed." Some scholars have questioned the relevance of Lord Coke's words because he, unlike Otis, was not specifically addressing constitutional interpretation, and because, as Bailyn ([1967] 1992, 177, 180) has argued, by the eighteenth century, parliament was viewed as being supreme, and itself no longer operated as a court that could annul legislation on the grounds of constitutionality. However, Waters (1975, 134) is surely correct that the citation of Coke remained valid as "a means to an end." For Samuelson, also, complaints of inconsistency in this respect miss the point:

> Unlike Adams, Otis knew that the American constitutional case had already lost when the Stamp Act Congress convened in 1765. The central intellectual project of his career was not a stalled effort to elaborate American rights, or to resolve the ideological tensions latent in the Whig tradition, but a failed effort to solve the imperial crisis.
> SAMUELSON 1999, 523

On the other hand, Wilcox (2012, 7) stresses the constitutional focus of Otis' written work, suggesting that *The Rights of the British Colonies Asserted and Proved* "vociferously attacked the Sugar Act and Stamp Act as not merely economically detrimental but as violations of "the fundamental principles of law.""

The almost immediate response to Jemmy's performance in this speech before the Superior Court of Judicature was his election to the lower house of the legislature, the Massachusetts General Court (Brennan 1939, 691–692). However, Otis was soon viewed as having changed his mind, and the apparent about-turn in his analyses came to be connected with the mental illness that would later afflict his life and which may have been occasioned by the attack on him by the customs collectors. For example, Waters (1975, 184) writes that he "had been one of the first to recognize the grounds for separation from England, but he had fled from his own reasoning." Breen (1998, 398) argues that, "it must be admitted that on the subject of parliamentary sovereignty Otis really was wildly inconsistent, sometimes calling for constitutional review of parliamentary statutes, a truly original argument, but just as frequently lavishly praising the British legislature." At the time, John Adams reported that "[h]e was called a reprobate, an apostate, and a traitor, in every street in Boston'" (John Adams, letter to William Tudor, March 11, 1818, in Adams 1856, 295; Ferguson 1979, 194). It is generally believed that Otis himself saw no such contradiction in his position, but many contemporaries viewed him as a turncoat for, notwithstanding his arguments in the writs of assistance case, insisting upon loyalty to the British crown. However, Brennan (1939, 700) argues that he was mainly objecting to "justifying revolution against arbitrary power"; such an explanation would not indicate any inconsistency in Jemmy's opinion. Samuelson (1999, 502–503) makes a similar argument, pointing out that, despite his radical argument in favor of natural rights, Otis believed also that it was wrong to attempt to usurp the British Parliament's authority by force. Ferguson (1979, 196, 197) sees this continued allegiance to the sovereign, even though he had capably delineated the monarchy's conspicuous failings, as evidence of a Hobbesian influence on Jemmy's thinking, whereby the initial act of consent to a government binds subjects forever to the decisions subsequently made by the Leviathan in question. Once again, such an interpretation would spare Mercy's brother from allegations that he contradicted himself.

Despite the problems caused by his mental illness, Jemmy came close to being elected as Speaker, an example that Ellen E. Brennan (1939, 724) uses to illustrate her point that he "continued his usefulness to the American cause, though with occasional instability, until 1771." Nonetheless, for John Adams, the fact that Otis gave long, often incomprehensible speeches was evidence that his illness was substantial. Adams points out that Jemmy spent an hour telling an anecdote that could be completed by someone else in three minutes (Adams [1768–1770] 1961, diary entry of January 16, 1770; McCullough 2001, 62). However, this focus on Otis' mental incapacity can be seen as an undesirable method of assessing his contribution to the intellectual thought of the late eighteenth century:

> It is here that we encounter a bizarre litany of charges leveled by historians more interested in Otis's character than in his ideas. Poor Otis, we are told, was always unstable, and perhaps even mad. It has been suggested that he lacked the imagination to anticipate the events of 1776. He wrote

in a crabbed, sometimes incoherent style. He mired himself in a tedious legal discussion over parliamentary sovereignty.

BREEN 1998, 396

Rather, like Breen, Samuelson argues:

The most interesting and underappreciated part of Otis's thought lies not in his madness, but rather in his efforts to think his way out of the imperial problem. His failure was so poignant not because he could not understand what was driving the crisis about him, as the conventional reading has it, but rather because he understood the problems of the day only too well.

SAMUELSON 1999, 493

Regardless of the disappointing final years of his life and the psychiatric issues that may have influenced his behavior, James Otis' intellectual contribution remains considerable even when looked at from the standpoint of the twenty-first century, and his influence on his sister, Mercy Otis Warren, was also substantial.

2   Jemmy's Sister: Never a Servile Servian

In November, 1754, at the age of 26, Mercy Otis married James Warren, a politically active lawyer and merchant, who would serve as a general in the Continental Army, fighting at the battle of Bunker Hill, and then become president of the Massachusetts Provincial Congress, the colony's autonomous legislature of the Revolutionary period. As might be expected, their union meant that Mercy must subvert some of her own interests to those of her husband. But, as Richards (1995, 4) observes, the Warrens were nevertheless "a loving, supportive, compatible couple, who, if they quarreled, never did so in public." Mercy had achieved self-development through interaction with her brother Jemmy, and she was able to continue that process from within a successful and high-flying marriage. As talk of rebellion increased, Mercy Otis Warren often found herself near the center of it, and she had some ability to contribute to the doctrines being evolved. Her home in Massachusetts was used for meetings of the Sons of Liberty Patriot group. Plymouth-born James Warren had possibly encountered Jemmy at Harvard, where he completed his studies two years after Mercy's brother had left (Baym 1991a, 31–32; Brown 1896, 31, 33–35; Cohen 1994, 9; Davies 2005, 188; Smith 1966, 36).

Both James and Mercy Warren were *Mayflower* descendants. Mercy was the great-great granddaughter of an indentured servant called Edward Doty (his name is also given as Doten or Dotey, and additional spellings are used in county records). Doty signed the Mayflower Compact, although, during the voyage, he had attempted to mutiny (Brown 1896, 13; Davies 2005, 183; Stuart 2008, 7, 20; Zagarri 1995, 5). Doty was also an ancestor of James Warren, so James and Mercy were cousins, with the 1662 marriage of Doty's son, also called Edward, to Sarah Founce producing sisters Sarah Doty, the grandmother of Mercy's husband, and Mary Doty, the grandmother of Mercy (Stuart 2008, 20). Brown (1896, 33) notes that James was also the descendant of Richard Warren who, like Doty, arrived in the Western hemisphere on the *Mayflower*, and Stuart (2008, 21) writes that "the Warrens descended from two Plymouth settlers, *Mayflower* passengers Edward Dotey and Richard Warren." Richard Warren lived in Plymouth, and had many surviving children and therefore many descendants. Mercy's husband, James Warren was a descendant of Richard Warren's son, Nathaniel, and his wife, Sarah Walker (Warren 1895, 6, 10, 11).

James and Mercy Warren had five children, all boys: James, Jr., Winslow, Charles, Henry, and George, three of whom died in their youth (Brown 1896, 37–38, 47; Cohen 1994, 8). Saxton (2009, 25) contends that Mercy's ability to contribute to ongoing political developments was harmed by a psychological condition that at times caused her significant self-doubt, a predicament that she shared with two of her sons as well as her brother Jemmy. Like Jemmy, James Warren was quite radical, even for an Anti-Federalist, and eventually his sympathy for the predicament of the farmers of the Shays Rebellion, if not for their methods, put him on the opposite side even to John and Samuel Adams, who saw all forcible resistance as a threat to their new republic (Cima 2000, 489; Cohen 1994, 8; Richards 1995, 19; Stoll 2008, 222, 228; Stuart 2008, 87).

It was Mercy's husband who had first suggested the creation of Committees of Correspondence in a private conversation that took place at his own house when Samuel Adams was visiting. The Committees were centers of opposition to colonial policies that eventually developed into informal government bodies, coordinating resistance to British rule. From its origins in Plymouth, this original medium for defiance swiftly spread to the other colonies. In Massachusetts, the state Committee, which was formed in 1772, consisted of fifteen persons, including both John Adams and James Warren. It was on this Committee that the arrangements for the First Continental Congress were developed (Brown 1896, 61; Smith 1966, 83; Stoll 2008, 108; Warren 1805a, 72; 324, fn. *). As Otis Warren noted in her *History*:

> Perhaps no single step contributed so much to cement the union of the colonies, and the final acquisition of independence, as the establishment of committees of correspondence. This supported a chain of communication from New Hampshire to Georgia, that produced unanimity and energy throughout the continent.
>
> WARREN 1805a, 71

Gradually, however, James Warren's influence faded reciprocally as the progress of revolutionary action increased. Ultimately, his commitment to the goal led to his dissatisfaction with the new institutions that developed during the Revolutionary War and after independence had been achieved. Smith writes:

> During the years after the war when his old friends looked upon him with suspicion, Warren undoubtedly felt that he was upholding the real principles of the Revolution and that men like John Adams had deserted the cause they had entered upon together.
>
> SMITH 1966, 37

Eventually, like Mercy and many other Anti-Federalists who opposed the new Constitution, he became identified as one of the "Old Patriots" or "Old Republicans" who believed that the new nation had left him and the revolt's original values behind. But although Mercy would in 1788 criticize the coming Constitution in her *Observations on the New Constitution and on the Federal and State Conventions. By a Columbian Patriot* [hereafter referred to as her *Observations*], eventually the addition of a Bill of Rights would make her more accepting of it, so the approach of her *History*, where she (1805b, 236) writes that "[p]erhaps genius has never devised a system more congenial to their wishes, or better adapted to the condition of man, than the American constitution," is quite different (Cornell 1999, 53, 55; Roberts 2008, 135; Shaffer 1975, 149; Smith 1966, 109; Warren 1805b, 214, 236; Zagarri 1995, 120). Consequently, she has been interpreted as follows:

> Her ambivalence was reflected in a rambling, sometimes contradictory commentary on the genesis of the national government.
>
> SHAFFER 1975, 146–147

Just as she had corresponded with her brother at Harvard, Mercy also wrote letters in the early years of her marriage, and her contacts came to include many important figures of the American Revolution. She corresponded with both John and Abigail Adams; Hannah Winthrop, who was married to Harvard science professor, John Winthrop; Catharine Macaulay, the author of the controversial *The History of England from the Accession of James I to that of the Brunswick Line* (completed in 1783, and referred to subsequently in this chapter as her *History of England*), and a supporter of independence for the American colonies; Martha Custis Washington; Dorothy Quincy Hancock, the wife of John Hancock; Thomas Jefferson; Elbridge Gerry; and John Dickinson (Baym 1991a, 27; Brown 1896, 55, 56; Cohen 1994, 10; Fleming 2009, 47; Shaffer 1975, 105). Later, she would write polemical plays and poems that advanced the Patriot cause, as well as the two political works referred to above: the anonymously published Anti-Federalist *Observations* ([1788] 1888), which was for a long time and sometimes still is attributed to Gerry, and the extensive *History* (1805a, 1805b). As Baym (1991b) points out, part of Otis Warren's significance is that of all "the many Massachusetts intellectuals who wrote to support the patriot cause before and during the American Revolution," she "was the only woman." Her personal intrusions into the intellectual activities of Massachusetts were largely anonymous until she reached her sixties and in 1790 published her book, *Poems, Dramatic and Miscellaneous*, under the name "Mrs. M. Warren" (Cima 2000, 492; Warren 1790, i).

Today, Otis Warren is mostly remembered for the originally three-volume *History*, which has today been re-divided by Lester H. Cohen into a two volume edition, which is the version used for the present chapter. Alice Brown, the author of the late nineteenth century, first biography of Mercy, notes that the latter would likely have felt it to be "the crowning labor of her life, the evidence through which it should afterwards be weighed" (Brown 1896, 191). It is the acuity of the remarks contained in that pioneering attempt at historical scholarship that persuades Stuart (2008, 6) to write that "[h]er strong beliefs, captured in print, made her muse of the revolution." Cohen (1994, 6) calls Otis Warren "the most formidable female intellectual in eighteenth-century America." However, political perspective and differing understandings of what constitutes good historical writing have long influenced the evaluations of her work.

Although the current president, Thomas Jefferson, subscribed to several copies and encouraged others in the federal government to do the same, and John Dickinson and the Harvard librarian, James Winthrop, both also liked her *History* very much, other political leaders declined to purchase it, either because they disagreed with her steadfastly polemical, Anti-Federalist, or allegedly "republican" views, or because another work appeared at the same time: John Marshall's *Life of George Washington*, published between 1804 and 1807; despite its name, Marshall's study is really an early history of the United States

(Baym 1991b; Fleming 2009, 195; Hutcheson 1953, 379; Reif 1960, 132; Roberts 2008, 134; Smith 1966, 38–40). Cohen (1994, 12) points out that some readers were disdainful of the work because its author was female, and Shaffer (1975, 3) argues that her gender was a reason why Otis Warren herself expected little political gain from the publication of her great creation.

For John Adams, what he saw as the *History*'s political slant, including its sympathies for the Jeffersonian Republicans rather than with the Federalists, was almost too much to bear, and he told its author that he felt that it "has been written to the taste of the nineteenth century, and accommodated to gratify the passions, prejudices, and feelings of the party who are now predominant" (John Adams, letter to Mercy Warren, August 15, 1807, in Adams [1878] 1972, 463; Cohen 1994, 318, fn. 27). In response, Otis Warren suggested that the real "party rancor" lay with those Federalists whose response to the publication of her book had been to attempt to assassinate her character (Mercy Warren, letter to John Adams, August 27, 1807, in Adams [1878] 1972, 489). For Smith (1966, 37), the Warren family's turn against the former president could not be explained completely independently of its own political decline, which was to some extent occasioned by Federalist disapproval, and by John Adams himself, as a result of the Warrens' sympathy for the Shays farmers. The issue of her husband's failure to be appointed to another political position by the second president would also be discussed in the correspondence between Adams and Otis Warren, with Adams telling Mercy that he was unable to nominate her husband, for example to be the customs dues collector in Plymouth, because it was certain that the Senate would overrule him (John Adams, letter to Mercy Warren, August 19, 1807, in Adams [1878] 1972, 476).

In her *History*, Otis Warren referred disparagingly to Alexander Hamilton, who was born on the Caribbean island of Nevis, as "a young officer of foreign extraction" (Warren 1805b, 216). She saw in Treasury Secretary Hamilton's economic ideas, in particular, a vision of a future United States where an intensely capitalist society would develop, rendering some people rich, but making it impossible for a much greater number to survive. In the early years of independence, such avaricious motivations had "created a rage for project, speculation, and various artifices, ... which finally ruined multitudes of unsuspecting citizens" (217). This characterization of Hamilton's monetary policy, which included developing a pro-business environment; acceptance of great differences between the wealth of citizens, with unlucky people being burdened by debt; and the planned creation of a national bank, as a boon for speculators and a danger to society – a phenomenon currently experienced in post-independence New England through the medium of inflation – was what prompted Mercy's vehemence here (Davies 2005, 254; Friedman and Shaffer

1975, 195; Hutcheson 1953, 398; Shaffer 1975, 13; Smith 1966, 112; Stuart 2008, 214–215). As an alternative, in the *History* she advocated "a confederacy which ought ever to be cemented by a union of interest and affection, under the influence of those principles which obtained their independence" (Warren 1805a, 28).

To evaluate Mercy Otis Warren's enterprise in her *History*, it is necessary to ask what she was trying to achieve. Disagreeing with John Adams, who had seen the work as being impaired by nineteenth-century, Jeffersonian concerns, Hutcheson instead locates its focus in an earlier time:

> Mercy Warren's work is a product of the eighteenth century, when the function of the historian was to record rather than interpret, and to trace the hand of God in events instead of the working of natural laws.
>
> HUTCHESON 1953, 397

For Richards (1995, 127), however, her message is instead timeless; Otis Warren is telling "a somewhat progressive moral story," in which the characters who framed the American Revolution present evidence, as demonstrated by their attitudes and behavior, of moral success and decline. Similarly, Cohen (1980, 203) comments that "her *History* is not merely a reflection of her personal concerns and convictions; it is also a work of moral art." However, from the perspective of Baym, the work is one of hyperbole:

> The *History* is a crabby, tendentious, outspoken work whose melodramatic narrative presents the monarchist British as monsters and the republican Americans as paragons.
>
> BAYM 1991a, 32

On the other hand, Shaffer contends that Warren was much more balanced, a critic willing to fight the Constitution's perceived defects from within the system, and essentially just a supporter of the Jeffersonians, who "was not advocating that the political or social system be changed. The implicit assumption bent of her criticism was simply to vote the rascals out" (Shaffer 1975, 41).

Clearly, a major thesis to be found in Mercy Otis Warren's *History* is one of American moral decline. At times, she hints at a stages theory of humanity's historical development, such as that of Adam Ferguson, the Scottish Enlightenment author of *An Essay on the History of Civil Society* (1767), with whose work she might been familiar.[2] Ferguson, like Mercy, saw the potential of

---

2   Unlike his intellectual ally, John Witherspoon, who moved to the United States in 1768, and would later be one of the signers of the Declaration of Independence, Ferguson was

luxury to undermine a developed civilization; he envisaged societies moving progressively through rude/savage, barbaric, and civil/polished stages, with the final stage being one of restrained capitalism (Ferguson 1767, part 6; Maloyed 2010, 65–85; Pocock [1975] 2003, 499–501). Otis Warren describes some human qualities as being instinctual, whereas other refinements such as patriotism grow along with the development of society. However, eschewing the optimism of many utopian writers who saw the final, most developed stage of humanity as being the most beneficial, Mercy is, like Ferguson, more concerned about the danger that, at a certain point in time, "refinement is wrought to a height that poisons and corrupts the mind" (Warren 1805a, 89). Greed and ambition may eventually develop to such a degree that the process can then be seen as reversing itself, as the more prosperous individual "reverts back to selfish barbarism, and feels no check to his rapacity and boundless ambition, though his passions may be frequently veiled under various alluring and deceptive appearances" (89). Otis Warren's skepticism, like that of Ferguson, tells her that conflict delivers social outcomes uncontemplated by those involved in the action. In the case of the American colonies, the goals of self-sacrificing patriots have quickly become eclipsed as the pursuit of wealth and luxury and rivalry to achieve political position have caused many to be unsatisfied with the limited bounty of the continent. This transformation has occurred at a pace that nobody could have anticipated (Warren 1805a, 30, 41, 1805b, 180–181). At first, the European settlers in the Western hemisphere lived in organized communities that also achieved a harmony with nature, particularly in New England, where class divisions were not great (Cima 2000, 494; Shaffer 1975, 76, 81; Smith 1966, 77, 79, fn 14). Smith (1966, 77) comments that, for Otis Warren, "[t]he archetype of the colonial citizen was the independent, educated farmer whose means were adequate to satisfy his desires." After all, for her (1805a, 89), the settlers in Massachusetts and nearby colonies "were as far advanced in civilization, policy, and manners ... in their ideas of government, the nature of compacts, and the bands of civil union, as any of their neighbors at that period among the most polished nations of Europe."

Davies (2005, 223) notes that Mercy's skepticism extended not only to the rapid development of commerce that she saw happening around her in Massachusetts, but also to the corruption of leaders' characters, of which John Hancock was a prominent example. For Otis Warren, Hancock symbolized the dangers of excessive luxury as well as illustrating the consequences of poor

---

dispatched to the colonies in 1778 to try and end the American Revolution. As President of the College of New Jersey (which would later become Princeton University), Witherspoon used Ferguson's *An Essay on the History of Civil Society* as a textbook in a course on moral philosophy that he taught; one of the students in that class was James Madison.

leadership. Lambasting him as a politician who had succeeded by the distribution of patronage, she commented in the *History* that he was, after all, not a natural leader, but a person "of more external accomplishments than real abilities" (Warren 1805a, 112; Zagarri 1995, 102, 103).

For Mercy Otis Warren, the settlers of North America – even if their standard of living was superior to that of their cousins back in Europe – were virtuous and hard-working, and lived relatively simple lives. She writes:

> Happily for America, the inhabitants in general possessed not only the virtues of native courage and a spirit of enterprise, but minds generally devoted to the best affections. Many of them retained this character to the end of the conflict by the dereliction of interest, and the costly sacrifices of health, fortune and life.
>
> WARREN 1805a, 99

As Barkalow (2009, 9) notes, "Americans were uncontaminated by foreign luxury, the intricacies of foreign policies, or the theological jargon of metaphysical skeptics of foreign extract." However, the pursuit of wealth that came with the American Revolution and the US Constitution soon became disruptive to society. For Otis Warren, the source of corruption lies in the character of the British government and its policies, and also in European manners and values, including the pursuit of opulence. With independence, such profligacy appeared to Otis Warren to be rapidly infecting the new nation (Davies 2005, 284; Richards 1995, 17; Smith 1966, 73; Zagarri 1995, 143, 144). She believed wealth and war had now corrupted Americans and made them more avaricious, while the past patriotic fervor was disappearing, an opinion shared by her correspondent, Abigail Adams, as well as by Mercy's husband, James Warren, who related how "fellows who would have cleaned my shoes five years ago" had swiftly "amassed fortunes and are riding in chariots" (McCullough 2001, 219; Stuart 2008, 141). In 1789, both Mercy and James had written to John Adams in Europe to warn him of the coming decline (McCullough 2001, 398). Consequently, in the *History*, she calls for a return to moral uprightness, because she believes that, without the persistence of virtue, the new Constitution (the legitimacy of which she has now come to accept) will not work very well. In fact, the danger is already that, "from the rage of acquisition which has spread far and wide, it may be apprehended that the possession of wealth will in a short time be the only distinction in this young country. By this it may be feared that the spirit of avarice will be rendered justifiable in the opinion of some, as the single road to superiority" (Warren 1805b, 205).

Therefore she asks whether it was worth making the sacrifices of the American Revolution if this inadequate quantity of virtue is now to form the basis of

American society in the future: "Shall a few designing men, for their own ag-
grandizement, and to gratify their own avarice, overset the goodly fabric we
have been rearing at the expense of so much time, blood, and treasure?" (Warren 1805b, 7). Furthermore, there is a certain inevitability to the transformation
being witnessed:

> It may be observed in this, as in innumerable instances in the life of man,
> that virtue and talents do not always hold their rank in the public esteem.
> Malice, intrigue, envy, and other adventitious circumstances, frequently
> cast a shade over the most meritorious characters; and fortune, more
> than real worth, not seldom establishes the reputation of her favorites, in
> the opinion of the undiscerning multitude and hands them down to pos-
> terity with laurels on their brow, which perhaps they never earned, while
> characters of more intrinsic excellence, are vilified or forgotten.
>
> WARREN 1805b, 14

A particular threat comes from the pursuit of wealth, power, or the "love of
distinction," in each of which Otis Warren sees the potential of arbitrary decision-making, the creation of an aristocratic class, and *de facto* slavery (Warren
1805a, 29, 36). Throughout human history, and notwithstanding the fact that
human beings enjoy "natural equality," leaders have assumed such great
amounts of personal power that the rights of the majority of people have come
to be worthless:

> Sanctioned by time and habit, an indefeasible right has been claimed,
> that sets so mischievous a creature as man above all law, and subjects the
> lives of millions, to the rapacious will of an individual, who, by the intoxi-
> cating nature of power, soon forgets that there are any obligations due to
> the subject, a reptile in his opinion, made only for the drudgery neces-
> sary to maintain the splendor of government, and the support of
> prerogative.
>
> WARREN 1805a, 119

In its treatment of the American colonies, the British government presents an
obvious example of this phenomenon (119). Her brother, James Otis, Jr., had
argued persuasively for a somewhat narrow sphere of natural equality, to
which Rossiter (1953, 374) refers as "an essential principle of libertarian political theory."

Equal to her dislike of John Hancock was Mercy Otis Warren's consternation
about the character of Thomas Hutchinson, who became the royal governor of
Massachusetts in 1771. In this respect, to some extent, Mercy took over the

agenda of her brother, James, who, as noted earlier, had made his argument against general writs of assistance before the presiding Hutchinson a decade before, and whose mental illness now limited his ability to contribute fully to the family project (Cima 2000, 472). In *The Adulateur, The Defeat*, and *The Group*, three plays that she wrote in the early 1770s, she satirized this politician quite savagely (Hicks 2005, 277; Shaffer 1975, 149). *The Adulateur* and *The Defeat* present him as Rapatio, the governor of a fictitious nation called Servia, where he sets out to destroy "the ardent love of liberty in Servia's free-born sons" (Hutcheson 1953, 384; Warren 1773, 23). In her *History*, Mercy describes Hutchinson as being "dark, intriguing, insinuating, haughty and ambitious, while the extreme of avarice marked each feature of his character" (Warren 1805a, 60). She sees him as a man who was fully aware of the constraints that ought be exercised on human behavior by considerations of virtue and patriotism, but who chose to instead opt for favoritism, as well as resisting measures that would have improved the condition of slaves in the colony. Moreover, Hutchinson's family, including in-laws with the last name of Oliver, held many prominent positions in Massachusetts government (Cima 2000, 477; Hutcheson 1953, 382; Warren 1805a, 69). For Gordon Wood, it had been important for Jemmy "to distinguish himself from those rich aristocrats like Thomas Hutchinson" who were hostile to the needs and concerns of ordinary people (Wood 1992, 136–137). Cima (2000, 493) argues that Otis Warren's portrayal of Hutchinson as Rapatio was an example of her "taking the place of her debilitated brother in the fight." In that role, Otis Warren ([1788] 1888, 6) notes that, in a letter to his patron, the Earl of Hillsborough, Hutchinson had revealed his desire to implement political changes "that might be executed in spite of opposition" (Bailyn [1967] 1992, 331–332). In *The Defeat*, Hayes (1976, 443) notes that "she took the image of the stage villain, the Vice figure of the English morality plays, and applied it to Hutchinson. She chose the Vice because he traditionally represents the hypocrite who wears a mask in public and "plays" at virtue." Thus in her plays, Otis Warren was able to promote her belief in the importance of virtue to political life, and the consequences that take place when it is inadequately represented. A similar concern is displayed in her poems. For example, in verse that she did not publish, titled "To J. Warren, Esq.," she writes:

> Come leave the noisy smoky town
> Where vice and folly reign,
> The vain pursuits of busy men
> We wisely will disdain
>
> WARREN [1766] 1981, 206

In 1760, the then-lieutenant governor was given an additional position, that of chief justice. This enraged both Mercy and Jemmy, because they believed that the colonial governor of Massachusetts Bay, William Shirley, had promised the position to their father, James Otis, Sr. Furthermore, they believed that Hutchinson and other members of Massachusetts' highest social stratum looked down on the Otises, and particularly upon their father, who, even though he was successful and had served as a colonel in the state militia, was self-educated. It was believed that Hutchinson had prevented him from being elected to the Massachusetts Governor's Council (an advisory body that still exists today) precisely because of his inferior origins. Consequently, it can be argued that some of the writings and activities of both James Otis, Jr. and of his sister to some extent reflect significant personal political rancor against Hutchinson (Brown 1896, 39–40; Waters 1975, 103, 105; Wood 1992, 62, 200). Thus Maud Macdonald Hutcheson (1953, 382) points out that, while "to Mercy Warren, he was a Machiavellian character with mediocre ability," modern historians may instead view Thomas Hutchinson as "a faithful public servant." Ironically, that would be an opinion supported by James Otis, Jr. himself when, in 1771, serving as a member of the state legislature, he said that the governor, who was under attack from Jemmy's political allies, was a "good man"" (Brown 1896, 46; Stoll 2008, 95). Additionally, Waters gives historical examples that suggest actual historical inconsistency in Jemmy's perspective:

> In January 1765 he voted for Richard Jackson as agent (with a three-year term), thus joining the Hutchinson men; while in February he provided the crucial vote that granted to Chief Justice Hutchinson £40 for what was termed the "faithful discharge" of his duties. This was in effect a partial restoration of the salary cut Otis had favored earlier.
> WATERS 1975, 153

The existence of this new political alliance seems to justify the view that Jemmy was inconsistent, with his change of heart being located, according to John Adams, in 1764, while others, like Waters give the date as 1765 (Brennan 1939, 692).

Despite the fact that the new nation had rid itself of a king, someone to whom Mercy refers as "a foreign Monarch" (Warren [1788] 1888, 3), in developing patterns of behavior, which, from her point of view, increasingly mirrored European societies, there was a certain danger that the creation of a different type of political system would become a change in name only:

> [B]efore many years roll over, some aspiring genius, without establishing
> the criterion or waiting the reward of real merit, may avail himself of the
> weakness, the divisions, and perhaps the distresses, of America, to make
> himself the designator and the fountain of honor and expectation. Such
> a sovereign without a crown, or the title of *king*, with his favorites and his
> instigators about him, may not be a less dangerous animal, than the *mon-*
> *arch* whose brow is decorated by the splendor of a diadem.
>   WARREN 1805b, 188

Hopefully, the fact that Americans have actually fought and made sacrifices in
order to have a more representative government will mean that the process
she is describing will not actually result in the permanent triumph of avarice
in the United States (Warren 1805b, 192), a new nation to which she nevertheless refers as "a degenerate, servile race of beings, corrupted by wealth, effemi-
nated by luxury, impoverished by licentiousness, and become the *automatons*
of intoxicated ambition" (203).

In explaining the many advantages of the society that are being lost, Mercy
Otis Warren does not sound like a republican as she praises the arguments of
her brother Jemmy, the first Earl Ludlow (an Irish-born Whig member of the
British parliament), Algernon Sydney, James Harrington, Milton, Locke, John
Dickinson, Thomas Jefferson, and Josiah Quincy, Jr., in favor of liberty in general, together with her insistence on the limited and contingent nature of political authority (Warren 1805b, 191–192):

> Princes, senates, or parliaments, are not proprietors or masters; they are
> subject to the people, who form and support that society, by an eternal
> law of nature, which has ever subjected a part to the whole.
>   WARREN 1805b, 191

The society currently being eclipsed enjoys many significant advantages,
Mercy argues, among which she enumerates respect for the general will, elections, the separation of powers, the right to a jury trial, the prohibition of religious tests to hold office, the free exercise of religion, and the absence of an
established church (191–192).

3   Subjugated People

One area where the interpretation of Otis Warren as a "republican" seems most
at odds is her consideration of dominated groups, where her sympathy for the

disadvantaged is surely more compatible with Lockean and Jeffersonian approaches to the protection of minority interests, a weak area in the conventional republican canon. Again and again, she argues for equal rights, a quite modern as well as classical liberal approach. When talking about the conditions faced by the Irish, for instance, she speaks of "native rights," "patriotism," and "virtues."

In regard to Native Americans, Otis Warren lauds the bravery and patriotism of people who have mistakenly been estimated to be fierce, and who may eventually face extermination in North America for the sin of seeking to preserve the property that has kept them and their ancestors alive. The argument that the original peoples of the continent are incompatible with the civilized values of Europeans, continues Mercy, is to ignore the history of Europe itself, where "the ancestors of the most refined and polite modern nations" were once "but rude, ignorant savages" Rather, the only difference between Native Americans and white people, she argues, is skin color:

> Nature has been equal in its operations, with regard to the whole human species. There is no difference in the moral or intellectual capacity of nations, but what arises from adventitious circumstances, that give some a more early and rapid improvement in civilization than others.
>
> WARREN 1805a, 232

Consequently, one of the tasks for the new nation of the United States will be to help Native Americans develop the skills and experiences that will allow them to integrate into the new nation (Warren 1805a, 231–232). Although Richards (1995, 143) summarizes her argument here in the *History* as being unfortunately an ethnocentric one, he points out that her comments about the "education" of Native Americans are nonetheless consistent with her view that the American Revolution has lifted up everyone on the continent. Furthermore, it can be noted that Mercy's view of the importance of education to improve opportunities for disadvantaged people is substantially consistent with the perspectives of many thinkers today.

For Mercy, the economic policies discussed earlier in the chapter, that were being pursued by her adversary, Alexander Hamilton, added to the woes of the continent's original inhabitants, leading to the loss of their homes (Stuart 2008, 214–215). Moreover, she sees the stereotypes of negative and hostile tribal behavior as being largely illusory. She explains that the Irish-born Colonel Guy Johnson, and other British patriots, coached the natives, with differing degrees of success, to adopt violence as a means of opposing the goals of the settlers, even before independence had been declared (Warren 1805a, 127); Johnson's

activities at the 1778 Battle of Wyoming would later be characterized as barba-
rous, following the torture of prisoners of war by Johnson's Iroquois soldiers.
Similarly, a British commander of French extraction, Philippe-François de
Rastel de Rocheblave, had apparently paid Native Americans to take the scalps
of Patriots. Mercy recalls that her son, Winslow Warren, had remarked that
ninety percent of the most reprehensible violence had been conducted by
white and not by native residents (Warren 1805a, 230, 233). The Caribbean island of St. Vincent, which she notes was taken away from the British (in 1779)
by Charles Hector, the Comte D'Estaing, the French ally of the Americans, "had
formerly cost much British blood to arrest and secure, by the cruel attempt
to exterminate the unfortunate and innocent Caraibs [Caribs]" (Warren
1805a, 249). Similarly, in colonial America, while it was true that the Patriots
had executed some of their Loyalist prisoners, a response that, Otis Warren
argues in the *History*, would seldom have been appropriate, the behavior of
the British, who transported their captives, forced them to labor, and in
some cases, allowed them to die was much more reprehensible (Warren
1805b, 83).

The example of Poland and its conquest by Russia should, Mercy feels, be a
cautionary example to all Americans. The presence of an aristocratic class, a
lack of patriotic feeling, excessive pursuit of personal goals, division caused by
the nature of differing interests – all potential causes of future trouble that she
witnessed in her own newly independent nation – were to be found in Poland,
its territories now divided between Russia, Prussia, and other German states,
as other nations passively looked on (Richards 1995, 140; Warren 1805a,
257–258).

Otis Warren also laments recent events on the small Caribbean island of
St. Eustatia, as it was generally called in her time, and referred to by James
Boswell. It is also known by its Dutch name, Sint Eustatius, and as Statia. With
a population of 1,800 in 1991, it is today a part of Curaçao. In 1781, the British
invaded the island and took it from the Netherlands, which was seen as an ally
of the Americans; the possession was returned to the Dutch in 1816. Following
the invasion, she notes the treatment of Samuel Hohen, a longtime and wealthy
Jewish resident of St. Eustatia, whose money and other possessions were taken
from him as he was loaded onto a ship bound for England, where, upon his arrival, he was unable to support himself, and despite the support of Edmund
Burke in the House of Commons, could not obtain any redress. All other Jewish
residents of the Caribbean island were unwillingly transported in this way
without their belongings, although some property was later returned to them.
As far as Burke himself was concerned, Otis Warren viewed him as a kindred

spirit in the matter of the rights of colonized peoples. Although she criticizes his rejection of the French Revolution, she admires his support for the American colonists and for people in India (O'Shaughnessy 2013, 306–307; Warren 1805b, 107).

Mercy notes that, following the St. Eustatia expulsions, Admiral Sir George B. Rodney and Major-General Sir John Vaughan spent their time on St. Eustatia selling the booty they had obtained by removing the island's Jews (Warren 1805b, 118–119). The only consolation for those robbed by the British was, as she mentions, the fact that Rodney's behavior was widely viewed back in England as being disgraceful: "his laurels stained by his avarice and cruelty, it was impossible, either by address, deception, or effrontery, to parry the severe reprehensions he received from some of the first nobility in the house of lords, as well as from many members of distinction and talent in the house of commons" (Warren 1805b, 120). Later, however, the reputations of both Rodney and Vaughan would still allow them to serve in the British parliament, Rodney in the Lords, and Vaughan in the Commons.

Otis Warren applies her criticism of Britain also to the Empire's treatment of Irish people and of Catholics in general. The Irish, she points out, were always viewed by the English as their inferiors, and Catholics punished more harshly than non-Catholics; Britain has, as it did to the American colonists, she notes, imposed controls on Ireland, limiting its ability to trade. In fact, "no means were neglected to rivet the chains in which they were held by the prejudices of Englishmen, with regard to their commerce, their police, and their religious opinions" (Warren 1805b, 142). Recently, Mercy adds, conditions have improved for the Irish, a factor that she attributes to the persuasiveness of the arguments advanced by defenders of Irish legislative independence who were also known as "patriots," people such as Henry Flood (1732–1791) and Henry Grattan (1746–1820) (Warren 1805b, 143). From her perspective, a parallel exists not only between the ideas advanced by Irish and American patriots, but also in the eloquence used to advance their causes.

In India, another area of the British Empire, Otis Warren comments, the atrocities perpetrated "against the innocent natives of India," which includes the conscious employment of genocide, resemble the crimes inflicted on Native Americans. All the various peoples of India, notwithstanding their rank and accomplishments, have been reduced to poverty and humiliation as the British have destroyed one of the great cultures of the world through their barbarism and by starving the inhabitants, as happened when they were battling Patriots in North America. For example, in Calcutta [today, Kolkata] in 1779, and in Madras, in 1781, 14,000 people were dying, she points out, every week

(Warren 1805a, 273). In some entanglements, British military leaders ordered that every Indian man be killed, while, in many others, not content with "butchery," which included the execution of prisoners and the rape and murder of women, the officers, having captured a territory, personally appropriated the wealth of its residents. Here, Otis Warren speaks of "the avarice of the officers," avarice being a quality that she particularly deplored (Warren 1805b, 165–166).

In the American colonies, meanwhile, respect for British authority might have sufficed to make residents accept their conditions of oppression due to the "narrow prejudices of national attachment" (Warren 1805b, 94) felt by the large numbers of settlers who viewed the colonial power as their original home and as the center of their culture. However, once Britain started to apply its familiar tactics of vicious conquest even to North America, there was no longer any need or much willingness to resist the call for independence. In fact, Mercy says, there had never been much necessity for the colonists to regard Britain as an ally, for, as in Ireland, the colonial power's economic restrictions seemed designed to achieve subjugation without need to resort to war. From the start, Americans were condemned to live in limited circumstances and unlikely to achieve the success that their hard work and commitment might warrant (Warren 1805b, 94). However, as soon as what Otis Warren sees as the initial wave of religiosity belonging to the Pilgrims had fallen off, the character of their society became superior to that of the more complicated set-up left behind in Britain, for the colonists had soon achieved a "just and happy medium between the ferocity of a state of nature, and those high stages of civilization and refinement, that at once corrupt the heart and sap the foundation of happiness" (Warren 1805a, 36). Thus a transformation took place rapidly in North America as settlers came to see the limitations of life as a colony:

> We look back with astonishment when we reflect, that it was only in the beginning of the seventeenth century, that the first Europeans landed in Virginia, and that nearly at the same time, a few wandering strangers coasted about the unknown bay of Massachusetts, until they found a footing in Plymouth. Only a century and an half had elapsed, before their numbers and their strength accumulated, until they bade defiance to foreign oppression, and stood ready to meet the power of Britain, with courage and magnanimity scarcely paralleled by the progeny of nations, who had been used to every degree of subordination and obedience.
>
> WARREN 1805b, 189–190

For Mercy, then, both the fact that there was an American Revolution, and the reason that resistance to the colonial power was considerable, are explained by the nature of the culture that had developed around the Americans. People such as the Loyalist general and governor of Massachusetts, Thomas Gage, underestimated the tenacity and fortitude of those born in New England, and the extent to which they would be willing to sacrifice their livelihoods for their principles (Smith 1966, 76, 85; Warren 1805a, 104). Accustomed to the passivity of the propertyless mass of people in Europe, ruled by class distinction and mainstream church dogma, British leaders failed to understand the nature of the new norms that had been spawned across the Atlantic, misunderstanding "the tendency of nature and society to preserve *freedom*, made more active by their opposition" (Warren 1805b, 104), imagining it to be the kind of "rebellion" it was customary for them to crush. Ultimately, the winners in the conflict would not be the side with the greatest army, but the combatants whom, paraphrasing Otis Warren, Smith (1966, 89) calls the ones who possessed "an enthusiastic belief in the cause of freedom." Moreover, the attempt to counter protests by military means, including the employment of standing armies, is likely to be counterproductive, Mercy writes, because decent people will decide that the moral and intellectual debasement that must follow their violent subjection can be best countered by resistance (Warren 1805a, 53, 1805b, 103–104).

Otis Warren concedes that the human race possesses a "certain supineness which generally overspreads the multitude" (Warren 1805a, 44) and resists the call to action in all but the most drastic cases, accounting for what she sees as the frequent enslavement of the majority by those in power. Once the situation is perceived as having reached a dire level, however, when an appropriate response within the existing political arrangements is unforthcoming – and, particularly, in North America, where colonists were forced to endure "the repeated attempts to reduce the colonies to unlimited submission to the supreme jurisdiction of parliament, and the illegal exactions of the crown" (68) – then the normal rules of appropriate behavior change (44, 83, 87), perforce "destroying all subordination" (86). For example, Mercy writes that the setting up of the First Continental Congress might in most times be interpreted as an act of treason, but, given the state of British rule in the American colonies when that event took place, it became instead a noble and entirely appropriate development:

> Firm and disinterested, intrepid and united, they stood ready to submit
> to the chances of war, and to sacrifice their devoted lives to preserve

inviolate, and to transmit to posterity, the inherent rights of men, conferred on all by the God of nature, and the privileges of Englishmen,
claimed by Americans from the sacred sanctions of compact.

WARREN 1805a, 82

Mercy Otis Warren is at her most radical when writing as "A Columbian Patriot," in her nineteen-page *Observations*, which was released anonymously during the ratification process. Here, she is most concerned about the nature of
the changes represented by the proposed US Constitution. At a time when little accurate information was in circulation, Mercy had read Luther Martin's
The Genuine Information, an account of what had happened at the Constitutional Convention in Philadelphia,[3] which opined that aristocracy was to be a
key element in the new government eventually transpiring from the proceedings (Cornell 1999, 52, fn 2). Thus, attacking the lack of specificity that exists in
the Constitution, a feature that many have viewed as having secured its survival, she notes that the document, "by the undefined meaning of some parts,
and the ambiguities of expression in others, is dangerously adapted to the purposes of an immediate aristocratic tyranny" (Warren [1788] 1888, 4). As explained later in the present chapter, in a conversation with Catharine Macaulay
and herself, John Adams's ill-considered comments also caused Mercy Otis
Warren to believe that he, too, intended a similar kind of transformation to
take place, and that, as president, he was actually taking steps to implement it.
Thus it is not surprising to find that she views the document to be a means of
creating despotism:

> And when patriotism is discountenanced and publick virtue becomes
> the ridicule of the sycophant – when every man of liberality, firmness
> and penetration who cannot lick the hand stretched out to oppress, is
> deemed an enemy to the State – then is the gulph [gulf] of despotism set
> open, and the grades to slavery, though rapid, are scarce perceptible –
> then genius drags heavily its iron chain.
>
> WARREN [1788] 1888, 2

Even though Mercy had disclosed her authorship of *Observations* in a December 18, 1787 letter to Macaulay, to whom she also sent a copy of the work, for
many years, Elbridge Gerry was incorrectly assumed to be its source. Despite
the fact that there were many rumors to the effect that the script was

---

3 Today, historians have the benefit of James Madison's own handwritten account, which was
   eventually published in 1840 as *Notes of Debates in the Federal Convention of 1787*.

distinctive of Otis Warren's prose, and that Paul Leicester Ford, the editor and writer of an introduction to a centenary edition that bears Gerry's name (Warren [1788] 1888), noted that the "florid" style had disturbed some of its potential readership, it was only in the 1930s that Mercy's great-great grandson, the Pulitzer Prize-winning lawyer, Charles Warren, read the old letter and realized that an error had been made. Subsequently Gerry's name was erased in some places, although it continues to remain in other sources (Cima 2000, 490; Hutcheson 1953, 393; Reif 1960, 132; Stuart 2008, 197; Zagarri 1995, 69–70, 70, fn. 1).

In her *Observations*, writing in what Zagarri (1995, 121) calls "her typically bombastic, convoluted style," Otis Warren made some familiar Anti-Federalist and Jeffersonian remarks that the failure to include a Bill of Rights in the original document would endanger residents' liberty. She listed many criticisms according to which she claimed that the Constitution was incompatible with "republicanism," particularly in the extent to which considerable power had now been given to the new federal judiciary, whose powers represented to her "a boundless ocean" (Warren [1788] 1888, 7; 9 is similar) – a criticism that has been made many times since, for example by opponents of judicial activism. Also (8), she expresses her fears of the provision for a standing army, a sign that, she believes, indicates a desire to replace civilian authority with the power of a monarch or of an aristocracy (Cornell 1999, 56; Smith 1966, 108, 109; Stuart 2008, 195–196; Zagarri 1995, 121–122). Indeed, she claims that it is impossible to discern either "Democratick or Republican" principles in the eventual document, it being a "many headed monster; of such motley mixture," and that the commitment to making every state maintain "a Republican form" is quite hollow given all the other measures that the document imposes (Warren [1788] 1888, 5, 8).

4   Defining "Republican"

From time to time, former students in US History or American Government classes have been known to write short though rather pointed letters submitted to newspaper editors in which they claim to have resolved an important political issue as they assert something like "Anyway, the United States isn't a democracy; it's a republic." But what exactly is a republic, or a republican, or republicanism? Some scholars have used the terms almost as facilely, without seeing any need to craft a definition, while others have noted the problematic nature of such words. Linda Kerber (1985, 480), for instance, writes that "'Republicanism' has become so all-embracing as to absorb comfortably its own contradictions."

John Adams attributed the appearance in Article IV of the US Constitution of a "guarantee to every state in this union a Republican form of government" to the participation of Charles Pinckney in the document's writing. Adams himself, however, reveals some skepticism about the concept when he tells Mercy Otis Warren that that "I confess I never understood it; and I believe no other man ever did or ever will." This, for the second president, is due to the word's vagueness, and the fact that different people use the term in various ways, with the consequence that any government at all can be deemed a republic (John Adams, letter to Mercy Warren, July 20, 1807, in Adams [1878] 1972, 352–353). As Kerber notes, a common original meaning of the words was a reference to a type of government that did not have a monarch, although, in *Federalist* #39, Madison widened the meaning slightly by stating the reciprocal version of the definition, that in a republic, power is ultimately held by the people, rather than the people being subjects (Kerber 1985, 475, 1988, 1663–1664). However, the very reason that Madison takes this stance is because of his near agreement with Adams that, in practice, there is "no satisfactory" answer to the question, "What, then, are the distinctive characters of the republican form?" (*Federalist* #39). Thus, Shalhope can conclude:

> Only one thing was certain: Americans believed that republicanism meant an absence of aristocracy and a monarchy. Beyond this, agreement vanished – what form a republican government should assume and, more important, what constituted a republican society created disagreement and eventually bitter dissension.
>
> SHALHOPE 1972, 72

For many, however, republicanism has assumed what Kerber calls "a moral dimension, a utopian depth" (Kerber 1985, 478; see also Wood [1969] 1998, 47–65). With the development of later, more grandiose formulations, Kerber notes, some researchers chose to ignore the "hyperbole," the more ideological formations of "republicanism" and related words (Kerber 1985, 477). This left a situation in which many writers still refer to concepts that are not well understood. Michelman comments:

> Republicanism is not a well-defined historical doctrine. As a "tradition" in political thought, it figures less as canon than ethos, less as blueprint than as conceptual grid, less as settled institutional fact than as semantic field for normative debate and constructive imagination.
>
> MICHELMAN 1986, 17

Explanations of the American Revolution that prioritize the influence of John Locke and other state of nature liberals have been challenged by the publication of works such as J.G.A. Pocock's *The Machiavellian Moment* (Pocock [1975] 2003), which stressed the importance of Italian Renaissance republicanism and the concept of civic virtue; and by the endeavors of scholars such as Gary Wills (1978), who have found parallel explanations in the ideas of the Scottish Historical School, one of whom, Adam Ferguson, was mentioned above, seeing, in Wills' case, the influence of the Irish-born Francis Hutcheson, rather than Locke, on Thomas Jefferson. Wills was not the first writer to make this connection to Scotland's Enlightenment – Howe (1989, 572) notes that "[b]ehind the flashy performance of Wills lay a long historiography, going back to ... 1907." Other putative civic republican sources include the writings (as "Cato" in *Cato's Letters*) of John Trenchard (1662–1723) and Thomas Gordon (1692–1750). The 144 "letters," which were rediscovered by historians in the 1950s, cite Hobbes and display what many scholars see as the influence of Locke, but for others, they also have a civic republican cast. Gordon translated works of Tacitus, the pessimistic Roman historian. Ferguson (1767, 36, 60, 66, 69, 73, 76, 190) also discusses Tacitus in his work, and a few commentators see the influence of Bernard Mandeville on both "Cato" writers, or perhaps just on the younger and more prolific of the two, Gordon, who may have attended the University of Aberdeen (Bailyn [1967] 1992, 35). Many emphasize the stimulus of James Harrington. For example, even the early constitution of the Carolina colonies, the Fundamental Constitutions of Carolina of March 1, 1669, which, while it was physically penned by John Locke, in his role as secretary to Lord Ashley (the Earl of Shaftesbury, who was one of the proprietors of the American territory), nevertheless reflects the ideas of Harrington and of Ashley himself, with the document seeking to balance the influence of different classes, echoing Harrington's "theory of the balance" which is to be found in his utopian work, *The Commonwealth of Oceana* (1656), and a facet that is shared with classical republicanism (Berthoff 1982, 582; Bloch 1987b, 40–41, Cohen 1983, 482–483; Kerber 1988, 1663–1664; Kramnick 1982, 632–633; Mitchell 2003, 291–294, 304; Pocock [1975] 2003, 515; Shalhope 1972, 57. For Pocock ([1975] 2003, 384), the publication of *Oceana* "marks a moment of paradigmatic breakthrough, a major revision of English political theory and history in the light of concepts drawn from civic humanism and Machiavellian republicanism."

For some scholars, such as Harpham (1984, 766, 771), it stretches the truth to imagine some of the Scottish Enlightenment thinkers such as Adam Smith or David Hume embracing a civic humanist concept of liberty that includes the participation of ordinary citizens in the political process, when many of those citizens would lack the psychological commitment to the society in which they toiled to keep themselves alive. For those who favor the revised understanding, however, the commitment to active citizenship is an important element of republicanism, an approach that has been advanced in recent decades as a contemporary jurisprudential philosophy. Sunstein writes:

> It is no longer possible to see a Lockean consensus in the founding period, or to treat the framers as modern pluralists believing that self-interest is the inevitable motivating force behind political behavior. Republican thought played a central role in the framing period, and it offers a powerful conception of politics and of the functions of constitutionalism.
>
> SUNSTEIN 1988, 1540

For Pocock, the tradition of civic humanism extends from Florence, influencing the Scottish thinkers, Harrington, and the American colonists. Of Mercy's friend and intellectual ally, Catharine Macaulay, Pocock says she "was a patriot, committed to the ancient primacy of civic virtue among the defining human values" (Pocock 1998, 251). However, his characterization of Macaulay as a republican has been criticized, for example by Barbara Taylor (2003, 297, fn 48) and Kate Davies (2005, 22–23), who comment that Pocock presents Macaulay as a republican without considering the feminist aspects of her thought. Although Pocock does not write specifically about Mercy Otis Warren in this regard, the implication, which has been adopted by many scholars who have written about her, is that Mercy's concern about the loss of virtue following American independence derives to some significant extent from this source, and thus they routinely refer to her as a "republican."

For Pocock and others, the term "civic humanism" describes the Renaissance revival in Florence of classical Greek and Roman ideas, which led to the commitment of that society to the idea that participation in politics was an important part of a citizen's life, and thus to be identified with virtue. Such an understanding of political life presents a rival explanation to the Lockean, individualistic, and emergent capitalist formulation which is often presented to explain developments in North America (Dickey 1987, 98–99). Thus, Bloch (1987b, 38) writes of "the recent interpretation of the American Revolution known as the "Republican synthesis,"" and explains that "the word "virtue" ... [refers to] the willingness of citizens to engage actively in civic life and to sacrifice individual interests for the common good," while Harpham (1984, 764) notes that "[f]ocusing upon the central role played by the concepts of virtue and corruption in the republican tradition, these studies have led to a striking revisionist understanding of an evolving Anglo-American tradition of political discourse." Pocock writes:

> The confrontation of "virtue" with "corruption" is seen to have been a vital problem in social and historical philosophy during that era [the eighteenth century], and its humanist and Machiavellian vocabulary is shown to have been the vehicle of a basically hostile perception of early modern capitalism.
>
> POCOCK [1975] 2003, ix

Elsewhere, Pocock calls the American Revolution "the last great act of the Renaissance" (Lewis 1987, 711, fn 81; Pocock 1972, 120). Kramnick explains as follows:

> Part Aristotle, part Cicero, part Machiavelli, civic humanism conceives of man as a political being whose realization of self occurs only through participation in public life, through active citizenship in a republic. The virtuous man is concerned primarily with the public good, *res publica*, or commonweal, not with private or selfish ends. Seventeenth-century writers like James Harrington and Algernon Sidney adapted this tradition, especially under the influence of Machiavelli (according to J.G.A. Pocock), to a specifically English context.
>
> KRAMNICK 1982, 630–631

According to the revised telling, it was these ideas that were the main influence on the American Revolution, as Berthoff points out:

> The peasant-smallholder or artisan-proprietor outlook of most European immigrants to America from the seventeenth century down to the early twentieth century bore a fundamental affinity to the classical republican ideals with which the American Revolution endowed the United States. The social values of early-modern English colonists evidently predisposed the patriots of 1776–1787, their descendants, to identify with classical republicanism.
>
> BERTHOFF 1982, 579

However, some writers have felt that the influence of classical republican ideas on the American colonists has been exaggerated by its best-known exponents, who include Gordon Wood as well as Pocock. For instance, Bloch observes:

> Wood and Pocock are vulnerable to the same criticism. ... all the conflicts
> they describe are essentially over issues defined by the classical republi-
> can tradition. All other currents of thought are either subsumed under
> the rubric of "republicanism" or explained as reactions against it.
>
> BLOCH 1987a, 552–553

Eventually the fight waged by Mercy Otis Warren and other alleged proponents
of civic virtue would be lost as the values of capitalism came to predominate,
and political existence was understood much more in terms of the individual,
a process now referred to sometimes as the "end of classical politics" (Davies
2005, 35; Kramnick 1982, 662; Pocock [1975] 2003, 523, 527; Shalhope 1991, 468).
Certainly, there had been a transformation in people's understandings of human society and politics over time, for Americans in the early 1800s no longer
shared the views of people on both sides of the Atlantic in the early 1700s, for
whom, Pocock points out, "it was far from clear how any group intent upon its
private interest could have any sense of the common good at all, and if it had
not it would be no more than a faction, driving its members to further and
further excesses of greed and frenzy" (Pocock [1975] 2003, 483). But while these
concerns, which may continue to be shared by many people around the world
today, provide much food for thought, they do not seem to be particularly "republican" in any significant way. In fact, even Pocock's rather original attempt
to characterize the concept requires him to distinguish between its application
to sixteenth-century Florence and its role in eighteenth-century North America, where citizens "were able to define corruption and irrationality in terms far
more positive, material, and dynamic" (486). So, were they really the same
phenomenon?

   In the present chapter, it is argued that the use of the term "republican" to
describe the work of Mercy Otis Warren is also to distort many of her main
points. After all, the scholarly interest in republicanism has waned in recent
years. Rodgers (1992, 11), for example, notes that, "[t]he concept of republicanism ... [b]y 1990 ... was everywhere and organizing everything, though perceptively thinning out, like a nova entering its red giant phase." Anyway, he writes,
"republicanism was a relatively modest paradigm" (12), one that scholars have
now shifted their interests beyond, finally recognizing the impracticality of "a
detritus of loose ends and things that would not fit the radical simplifications
that paradigm construction entails" (34). Today, Rodgers notes, "its ontological
status grows fainter and more confused" (37). Given the fact that the consequences of this paradigm shift have perhaps not had much influence upon
more recent commentary on the topic of Mercy Otis Warren, perhaps it is appropriate that her writings now be reexamined, which is, of course, the purpose of the author here.

The attributions of classical republican influence upon colonial America were always somewhat limited. For example, Barnard Bailyn, the author of *The Ideological Origins of the American Revolution*, one of the works credited with starting the "republican" paradigm, himself points out that, among the architects and pamphleteers of the American Revolution, the "elaborate display of classical authors is deceptive. Often the learning behind it was superficial" (Bailyn [1967] 1992, 24). Concerning Mercy Otis Warren's knowledge of Enlightenment-era authors, Bailyn (29) comments that she "listed the contents of a hypothetical Tory library in her play *The Group*; but with the exception of Filmer none of the authors she mentions there were in fact referred to favorably by the Tories." Actually, Filmer's name is absent from *The Group*, and the somewhat whimsical onstage library in the stage directions to which he refers includes Mandeville's *The Fable of the Bees* and Hobbes' *Leviathan*, both of which works that were heavily criticized by the conservatives of the time (Warren 1775). But Bailyn's more important point is that the colonists would not have interpreted their endeavors in the way we do today:

> They would have been astonished to hear that they were initiating a change from something scholars would later call "civic humanism" or "classical republicanism" to another, something that would be called "liberalism," or that they were chiefly interested in preserving patrician rule derived from the older tradition.
>
> BAILYN [1967] 1992, 351–352

In *The Machiavellian Moment*, Pocock defines "republic" in relation to that "Machiavellian moment" in sixteenth-century Florence (and more specifically, between 1494 and 1530), when political authority came to be understood not as a consequence of eternal divinity (Pocock [1975] 2003, 333), but in terms of the existence of the republic of Florence, a contingent arrangement, "affiliated only with other republics and with those moments in past time in which republics had existed" (53). With the coming of this new era of civic humanism, citizens were now in some circumstances able to supplement their religious obedience with an awareness that, "only as a citizen, as political animal, ... could he fulfill his nature, achieve virtue, and find his means rational" (114). In the 2003 afterword to that detailed and extraordinarily influential work, Pocock also presents us with a "republicanism' that is formulated as "an advocacy of "ancient liberty," whose survival must be ensured under "modern" conditions" (576). These are Pocock's original attempts to craft an explanation, but his formulations are quite different from more common accounts. Elsewhere, in his discussion of Trenchard and Gordon's *Cato's Letters*, Pocock writes that "Cato" has written that, "England ... is a republic of that peculiarly happy kind which has a king as its chief magistrate" (468). As Nelson (2004) has pointed out, Pocock's source here is the letter of July 15, 1721, "Character of a good and of an evil Magistrate, quoted from Algernon Sidney, Esq.," but the words Pocock paraphrases here are somewhat tricky, for their author is making what Nelson calls "a play on words" (2004, 140). What "Cato" writes is:

> I shall only take notice, that the passages which I take from him are not republican passages, unless virtue and truth be republicans: That Mr. [Algernon] Sidney's book, for the main of it, is eternally true, and agreeable to our own constitution, which is the best republick in the world, with a prince at the head of it.
>
> GORDON [1721] 1995

As Nelson observes, England is only a republic for Cato (in this case, Gordon) if republicanism happens to be about virtue and truth, but that is not the complete definition that Trenchard and Gordon, writing from a somewhat Harringtonian perspective, wish to employ. Nelson continues:

> [W]hile Cato argues that England is not a republic, and that liberty can be secured by non-republican governments, he is clear that liberty in any regime requires the absence of disproportionate wealth in individuals.
>
> NELSON 2004, 142

Nelson points out that Cato does not really believe that England is a republic – rather, it is a kind of monarchy (140–141).

Again, we see Pocock implicitly and explicitly defining "republic" in a way that differs significantly from the way that the term has often been understood (as an alternative to hereditary government), as he does when he writes that "[Thomas] Paine was no classical republican, only a hater of monarchy" ([1975] 2003, 575). Also, Nelson points out that in arguing for a continuous tradition of "republican" thought, Pocock has assumed an unwarranted similarity between Greek and Roman political theory, and also made another argument that "is difficult to sustain" (Nelson 2004, 4) regarding the sixteenth century thinkers, Machiavelli and Francesco Guicciardini (1483–1540), that they were committed followers of Aristotle. While these objections to Pocock's enterprise fall beyond the scope of the present topic, they constitute additional indications that there are many ways in which the characterization of a "republican" current running through history may be flawed (Nelson 2004, 3–4).

The idiom of republicanism has also occurred in discussions of the nature of the Republican Mother, a term that has been used to delineate Mercy Otis

Warren's contributions. First defined by Linda Kerber (1976, 202), the phrase relates to an alternative understanding of the correct way for women to act that Kerber (201–202) argues first appeared in the 1790s, and which she associates with the ideas of the early feminist, Judith Sargent Murray (1751–1820); the Massachusetts-based novelist, playwright, and actress, Susannah (or Susanna) Rowson (1762–1824); and the American revolutionist signer of the Declaration of Independence, Benjamin Rush (1746–1813). Mercy lived during the same time period as these thinkers, but, in Kerber's pioneering article, she is assigned a minor, supporting role in this new paradigm, with the author arguing that Otis Warren failed to "deal with the questions" about the rights and role of women that her brother Jemmy had raised (199). However, as this new Republican Mother sub-paradigm has swelled out, Lewis (1987, 690, fn 2) points out that Kerber's concept "has taken on a life of its own and is often assumed to say more about motherhood than Kerber herself ever claimed." As part of that development process, Mercy's work has increasingly been interpreted as a major element of its thinking. For Saxton (2009, 24), then, Otis Warren's "life in many ways anticipates Republican mothering." Similarly, Zagarri (1995, 28) writes that, "Motherhood essentially assumed a political, or protopolitical, function. Mercy Otis Warren's writings suggest that the roots of the concept go deeper. Republican Motherhood may have originated well before the Revolution."

The concept of Republican Motherhood is intended to explain the contradictory commitment to expansion of women's roles during the 1790s, an understanding that largely restricted them to the domestic functions of child-rearing and making a home for their husbands, a formulation believed to be somewhat loosely related to classical republicanism (Kerber 1976, 203–205), an attribution made in tentative statements such as "the answer, in part, may be that Roman women showed them how to participate in republican political life" (Hicks 2005, 291).

Zagarri (1992, 192) writes that "Republican motherhood preserved traditional gender roles at the same time that it carved out a new, political role for women." Norton explains:

> The ideal American woman was to be the nurturant, patriotic mother who raised her children, and especially her sons, to be good Christians, active citizens, and successful competitors in the wider arena of life.
>
> NORTON 1984, 617

The raising of sons allowed women to play an indirect role in politics, through the political socialization of the boys in their families. Thus, Kerber writes:

> The Republican Mother's life was dedicated to the service of civic virtue;
> she educated her sons for it; she condemned and corrected her husband's
> lapses from it.
>
> KERBER 1976, 202

However, scholars have disagreed about the focus of Republican Motherhood
during Mercy's lifetime. Jan Lewis, for example, has argued that the original
focus was upon women's role as a wife, with the concern about motherhood
not arriving until the 1830s (Lewis 1987, 689–691; Zagarri 1992, 209). Another
problem with the perspective is that, not only is it not markedly about motherhood, particularly if looked at chronologically, as a means of explaining Otis
Warren's ideas, but neither is it is a portrayal of women that is especially
"Republican." In the context of the present chapter, the best, though limited
conclusion to be made here is that explanations in terms of Republican
Motherhood also fail to advance the hypothesis that Mercy Otis Warren was a
republican. Moreover, even to the extent that Republican Motherhood is a useful explanatory vehicle, Rabinovitch (2001, 360), points out that there were
always women who opposed this modeling of their role and who could see
beyond the limits it imposed on their thinking, and thus to characterize their
activity at this time in terms of its influence must be flawed.

5   Mercy Otis Warren as a "Republican"

In response to the criticisms of John Adams and others that "republic," "republican," and "republicanism" were concepts that had little precise meaning, Otis
Warren attempted to show that the words did have a specific function. Additionally, she argued that the attempt to portray republicanism as a hollow
doctrine was a deliberate and disingenuous attempt to undermine it and its
supporters (John Adams, letter to Mercy Warren, July 30, 1807, in Adams [1878]
1972, 390; Rodgers 1992, 38, Stuart 2008, 250; Warren 1805b, 168–169; Mercy Warren, letter to John Adams, July 30, 1807, in Adams [1878] 1972, 398).

For Cass Sunstein, not only Anti-Federalists such as Mercy Otis Warren, but
also Federalists, who included James Madison, were committed to this ancient
idea of civic humanism. It was, he argues, for this reason that, in *Federalist* #10,
Madison, fearing that not many Americans would be able to apprise the public
good and behave virtuously and on behalf of society as a whole, sought a
system of remote and indirect government so that only those committed to
civic virtue – actors whom Pocock ([1975] 2003, 520) terms "a Few ... if possible,

... members of the patrician elites" – would be likely to serve (Gerber 1994, 988; Kerber 1988, 1666; Michelman 1986, 59; Sunstein 1988, 1547–1548, 1558–1559). An obvious weakness with this approach is that many interests are thus excluded from participation since they do not agree with the "best" resolution, a conclusion that is acknowledged even by Michelman, a contemporary advocate of republican jurisprudence who notes the imposition of the majority's view of morality in *Bowers v. Hardwick* (1986), where Justice Byron White argued that the fact that half the states banned sodomy made it difficult to legalize it.[4] Nonetheless, Michelman (1988, 1495) argues "that republican constitutional thought is not indissolubly tied to any such static, parochial, or coercive communitarianism" and he attempts to show how legal analysis that has a commitment to modern civic virtue could have produced the opposite result (1988, 1495, 1532–1533).

As was noted above, Mercy Otis Warren is often identified as a "republican." Stuart, for example, speaks of "her commitment to the unpopular republican values of the early Revolution" (2008, xii). Davies speaks of "Warren's use of a republican discourse" (2005, 21), and states that, "Mercy Warren was at the centre of a correspondence network that connected republican women across Massachusetts" (2005, 186). Baym (1991a, 34) comments: "Believing that only the republican form of government valued domesticity, Warren gives women particular reason to be loyal and grateful citizens." Zagarri writes that, in Mercy's *History*:

> Drawing on classical republican tropes, she sought to remind the next generation of the principles of liberty and virtue that had made success against Britain possible and republican government viable. ... She thus wrote from a well-defined point of view: as a patriot, an "old republican."
>
> ZAGARRI 1995, 142

Certainly, for Mercy Otis Warren, there was an identification of what she admired about the American colonial society in which she had grown up with aspects of the ancient societal organizations that she had studied, because, in her *History*, she warns the reader, as follows:

> If, instead of the independent feelings of ancient republics, whose prime object was the welfare and happiness of their country, we should see a

---

4 The decision was eventually overturned in *Lawrence v. Texas* (2003).

dereliction of those principles, and the Americans ready to renounce their great advantages, by the imitation of European systems in politics and manners, it would be a melancholy trait in the story of man.

WARREN 1805b, 205

On the other hand, when John Adams had told Otis Warren and Catharine Macaulay at a social gathering at his home that, for him, the ideal constitutional structure for the United States would be "King, Lords, and Commons," it was necessary, in response to Mercy's outrage that he would consider a system that had any hereditary governmental institutions, for him to refine what he had said, claiming that all he had intended to say was that "mixed government is the only one that can preserve liberty" (John Adams, letter to Mercy Warren, July 11, 1807, in Adams [1878] 1972, 325). Here, we find Adams employing the Harringtonian and "republican" language of the balance of power between the traditional classes (327), whereas Otis Warren is the one who is offended. For what can a monarch or an aristocracy be but hereditary? Kerber (1985, 480) points out that, in such a system, "[i]n the antique balance between "the one, the few, and the many," the cards were stacked in favor of the few." Moreover, as Berthoff observes, the formulation is fundamentally unequal and discriminatory:

> The Aristotelian categories of the one, the few, and the many – read in England as King, Lords, and Commons – each had its appropriate form of republican virtue, in which all were superior to noncitizens, who did not. ... they could not be relied upon for civic virtue and so should not be citizens.
>
> BERTHOFF 1982, 582

For Cornell, even though Mercy spoke frequently about the decline of virtue, and in her work as "A Columbian Patriot" referred to the ideas of French republican theorist Gabriel Bonnet de Mably, she is not best understood as a disciple of classical republicanism:

> Warren's constitutional vision did not require the creation of a Christian Sparta: her republicanism was decidedly Whig, not classical, in conception. As long as men of wisdom guided the ship of state and representative institutions functioned to refine the public will, republicanism would thrive.
>
> CORNELL 1999, 56

When Shaffer points out that Otis Warren never defined the republican government that she desired, he notes that she nevertheless gave readers "a number of precepts, such as sovereignty of the people, the protection of personal liberty, private property, and freedom of conscience, and the separation of powers" (Shaffer 1975, 158). However, such requirements appear to owe little to classical republicanism, and much to Locke, Jefferson, and the Bill of Rights, with the approval of the latter, of course, putting an end to many of Mercy's reservations about the workability of the US Constitution (Shaffer 1975, 26). Often, Mercy speaks only in the most general way of a contrast between "a republican form of government and more despotic modes" (Warren 1805b, 183). Brown (1896, 219) comments that, "Mrs. Warren adhered to what she considered an ideal and abstract republicanism."

For some scholars, it is Otis Warren's insistence on the need to sustain public virtue that by itself warrants the attribution of republicanism to her political philosophy. Cohen (1983, 481), for example, portrays virtue as "the genius of republicanism; it was a quality of human character and conduct that manifested the confluence of personality and public behavior, such that civic values and practices were continuous with individual values and practices." For him, the desirable principles are instead "patriotism, self-discipline, autonomy, simplicity, moderation, prudence" (482), and their antonyms in a political sense are "self-aggrandizement, luxury, glory, commerce, refinement, and artifice" (482). But even with these categories it can be asked whether the connection to Florence and Aristotle, etc. is anything more than superficial. When Bailyn ([1967] 1992, 344) observes that the Anti-Federalists believed "that the animating principle of republics was virtue," the presence of "republics" seems to be a much less critical factor than "virtue."

For Mercy Otis Warren, the Society of the Cincinnati,[5] a group recently founded to celebrate and memorialize the War of Independence, presented a particularly irritating example of the moral decline of the United States; she saw in its newly created traditions and values a longing for a European type of hereditary aristocracy, and a clue that the Federalists secretly desired to have a monarch, both of which Alexander Hamilton had proposed at the Constitutional Convention as part of his swiftly rejected plan (Baym 1991b; Friedman and Shaffer 1975, 202; Shaffer 1975, 147). It might seem ironic that Mercy, a thinker who had read about, and was evidently impressed by, Roman civilization, would dislike the Cincinnati, while Cincinnatus himself, after whom the

---

5 Davies (2005) misspells Cincinnati and Cincinnatus throughout her book and its index (as Cincinatti and Cincinattus).

Society was named (certainly in the way that the Roman Dictator's actions are presented in the writings of Livy, as a reluctant hero, disdainful of holding office any longer than necessary, and as soon as possible returning to his own small farm that he plowed by himself) is as expected a model of moral citizenship for her (Livy 1905, book 3). In her *History*, Mercy clearly credits "the humble and disinterested virtues of the ancient Roman" (Brown 1896, 209; Warren 1805b, 182), and she also notes that many of the Patriots who had assembled to overthrow the King had quickly sought only "to return to the plough, or to the humbler occupations of their former life" (Warren 1805b, 182). Indeed, "Cincinnatus" was the pseudonym behind which another Anti-Federalist, Arthur Lee, the brother of Richard Henry Lee, had concealed his authorship. For Mercy, the lessons to be learned from the example of Cincinnatus were the opposite of what was signified by the creation of the Cincinnati. Smith (1966, 102) points out that Otis Warren saw the Cincinnati as "[a]n hereditary privileged order," one that would not have been tolerated at the time that independence was declared, and she viewed the organization as yet another example of the new nation reverting to older, European types of cultural practices, one where "this institution would give a fatal wound to the liberties of America" (Warren 1805b, 183). In fact, even retired officers and aristocrats from Europe were able to join that organization, and the last thing that the new nation needed, she felt, was an aristocracy (Pocock [1975] 2003, 527–528; Smith 1966, 102–103, 105; Zagarri 1995, 144). Otis Warren writes:

> [I]t might have been expected ... that they would have retired satisfied with their own efforts to save their country, and the competent rewards it was ready to bestow, instead of ostentatiously assuming hereditary distinctions, and the insignia of nobility. But the eagle and the ribbon dangled at the button-hole of every youth who had for three years borne an office in the army, and taught him to look down with proud contempt on the patriot grown grey in the service of his country.
> WARREN 1805b, 182

For the early biographer of Otis Warren, Alice Brown (1896, 208–209), Mercy "never deviates from the sternest patriotism," in her *History*, "which displays itself nowhere more plainly than in her prevailing distrust of the Order of the Cincinnati." It is difficult to predict what Mercy Otis Warren would have to say about her own memorialization in the activities and the name of the oldest Massachusetts chapter of the Daughters of the American Revolution, a group that, like the Cincinnati, still exists today (Chapman 1896).

The virtuous character of Cincinnatus in the legend depicted by Livy has often been likened to that of George Washington, a president similarly reluctant to assume power, a comparison that is explored, for example, in Gary Wills' book, *Cincinnatus: George Washington and the Enlightenment* (Wills 1984). Lillian B. Miller (1985, 527) says of that work that, "it is the Cincinnatus metaphor, in Wills's opinion, that became the key to the Washington legend." Although Mercy Otis Warren does not note such a direct correlation, George Washington is also, for her, an exemplary leader who resists the temptations of power and luxury. For example, she notes that, "Washington resigned his commission to congress [sic], and, after acting so conspicuous a part on the theatre of war, retired from public scenes and public men, with a philosophic dignity honorary to himself and to human nature" (Warren 1805b, 196). The concern, of course, would have been that, given human nature, following the violent overthrow of British rule, the first president might have sought to hold on to his position. But for Mercy, herein lies the great strength of Washington's personality, that notwithstanding his popularity, which might have allowed him to rationalize continuing in the station, he knew that he needed to do the right thing and so he pleasantly and politely retired (Warren 1805b, 214).

When Mercy uses the word "republican," one of the meanings she intends is just its older, simple meaning of not being a monarchy. Thus she rebukes President Adams because he now appears to like the idea of having a king, and has even, from her perspective, started behaving like one. However, this identification seems to Shaffer to be flawed since Mercy is apparently making the assumption that because Adams behaves like a monarch, he is now no longer a republican, which "illustrates a fundamental weakness in Warren's analysis" (Shaffer 1975, 148; Friedman and Shaffer 1975, 203 is similar). Certainly, it is correct that Mercy based her conclusion significantly on Adams' behavior, and she told him in a letter that, "There certainly was then an observable alteration in your whole deportment and conversation. Many of your friends saw, felt, and regretted it" (Mercy Warren, letter to John Adams, July 28, 1807, in Adams [1878] 1972, 361). Furthermore, in the same document, she notes that Adams' actions as president, in restoring some of the restrictive practices of colonial days, "[s]edition, stamp, and alien laws, a standing army, house and land taxes, and loans of money at an enormous interest, were alarming symptoms" (363) at the expense of Americans.

Smith notes that, in response to Adams' skepticism about whether "republican" meant anything at all (John Adams, letter to Mercy Warren, July 30, 1807, in Adams [1878] 1972, 390), Otis Warren, in a letter, presented a definition, but that definition was different than the one she gave in the *History*. In the letter, he writes, she bases her characterization on allowing the right to vote and using that right responsibly. However, in the *History*, Smith (1966, 104–105) argues that her approach is based on more holistic categories, such as human beings' natural equality and sovereignty – this would certainly be a rather more negative enumeration of freedom. Somewhat paradoxically, Adams writes in the same letter:

> I was always for a free republic; not a democracy, which is as arbitrary, tyrannical, bloody, cruel, and intolerable a government as that of Phalaris[6] with his bull is represented as being. Robespierre is a perfect exemplification of the character of the first bell-wether in a democracy.
>
> JOHN ADAMS, letter to MERCY WARREN, July 30, 1807, in ADAMS [1878] 1972, 394

However, the way that Otis Warren delineates "republican" in her own missive is not actually inconsistent with the "holistic categories" of the *History*, but rather seems to match them quite well. She points out to Adams that, in the *History*, she has (1) argued that people should not abuse the vote by using it to achieve personal or partisan benefit; and (2) emphasized the need for "electing such men to guide the national councils, whose conscious probity enable them to stand like a colossus on the broad basis of independence, and by correct and equitable arrangements endeavor to lighten the burdens of the people, strengthen their unanimity at home, command justice abroad, and cultivate peace with all nations" (Mercy Warren, letter to John Adams, July 30, 1807, in Adams [1878] 1972, 398–399). The political goals of responsiveness to the citizenry, peace, consensus, and global justice seem well-attuned with a philosophy that promotes natural equality and natural sovereignty. As Richards notes:

> Given the attributes Warren assigns to human nature, or humanity, she can support only one form of government: the republic. This word would be the cause of much conflict between Warren and John Adams, but we can draw some conclusions about what Warren believed. ... A republic ... is that form of government which intrudes least on its citizens, but the implication is that it must also be that form of government which most activates a contrary tendency to the "supineness" that leads to loss of liberty.

---

6 Phalaris was a sixth century BC tyrant believed to have ruled the whole island of Sicily, burning opponents alive in a metal chamber known as a bull.

In Warren's view, a republic is essentially a system whereby the people (though in real terms, white men) freely chose their representatives and leaders.

RICHARDS 1995, 139

Within such a demarcation, there seems to be little or no influence from classical republicanism, and the desire to have elected leaders be persons of higher moral values was shared by other great minds of the day, including James Madison. It is surely an exaggeration to interpret this as Baym (1991b) does, as "Warren is no democrat. She frequently contrasts the excitable and turbulent multitude to the enlightened and prudent few so as to distinguish the well-born heroes from the mob."

Furthermore, when Hicks attributes the main influence on Otis Warren's politics to role models in the women of Rome, as in the following statement, the hyperbole is quite profound:

The Roman matrons were political heroines who had made key contributions to the Roman republic and had defied the corruption of imperial Rome. In them, American women discovered stirring examples of learning, courage, and patriotism – and a precedent for their own empowerment. Indeed, though Warren's pose was verbal rather than sartorial, intimate rather than public, republican history proved instrumental to the formation of her political identity.

HICKS 2005, 265–266

There is little evidence that, beyond reading classical authors and using pen-names with classical antecedents, such as Mercy's pseudonym, Marcia, that Otis Warren was a republican in the way, for instance, that Pocock intends. Another of Mercy's pseudonyms, "A Columbian Patriot," portrayed Whig and Anti-Federalist, not classical ideals, while her use of "A Lady from Massachusetts" was merely descriptive. If Mercy and her correspondents had named themselves after Smokey, Whiskers, and Miss Kitty, or other favorite cats, would political theorists and historians today assume the influence of feline philosophy on their writings? It does not follow from the fact that she set her plays in different centuries and fictional or anachronistic locales, putting the emphasis on virtuous behavior, that "republican" ideas had much influence on her at all (Cornell 1999, 37; Hicks 2005, 290). Richards (1995, 79) is of course correct to point out that "Warren's literary allusions are drawn largely from the classics or English and Continental writings," but this may mean nothing more than the fact that these were the sources that existed at the time, which she had read;

these were, after all, the kinds of work that were sitting in her uncle, the Rev. Jonathan Russell's library, which, when she was young, was her main source of intellectual material. Certainly, it is possible for someone to note, say, the Roman women protesters described by Livy (1905, book 34), an author with whom Mercy was familiar, wives who were prohibited under the Oppian Law from owning much gold or from wearing purple, and who rallied and succeeded in overturning the regulation, which was based on the supposition that women were naturally profligate, and would waste resources that were needed to rebuild Rome following its defeat by Hannibal in the Second Punic War. Today, we might view the women's actions as an admirable precursor to modern feminism, but though the Roman women had an appropriate desire for greater liberty for themselves, and staged a street demonstration to achieve what they wanted, Mercy Otis Warren had a rather dissimilar agenda, is not often regarded as a radical feminist, and would certainly view skeptically the sacrifice of money on human adornments and other extravagances that could be better used for the public good. In fact, when Catharine Macaulay visited her in 1784, the two "republicans" had quite different opinions about the *Sans Souci* tearoom that had opened in Boston, where music was played and fashionable members of society might meet. Macaulay had no problem with this new attraction, but Mercy viewed its appearance as a reversion to "European" values, disapproving of the opulent lifestyles that she felt were promoted by its style (Davies 2005, 238, 244).

The disagreement between Otis Warren and Macaulay about the character of the *Sans Souci* may therefore be explained in terms of an emerging bifurcation between the values of Britain and those of its former colony, with virtue in the United States being prized by many above overindulgence, though it is not necessary to justify that preference in terms of a "republican" commitment. Moreover, what Otis Warren valued is not to emulate what Roman women desired. In the introduction to "The Sack of Rome," an historical tragedy that is included in her 1790 book of poems, Otis Warren explains that her purpose in setting the work in that classical time and place is, rather, because it presents an extreme example of a general tendency of human beings to be seduced by opulence and other vices. "Perhaps," she writes, "at that period, the character of man was sunk to the lowest stage of depravity" (Warren 1790, 9), a debility that would eventually lead to the destruction of the Roman Empire (10). The message for the young United States is to be found in the words of one of the play's characters, Gaudentius, who says:

> If party rage and luxury should cease,
> And peace give time to make a just reform
> Through each corrupted channel of law;

Or if simplicity returns,
And government more energy assumes,
Her ancient codes restor'd on equal terms,
She might yet reign
WARREN 1790, 16

Otis Warren is concerned to show the dangers of the retreat from virtue that she believes she witnesses in her lifetime as in Roman times, and this is an important component of what is often depicted as her "republicanism." As Zagarri (1995, 100) observes, Mercy's point in "The Sack of Rome" is indicated in the line, "Empire decays when virtue's not the base" (Warren 1790, 80). In making her case, Otis Warren looks to classical antiquity to give examples, many of which are negative. For instance, in the *History*, she makes parallels between the present situation and isomorphisms from earlier centuries, so it is unsurprising that she discusses the historical passage "from the rise of the Roman republic to the destruction of her splendid empire" (Warren 1805b, 226). Thus we find that by the time of Rome's demise:

Beneath incrusted roofs, emboss'd with gold,
Egyptian pearls and emeralds of the East,
The sword alone is all that Rome can boast
That bears affinity to former fame
WARREN 1790, 17

Similarly, she mentions ancient Athens, which, "corrupted by riches and luxury, was wasted and lost by the intrigues of its own ambitious citizens" (1805b, 227). Her goal here is to identify societies that once were viewed as admirable and which comported to her own values, and to delineate what "history and experience have proved" (226), rather than to extol a specific classical period. She describes the Roman transition as that empire moved away from "the sacred obligations of virtue" (226), not indicating it to be a society that ought to be recreated in the nineteenth century United States. These ancient cultures were at the time she admires them, just for the interim, places of virtue, and Mercy also praises them because they "boasted their freedom" (227). Moreover, she contends, it is wrong for people to view the decline of such societies as having been caused by "the spirit of free inquiry" (228), when in fact, she argues, the real villains were ambition, wealth, monarchy, and aristocracy (228–229). Cohen points out:

While, for Warren, history may have been easy enough to categorize into strict oppositions, its outcomes were neither obvious nor inevitable. If history revealed any consistent tendency, it was that arbitrary power, corruption, and irrationality tended to defeat enlightened principles. That was why most of the world remained enslaved.

COHEN 1994, 7

Applying her argument against luxury and vice specifically to the new United States in her poem, "The Genius of America," Otis Warren writes:

While luxury in high profusion reigns.
Our country bleeds, and bleeds at every pore,
Yet gold's the deity whom all adore

WARREN 1790, 246

In fact, for her, even the peacefulness of the American colonies and the progression toward independence had been nourished by "a few prostitutes of power, nurtured in the lap of America" but willing to betray their neighbors and friends to pursue personal ambition, with the assistance of the British (Warren 1805a, 43). Surprisingly, perhaps, the majority of colonists allowed just some among their number to benefit from this situation. As might be expected, Mercy mentions Thomas Hutchinson in this regard; his influence was used to obtain positions for his sons with the East India Company (68, 69) and she rues the consequence that, in Massachusetts, "almost every department of high trust as it became vacant by resignation, suspension or death, was filled by some relation or dependent of governor Hutchinson" (74). Of course, Mercy was somewhat disingenuous here, for she had also, from time to time, sought patronage positions for her husband and sons (Bailyn [1967] 1992, 109; Fleming 2009, 168, 194; McCullough 2001, 411; Roberts 2008, 135). Consequently, some of her criticisms of John Adams after he became president have been attributed to what Saxton (2009, 25) calls "personal disappointment in the friendship."

This criticism of the second president's apparent sympathies for royalty, despotism, and other faults in Otis Warren's *History* and later in the personal correspondence between the two of them has attracted scholarly attention. For Pocock, Mercy was attempting to analyze the actions of contemporary statesmen without having access to the details and circumstances under which leaders labored, and thus the conclusions she formed about the president were uninformed, and so Adams was merely "objecting quite justly" (Pocock 1998, 253) to what she wrote, whereas her friend, Catharine Macaulay, whose scholarship in her *History of England* instead employed "documents and narratives" (253) about the past, was better entitled than Otis Warren to see her work as being that of an historian. This is a controversial conclusion, differing substantially, for instance, from those of modern writers who have devoted whole books to explicating Mercy's life and writings. Moreover, her ability to perceive threats to the new society for which she had strived was not very complicated to achieve: she needed only to observe changes that were taking place around her, negative developments that were apparent to Jefferson and other contemporaries, and which, it can be argued, persist in the present day, notwithstanding the protections that were added to the Constitution via the Bill of Rights. Consequently, it is not surprising that she would write in her earlier polemic against ratification:

> Self defence is a primary law of nature, which no subsequent law of society can abolish; this primæval principle, the immediate gift of the Creator, obliges every one to remonstrate against the strides of ambition, and a wanton lust of domination, and to resist the first approaches of tyranny, which at this day threaten to sweep away the rights for which the brave sons of America have fought with an heroism scarcely paralleled even in ancient republicks.
>
> WARREN [1788] 1888, 2

Today, the wisdom revealed by Mercy Otis Warren in her historical writings, letters, plays, and poems remains a valuable source not just for political theorists and historians, but for anyone concerned about the twenty-first century loss of liberty and triumph of greed. Mercy may not have been a "republican" in any meaningful regard, but she did perceive multiple ways that a nation, once dedicated to the highest principles, and willing to endure great risk and suffering to free itself from tyranny, could then retreat, and sink, and eventually reach the point at which abandonment of the values that inspired that fight and the attendant triumph of a cruel plutocracy are all but complete.

ILLUSTRATION 2   Louise Michel, unknown photographer
PHOTO, 1880. WIKIMEDIA COMMONS.

CHAPTER 2

Louise Michel: Neither a Red Nor a Virgin?

Clémence Louise Michel (1830–1905), now known almost ubiquitously simply as Louise Michel, the anarchist feminist heroine of the Paris Commune, who repeatedly claimed that the year of her birth was 1836, was born in the French countryside in a village called Vroncourt-la-Côte in the *département* of Haute-Marne. Her mother was a domestic worker named Marie-Anne "Marianne" Michel, who lived and worked on the prominent Demahis family's estate. Louise's father is believed to have been Laurent Demahis, the son of the family patriarch and mayor of Vroncourt, Étienne-Charles Demahis, or possibly Étienne-Charles himself. Laurent departed the household for a nearby farm following the birth, and Michel believed he was the person most likely to be her father, as do most scholars today. Although she was the daughter of a poor peasant woman, and despite the fact that the Demahis family was not wealthy, Louise enjoyed the benefits of being raised in the château, even though she describes it as "tumbled-down," lacking some windows, and known as "the Tomb," a castle that later in her life she would note had become a ruin (Michel [1886] 1981, 4, 15). She was treated as though she were a granddaughter of Étienne-Charles and his wife, a circumstance that meant she attended the two-roomed Vroncourt school and was later trained as a teacher, and grew up with a knowledge of music and poetry; her "grandparents," which was how Louise referred to them, even offered a dowry in case, despite her illegitimacy, she wished to marry. That privileged situation whereby Louise was referred to locally as "Mademoiselle Demahis" lasted until Laurent's father died, and his mother, the former Louise-Charlotte Porquet, objected to Louise publishing poetry under the name "Louise Michel Demahis"; when Louise-Charlotte died in 1850, Laurent inherited almost all his parents' property, at which time he expelled Louise from the estate, although she retained a piece of land of about twenty acres, which later she had to sell to pay off debts after she was deported to New Caledonia. Benefiting from her access to education, and after qualifying as a teacher in nearby Chaumont-la-Ville, where she lived in a boarding house, Michel then in 1853 opened her own free school in Audeloncourt, where some of her mother's family lived, and which was also not very far from Vroncourt, before moving to Paris where she worked as a teacher for nine years, eventually purchasing a school in Montmartre with the financial help of her mother, who sold most of the land she herself had inherited from the Demahis family. Louise describes the stagecoach trip between Chaumont and

Audeloncourt as being somewhat arduous, winding around a mountain, Mont Chauve, and passing the ruins of an inn inside which travelers were rumored once to have been slaughtered.

Michel's experience of poverty contributed to her sympathy and identification with the most disadvantaged members of society, while her roots in Haute-Marne presented a symbolic association with the simpler local culture of her birth and its Celtic intonation, vocabulary, and roots, and an attachment to "the unconquered, long-haired Gauls" (Michel [1886] 1981, 17) who had fought a failed rearguard action against Roman conquest and civilization (Girault 1906, 2–20; Hart 2001–2002, 110, 114, 2004, 132–134; Lowry and Gunter 1981b, vii; Maclean 2003, 126–127; Michel [1886] 1981, 12, 16–17, 23, 31–34, 45; Mullaney 1984, 112, fn 30, 112–113, 120, 1990, 301–302, 317; Stivale 1986, 42; Thomas 1980, 14–25, 30, 67). She grew up influenced by diverging perspectives. Greenberg notes:

> Because she was the issue of two opposing social classes, Michel was able to both experience and record "misery."
>
> GREENBERG 1999, 163

Thus, to some extent, Higgins argues, she invented the persona with which she wished to be identified:

> [I]n her life and writing, she is posing for the person she wants to be, and to a great extent that is whom she became. Michel's contributions to her own public image were thus largely a case of self-invention: she created her legend and then lived it.
>
> HIGGINS 1982, 214–215

However, some of her feelings derived from her actual experience watching farm workers and farm animals being cruelly exploited by the persons they labored for, and seeing local children, no matter how hard their parents toiled, die of starvation. In her *Memoirs*, she writes:

> I know the woes of the peasant. He is incessantly bent over land that is harsh as a stepmother. For his labor all he gets is leftovers from his master, and he can get even less comfort from thought and dreams than we can. Heavy work bends both men and oxen over the furrows, keeping the slaughterhouse for worn-out beasts and the beggar's sack for worn-out humans.
>
> MICHEL [1886] 1981, 27

Another true quality of her background that influenced her personality was certainly not the product of her imagination, which was the fact that she was illegitimate, and the consequences of this continued to haunt her throughout her life:

> In her *Mémoires*, in the passages relating to her childhood, she elides the facts of her birth – indeed, the place and name of the father are marked only by an absence, a lack in the text. She is named as a bastard only once, towards the end of the book.
>
> MACLEAN 2003, 126

Early on, she knew, too, that she did not wish to marry at the age of twelve or thirteen, which was when she rejected two suitors, a decision her "grandparents" had fortunately given her the option to do:

> There have been unfortunate children who were forced to marry old crocodiles like those. If it had been done to me, either he or I would have had to jump out the window.
>
> MICHEL [1886] 1981, 21

At 56, her views remained consistent with this earlier perspective:

> There are enough tortured women in the world without my becoming another one. ... I have always looked upon marriage without love as a kind of prostitution.
>
> MICHEL [1886] 1981, 39

At a meeting at the Salle Rivoli, a ballroom in Paris, in 1880, she said, "We want free marriage, in which men no longer hold propriety rights over women" (Michel, quoted by Thomas 1980, 175; see also Mullaney 1990, 316).

1   Michel the Heroine of France

The principal biographical work about Louise Michel is *Louise Michel* by Édith Thomas, which has been translated into English by Penelope Williams (Thomas 1980); the original French version (Thomas 1971) has a longer title, *Louise Michel ou La Velléda de l'anarchie*. Thomas' work has received some criticism, including its tendency to dwell on theories concerning its subject's romantic life (Mullaney 1990, 314), and its focus on historical detail at the expense of a more extensive exposition of Michel's philosophical ideas (Crichfield 1972, 54). The latter point is echoed by Marquant (1971, 178–179), and also by Kinsman (1982, 155), who additionally complains that more explanation of key events from French history should have been included in the English-language version. In her biography of Thomas, Dorothy Kaufmann suggests that she to some extent grew less approving of Michel as she grew older. In 1939, three decades before the publication of her biography of Michel, which was her last project and was released after her death, Thomas had written a much more enthusiastic though unpublished account, quite unlike the later version, in which Kaufmann (2004, 187) says "Thomas's irritation with her protagonist is at least equal to her admiration." Kaufmann (206) complains that Thomas' book is too long, and points out that the publisher of the French language rendering, Gallimard, had also suggested that she shorten it, which she refused to do.

Louise's *Memoirs* have been translated into English under the name *The Red Virgin: Memoirs of Louise Michel* (Michel [1886] 1981). There are also a number of other extant works written by Michel, including *Légendes et chants de gestes canaques* (Michel [1885] 1980), which is an account of her time living as a déportée in New Caledonia, and which describes the local fauna, vegetation, and weather of the colony's islands, as well as the language of the Kanaks, the native people there. Her concerns about child poverty are addressed in a novel, *Le claque-dents* (Michel 1890). *Avant la Commune* (Michel [1905] 1987) is a collection of some of her poetry, as is *Au gré du Vent: Poesies* (Michel 1912). She wrote other fiction, including plays and children's stories, as well as articles advocating her feminist and anarchist views, some of which were included in *la Révolution sociale*, an anarchist paper that was published in Paris from 1880 to 1881. Some of her personal letters have been collected, but other published works have not survived.

Michel was one of the leading lights of the Paris Commune, a valiant attempt to create an autonomous democracy in that city which began on March 18, 1871 and lasted for little more than two months before being overwhelmed by the army of the Third Republic. Though about 25,000 residents perished in the experiment, it remains celebrated by anarchists and others of like values for its creation of what Ross (1989, 751–752) calls "the free organization of its social life." Maclellan writes:

> It inspired a range of anarchists, socialists and communists in the decades leading up to the Russian Revolution of 1917, and was a source of ideas about the replacement of capitalistic political structures with those that could assist a transition to a socialist society.
>
> MACLELLAN 2004a, 10

For Peter Kropotkin, one of the reasons for praising the Commune and seeing it as a model for the future was that it had taken over the city almost without violence, and was the collective act of a community:

> When the armed people came out into the streets, the rulers fled away,
> the troops evacuated the town, the civil functionaries hurriedly retreated
> to Versailles [where France's new Third Republic national government
> was located], carrying everything they could with them. The Government
> evaporated like a pond of stagnant water in a spring breeze, and on
> the 19th the great city of Paris found herself free from the impurity
> which had defiled her, with the loss of scarcely a drop of her children's
> blood.
>
>   KROPOTKIN 1909, 3

Ross continues:

> The Commune was not just a political uprising; it was perhaps even more
> a revolt against deeply entrenched forms of social regimentation.
>
>   ROSS 1989, 751–752

Michel worked on behalf of the venture's success as nurse, teacher, and soldier,
as well as by motivating her fellow-revolutionists with her impassioned rhetoric, one consequence of which is that Mullaney (1984, 104) writes that she "is
generally regarded as the greatest female revolutionary that France ever
produced," while Harison (2007, 14) proclaims her "virtual embodiment of revolution in France." In addition to assuming roles suggested by the customs of
gender segregation, such as teaching students, taking care of the injured, and
running a soup kitchen, Michel also gave speeches advocating women's rights,
and as a combatant she dressed in the uniform of the National Guard,
while on sentry duty she wore *godillots* [military boots] (Mullaney 1990, 302;
Ross 2015, 12–13). Ironically, the gender segregation may have worked to her advantage when, at her trial, future prime minister Georges Clémenceau, the
mayor of Paris' eighteenth arrondissement (Montmartre), who had been de-
posed by the Communards, disputed some of Louise's responsibility for her
actions because she was a woman, as follows:

> She was sometimes deranged: for instance, I have seen her cry and la-
> ment because she did not receive the quantity of food and clothes that
> she wanted to distribute.
>
>   Testimony of Georges Clémenceau, quoted in TAITHE 2001, 112

In fact, gender segregation was also a factor in the way that the Vigilance Committee of Montmartre (*Comité de Vigilance de Montmartre*), a radical political group existing (in Montmartre, a district not yet formally part of Paris) since before the instigation of the Commune, was organized: it was separated into a men's committee and a women's committee, with Michel being the leader of the latter, but also participating in the men's group (Eichner 2004, 148; Michel [1886] 1981, 58–59; Stewart 2006, 304; Thomas 1980, 67, 71).

One aspect of the Commune's ethos is of particular relevance to Michel's activities on its behalf, especially in the light of her impoverished origins and her self-chosen Gallic identity. Hart (2001–2002, 115) notes that, "The 1871 Commune was a time when the boundaries between art and life, as well as between "high" and "low" culture were temporarily displaced." The revolt offered an opportunity to recreate cultural norms in a fashion that reflected the goals of its activists, who were generally republicans personally familiar with the strains of labor, and often influenced by the goals of Karl Marx's First International. For that reason, they implemented the separation of church and state, removing crucifixes in particular, and the influence of the Catholic Church in general from their schools, beginning a process of modernization and diversity that would result in a very different France today from the one they briefly supplanted in Paris. The Communards' investment in a literature and art of universal appeal, no longer serving to emphasize the differences between people's position in society, would become a key facet. In much the same way, Argentinian novelist Julio Cortázar describes the zeal of college students and others in the early days of the Sandinista revolution in Nicaragua in the 1980s, setting out cheerfully for the countryside to expand literacy, together with the implementation of a deliberate policy of publishing affordable copies of works of literature (Cortázar 1989; Gopnik 2014; Hart 2001–2002, 115; Ross 1989, 751, 2015, 12–13; Stopes 2015).

Eventually, the army of the government in Versailles invaded Paris, a development that led to many fires, some of which at least are believed to have been deliberately caused by Communard women, ever since dubbed *pétroleuses*, one of whom was Michel; the attribution to her, however, is viewed by Michel's biographer, Édith Thomas (1980, 11–12), as a slur. Following this crushing of the Commune, a large number of the rebels were simply killed on the spot, while others, including Louise, were put on trial. She, along with some other female leaders, including feminist Paule Minck (also spelled Mink, birth name, Adèle Paulina Mekarska); the novelist André Léo (real name, Victoire Léodile Béra Champseix), who was somewhat skeptical about the direction the commune took, particularly of many of its male leaders' less enlightened views about women; and Elizabeth Dmietrieff, a friend of Marx, who like Michel suffered from the disadvantage caused by her illegitimacy, had not been arrested. Minck and Léo moved to Switzerland for a while. However, Louise's mother, Marie-Anne, was found to be in detention, and when she tried to free her, she was herself captured. Louise writes:

> Somehow I managed to escape from the soldiers trying to arrest me. Finally the victorious reactionaries took my mother and threatened to shoot her if I wasn't found. To set her free I went to take her place, although she didn't want me to do it, the poor, dear woman.
> MICHEL [1886] 1981, 69

In some respects, this is a scenario that resembles the later example of the Chicago anarchist leader, Albert Parsons, who was not originally arrested in the Haymarket Tragedy, but was when he announced at the trial of the others that he was present in the courtroom; eventually Parsons would be hanged.[1] On the other hand, Michel's interpretation that her mother was a hostage tells a slightly different story. On December 16, 1871, following her arrest, Louise Michel stood before a military tribunal, charged with subversion, torture, murder, forgery, wearing a military uniform, possession of arms during an insurrection, and, she admitted, conspiring to assassinate Adolphe Thiers, the leader of the new Third Republic (or, as Kropotkin (1909, 8) termed it, "the traitor government which raised itself to power at the downfall of the empire"), which had begun following the humiliating defeat of France by Prussia; fellow-Communard Théophile Ferré (whom, as is discussed later, she admired) had persuaded her not to go ahead with this plan. However, the Communards did destroy Thiers' Paris house. On trial, wearing black, she stood out as someone exceptional for her unapologetic defense of her actions and those of the other Communard leaders, even admitting to activities in which she had not participated, while denying the guilt of anyone else. Refusing to plead for forgiveness or leniency, and saying that she took full responsibility for her actions, she demanded execution, a request that, perhaps because the prosecutor, a Captain Dailly, in summation formally withdrew all of the charges except for the weapons offense; or, due to the Court's own obstinacy; or, perhaps because she was a woman; or because she was a woman whom her judges viewed as being arrogant and behaving in an insufficiently deferential manner; or maybe because of her great eloquence; or due to some combination of some or all of these factors, the Court declined to do. She had served as her own lawyer, rejecting the assistance of a Court-appointed defender called Haussman, and when she

---

1   At a Haymarket Square, Chicago anarchist meeting on May 4, 1886, the throwing of a bomb by an unknown assailant, killing a policeman, became the pretext for the judicial murder of four anarchists now known as the Haymarket Martyrs.

was eventually silenced by the judge, she responded, "Si vous n'êtes pas des lâches, tuez-moi" ["If you're not cowards, kill me!"] (Bullard 2000, 79; Danaswamy 2006; Fetridge 1871, 111, 255; Girault 1906, 78–88; Gopnik 2014; Greenberg 1999, 161; Gullickson 1996, 125, 209–212, 2016; Hart 2001–2002, 107, 2004, 138; Higgins 1982, 214–215; Leighton 1990, 26; Michel [1871] 1986, 81, 85–88; Mullaney 1990, 305; Thomas 1980, 83–84, 88–89, 124–126; Wright 2017, 107). At this point, Gullickson argues, Michel was so exhausted and despondent that she actually wanted to die:

> But claiming responsibility was more than a way of defending the Commune for Michel. It was also an attempt to control her own destiny. She wanted to die. She had had enough, especially after the government had executed Ferré.
>
> GULLICKSON 1996, 210

Louise Michel was saved from execution by the Court, but as punishment was instead transported on a frigate called *la Virginie*, a trip that took four months, stopping in the Canary Islands and Brazil, before arriving in New Caledonia, a French dependency that until 1895 was used as a penal colony (Michel [1871] 1986, 90–95). In *Légendes et chants de gestes canaques*, Louise points out that her new home lay isolated – as Paul Mason (2017a) notes, "about as far as you can physically get from France" – to the east of Australia, to the west of Fiji and the Loyalty Islands (the latter are now part of New Caledonia) and south of the New Hebrides (now called Vanuatu) and the Belep Islands, which are now also a part of New Caledonia (Michel 1885, 6). In 1880, the Communards were freed following a general amnesty, the only condition under which Louise said she would be willing to leave her comrades, and she returned to the French mainland. While she was there, however, eschewing quiet acceptance of her predicament, she found another population, the Kanaks, who were much in need of an advocate. She started a school for them, teaching them how to write, an effort that was to some extent a continuation of her efforts as part of the Commune; she also taught the children of the French residents. Additionally, she connected with and sympathized with Arab déportés from the French colony of Algeria. Near the end of her life, in 1904, Louise visited Algeria. She was consistently an internationalist, an opponent of colonialism; Thomas describes these sentiments as follows:

> Louise aime les indigènes algérians, comme elle aimait les Canaques et hait la morgue des Français, qui sont installés là-bas et qui se considerèrent commes des êtres supérieurs. (Thomas 1971, 438) [Louise liked

the indigenous Algerians in the way she was fond of the Kanaks and loathed the arrogance of the French, who had installed themselves over there and who considered themselves superior creatures.]

In New Caledonia, she supported the indigenous people's pro-independence revolt of 1878, one of the causes of which was conflict between French settlers and local Kanaks over land (Thomas 1980, 148, 159, 162–164). Hart writes:

> Her compatriots are shocked when she professes admiration for supposedly "savage" and "uncivilized" Kanakan music and dance, and she outrages them with the suggestion that they start a Kanakan theater, blowing through horns, shaking palm leaves, and striking bamboo reeds. Whereas other exiled communards wished to take up arms against the Kanaks, Louise Michel actively supported their revolt.
>
> HART 1999, 159

Pressure to establish complete independence of New Caledonia from France continues to this day, as Mason observes:

> The apartheid system is gone – you will see middle-class Kanaks eating in restaurants alongside the descendants of white settlers. But the discontent is not. ... there is tension: the township of St. Louis, just outside the capital, Noumea, has become a partial no-go area, with sporadic carjackings and alleged hostage-taking by the indigenous population.
>
> MASON 2017a

With the exception of the Kanaks' cannibalism, Michel's assumed minority identity made her naturally sympathetic to them, more so than was the case with the other déportés (Bullard 2000, 162, 274–275; Greenberg 1999, 161; Hart 2001–2002, 107–108, 116–117; Mullaney 1984, 134, 1990, 303). Bullard comments:

> Perhaps as a woman in a strongly patriarchal culture, Michel in fact felt less infinity for French "civilization" and could more easily perceive the virtues of the Kanak.
>
> BULLARD 2000, 274

Armogathe takes the same position:

> Louise Michel s'est passionnée pour les Canaques, parce qu'ils sont « l'autre », et qu'elle aussi, bâtarde et réprouvée, parle d'une position autre.

Ce n'est pas de la simple curiosité pour eux. Elle les « *comprehend* ». Ce faisant, elle ouvre la voie au respect des races. (Armogathe 1985, 2) [Louise Michel became passionately fond of the Kanaks because they are "the other," and because she, a bastard and an outcast, also speaks from an alternative perspective. This isn't ordinary curiosity about them. She "understands" them. For that reason, she is opening the way to respect between the races.]

On the other hand, Louise saw clearly that Kanak culture was "other" to what she had learned in her own privileged French educational environment:

La musique canaque avec ses quarts de tons ressemble au vent, aux bruits de bois, aux flots, souvent elle est douce, quelquefois rauque, parfois on dirait des gouttes d'eau tombant sur les feuilles.

Des bambous frappés en cadence, une flûte de roseau, les branches de palmiers grattées, une feuille qu'ils s'appliquent sur la bouche, tels sont leurs instruments.

Souvent encore ils accompagnent, ensifflant ou en soutenant la voix sur une seule note, tandis que l'air est chanté; ces sons filés produisent un effet étrange. (Michel [1885] 1980, 124–125) [Kanak music with its quarter-tones resembles the wind, the clatter of timber, waves; often it is gentle, sometimes harsh, now and then it sounds like specks of falling water on leaves. Bamboos struck in cadence, a reed flute, scraped branches of palm trees, a leaf that they stick over their mouths, such are their instruments. Often, also, accompanying them, whistling or a single vocal note, while the melody is sung, these spun out sounds produce a peculiar effect.]

Moreover, commitment to a theory of Michel's otherness obscures positive feelings she retained about her gentle upbringing. In her *Memoirs*, she writes of her château experience effusively as follows:

What peace there was in this place, and what peace there was in my life at that time! Maybe I did not deserve it. How I love to dream of this little corner of the earth.

MICHEL [1886] 1981, 7

As a teacher, Michel acquired a thoughtful awareness of the limitations of education as customarily practiced, and even as a child, some of the defects were quite apparent, and apprised in a manner that is consistent with feminist and anarchist perspectives:

> I'm convinced that my first impressions were correct; adults give girls a
> pile of nonsense supported by childlike logic, while at the same time they
> make our "lords and masters" swallow little balls of science until they
> choke. For both of us, it is a ridiculous education. A few hundred years
> from now people will see it all as a heap of trash – even the education of
> men.
>
> MICHEL [1886] 1981, 20

She continues:

> I have never understood why there was a sex whose intelligence people
> tried to cripple as if there were already too much intelligence in the
> world. Little girls are brought up in foolishness and are expressly dis-
> armed so that men can deceive them more easily. That is what men want.
>
> MICHEL [1871] 1986, 140–141

Of course, since the fact that education steadily reinforces the *status quo* and
the inequalities that are embodied therein, preparing the vast majority of
students for future lives of compliant discontent and abject inferiority is no
accident, so it follows that even to try to overcome the inevitability of its perpetuation would require the kind of leadership and strength of character demonstrated by Michel throughout her life. It is likely she would have embraced the
opinion of the German anarchist, Max Stirner, whom she is not believed to
have studied, on the subject of what would constitute a non-ridiculous, thoroughly anarchistic approach to education. Stirner writes:

> Truth itself consists in nothing other than man's revelation of himself,
> and thereto belongs the discovery of himself, the liberation from all that
> is alien, the uttermost abstraction or release from all authority, the re-
> won naturalness. Such thoroughly true men are not supplied by school.
>
> STIRNER [1842] 1967, 21

Furthermore, in characteristically anarchist fashion, Louise could also see the
role that ignorance, misinformation, and lack of educational opportunity play
in undermining fairness and democracy. She wrote:

> Throughout the world there are too many minds left uncultivated, just as
> good land lies fallow while much of the old cultivated land is exhausted.
> It is the same for human races. Between those who know nothing and
> those who have a great deal of false knowledge – those warped for

thousands of generations by infallible knowledge that is incorrect – the difference is less great than it appears at first glance.

MICHEL [1886] 1981, 118

As for Karl Marx and Alexander Berkman among others, the failure of ordinary people to apprehend the true nature of their circumstances perplexed and aggravated Michel:

> This time the people must be the masters. The feeling for liberty will develop. Perhaps it would be better for the people if all of us who lead the fight now should fall in battle, so that after the victory, there will be no more general staffs. Then the people could understand that when everyone together shares power, then power is just and splendid; but unshared it drives some people mad.
>
> MICHEL [1871] 1986, 131

Of course, as she appreciates, in the absence of a widespread desire for freedom and the equitable sharing of power, the underlying risk is that the masses, remaining thoroughly ignorant and believing untruths, will embrace a tyrannical populism that makes the situation even worse. For Michel, instead, a key part of the revolution that she wanted to see was the establishment of equal rights for men and women alike (Michel [1871] 1986, 139–142).

2   Michel the Anarchist

Like Kropotkin ([1927] 1970, 147), Michel believed that human nature was basically good, while modern society prioritized distorted values that stressed competitiveness and power at the expense of the innately cooperative spirit of human beings. Though somewhat skeptical about its accuracy, Thomas describes her philosophy as follows:

> La foi de Louise était assez simpliste: l'homme est originellement bon. C'est la société et le pouvoir qui la corrompent. La dernier avatar de cette société coercitive et malfaisante, c'est la capitalisme, héritier de toutes les formes de domination. ... La société capitaliste, c'est aujourd'hui l'ennemi qu'il faut détruire. (Thomas 1971, 452) [Louise's faith was rather simplistic: humankind is fundamentally good. It is society and power that corrupt it. The latest embodiment of this coercive and harmful society is capitalism, the inheritor of all forms of domination. ... Capitalist society is today the enemy that must be demolished.]

Louise, an active anarchist who described herself in that way, lectured to
large numbers of people in the 1880s and 1890s in Belgium and the Netherlands
as well as in France and England about the virtues of anarchism, but she is not
believed to have read the works of many contemporary revolutionaries,
Proudhon probably being an exception, whose theories she talked about while
she was imprisoned in New Caledonia with a fellow déporté, a journalist
named Auguste Passedouet, who would die in the colony; also, in her *Memoirs*,
she criticizes Proudhon for not taking women's equality seriously. Nonetheless,
her ideas were often compatible with those of Emma Goldman (Leighton 1990,
22; Lowry and Gunter 1981b, ix; Mason 2017b ; Michel [1886] 1981, 110–111, 142,
143; Thomas 1980, 153). In 1895, traveling to Vienna from the United States,
Emma stopped off in England, and one of the first people she met upon arriving in London was Louise Michel, who was someone she admired. Goldman
wrote:

> Ever since I had read about the Paris Commune, its glorious beginning
> and its terrible end, Louise Michel had stood out sublime in her love for
> humanity, grand in her zeal and courage. She was angular, gaunt,
> aged before her years (she was only sixty-two); but there was spirit and
> youth in her eyes, and a smile so tender that it immediately won my
> heart.
>
> GOLDMAN [1931b] 1970, volume 1, 166; the quotation is reprinted in MACLELLAN
> 2004b, 109

Some years later, in the text of a speech that she planned to deliver in Chicago
until she was prevented from doing this by police, describing Michel as the
epitome of everything that anarchists stood for, Goldman wrote:

> Again, let us take a type of human being with the social instinct devel-
> oped to the extreme – Louise Michel, the world-renowned anarchist,
> "Mother Louise," as she was called by every child of the gutter. Her love
> for man and beast knew no bounds.
>
> GOLDMAN [1908] 2005, 292

On September 13, 1895, Michel and Goldman appeared on the same platform at
a meeting at the South Place Institute in Finsbury, London, the title of which
was "Political Justice in England and America," although Louise spoke about
conditions in her own country in French (Drinnon 1961, 64–65; Falk 2005a, volume 1, 221, volume 2, 535; Falk 2005b, volume 1, 38; Goldman [1931b] 1970,
volume 1, 166; Thomas 1971, 375–376). In *Louise/Emma*, a play by Anne Roche
and Françoise Chatôt (1982) that was first staged in Marseille, France in 1983,

the writers build on the written works of the two women anarchists to create imaginary encounters between them that indicate the shared significance of, and interrelationship between, the values expressed by Michel and Goldman. Moss writes:

> In talking about their personal and political lives, their feminist and revolutionary ideals, Louise Michel and Emma Goldman speak for all women and all oppressed people. ... *Louise/Emma* succeeds in making these two passionate women come alive to serve as symbols of women's struggle for freedom.
>
> MOSS 1987, 556

Ironically, given her nickname "the Red Virgin," a phrase which has also been used as the title of her English language *Memoirs* (Michel [1886] 1981), one of the contributions that Michel would make to anarchism was actually to adopt the black flag as the symbol of the creed, in preference to the red color favored by Kropotkin and others. At a March 9, 1883 demonstration by unemployed people in France at the Esplanade des Invalides in Paris led by Michel and Émile Pouget, a fellow-anarchist, who would later become one of the leaders of the Confédération générale du travail (CGT) congress of labor unions, an organization that, in the beginning of the twentieth century, was strongly influenced by syndicalist ideas, Michel and Pouget brought along a black banner to draw attention to the damage done by the crushing of the Paris Commune; they were both charged, Louise after having stayed hidden for three weeks before turning herself in. Of the new color, she said at her trial, "We have used the black flag because this was a peaceful demonstration, because it is the flag of strikes and starvation" (Michel, quoted by Thomas 1980, 221). However, she had suggested that starving workers should break into bakeries and steal bread, which some of those in attendance did in fact carry out, although Louise pointed out that she had not. Although the jury recommended leniency, she received six years' imprisonment in solitary confinement, of which she would serve three, and Pouget was given eight years in solitary, and was also incarcerated for three before being released (Chincholle 1885, 182–188; Falk 2005a, volume 1, 144, fn 3; Girault 1906, 147–150; Lowry and Gunter 1981b, ix; Maclellan 2004a, 19–20, 2004b, 105–107; Michel [1886] 1981, 158–171; "The Trial of Louise Michel" 1883; Thomas 1980, 206–227). Fortunately, this period of imprisonment gave Louise the opportunity to write her *Memoirs*, which, though not organized in the most systematic way, are of great value to researchers today, showing not only many of the factors that shaped her life, but also the beliefs that were embodied in her desire to participate in revolution (Hart 2001–2002, 109).

The conventional wisdom is that Michel became more of an anarchist, and less of a socialist, after the Commune, and this is what, at times, Louise also indicated (Leighton 1990, 27–29). But if "red" is no longer the best color with which to describe her views, some scholars have gone to pains to suggest that neither is the word "virgin." Greenberg writes:

> It is interesting that Michel has always been nicknamed the "red virgin," a reference to her revolutionary politics. A committed *communard*, she sublimated the passion of a sexlife [sic] that according to historians was non-existent, except for the rumor of an involvement with [Victor] Hugo during her visit to Paris on September 13–18, 1870.
>
> GREENBERG 1999, 166

However, other writers would not agree. Emma Goldman, for example, became actively involved in discussion of Michel's sexual orientation (Mullaney 1984, 149–150). In an article in the *Jahrbuch für sexuelle Zwischenstufen* of 1906, its author, a physician named Karl von Levetzow, had argued that Louise's atypical behavior indicated that she was a lesbian. In her response some time later, denying the attribution of lesbianism to Michel, but pointing out that she was not prompted by any dislike of homosexuality or of those who practiced it, Goldman wrote that "it may be psychologically conditioned in all persecuted peoples to cling for support to the exceptional types," which suggested that, in this case, the attractiveness to him of Michel's persona and his desire to appropriate it implied that "von Levetzow suffers from an overdose of homosexual sectarianism." While von Levetzow had explained Louise's rejection of male suitors as a young teenager as a sign of her lesbianism, Emma assured him that this was not the case, but was instead just the rejection of marriage and a commitment to the real love of her life, which was revolution (Goldman 1923a, which is also reprinted in Goldman 2016; Goldman 1923b is similar; Maclellan 2004, 112–115, contains an abbreviated version of Goldman 1923b; Mullaney 1990, 312–313). Mullaney provides a justification for Goldman's view, painting it in a sympathetic light as follows:

> Determined to demonstrate the widespread nature of homosexuality, researchers were anxious to unveil the sexual preferences of as many acclaimed individuals as possible. They were also particularly interested in the relationship between feminism and lesbianism. The spirit of civil libertarianism that motivated members made them especially sympathetic to radical movements of the kind Michel had long embraced, those that put a premium on human freedom and social change.
>
> MULLANEY 1990, 309

Elsewhere, Mullaney comments:

> Those anxious to prop up the myth of the saintly and pure "Red Virgin"
> devoted only to the revolution adamantly insisted on her platonic
> relationships with men. Political opponents, however, were eager to see
> something "pathological" in her refusal to marry, her masculine manner-
> isms, "tomboyish" youth, and decidedly "manly" interests.
>   MULLANEY 1984, 149

Michel was suspected of having a relationship with Charles-Théophile Ferré,
usually known just as Théophile Ferré, who was a member of the men's
Vigilance Committee of Montmartre, and who became the first Communard
leader to be executed, having been convicted of ordering the firing squad killing of Georges Darboy, the Archbishop of Paris and five other hostages (Mullaney 1984, 141, 1990, 306). In her *Memoirs*, Michel tells of her friendship with
Marie Ferré, Théophile's sister [another friend of Louise, Ernest Girault (1906,
57, 59) refers to her as Maria Ferré] who, under pressure to reveal the location
of her brother, during her subsequent week-long imprisonment lost control of
her reason, a debilitating condition from which she never recovered, dying a
few days later (Bullard 2000, 82; Michel [1886] 1981, 74–75, 135–138). Although
Théophile Ferré was an admirable figure to Louise and other Communard supporters and participants, other commentators saw him quite differently. For
example, in a review of a biography of Darboy by the Archbishop of Lyons, the
anonymous writer sees him, notwithstanding his first name, as being in no way
a friend of God:

> Théophile Ferré was, if possible, even more odious than [Raoul] Rigault
> [an atheist Communard]; his claim to distinction lies chiefly in his having
> led the firing party which put Mgr. Darboy and the other hostages to
> death. *Théophile Ferré* – there seems to be a sort of irony in his having
> borne such a name – was, it appears, unlovely in form and feature, and to
> this peculiarity, M. [Maxime] Du Camp [the author of a history of the
> Commune, *Les Convulsions de Paris*] is inclined to lay the blame of much
> of his bloodthirstiness and cruelty.
>   "In the Ninety-Second Year of the Revolution" 1889, 276

His last name, Ferré, does have the meaning of "steel-tipped," which might
be an appropriate depiction of the militancy of some of the Communard
leaders, and which may also describe Michel's military-style footwear. But not
everyone would view the identification of the goals of the Commune with the

behavior of Rigault. Gopnik notes that the latter enjoyed the finer things in life, particularly when it came to food and wine. However:

> If Louise Michel represents the forward-looking aspect of the Commune, Raoul Rigault represents the backward-looking aspect – he is a kind of [Georges] Danton reborn.
>
> GOPNIK 2014[2]

At the tribunal, Louise denied having had a relationship with Ferré, which members of the tribunal who tried her, familiar with gossip that claimed she had been his mistress, considered that, since she was a woman, was her most likely motivation for having participated in the Commune. Her denial, meanwhile, fueled an alternative hypothesis that she was romantically involved during the Commune, and later when they were exiled to New Caledonia, with a fellow-anarchist Natalie Lemel (also known as Nathalie Duval), who had left her husband. Later, she was believed to have a relationship with another woman she had worked with during the Commune, Paule Minck, who was the person some scholars believe fully converted Louise to the doctrines of anarchism (Mullaney 1990, 305–307). Not surprisingly, Gullickson comments:

> What Michel's relationship was with Théophile Ferré is an often asked and largely unanswerable question.
>
> GULLICKSON 1996, 210

Nonetheless, some of her biographers have not been deterred from attempting to answer it. Her affection for Ferré is clear from the poem she dedicated to him titled "To Th. Ferré" [À Th. Ferré], which contains the following lines:

> In the final days of the Empire,
> When the people were awakening,
> It was your smile, red carnation,
> Which told us that all was being reborn.
>
> MICHEL [1871] 1986, 51; the French version is reproduced in GIRAULT 1906, 65

Édith Thomas, writing from what may seem to the reader to be a somewhat dated perspective, makes much of the fact that Michel was sixteen years older

---

2 Danton was guillotined by some of his fellow French Revolutionists for corruption and his extravagant lifestyle.

than Ferré, though she implies that Louise probably never told him how old
she actually was; despite Louise's feelings, she doubts that they were ever romantically involved:

> This feminine deception of hers looks to me like another indication of
> her love for Ferré. ... This great passion by a spinster in her forties for a boy
> of twenty-five could only be platonic.
>
>   THOMAS 1980, 67, 69

Similarly, Girault writes:

> L'homme, le seul je crois, qui fit vibrer le cœur de Louise Michel, était
> Théophile Ferré. [The man, the only one, I believe, who thrilled the heart
> of Louise Michel was Théophile Ferré.]
>
>   GIRAULT 1906, 57

However, he also notes (1906, 63) that this was a one-sided attraction, speaking
of "la non-réciprocité de son amour pour Théophile Ferré" [the non-reciprocity
of her love for Théophile Ferré]. According to Louise's *Memoirs*, in the final letter to Michel that Théophile wrote at 5.30 a.m., shortly before he was executed
on November 28, 1871, he addressed her as "[m]y beloved sister," and called
himself "[y]our devoted brother" (Michel [1871] 1986, 77). However, in the original French language version of her biography of Michel, Thomas (1971, 130,
1980, 120) writes that in this last letter Théophile opened and closed much
more formally with "*Chère citoyenne*" (in the English version, "Dear *citoyenne*"),
which raises the issue of whether they were describing the same letter, only
one of which can have been the final missive. The issue of whether or not Louise had an affair in Paris with Victor Hugo, which Thomas (1980, 62) believes
was the case, is similarly difficult to discern, although Hart offers the following
lukewarm validation:

> While this cannot be confirmed, it is worthwhile to recall that Hugo loved
> young girls and possibly expressed an amorous interest in Michel that
> may or may not have been reciprocated.
>
>   HART 2004, 134

Consequently, in the light of the existence of all these speculations, Leighton's
conclusion (below) seems difficult to validate, and also for the additional reason that even though Louise liked music and sang in church choirs, the characterization of her as celibate due to her profound religious faith seems doubly
unlikely:

> Her sexual asceticism (for which there are also obvious social reasons such as the total unavailability of contraceptives and societal taboos on female sexuality) made her even more the ministering angel, the *sœur de charité*, which was still a powerful symbol in the very much Catholic-influenced France of the 19th Century.
>
> LEIGHTON 1990, 24

The fact that Louise's mother, Marie-Anne, was unmarried should perhaps point the reader to the truly obvious fact that many people seldom behave in a way that is in complete accordance with their own values nor in compliance with contemporary taboos, and responding to this reality and its more negative consequences is a constant component in the narrative of humankind. For Thomas (1980, 36, 45–46), when Michel was younger, she appears to have been a deeply committed Catholic of a spiritual bent, a fact that she began to deny when she became more politically radical, including in the accounts of her life that she penned in *Memoirs*, thus keeping secret from her devotees "the inherent logic of her evolution from compassion and religious fervour to a sense of justice and revolutionary fervour" (Thomas 1980, 36). Later, Louise turned "furiously anticlerical" (Thomas 1980, 65). But for another Michel biographer, she was maybe mystical at times, in a general, pantheistic way, but never at any time in her life was she a Catholic:

> Louise ne fut jamais une catholique, ni une déiste orthodoxe; mais, quant à affirmer qu'elle professa toujours un athéisme et un matérialisme absolus, ce serait peut-être lui donner une conception scientifique qu'elle n'avait pas, lui accorder des idées quelle ne mûrissait nullement. (Girault 1906, 31) [Louise never was a Catholic, nor a conventional deist; but, as for asserting that she always practiced atheism and absolute materialism, that might be to embrace a scientific concept which she never had and apply it to ideas that that were never thoroughly thought out.]

On her return to the French mainland from New Caledonia in 1880, Louise smuggled five of her cats on the ships that took her from Nouméa to Sydney and then to London and Dieppe, demonstrating her well-known commitment to animal welfare, and also showing that her courage and self-determination in the face of power remained strong (Michel [1871] 1986, 121–122). Naturally, she immediately became involved again in radical politics. In October 1886, Michel became rather briefly involved with the Symbolist/Decadent movement and its self-conscious attempt to decide where it stood in terms of politics. She appeared at two Symbolist conferences that were held in Paris, which, Shryock (2000, 292, 296) writes, indicates that anarchists of the time were attracted to the radical character of that burgeoning art form, with Louise as a poet and teacher being particularly open to the value of literature as a means for transforming the consciousness of the masses. More generally, Thomas points out:

> Anarchists were attracted to the Decadents and to anybody else seeking new directions in literature because they, too, rejected the principle of authority, distrusted the bourgeoisie and its literature, and demanded the freedom to study any subject and reach any conclusion.
>
> THOMAS 1980, 272

However, at the first of the meetings, Louise said little about Symbolism and spoke mostly about literature in general, stressing the commonality of goals between Decadents and anarchists; at the second conference, in front of an audience containing some less tolerant Symbolist advocates who resented the intersection of poetry and politics and kept interrupting her, she revealed that, while she thought that symbols could be utilized as a novel way to help educate the masses, she did not really understand what the movement stood for. Though scheduled to appear at a third conference, Michel did not show up again (McGuinness 2015, 54; Shryock 2000, 300–303; Thomas 1980, 270–273). Although like anarchism, Symbolism opposed conventional understandings of reality, it deliberately sought out complicated explanations that were not easy to understand, resulting in styles of poetry that were very different to the verses that Louise wrote. McGuinness writes:

> Louise Michel's poetry is an interesting example of this crossover between literary avant-garde and radical political forums: she had been published regularly in Decadent/Symbolist magazines such as *Le Scapin*, and wrote formal, demotic, idealistic poetry with a strong utopian strand that would have been considered little better than doggerel by the Symbolists and Decadents.
>
> MCGUINNESS 2015, 53

So, given the difference in perspective between the two philosophies, why had Michel's work appeared in *Le Scapin*, even on its front page? There are several explanations: it was partly a pragmatic decision, because journals such as *Le Scapin* sought readership and notoriety; also, the publication was open to criticism of Symbolism; and it is likely that its editor, René Ghil, was sympathetic to Michel's ideas because he was a socialist (Brooker et al. 2013, 64; McGuinness 2015, 53; Shryock 2000, 299).

In 1888, while she was giving a speech in Le Havre, a man called Pierre Lucas, a former circus clown who was opposed to anarchism, shot her twice and wounded her in her ear, causing him to then be beaten by the audience. Louise, who initially claimed that Lucas had only fired blanks, continuing with her address, spoke up on his behalf, and refused to file charges against him. A contemporary anarchist, Voltairine de Cleyre, similarly refused to prosecute one of her students, Herman Helcher, after he shot her in 1902. Partly because of this sense that she did not embody a traditional lifestyle and, like de Cleyre, did not seek vengeance for sleights and attacks, but recognized like many anarchists that most crime and violence are societal rather than individual problems, Michel was often viewed as being dangerous – so much so that she was not allowed to join the thousands of other mourners at her mother's funeral ("Attempt to Kill Louise Michel" 1888, 1, 8; Avrich 1978, 173; Lowry and Gunter 1981a, 198; Sartwell 2005, 7; Ross 2015, 97; Thomas 1980, 279–284). For a time, this perceived lack of decorum on the part of women leaders of the Commune caused their role in that event to be underappreciated and its true extent went unacknowledged until recent decades (Higgins 1982, 212). In January 1881, she attended the funeral of the radical Auguste Blanqui, who, like her, had been imprisoned for his ideas, and, in July of that year, along with Peter Kropotkin, Errico Malatesta, and those of similar minds, participated in an Anarchist Congress in London. In the last part of her life, from 1890 onwards, Louise lived in London a lot of the time, where she was much less bothered by police surveillance than she was when in France, and she worked with the poor in the Whitechapel area, taking care of abandoned animals, and teaching the children of refugees; in 1895, she returned to France for a while, and from then onwards, she traveled more widely (Bantman 2006, 965; Maclellan 2004a, 21–22; Mullaney 1984, 130, 134; Thomas 1971, 361–363; Watson 1978, 396–397). For Ernest Girault, a fellow-anarchist, who knew Michel well and visited Algeria with her shortly before her death, the earlier years of this period with their time spent away from France had not been the most productive era for Louise:

> Son exil à Londres rendit Louise silencieuse, à son grand regret, pour quelques années. À part ses nombreuses visites aux juifs de Whitechapel qu'elle aimait beaucoup, sa vie est pour ainsi dire nulle de 1890 à 1895. (Girault 1906, 163) [Her exile in London made Louise silent, to her great regret, for a few years. Apart from her numerous visits to the Jews of Whitechapel, whom she liked a lot, her life is virtually zero from 1890 to 1895.]

However, when she arrived in London in the summer of 1890, Michel soon made contact again with Kropotkin and was able to focus on writing and participating in conferences (Thomas 1971, 355–358).

Along with the fact that she was a revolutionary, an anarchist, the tendency of some evaluators of Michel's life to be critical of some or all the many things that she attempted, or to argue that she wrote too much too quickly, resulting in the publication of some work of poor quality, or to see her as being psychologically aberrant in some way and unable to control her actions has meant that along with her admirers, there have also been many critics. In the introduction to his biography of her, written the year that she died and published the next, Girault (1906, vii–ix) attempts to refute some of these criticisms which, he argues, are responsible for reducing her historical importance to the Commune and to anarchism, and for her becoming inaccurately designated the Red Virgin. He comments:

> Si l'on prend la vie de Louise Michel en bloc, avec ses impulsions, ses actes de violence, ses écrits parfois décousus, ses rêveries poétiques, son art incomplet, sa pédagogie inachevée et son originalité intime, on est tenté de la considérer comme une abracadabrante et une abnormale. – C'est une erreur." (Girault 1906, vii) [If we take the life of Louise Michel as a whole, with her impulses, her acts of violence, her sometimes rambling writings, her poetic reveries, her incomplete art, her unfinished pedagogy, and her inner eccentricity, one is tempted to consider her a joke and an abnormal person. This is an error.]

Above all, she was a disciple of liberty. In her poem, "Libre," she identified with a caged bird that became exasperated with its imprisonment:

> Il cesse ses chansons pour frapper avec rage,
> A s'en rompre le bec, les grilles de sa cage,
> La liberté, pour lui, c'est le bien le plus doux! (Michel 1912, 27)
> [He leaves off his chirping to strike with rage,
> Breaking his beak, the bars of his cage,
> Liberty, for him, it's the sweetest thing!]

Ferretti (2016, 83) is certainly correct that "Louise Michel struggled not only against patriarchy, but against all oppression and all exploitation." Moreover, her ideas and exploits appealed to many, as they do today to many of the much smaller number who are familiar with her. Her funeral on January 22, 1905 in Paris attracted a large number of people, which has been estimated at from

50,000 to 120,000 people; it was believed at the time to have been the largest funeral attendance in France so far save for that of Victor Hugo, following which she was buried next to her mother at Levallois-Perret cemetery, where Théophile Ferré is also laid to rest (Harison 2007, 14; Leighton 1990, 22; Mullaney 1990, 303; Thomas 1971, 446–447). When Michel was still alive, John Bell wrote about her accurately, but somewhat scathingly, as follows:

> Politics rather than love and marriage monopolised her attention, and to such an extent that, like Joan of Arc, the schoolmistress of Montmartre imagined that she was called upon to play a role in shaping the destiny of her country.
>
> BELL 1903, 75

With the advantage of hindsight, Louise Michel appears today to have in fact starred in that role, and to be justifiably remembered for assuming it.

Victoria C. Woodhull.

BRADLEY & RULOFSON.

SAN FRANCISCO

ILLUSTRATION 3   Victoria C. Woodhull, by Bradley & Rulofson, San Francisco
PHOTO, UNDATED, CIRCA 1870. WIKIMEDIA COMMONS.

CHAPTER 3

The Originality and Political Philosophy of Victoria C. Woodhull

If she is not remembered today as a scandalous libertine who shocked nineteenth century society, then it will be as the first woman to run for president. Victoria Claflin Woodhull (1838–1927) is also the subject of quite a number of detailed historical biographies, some crafted more consistently with scholarly norms than are others, with many containing details that are difficult to verify. In her day, she was known as the person who "outed" an adulterous preacher, and together with her sister, Tennie C. Claflin, they are celebrated as the first two women to work as stockbrokers. Despite the obvious interest of researchers in a person whom *Harper's Weekly* satirized in a cartoon as "Mrs. Satan," and Harriet Beecher Stowe in her novel, *My Wife and I: or, Harry Henderson's History* (1871), turned into the character Audacia Dangyereyes, an outrageous women's libber who behaved rather inappropriately, Victoria's political ideas have received somewhat more restricted notice. While it is inaccurate for Horne (2016) to say that "[h]istory has reduced Woodhull to a footnote – a curiosity more than a contender," it is disturbing that an ardent radical, who became well-known to (though she was also feared by) Susan B. Anthony, the latter being jealous of Victoria's charisma, should be evoked so consistently for her less intellectual contributions, and, as Underhill (1995, 309) points out, "written out of the suffrage movement during her lifetime," an intentional goal on the part of Anthony. In contradistinction, therefore, much of the focus of this chapter is on Woodhull as a feminist political theorist, an aspect of her many accomplishments that is surely deserving of more attention. But first, who exactly was she, and for which ideas, in all probability, was she responsible?

1 The Originality of Victoria C. Woodhull

Victoria Claflin Woodhull was born on the frontier in Homer, Ohio in 1838. Married three times, she died in Worcestershire, England, in 1927, a wealthy woman who had repudiated many of her earlier, more radical ideological positions and even denied having once held them. In 1872, she ran for president as the candidate of the Equal Rights Party, the first woman to seek election to that office. She was an opponent of slavery and an advocate of free love. She was named in honor of Queen Victoria, as a baby being known as "the Little Queen," but she is referred to by some modern authors consistently as "Vicky," and she was identified by many during her most politically active years as "The Woodhull," which Meade ([1976] 2000, 81) suggests was used "as if she were a ship or a public monument." The fifth, sixth, or seventh, and most successful child of a very individualistic family of ten children, Victoria received little formal education. Sources give different counts, and, as Underhill (1995, 15) points out, three sisters died as children, which adds to the confusion; she names all ten but does not cite any sources for this information, an issue that has plagued many works less erudite than her own much-praised book. Victoria's father was Reuben Buckman Claflin, originally from Massachusetts and usually known as "Buck," an itinerant confidence man who posed as a doctor while selling remedies for a range of medical complaints. His wife, Roxanna Hummel Claflin, who prior to marriage had worked in a family bar in Pennsylvania (her name is sometimes spelled "Roxana," and the nicknames Annie, Anna, and Roxie are also used) was very religious, a German-American who could speak German and sometimes used it to curse. By the age of fourteen, Victoria was working as a fortune-teller and faith healer and, it has been argued, occasionally as a prostitute, to help support her family (Auerbach 1998, 21; Havelin 2007, 11–13; MacPherson 2014, 3; Marberry 1967, 5, 11, 58, 268; Meade [1976] 2000, 2; Sachs [1928] 1978, 4; Stinchcombe 2000, 8; Tilton 1871, 3, 7).

Victoria became married for the first time at the age of fifteen (some sources say fourteen) to her physician, Canning Woodhull, a man with a serious drinking problem as well as a pregnant mistress and an ongoing penchant for dalliances with prostitutes; he is reported to have spent the third night of his marriage visiting a brothel. Throughout their marriage, the doctor is believed to have expended much of his time with, and money on, other women. Their son, Byron, who was born in 1854, was severely brain damaged, a condition that would limit his understanding throughout his life, possibly due to the fact that his father, who helped bring him into the world, was drunk at the time. The feverish baby almost died, with Victoria managing to nurse him into health, a feat so against the odds that it would add to her feeling that she was a natural healer; later, her spiritualist-influenced thinking told her that Byron's disabilities were caused (in a metaphysical sense) by a marriage that was not made in Heaven, though she also blamed herself for giving birth at sixteen, when she "knew no better than to surrender my maternal functions to a drunken man" (Woodhull [1874d] 2010, 242). This happenstance began the process by which she soon came to view the legal institution of marriage in a critical way (Carpenter 2010a, xv; Havelin 2007, 15, 20–21; Perry 2005, 135; Robinson 2010, 13;

Tilton 1871, 1–13, 21; Underhill 1995, 24, 260). For her contemporary, Charles Sutton, the warden of New York's prison, The Tombs, where later on Woodhull would spend two nights behind bars, Victoria's pregnancy and the birth of Byron were the key to understanding the development of her life:

> At an early age Victoria married a man named Woodhull. To them was born an idiotic son, whose birth seems to have cast a blight over all her life. At any rate she soon began to evolve peculiar ideas relative to the marital relation, and struck out into that erratic groove in which she now is.
>
> SUTTON 1874, 508

In a speech titled "The Scare-Crows of Sexual Slavery," Victoria recalled her experience with her first husband evocatively and poetically, albeit also quite probably anachronistically:

> I have traveled the icy pavements of New York in mid-winter, seeking employment, with nothing on my feet except an old pair of india-rubber shoes, and a common calico dress only to cover my body, while the man who called me wife and who made me his sexual slave, spent his money on other women.
>
> WOODHULL [1873e] 2010, 210

By 1857, Woodhull was in San Francisco, where she had an opportunity to work as an actress, playing the role of the "Country Cousin" in a dramatic version of newspaper reporter George G. Foster's *New York by Gas-Light*, a book which, ironically, explored the themes of drunkenness and prostitution in the swiftly modernizing metropolis that would become Woodhull's home. For this role, Victoria was able to make use of her photographic memory, a skill that would help her many times later when preparing to give political speeches. Suddenly she was making $52 a week in a somewhat respectable profession. Later, in the middle of acting a scene in Alexandre Dumas' *The Corsican Brothers*, she understood herself to have been summoned by the spirit world – by an apparition of her younger sister Tennie, who was imploring her to return to the family, currently resident in Columbus, Ohio. Victoria, who had not really wanted to be an actress, immediately walked off the stage, returning to her mother, along with Dr. Canning and Byron, by ship. (Havelin 2007, 17; MacPherson 2014, 13; Meade [1976] 2000, 19–20; Tilton 1871, 17–19).

Woodhull resumed her more usual activities as a fortune-teller, medium, and seller of treatments. After the birth of her second child, a girl whom she called Zula Maud, she left her husband. One of her customers as she worked in St. Louis as a channel called "Madame Holland" was a man known as Colonel James Blood, the city auditor, who would become her second husband in name, although no paperwork was ever filed. Blood was a wounded Civil War veteran, although some authors dispute whether he had actually been a colonel. Influenced by the example of Lucy Stone, Victoria decided to keep the name "Woodhull." Blood's influence on her was profound, for he was an advocate of free love and Victoria was the survivor of a bad relationship. Despite his elevated position in local society, he was also a decrier of capitalism (Buescher 2002, 580, fn 7; Havelin 2007, 18–19, 22, 24; MacPherson 2014, 24; Meade [1976] 2000, 25, 29, 31–32; Sachs [1928] 1978, 43; Stinchcombe 2000, 9; Tilton 1871, 24, 25; Underhill 1995, 35).

In 1868, Victoria and Tennie moved to New York where they encountered wealthy Commodore Cornelius Vanderbilt, who sought their services as mediums to contact dead members of his family; he was, like Woodhull, increasingly interested in spiritualism. This relationship proved profitable to both parties. With her contacts, Victoria was able to obtain inside information about businesses that she passed on to Vanderbilt, allowing him to make money from investments while he gave her stock tips that her husband took advantage of. Then, with Vanderbilt's support, Victoria and Tennie became the first female stockbrokers when, with Col. Blood, they opened the Wall Street office of "Woodhull, Claflin & Company" (Auerbach 1998, 21; Gabriel 1998, 36; Havelin 2007, 26, 28, 31–32; Johnston 1967, 47). Smith notes that this earned the sisters some immediate attention:

> On coming into the street, the lady brokers created a great sensation. All day long crowds were around the doors. Men flattened their noses against the plate glass, peeping in, and every imagined excuse was invented by parties who wanted to walk inside and look at the sights.
> SMITH 1871, 273

Similarly roused by the outlandish development, Charles Sutton reflected:

> Two women, from the Prairies of the West, had pitched their tents in Gotham, and openly announced themselves as being engaged in the buying and selling of stocks and gold—in a word, as female bankers.
> SUTTON 1874, 506

Also intrigued by the sisters' accomplishment, Susan B. Anthony, who was not yet personally familiar with them, visited their office and reported the event for her publication, *The Revolution*, commenting that "[t]he advent of this *woman* firm in Wall Street marks a new era" (Anthony 1870, 154). Anthony's present lack of acquaintance with the women who would later come to be seen by her as rivals was revealed in this article by the fact that she gave Tennie's name as "Jennie," and her initials as "J.C.C." (154–155), a happening made stranger by the realization that, as Underhill (1995, 67) points out, "[i]t was with Tennie, not Woodhull, that Anthony talked."

In 1870, Victoria and Tennie generated another first, with the introduction of their provocative newspaper, *Woodhull & Claflin's Weekly*, which would quickly become a vehicle for Victoria's presidential campaign. 50,000 copies were printed of the first issue, and eventually, the paper had 20,000 subscribers. It would survive for six years, ending at the same time as Victoria's second marriage also folded. When times were tough, Woodhull would pen an urgent appeal for funds, and once she implored Vanderbilt to again help the publication out (Gabriel 1998, 235–236; Havelin 2007, 38; MacPherson 2014, 250; Meade [1976] 2000, 64; Woodhull and Claflin 1872, 4–5). When, in 1872, ostensibly outraged by his hypocrisy, the *Weekly* blasted Congregationalist Rev. Henry Ward Beecher, brother of Harriet Beecher Stowe and pastor of the Plymouth Congregationalist Church in Brooklyn, for having an affair with Elizabeth "Lib" Tilton, the wife of Theodore Tilton, the sense of scandal was considerable. Though Victoria would insist that "to sustain the indictment of disloyalty to truth, I was necessarily compelled" (Woodhull 1873a, 8) to expose the adultery, there was underlying what would quickly become one of the major news stories of the decade a reciprocal suspicion that not only had Victoria at one time had an affair with Tilton, but she had also been romantically involved with Rev. Beecher (Johnston 1967, 208). Nonetheless, Victoria explained her own motivation as follows:

> [H]e [Beecher] has permitted himself ... to profess to believe otherwise than as he does believe, to help, persistently, to maintain, for these many years that very social slavery under which he was chafing, and against which he was secretly revolting both in thought and practice; and that he has, in a word, consented, and still consents to be a hypocrite.
>
> WOODHULL [1876b] 2010, 108; WOODHULL, quoted in DOYLE 1875, 24 is very similar

Anthony Comstock, the crusading opponent of what he saw as obscenity, which often included advocacy of women's rights, had Woodhull and Claflin arrested for the misdemeanor of sending obscene material (the *Weekly*) through the mail; in his eyes, and in those of US Attorney General Benjamin F. Tracy, a friend of Beecher, accusing an important person of adultery was obscene. As Woodhull would later testify to the US House Committee on Claims, the prosecution was "backed up by a powerful body of sectarian Christians, to save the then most powerful Christian minister in the world" ("Woodhull & Claflin" 1876, 4). Brookhiser comments:

> Beecher's reputation was important to Protestantism in general, to the liberal wing of the Republican Party, to the backers of Plymouth Church and to Beecher's publisher, who had given him a big advance for a life of Jesus.
>
> BROOKHISER 1998

Meanwhile, Victoria's reputation was also of concern to them, as she alluded in a speech at Manhattan's Cooper Institute immediately before her arrest:

> The District Attorney, and everybody concerned in this nefarious matter have … already accomplished all they aimed at, by covering my sister and me with the odium of being prisoners and accused of a scandalous offense.
>
> WOODHULL [1871c] 2010, 127

Indeed, the way that the charges of "obscenity" were described in the press appears to reflect a lack of due process in the treatment of those who criticize elite members of society. The *New York Daily Tribune*, for example, reported the arrests of Victoria and Tennie in the following manner:

> The case is attended with peculiarly aggravating circumstances, because the defendants have not only circulated obscene literature, but they have attacked in a most abominable manner the character of one of the best and purest citizens of the United States, and it is well worth while [sic] for the Government of the United States to vindicate him.
>
> "Woodhull and Claflin in Jail" 1872, 2

Here, the reporter's hyperbole matched very closely the rhetoric of General Henry E. Davies, the U. S. Assistant District Attorney for the Southern District of New York, as he was suggesting an amount that should be fixed for bail. In reality, there was only one charge, because the so-called obscene literature was itself the attack on the preacher's character, and he did happen to be an adulterer as claimed; also, as the sisters' attorney, James D. Reymert, pointed out to the judge at the time, it was not the job of the government to use the federal court system to vindicate anyone ("The Claflin-Woodhull Difficulty" 1872, 6). Rumors of Beecher's affair had circulated for a while, and Woodhull had at times referred to them in speeches and, it is believed, attempted unsuccessfully to sell the details of the dalliance to mainstream newspapers; eventually, when no defamation suit was filed against her by Beecher, the federal charges were dropped, although upon the arrest of Victoria, Tennie, and Blood, the *Weekly*'s presses and other office equipment had immediately been destroyed by the authorities. It was thus that the first woman to run for president of the United States spent about a month, together with her sister, in a four feet by eight feet cell in New York's Ludlow Street Jail. Later, *Tilton v. Beecher* (1875), an alienation of affection case in which Woodhull was called to give evidence, resulted in a hung jury (Bradford 2006, 79, 188; Carpenter 2010a, xxvi–xxvii; DeVoto 1928; Doyle 1875, 13; Frisken 2008, 538; Gabriel 1998, 186–188; Havelin 2007, 40; Hibben 1927, 283–284, 310, 311; Horowitz 2000, 420–421, 433; Stern 1968, 128–129; Train 1902, 324). Despite Victoria's dislike of Beecher's two-facedness, the way she had apparently tried to make use of his duplicity casts doubt on the purity of her own motives. Stoehr writes:

> Those in the know claimed that her actual motive in baring Beecher's indiscretions was revenge; he had repeatedly refused to countenance her work by introducing her on a public platform, and she had finally passed from threats to punishment.
>
> STOEHR 1979b, 41

A seemingly minor incident became the cause of additional criticism of Victoria's character. For a few weeks, her first husband, Dr. Woodhull, suffering effects from his alcoholism and maybe morphine use, stayed with her and Col. Blood in Cincinnati as they took care of him. This event and some later contacts with him were turned into a scandal by the press with Victoria being vilified as a woman who lived with, and by implication slept with two husbands (Johnston 1967, 61–62; Tilton 1871, 25–26). Some of this criticism reflects a social conservatism on the part of writers who would have been incensed, at least in their scribblings, by the activities of many women far less outrageous than Victoria, as a dispatch from the New York City correspondent of the *Charleston Daily News* indicates:

> Mrs. Woodhull keeps two husbands by her. She bears the name of one and lives with the other. She acknowledges this openly and glories in what she protests is an act of charity. Why, she asks, should she refuse to

support a sick and helpless husband merely because she has got a divorce from him?

"Glimpses of Gotham" 1871, 1

Meanwhile, an editorial in the Sweetwater, Tennessee newspaper, *The Enterprise*, knowing that Woodhull was running for president, and aware that Victoria and Tennie had not paid an advertising bill that dated back to their questionable "magic medicine" business activities of 1866, whimsically opined:

Perhaps in Mrs. Woodhull's case, as she has two husbands living, it might be proper to exact an agreement that neither of them shall be appointed to any office after her inauguration.

Editorial 1871b, 2

Apparently mocking the way that Victoria spoke as perhaps revealing her rather humble origins, the *Belmont Chronicle*, a paper from Ohio, the state of her birth, commented:

Victoria C. Woodhull – who lives with two husbands, and edits *Woodhull & Claflin's Weekly*, – don't want any "intrusive inspection of family affairs."

"The Woman With Two Husbands and a Newspaper" 1871, 1

When he was contacted by author Emanie Sachs, Benjamin R. Tucker, the major contributor to the political philosophy often referred to as American Anarchism, who edited the leading anarchist newspaper, *Liberty*, in Boston and then in New York, revealed his brief sexual liaison with Woodhull, and also explained his growing disaffection with her ideas. Tucker also contributed to the theory that, as a person who had only ever received three years of schooling, Victoria was essentially illiterate, and thus to view her as the intellectual force behind her speeches and what are known as her writings is an error. Tucker told Sachs:

Not once did I ever see Victoria have a pen or pencil in her hand. Never did she read a book or give more that a cursory glance at the contents of a newspaper. I was told (I forgot by whom) that she could manage to write her own name with difficulty.

BENJAMIN TUCKER, quoted by SACHS [1928] 1978, 259

Disputing whether Victoria could really explain any of the issues upon which she campaigned except for free love, an ironic concession since they had once been intimate together, Tucker also doubted that she was capable of producing the elaborate signature that appeared in the beginning of her work, *The Origin, Tendencies, and Principles of Government* (Tucker, quoted by Sachs [1928] 1978, 259). Another contemporary, her former ally, who had been an editor of the *Weekly*, Dr. Joseph Treat, had made a similar accusation, saying in an 1874 pamphlet titled "Beecher, Tilton, Woodhull, the Creation of Society" that "you write nothing, not a word," at the same time questioning her sexual morality and claiming that she admitted being a prostitute (Meade [1976] 2000, 142). Likewise, for MacPherson (2014, 52), it is not possible for "the uneducated, unlettered sisters," Victoria and Tennie, to have written much of the content of the speeches and writings that bear their names. The exception again, for MacPherson (2014, 55), is the experience of women as second-class citizens and in their oppressive marriages, where it was obvious they each had considerable practical experience of what they described. Presenting her more sympathetically, Stinchcombe (2000, 118) writes that "she found writing difficult," and points out that she was also a very busy woman who needed assistants to help her with her many projects. Similarly, Townley (1948, 9) comments that, "Victoria hardly could write even her name and Tennessee was little better, but they accomplished things"; in this context, he mentions their marriages in England to very wealthy men. The riddle seems difficult to rectify even from consideration of Victoria's own words and actions. In Tilton's early biography of her, written under her influence and with her approval, her erstwhile lover comments:

> I wish to add that ... [Victoria] is a person of no special literary training; indeed, so averse to the pen that, of her own will, she rarely dips it into ink, except to sign her business autograph; nor would she ever write at all except for those spirit promptings which she dare not disobey.
> TILTON 1871, 10

Carpenter (2010b, x) observes that Woodhull's published pieces are better written than works in her own handwriting but, as she points out, that may be true of many authors who wrote everything that bears their name. Sachs ([1928] 1978, 126) credits Stephen Pearl Andrews, the anarchist thinker who would come to have much influence on Victoria for her speech, "The Principles of Social Freedom, involving the Question of Free Love, Marriage Divorce and Prostitution" (Social Freedom 1871, 12) given at Steinway Hall before three thousand people in New York on November 20th, 1871, but she also ([1928] 1978, 137) praises the delivery that Woodhull made, and it is clear that the success of the endeavor owed much to the speaker, who proudly proclaimed that "Yes! I am a Free Lover!" Andrews was not very accomplished at public speaking, but in her hands, his writings acquired a new resonance. In fact, Stoehr (1979b, 42) comments that, "Andrews had never written so well under his own name." Sachs ([1928] 1978, 58) calls Woodhull "the ideal trumpeter for his ideas.... Her voice was musical and captivating." Scholars have debated whether or not that combative line, often associated with Woodhull's ideas, was in the original text, or whether it was an improvisation, perhaps in response to something someone in the audience said. For Horowitz (2000, 414) and Sachs ([1928] 1978, 135–136), the remark was an amendment to the script. For Tucker, on the other hand, the fact that Woodhull repeated it in another appearance, at the Boston Music Hall, convinced him that it had always been intentionally part of the speech (MacPherson 2014, 133).

Additionally, while MacPherson (2014, 51) argues that many early position papers published in the friendly *New York Herald*, ostensibly written by Woodhull, were actually the work of Stephen Pearl Andrews, she comments also that "Victoria's ability to electrify, either with her words or those composed for her, was exceptional – especially regarding radical women's rights" (2014, 130). For J.E.P. Doyle, writing during Victoria's early and mid-1870s heyday, the intellectual influence of Col. Blood was also to some extent a possibility:

> It has been said, and is by many believed that he is the "power behind the throne," or the [Richard, Earl of] "Warwick" of the Woodhull kingdom, and that he writes the speeches, editorials, etc., of Victoria and Tennie. But we have personal assurance that such a suspicion is not well founded.
> DOYLE 1875, 433

Sachs ([1928] 1978, 60–61, 71), too, credits Blood, along with Andrews, for writing material attributed to Woodhull that appeared in the *Herald*, concluding:

> It is a fact that every man who wrote over Victoria's signature, every reporter who interviewed her, everyone who came in contact with her, expressed themselves with more than their usual vividness, while they were under her spell.
> SACHS [1928] 1978, 62

Marberry (1967, 13) writes that Andrews "found in Victoria a willing sponge who quickly soaked up his involved notions once they were put in writing and studied." Underhill (1995, 259) argues that Woodhull herself was the author of "Tried as by Fire, or the True and the False, Socially," a speech she delivered repeatedly on an extensive tour of the US in 1874, "[w]ithout Stephen Pearl Andrews's influence" (259; see also Hayden 2010, 126, fn 10). On the other hand, Stoehr keeps an open mind about that work's origins, writing:

> Perhaps it was written by Stephen Pearl Andrews ... or by Victoria's husband Col. Blood, who also ghosted much of her work; or possibly she dictated much of the speech to Blood, for her extemporaneous powers were great, and on the issue of free love she was never at a loss.
>
> STOEHR 1979C, 352

For Horowitz:

> Although Victoria Woodhull probably wrote few words of the articles she signed or the speeches she delivered ... she represented and defended the ideas and positions under her name and accepted legal accountability for them. In the case of the words for which she was arrested November 2, 1872, it was Woodhull who made the critical decision to print them.
>
> HOROWITZ 2000, 413; HOROWITZ 1999, 88 is similar

When we speak of "Victoria C. Woodhull," we invoke a depiction of a person as revealed by her actions, in her speeches, and from the perspectives she adopted at different stages of her life. That Col. Blood or Stephen Paul Andrews or others who surrounded her for a portion of her life contributed and/or scribed ideas identified with Woodhull is of continuing intellectual interest, but it should not be allowed to eclipse the phenomenon of "Victoria C. Woodhull" and what she represented and continues to stand for today. Everyone's perspective builds on a range of intellectual or other influences, and little thought is truly original, with much inventiveness lying solely in the manner that existing patterns of thought have been reengineered in a creative way. Even jazz improvisation merely rearranges notes and themes that have occurred and been heard elsewhere, played in a different order and in a different way. As Kropotkin argued:

> There is not even a thought, or an invention, which is not common property, born of the past and the present.
>
> KROPOTKIN [1906] 1990, 70

For example, what we know of Socrates is based on what Plato wrote about him, or to a lesser extent the rather different representations of him by Xenophon and Aristophanes, and what is contained in the *Magna Moralia*, which itself, according to scholars, may or may not have been written by Aristotle. The ideas of Confucius are presented quite differently in the main source for Confucius' ideas, the *Analects*, and by his most important followers, Mencius (Mengzi) and Hsún Tzu (Xunzi). Shakespeare will always be considered a thinker of the first rank despite doubts about which parts of his *oeuvre* he wrote, what works should be attributed to Edward de Vere, Christopher Marlowe, Francis Bacon, or others, or whether his writings were actually produced by a collective. John Locke contradicted himself concerning the existence of innate ideas in his two major works, *An Essay Concerning Human Understanding* and *Two Treatises of Government*. Reporters refer to the Bush Doctrine, the Obama Doctrine, etc., and amusingly even the Trump Doctrine, though much of what presidents appear to think comes from speech writers and other assistants – and it is essentially just the reporters who cluster around presidents who frame what they claim to be a "doctrine."

Another issue is that, although there have been many books published about Victoria C. Woodhull over the years, the majority have been directed at the general reader, have focused on the more scandalous aspects of Victoria's life, and have not been crafted in accordance with academic standards. Thus, MacPherson comments:

> For much of the twentieth century, Sachs's book – which contains no attributions, notes, or index – was followed as fact or used in fictionalized books masquerading as biographies, with made-up scenes and dialogue.
> MACPHERSON 2014, xxiv

On the other hand, many of those somewhat flawed works provide information that is likely accurate and in fact MacPherson draws extensively on these sources in her own book, a work of great scholarship in general, and a significant contribution to the Woodhull literature, but one that is itself rather inadequately referenced. Furthermore, in general, works of historical fiction and history books intended for the ordinary reader to access at public libraries have often not included notes. This can be a frustration, but it is hardly a drawback related solely to volumes about Victoria. Like MacPherson, the present author makes use of such sources where necessary. She concludes:

> After generations of mythmaking, it is difficult, if not impossible, to separate fact from fiction regarding the sisters. Everything written about them is a snarled knot of conjecture, hearsay, fabrication, perceptions of the times, and, yes, some facts.
> MACPHERSON 2014, xxiii

It is difficult to know what Woodhull actually wrote, or the extent to which Andrews, Blood, or others contributed, and there is the additional complication that Victoria repudiated and lied about what she had once said, disowning her more radical ideas. Then, there are elements of historical fiction in some of the biographies, with improvised dialog to convey what life must have been like in the Claflin family. However, MacPherson probably exaggerates the extent of the damage that this third issue adds to the problem – after all, we have Victoria's books, pamphlets, and speeches, as well as court testimony and newspaper articles of the time, and much of what has been written in more questionable formats concurs with other, more reliable accounts; her speeches were published and later brought out in collections such as *The Origin, Tendencies and Principles of Government*. Furthermore, many of the earlier writers were aware of these issues. Johanna Johnston (1967, 7), for example, begins her book about Woodhull with the comment that "This book is not fictionalized biography, except as its chief subject did some fictionalizing herself," noting her own extensive bibliography and emphasizing that her work contains no invented conversations; however, Johnston provides no in-text citations, and only the titles of newspapers and periodicals are given.

MacPherson is particularly critical of Sachs' scholarship in the latter's book, *The Terrible Siren* (1928), to which she refers as "[t]he first biography of Woodhull" (MacPherson 2014, xxiii). In reality, this was not the first such profile of Woodhull. Theodore Tilton's work, *Biography of Victoria C. Woodhull*, was published in 1871, with its content probably to some extent dictated by Victoria herself; elsewhere, MacPherson (5) refers to him as Victoria's "biographer, Theodore Tilton, a writer thought to be her lover." Even at the time, this effort was considered somewhat notorious: a book review of Tilton's work in *The Saturday Review of Politics, Literature, Science, and Art* commented that "it is difficult to say which most excites our amazement – the lady's career, or the manner in which it is described" ("A Free-Love Heroine," 1871, 751). In particular, MacPherson lambastes Sachs for:

> paying anarchist Benjamin Tucker, a friend turned enemy of the sisters, $3,500 to produce his account of losing his virginity at nineteen to thirty-four-year-old Victoria, and to describe Tennie's sexual advances. Tucker was an old man when he told his tale to Sachs, who used his material lavishly and did not divulge to readers the hefty price she had paid for it.
>
> MacPherson 2014, xxiii

Actually, far from using the material from Tucker "lavishly," Sachs presented the sections of Tucker's letters that she wished to use within quotation marks, allowing the reader to independently assess what is there; as Underhill (1995,

258) observes, "Sachs has simply printed Tucker's words." If she had wanted to libel Victoria, why would she have bothered to contact Tucker in France and pay him to make up a yarn? It is a fact that reporters offer remuneration for stories so that, as in this case, they have an exclusive. Meanwhile, Johnston (1967, 7) refers to Sachs' tome as "an invaluable sourcebook for any study of the lives of both sisters."

When he first met Victoria Woodhull, Benjamin Tucker was a nineteen year-old student at the Massachusetts Institute of Technology who had previously attended her "Social Freedom" speech in Boston, about three months after the Steinway Hall event. Tucker was already generally interested in anarchist and other radical perspectives and attended political conferences when he could. However, some of the accounts of the encounter between Woodhull and Tucker seem to have been crafted to demonize Victoria, with Stern (1968, 135) referring to Tucker as being "still in his 'teens,'" and Marberry (1967, 156) telling the story of innocent "Bennie" or "Young Bennie" meeting the seductress. Apparently, Dr. Blood left them alone for a while, and Victoria hung her jacket on the hotel room doorknob to prevent anyone observing what followed through the keyhole (Brough 1980, 244; Johnston 1967, 208–211). In their novel based on Woodhull's life, *Victoria la Scandaleuse*, Nicole Blondeau and Jean-Paul Feuillebois stage the moment spicily:

> – Venez près de moi, je veux vous dire quelque chose.
> Rouge comme une pivoine, il demanda:
> – Là? A côté de vous?
> – A côté de moi, ces choses-là ne se disent pas de loin. Voilà. Donnez-moi votre main. Benjamin, je vous trouve beau. J'ai très envie de vous. (Blondeau and Feuillebois 1979, 288)
> [Come close to me, I want to tell you something.
> Red as a peony, he asked:
> There? Next to you?
> Beside me, I can't discuss these matters with you from so far away. There you are. Give me your hand. Benjamin, I think you're handsome. I desire you.]

Amusing, pathetic, or erotic as this dramatization may strike the reader, in the twenty-first century it is hard to see the significance of Woodhull seducing Tucker, or of her sister Tennie flirting with him, or of a college student losing his virginity. This behavior is nothing unusual today, and no longer scandalous, precisely because women's rights and roles have progressed due to the influence of many feminists, including the Woodhull sisters, and the pervasiveness of oppressive moralizing ideals has waned.

It is generally believed that Victoria Woodhull and her sister Tennie Claflin moved to England in August of 1877 because they were paid to do so by William Henry "Billy" Vanderbilt, the son of Cornelius Vanderbilt, who had died in January of the same year, leaving almost all of his $100 million fortune to his favorite child, Billy, which prompted a lawsuit on behalf of the latter's siblings, who claimed their father had been insane, citing as evidence his interest in spiritualism. This development raised the question of what role Cornelius' erstwhile companion, Tennie, would play in a sensational trial, especially if she also tried to get hold of more of the inheritance than she had actually received, which was just the return of a painting titled *Aurora* that she had given to the Commodore for his seventy-fifth birthday. To explain the reasons for their departure, much is made of the fact that Victoria and Tennie were out of funds at this point, whereas they were conspicuously not poor soon after. In a December 1874 appeal for donations, Victoria noted that she had been personally subsidizing the production of the *Weekly*, writing that, "the renewals of subscriptions have fallen off about fifty per cent" (Woodhull 1874b, 8). In another urgent solicitation of funds to rescue the paper at the end of 1875, she and Tennie wrote that, "we wish to say that this will be the last emergency over which the *Weekly* will require to be assisted" (Woodhull and Claflin 1875, 4). The sisters may have collected $100,000 from William to go away, but they denied receiving anything, with reporters asking them this question even as they waited to board the ship that would transport them first class to England, the *Lafayette* (Brough 1980, 264; Havelin 2007, 81; Hoyt 1962, 218–222; Johnston 1967, 253–256; MacPherson 2014, 256; Marberry 1967, 191, 196; Meade [1976] 2000, 153; Sachs [1928] 1978, 288; Stinchcombe 2000, 18–19; Underhill 1995, 49). Sears comments that:

> In 1877, "The Woodhull" left America for England, denied her earlier work, and married into respectability, leaving behind her a string of adventures which several biographers have delighted to tell.
>
> SEARS 1977, 23

Indeed, what is most surprising about her final half century is the diligence with which Victoria attempted to erase the majority of her past, including most of the principles that she had up to then advocated. In a sense, then, there is created, following her departure from the United States, an entirely different "Victoria C. Woodhull" than the one responsible for so much apparent scandal. Thus, Fowler (1996, 634) refers to the other, more neglected part of her story, "the fifty years Woodhull spent in England (1877–1927), where she metamorphosed into a rather different Mrs. Woodhall." Probably to hide her identity and distinguish her present self from the person suggested by her reputation, Victoria had indeed for a while referred to herself as "Woodhall" instead of the more notorious Woodhull (Stinchcombe 2000, 19, fn 4).

Woodhull became more and more interested in eugenics. Attending an agricultural show in England, she praised the effects on the horses being displayed of breeding techniques designed to produce an outline of beauty and other desired characteristics, while at the same time, she criticized the physical characteristics of their grooms and the aristocrats who owned the horses (Woodhull 1892b, 12–13).

> Among wild animals and savage races, natural selection eliminates the unfit and leaves the fittest to procreate their kind, but among civilized races those who procreate and multiply are the unfit, the devitalised are not eliminated but are nurtured by civilization.
>
> WOODHULL 1892b, 15

Though still committed to the basic equality of all human beings, her growing allegiance to theories of selective breeding led her to question the practice of one person, one vote, because it increasingly seemed apparent to her that the doctrine much praised in the United States and enshrined in its amended Constitution, "[t]he theory that the vote of one man is of equal value with that of another, is untrue" (Woodhull 1892a, 34). For Victoria, this situation had its roots in the long hours worked by many ordinary people, and their tendency to have children earlier in life than their more affluent neighbors. Ultimately, society could be undermined if many voters lacked the mental acuity to participate in an election, and thus "to decide the destiny of a nation" (34), and therefore efforts should be made to improve the conditions and quality of the working classes. But at present, "[r]epresentation is determined by the quantity of individuals, and never by the quality" (36). Moreover, in a hierarchical society based on money, the percentage of people making enough income to be able to live well and take care of their progeny will be small, while the vast majority will not be able to do this. Consequently, many of their children will be weaker than those of the affluent, and will not have been raised in the optimal way, and will themselves probably not experience upward social mobility; thus, the situation is likely to deteriorate increasingly since, "in a polity ruled by a majority vote, the latter will determine who shall and who shall not be put into office" (Woodhull 1893, 51). For her, it was hard to see how this situation, if left to itself, could lead to societal progress (49–54).

Victoria and Col. Blood had divorced in 1876, and a more mundane reason for the increasingly reactionary nature of Woodhull's ideas lies in her desire not to outrage the man she wished to marry next, the banker, the very wealthy and cultured John Biddulph Martin, who would later become the president of the Royal Statistical Society, or his family. Meade ([1976] 2000, 157) comments that "[f]rantic at the prospect of losing John, Vicky embarked on a remarkable campaign of denial. Except for women's rights she disavowed nearly everything she had ever said or done. Vicky knew what she wanted. To get it, she was willing to lie." MacPherson (2014, 261) writes that "Victoria ... would do anything to gain the peace, security, and respectability she saw in Martin." Her contemporary, Henry Clews, no friend of women's rights, opined:

> Perhaps, her Wall Street experience may have assisted her, in a great measure, to accomplish this feat. Compared with her two former marriages, however, her happy union with the London banker is a decided success. It is probably only in the matrimonial line that women can become successful speculators.
>
> CLEWS 1886, 444

Before she died, John's sister, Penelope, had been an admirer of Victoria, and this prompted him to attend one of the lectures Woodhull gave in London. Although John was immediately romantically interested in her, for a long time it was uncertain, due to Victoria's reputation, if they would be married. Some details of her past had followed her across the Atlantic, creating concern on the part of the Martin family, the owners of Martin's Bank, and especially of John's mother; when they were finally wed in October 1883, his parents did not attend the ceremony. It was at least partly for this reason that Victoria started to disown many of her earlier positions, including free love, particularly as advocacy of free love was often misunderstood as an indication that one was a person of loose morals. She started to claim that views had been falsely attributed to her by various men with whom she had worked, including her second husband, and seems to have been responsible for publishing materials in England that promoted a whitewashed background (Carpenter 2010a, xxxiii; Havelin 2007, 85; Johnston 1967, 291; Sachs [1928] 1978, 290–291; Stinchcombe 2000, 19–21). Pirok writes:

> Woodhull's life in England was not fully cleansed of the soils of her past; the issues from her life in New York haunted her wherever she went. Still, once she became wealthy in England she attempted to erase the blots on

her reputation by dedicating her life to social reform, and by adhering to social norms.

PIROK 2011, 35

From now on, the cultivated picture of Victoria's life retained only the commitment to women's rights and additional unsuccessful attempts to become president of the nation where she no longer lived. Sachs ([1928] 1978, 298) notes that even with respect to that impossible aspiration, her goal was likely to "impress the Martins with her importance and assure them of her respectability."

The desire to secure the reputation of Woodhull, notwithstanding the reality that she had always been controversial, and despite the fact that doing this would mean obscuring and denying many of the positions that she had once advocated and with which she had long been associated, became such a preoccupation of Victoria and of her third husband that eventually, in February 1894, it spawned a libel case against the library of the British Museum (now known as the British Library). Ironically, such an act resonated at the time with an outrageousness that had in the past led to stigmatization of a younger Woodhull. A friend of Woodhull, George Washington Moon, discovered that the library contained a number of publications accessible to the public that contained references to Victoria that she now found to be disparaging, even if she had previously written them, spoken them, or authorized their publication. Accounts of the sensational Beecher-Tilton case, which included the accusation that Victoria had defamed the Rev. Beecher, were available to the public in the library, along with Tilton's biography of her, which she had apparently helped him to write, but in which she had portrayed her parents in a negative light, a perspective she now wished to conceal, as she did details of her relationship with the married Tilton. Although, following a request by Moon, a couple of the titles were withdrawn from public access, others continued to be available, although they were rarely sought by patrons (Marberry 1967, 283; McCrimmon 1975, 355, 355, fn 1, 357; MacPherson 2014, 284).

Due at that point to their only limited success, the Martins decided to file suit against the Museum with respect to two books that dealt with the Beecher-Tilton matter, arguing that many of the statements about Victoria in these challenged materials were untrue. The trial in the case, which lasted four days, *Martin et uxor v. the Trustees of the British Museum and E.M. Thompson* (1894), employed an advisory jury; under this type of configuration, the judge receives feedback from the jurors, but any decisions they make are non-binding on him or her. The judge was Sir Charles Edward Pollock, a correspondent of Oliver Wendell Holmes, with Victoria and her husband being represented by Sir Richard Webster, Q.C., and the British Museum by the Attorney General, Sir

Charles Russell, Q.C. (Marberry 1967, 288; McCrimmon 1975, 361, 1986, 68–69; Pirok 2011, 43; Stinchcombe 2000, 21–22).

Since it was clear that the Museum had obtained the distrusted materials and made them accessible to patrons, the central issue in the trial was whether or not they could be blamed for possessing texts that they did not know were libelous, simply because they had "selected" them. As an editorial in the Welsh newspaper, the *Western Mail*, pointed out at the time, giving a modern perspective: "If nothing is to go in the British Museum except what nobody takes any exception to it might as well be closed" (Editorial 1894, 4). Victoria's response to questioning from the Attorney General was to commit perjury, rejecting even some of the most obvious facts of her prior life. For instance, she denied that she had exercised editorial control over items that appeared in *Woodhull & Claflin's Weekly*, that she had been in favor of free love, or that she had even known Theodore Tilton, still less been his lover. Yet, Sachs ([1928] 1978, 106), points out that Victoria had once told a *Chicago Times* reporter that "he was my devoted lover for more than half a year." (Marberry 1967, 289; McCrimmon 1975, 361, 363, 1986, 68–69; Sachs [1928] 1978, 115; Stinchcombe 2000, 21–22).

Notwithstanding Victoria's dubious testimony, the jury decided that the materials were libelous, while, on the other hand, there was no negligence involved, for the Museum could not check the contents of every book they possessed to see if it contained any potential for a defamation complaint; they suggested damages of one pound (twenty shillings). The judge awarded court costs to the Museum. Victoria and her husband eventually decided not to appeal the split verdict, claiming victory, although, as Marberry (1967, 290) comments, "[f]or the Martins it was a Pyrrhic victory. They won a few shillings, and the fee of the expensive Sir Richard Webster, Q.C., was said to have been two thousand pounds" (Havelin 2007, 90–91; "Libel – Against British Museum" 1894, 113–114; MacPherson 2014, 285–286; McCrimmon 1975, 367).

2   Victoria C. Woodhull as a Political Theorist

It was noted earlier that, although many scholars and contemporaries of Victoria C. Woodhull deemed her unable to understand or compose a speech about most of the political issues that she nonetheless addressed articulately in her performances and in articles that were allegedly composed by herself, exceptions are generally made in the areas of women's rights, free love, and the misery experienced by many women at the hands of the marriage institution – or literally at the hands of their husbands, facets with which she was well familiar and about which she was genuinely articulate. Although the present author has attempted to lessen the significance of that view, it is the fact that, in the light of the exception generally made with respect to women's issues, it is thus uncontroversial to consider this particular area as being the one in which Victoria capably and knowledgeably developed her own viewpoint. In the rest of this chapter, therefore, the focus is on Woodhull not as she has most often been portrayed, as a lively and notorious historical character, but as a contributor to political theory.

Victoria's philosophy was influenced by the idea of the "New Departure," but she took that doctrine beyond its original premise. Originally presented by Virginia Minor in 1869 at a meeting of the Woman Suffrage Association of Missouri, the New Departure contended that, since women were citizens under the US Constitution, they were automatically entitled to vote. Minor and her husband, the attorney Francis Minor, pursued the argument in the courts, a strategy that culminated in the US Supreme Court case of *Minor v. Happersett* (1875). In her "Second Pronunciamento," which is included in her book, *The Origin, Tendencies and Principles of Government*, Woodhull argued that "to vote is not a privilege conferred by a State upon its citizens, but a constitutional right of every citizen of the United States, of which they cannot be deprived" (Woodhull 1871f, 37). Here, like the Minors, she argued that passage of the Fourteenth Amendment meant that the Constitution, while allowing women the right to vote as "persons born or naturalized in the United States," also preempted the ability of states to determine who could vote; at this point, only Wyoming Territory allowed woman suffrage. There were grounds for believing that citizenship did not entitle the right to vote, since the Fourteenth Amendment had also given the states the authority to manage elections. The Minors had also argued that the Fifteenth Amendment, by mandating the right to vote, had removed that ability to deny voting to women, although the US Supreme Court decided *Minor v. Happersett* solely on the question of what, if anything, had been altered by the Fourteenth Amendment. Thus, although Victoria did add additional reasons why women should be able to vote, DuBois is perhaps not technically correct to present her discussions of the Fifteenth Amendment as adding to the Minors' contributions:

> Woodhull's constitutional argument that the right to vote was inherent in national citizenship was even stronger than the Minors.' Woodhull asserted that the newly ratified Fifteenth Amendment established the "right of any citizen of the United States to vote," a right that could not be abridged by state law "neither on account of sex or otherwise.
>
> DUBOIS 1987, 855

At times, Victoria referenced the Thirteenth, Fourteenth, and Fifteenth Amendments, arguing that the Fourteenth Amendment had preempted the states' right to determine who could be a citizen of their state. Therefore, limits were instituted on the power to regulate elections: in consequence, she asks, "what business have the States to meddle with the rights, privileges and immunities of citizens, who obtain their conferment from a higher power?" by refusing to allow the largest group of citizens, women to vote (Woodhull 1871h, 8). Apprehending the ever-evolving structure of federalism, she perceived the Fourteenth Amendment as taking power away from the states, who had once been the dominant members of the partnership. Consequently, she presents its clarification of citizenship rights as mandating "first, citizens of the United States; and, secondly, of the States wherein they reside, which ultimately reverses the order of things" (8). Woodhull also invokes the original Constitution, pointing out that it had included no gender discrimination, and the Fifteenth Amendment, saying:

> [T]he right to vote is denied to women citizens of the United States, by the operation of Election Laws in the several States and Territories, which laws were enacted prior to the adoption of the said Article xv, and which are inconsistent with the Constitution as amended, and therefore are void and of no effect; but which, being still enforced by the said States and Territories, render the Constitution inoperative as regards the right of women citizens to vote.
>
> WOODHULL [1870b] 1919, 17–18

Additionally, citing also the equal protection clause of the Fourteenth Amendment, she mixes in the issues of racial and gender discrimination, adding the perspective that it was as members of the white and black races that women were entitled under the Fifteenth Amendment to vote; if it had been intended to exclude women from the category of "race," or to permit states to deny it, this would have to have been clearly indicated at the time, which it was not (DuBois 1987, 855; Woodhull 1871d, 15). In any case, Congress has reserved the power to overrule the states in the matter of elections rules. Unfortunately, she continues, rather than having a legitimate constitutional justification for denying women the right to vote, the states seemed intent on preserving the privilege of men:

> Nobody would think of denying a negro woman the right to register a ship, or to pre-empt land, or to obtain a passport. She is a citizen and entitled to these citizen's rights; but the moment another citizen's right is

involved – that one by which men held their usurped power – then they are denied the exercise of that right and are quietly informed that that right may be denied on account of sex.

WOODHULL 1871e, 8

Woodhull desired Congress to pass a law that authorized her interpretation. The Minors' first broaching of the argument had prompted women to attempt to vote or register to be able to do this, and, in 1871, both Victoria and her sister, Tennie made attempts to vote too (Brough 1980, 165; Carpenter 2010a, xvii–xviii; Doane 1896, 538–539; DuBois 1987, 852–858; Gaskell 2008, 20, 22; Havelin 2007, 42–43; Jones 2009, 352, 356–357; MacPherson 2014, 67; Woodhull [1870b] 1919, 1871d). In a letter to the *New York Times*, Woodhull complained that, having been denied the opportunity to participate by local officials of the Democratic Party, either they or she should be prosecuted, depending on which of the two were actually breaking the law; the Republicans had wanted her to be allowed to cast her ballot ("Women at the Polls: Their Experiences at New York" 1871; Woodhull 1871g).

US Rep. Benjamin Butler had persuaded Victoria that the best way to get Congress to act and declare that the Constitution as presently amended required that women be given the vote, would be to submit a petition to the legislature. This Victoria had attempted on January 11, 1871, wearing a blue sailor suit and testifying before the House Judiciary Committee, presenting what is known as her "Memorial" (Woodhull [1870b] 1919). The sensation of her being the first woman to testify before Congress guaranteed that the Memorial would be printed in newspapers throughout the United States. First, however, she formulated her arguments in an article that she published in *Woodhull & Claflin's Weekly*; some contemporaries and some scholars have debated the extent to which Woodhull wrote the Memorial and to which Rep. Butler may have contributed to it (Darwin 1919, 15; Havelin 2007, 43–44; Meade [1976] 2000, 70, 73; Squire 1911, 173–181; Stern 1968, 117; Wyman 1952, 386). In his biography of Woodhull, Theodore Tilton argues that the sophisticated reasoning the Memorial demonstrated was the product of spiritual guidance:

One night in December, 1869, while she lay in deep sleep, her Greek guardian [Demosthenes] came to her, and sitting transfigured by her couch, wrote on a scroll (so that she could not only see the words, but immediately dictated them to her watchful amanuensis) the memorable document now known in history as "The Memorial of Victoria C. Woodhull."

TILTON 1871, 28

In fact, Victoria claimed to commune with four spiritual guides, all persons of historical significance: Demosthenes, the Athenian orator; Demosthenes' enemy, Alexander the Great; Napoleon Bonaparte; and Napoleon's first wife, Joséphine de Beauharnais (Woodhull 1875b, 5). Somewhat whimsically, having encountered Tilton's biography, an editorial writer at an Indianapolis newspaper commented as follows on Victoria's fitness to become a Congresswoman:

> We may love Mrs. Woodhull, but we could not support Demosthenes, who is a foreigner and a bad man besides. It is bad enough to take Mrs. Woodhull with her two husbands, but to have a sinful old Greek hanging around can not be endured.
>
> Editorial 1871a, 2

In support of Woodhull, former Congressman Albert G. Riddle told the House Judiciary Committee that self-government was generally accepted in the United States as being a natural right, and perusal of any of the state constitutions would confirm this fact. So the issue boiled down to whether or not women were "persons." Moreover, he continued, since the Constitution largely restricts most people's participation in government to just voting, the failure to recognize this permission is to deny the natural right of self-government. With the passage of the Fourteenth Amendment, it was clear that, since its first section says neither all male persons, nor all white persons, but "all persons born or naturalized in the United States, subject to the jurisdiction thereof, *are citizens* of the United States and of the States where they reside," women, if they are citizens, must have the right to vote. Having a minimum age for voting, on the other hand, Riddle (1871, 7–8) argues, is merely reasonable and is not discriminatory, even though his argument on behalf of women could be raised, and had at the time been used, to question the restriction of voting to persons who were at least twenty-one years of age. In fact, passage of the Twenty-Sixth Amendment in 1971, which lowered this age to eighteen, suggests that the question may not be so simple. For Riddle, however, gender discrimination, was fundamentally wrong:

> I will never tolerate hearing it said, that my son is born to empire and sovereignty, while his sisters are born to be hidden away and yarded in some solitary desert place, as their proper sphere.
>
> RIDDLE 1871, 5

Of course, the question of whether or not women were persons in this context was not decided affirmatively by the US Supreme Court until its ruling in *Reed v. Reed* (1971), a unanimous decision that established that the equal protection clause applied to matters of gender discrimination. When Riddle argued that the Fourteenth Amendment's reference to "person" included all adults, others asked him why, then, it had been necessary to add the Fifteenth Amendment (which granted the right to vote to all men over 21 regardless of race), since this would seem to have already been achieved by its predecessor; his response was that the purpose of the Fifteenth Amendment was to prevent the denial of a preexisting right, not an act of conferral. In attempting to prevent the abridgement of the right, the writers of the Fifteenth Amendment were conceding that it already existed (Riddle 1871, 10–12).

Unfortunately, the committee's majority report, authored by US Rep. John Bingham, repudiated Woodhull's and Riddle's arguments with respect both to the Fourteenth and Fifteenth Amendments, denying that the states' authority over election rules had been changed by them, claiming that Article I, Section 4, Paragraph 1 of the Constitution, while allowing Congress to overrule states on matters concerning elections, did not give it the power to change requirements for being able to vote, which were still under the jurisdiction of the states; moreover, being included in the category of "citizen" did not confer to women any rights ("Woman Suffrage," 1871). Federal courts, emboldened by this congressional interpretation, soon became less tolerant of cases in which women's right to vote was raised (DuBois 1987, 857). In *Minor v. Happersett*, Chief Justice Morrison Waite for a unanimous Court readily conceded that, in the United States, women had always been "persons" and "citizens," providing a number of examples to make his case. However, he continued, the Fourteenth Amendment did not directly add anyone to the lists of voters that states had created, but simply provided additional protection for those who already possessed that right; without exception, the original states had restricted voting using gender, age, property qualifications, and, in South Carolina for example, race, whereas the US Constitution made no attempt to give the vote to all adults, while "[w]omen were excluded from suffrage in nearly all the States by the express provision of their constitutions and laws."

If this had been Victoria's only contribution to the fight for women's rights, it would still be a significant accomplishment, but, as Jones notes, she has not been adequately recognized for this (or many of her other) successes:

> Although Woodhull was the first woman to address such a high-level federal committee, an address that captured the attention of her contemporaries, editors have omitted Woodhull in the many anthologies that seek to reshape or rewrite histories of rhetoric.
>
> JONES 2009, 352

Certainly, for Woodhull herself, her triumph, such as it was, also included breathing new life into the national campaign for women's suffrage. By the end of the year, she was writing:

> And to-day the suffrage movement owes the rapid advance it has made during the past year, as well as its present promising attitude, to this movement thus inaugurated by me in Congress.
>
> WOODHULL 1871b, 10

Scarcely more than a year after her defense of women's rights before the Judiciary Committee, Messer-Kruse (1998, 211) writes that Woodhull responded scathingly to congressional opponents of slavery who now opposed naturalization of persons of Chinese ethnicity. While this is likely a view that was held by Victoria, the majority of the articles in the *Weekly* were not written by her or by her sister, Tennie, and the item in question bore no title and no writer's name (Untitled News Item 1872). But following her appearance before Congress, she certainly did develop the argument that discrimination in matters of voter eligibility was generally wrong regardless of the group that found itself disenfranchised. Based on the argument of James Otis, Jr., (whose ideas are discussed in Chapter One of this volume) that taxation without representation undermined the liberty of the American colonists, Victoria points out that this was a valid argument in the case of the slaves in the United States, and therefore, to be consistent as well as fair, it should be considered convincing in the case of women (Woodhull 1871d, 7–8, 13). Also in the same article, Victoria issued an important warning to those in Congress should they continue to impair the liberty of women by preventing them from voting, underestimate the significance of this matter, and still refuse to take them seriously. In such a case, then only one alternative would be possible, which is as follows:

> We mean treason; we mean secession, and on a thousand times grander scale than was that of the South. We are plotting revolution; we will overslough this bogus republic and plant a government of righteousness in its stead, which shall not only profess to derive its power from the consent of the governed, but shall do so in reality.
>
> WOODHULL 1871d, 32

Victoria C. Woodhull did anything but fade into the background following her failure to convince the Judiciary Committee of the need to allow women the right to vote. As she had already announced some months earlier, in the *New York Herald*, she intended to seek greater fame:

> I have deliberately and of my own accord placed myself before the people
> as a candidate for the Presidency of the United States, and having the
> means, courage, energy and strength for the race intend to contest it to
> the close.
>
> WOODHULL 1870a, 8

This was apparently a strategy to which Tilton (1871, 28) referred as a "self-nomination, ... mainly for the purpose of drawing public attention to the claims of woman to political equality with man." Given the *Herald*'s willingness to promote Victoria's ideas, a series of policy positions followed, and these were then collected into a book, *The Origin. Tendencies and Principles of Government* (Woodhull 1871f). As Meade ([1976] 2000, 53) notes, the effect of this publishing drive was to make Victoria appear scholarly and capable of becoming president.

Despite the many changes and deletions that characterized Victoria C. Woodhull's statements of what she believed, and despite denying that she had ever advocated "free love" – including when she was testifying in court – she always remained committed to the underlying principles that inspire an accurate definition of what that phrase truly means. Women advocates of free love were frequently accused of being promiscuous, when what they really desired was to have partnerships based on mutual love and commitment (rather than the existence of a legal contract that conferred obligations), in which women would have the same rights as men, would not be raped by their husbands, and would be able to end the relationship if they wished (Meade ([1976] 2000, 28; Woodhull [1874d] 2010, 225). Thus Woodhull ([1894] 2010, 55–56) complains that her critics "are shouldering upon Free Love the results that flow from precisely its antithesis, which is the spirit, if not the letter, of your marriage theory, which is slavery, and not freedom." To some extent, this paradox results inevitably from the way that "free" and "love" are otherwise used, with the consequence that even when a contemporary author who well understands the true meaning of the phrase describes it, a haziness creeps in, as follows:

> The sisters not only preached free love – which was also referred to by the
> more demure name of "social freedom" – but also practiced it, discarding
> husbands and lovers as they liked.
>
> MACPHERSON 2014, xxi

Moreover, Woodhull's own most inspirational words, delivered at Steinway Hall in New York, and then reiterated in her 1873 pamphlet, "The Elixir of Life," that "Yes! I am a Free Lover. I have an inalienable, constitutional and natural right to love whom I may; to love as long or as short a period as I can; to change this love every day if I please, and with this right neither you nor any law you can frame have any right to interfere," hardly makes the distinction clear (Hasday 2000, 1445, fn 236; Johnston 1967, 14, 133; Woodhull 1873c). As she soon discovered, the newspapers, and many of their readers, immediately interpreted it to mean, "Mrs. Woodhull confesses that she lives an utterly abandoned life; she lives and sleeps with two or three or five hundred or some other egregious number of men" (Woodhull [1873e] 2010, 138). She had in 1871 been chosen, almost accidentally, to be the president of the National Association of American Spiritualists. She would comment afterwards:

> I went to this convention merely as a spectator, with no previous concert or machinery of any kind, and was myself as absolutely taken by surprise by my nomination and election as could have been any one present.
>
> VICTORIA WOODHULL, quoted by DOYLE (1875, 20)

However, when, in 1873, she delivered "The Elixir of Life" as a speech to the Chicago Convention of Spiritualists, spiritualists, as well as feminists (both of whom sought the right to vote for women) became divided about whether she was an ally or a frivolous and dangerous enemy (Gutierrez 2005, 187–189). At other times, Victoria attempted to clarify the division, rejecting what she referred to as "free lust" (Carpenter 2010a, xxii), saying that, "I prefer to use the word *love* with *lust* as its antithesis, *love* representing the spiritual and *lust* the animal" (Woodhull [1894] 2010, 63). Even in 1873, Kent could lucidly articulate the difference that Woodhull and other advocates of free love were making:

> In her lectures she has made as clear a distinction between love and lust as any of us can make between pure and impure religion, or between true and false worship. But she thinks it wisest and best to leave both conditions – love and lust – free, with only such exceptions as her opponents generally make on religious matters.
>
> KENT 1873, 2

Nonetheless, she would eventually become exasperated trying to make critics understand the difference, and Marberry (1967, 183) suggests that, perhaps by 1874, she decided to give up constructing what had become a hopeless case. At the end of 1874, responding to an editorial in the Norristown, Pennsylvania *Daily Herald*, she began as follows:

It is a constant source of wonder to me how it is that people who pretend
to have a moderate degree of common sense can so misunderstand the
real meaning of my views of free love as stated in my lectures as the various criticisms that appear would seem to indicate that they do.

WOODHULL 1874a, 11

For Benjamin Tucker, however, the problem lay in the fact that no agreed upon
definition of "free love" existed and thus talking about it would always lead to
misunderstandings. Victoria, he noted, "while defining marriage in her own
way, and arguing therefrom, grants each and every other person the right to
define it in their own way, and judges their utterances by their definition"
(Tucker 1874, 6), a tolerant approach but one that did not enhance precision.
Indeed, such reasoning emboldened Woodhull's resolve, for a few years, to persist with the terminology she used. Of course, it turned out that she was undermined throughout the rest of her life because of her use of that phrase, and she
later did everything she could to deny that she had ever advocated what people
mistakenly believed she meant by it. She was frequently mocked. In 1870, for
instance, the *New York Herald* had supportively printed policy papers bearing
her name. Three years later, when she gave a speech at the Cooper Institute in
New York, a *Herald* reporter ridiculed her and her audience as follows:

The obscenity which was expected from Woodhull and her sister was not
afforded, and the vast congregation of prurient minds was happily disap-
pointed. However, there was enough of blasphemy substituted to make
up for the omission of the other article and gratify the many corrupt and
hoary headed old sinners who came to listen.

"Woodhull at Cooper Institute" 1873, 3

In his early biography of Victoria, Tilton made a distinction that was often
missed:

[O]n social questions, her theories are similar to those which have long
been taught by John Stuart Mill and Elizabeth Cady Stanton, and which
are styled by some as free-love doctrines, while others reject this appellation on account of its popular association with the idea of a promiscuous
intimacy between the sexes – the essence of her system being that marriage is of the heart and not of the law, that when love ends marriage
should end with it, being dissolved by nature.

TILTON 1871, 32

Indeed, this sense of the existence on the left of a not particularly radical common social agenda is reflected in the open-mindedness of the *Weekly*'s subject matter. Similarly, an article in the *Newark (N. J.) Register* commented when reviewing Tennie's *Constitutional Equality: A Right of Women* and Victoria's *The Origin, Tendencies and Principles of Government* that:

> [The books] advance many strong arguments for giving the women the right to vote, for a remodeling of the marriage laws, and, in fact, for the general renovating and making over of society. Some of these are new, and some not so new, but they are very well put, and will be found not uninteresting. even to those who are opposed to the doctrines advocated.
> "Woman's Rights – New Books" 1871, 15

When the first major American Anarchist, Josiah Warren, died, his admirer Stephen Pearl Andrews (1874, 11) reflected on the mutual respect felt, despite some disagreements, between Warren and John Stuart Mill. At the time, writers such as Henry James in his novel, *The Princess Cassamassima*, debated the merits of "the social question" and the legitimacy of anarchist violence. In *The Bostonians*, James seems to have based the character of Verena Tarrant on Woodhull. In the twenty-first century, the social question remains no less urgent. Why does almost everyone in the world live in poverty, and despite the ever-increasing, ubiquitous, and pervasive presence of administrative interference and hegemony, is no serious attempt made to satisfy the basic needs (food, housing, health care) of all? Why are the victims of this predicament, the overwhelming majority of the global population, and many millions of those living in the United States, blamed for their condition, which they have little ability to control, as though it were a defect of character, rather than what it is, a failure of government?

Woodhull was troubled by this social question. She understands liberty as having developed in the United States historically as the republic has grown. From the first, she notes, people were able to appreciate the advantages of religious freedom, and then came political freedom, but the third part of general freedom that is not yet extant, social freedom, remains to be achieved; it is toward the attainment of social freedom that Victoria directs her attention. She ([1894] 2010, 53) evaluates polemically the effects of religious and political freedom: allowing them has led only to positive results. Her argument might have been strengthened if she had said, more realistically, that the consequences were mostly positive, because even for the most libertarian advocate of freedom, there must be some negative consequences along the way. Anyhow, she contends, anyone who agrees with her must concede that social freedom should also be given a chance. Unfortunately, though, everyone "is ready for freedom, but regards everybody else, collectively, as being in danger" (Woodhull [1874d] 2010, 223), and is therefore potentially unable to handle the lack of restraint.

Individual freedom does not give people the ability to override the forces of nature but, within those limits, which may vary from place to place, each person should be given the power to make their own decisions, and not be subject to those imposed by society or by others. Moreover, it is only on the basis of liberty that one's word can be expected to be given honestly. Resembling J.S. Mill's observation that failure to allow atheists to give court testimony means that some dishonest atheists will pretend to be believers, whereas honest atheists will own up and thus be excluded (Mill [1859] 1956, 37), Woodhull complains that oaths in general reflect a society based on force that assumes that its citizens will lie if not threatened by the government: "Anything that is accompanied by compulsion is no proof of individual honesty" (Woodhull 1873d, 13). For Victoria, the prioritization of each individual's ability to make his or her own decisions, a commitment she shared with Mill and Tucker, rather than allowing others to impose their own opinions, religiously motivated or otherwise, onto people who do not really agree with them, is amply rewarded with a state of "peace and harmony" ([1894] 2010, 63) markedly different to life in other countries. This is an argument that continues to have merit with respect to those evangelical, "born again," Islamist, and fundamentalist doctrines that claim some pressing need to reform and indoctrinate the rest of us flawed, but peaceful individuals. She notes that allowing freedom of religion has not led to the development of absurd consequences in the way that critics of allowing people to live their lives more in line with what they personally desire claim will happen. For instance, she points out that religious tolerance in the United States has never created a huge expansion of Satanism. In fact, for Americans, pursuing one's own liberty and insisting that others, even those whose beliefs and choices we dislike, must be equally free, has in a way become the true religion of the United States, even if most of its citizens are not so far able to recognize this. Yet, while this tolerance allows an uncomplicated right "to say that everybody has the right to be a Catholic" (Woodhull [1874d] 2010, 229), transferring the debate from an issue about religious freedom to one of sexual freedom makes the advocate seem suddenly so much more outrageous, and hence she has been identified with the most extreme behavior that might happen once people's liberty to engage in it is recognized. Of course, in utilizing the parallel between religious liberty and the social freedom that she

wishes to bring into being, Victoria herself to some extent perforce creates the
misunderstanding, because many people who have different opinions to those
they deem to be "infidels" believe them to be wicked, and many Christians at
the time she was speaking believed promiscuousness to be immoral:

> I advocate the freedom for religion, to be enjoyed equally by the Chris-
> tian, the Infidel, the Pagan and the Jew; but I am neither one or the other
> of any of these, but a Spiritualist. Now why is it not charged, because
> I advocate this freedom, that I advocate Paganism? Simply because I do
> not – and people are so well versed in religious affairs as not to make so
> ridiculous an assertion; but the same persons who would never think of
> charging me with the advocacy of fire-worship, because I advocate the
> right of the fire-worshiper, do not hesitate to charge me with promiscu-
> ousness because I advocate the right to that condition for those who
> desire it. Is there anybody here who fails to see the analogy or the incon-
> sistency of my would be judges?
>
> WOODHULL 1873c

Liberty can not exist in a vacuum. Perhaps foreseeing an unending issue for the
United States, where people from time to time "yelp out Freedom with all their
might, without the least idea as to what is really going on about them in the
world" (Woodhull [1873b] 2010, 156), she writes:

> The people have fought for freedom, and become drunk upon the name.
> They have forgotten that this blessed boon cannot exist unless equality
> and justice also obtain.
>
> WOODHULL [1873b] 2010, 156

Equality for Woodhull should extend to the point at which it facilitates the exercise of personal liberty. Sounding like Kropotkin, she comments that each
person, is entitled, based on their existence (a natural condition that they did
not choose) rather than on the contributions they are able to make to others,
to a fair share of the resources of the world, to education, and to be able to live
a life in which they will not be overworked (Woodhull 1872e, 4). In the case of
minors, they are entitled to the same opportunities as any other child, including a share of the resources that will allow them to grow up and become a
functioning citizen of society (Woodhull [1874d] 2010, 223). Much later in her
life, she would pen an editorial that emphasized the significance of people
wanting to get by financially, and thus doing too much work:

The gravest social truth of the nineteenth century is, that overwork pro-
duces the unfit, because sufficient rest is not allowed for recuperation
and the elimination of the waste products of the body.
      WOODHULL 1892d, 1

Kropotkin also criticized overwork:

Overwork is repulsive to human nature – not work. Overwork for supplying the few with luxury – not work for the well-being of all. ... four hours
of useful work every day would be more than sufficient for supplying everybody with the comfort of a moderately well-to-do middle-class house,
if we all gave ourselves to productive work, and if we did not waste our
productive powers as we do waste them now.
      KROPOTKIN [1927] 1970, 71

In a speech to the Equal Rights Party, Victoria argues that the purpose "of government should be to foster, protect and promote the possession of equality"
(Woodhull [1872d] 2010, 91). However, in contemporary society, the most intelligent workers are those able to purchase better quality food than others, the
"muscle workers," including the people who grow and prepare the food, with
the effect that the former's brains function at a higher level, allowing them to
perpetuate their dominance, making social equality impossible (Woodhull
1892c, 2–3). Moreover, the law also distinguishes between different classes of
people, and protection of property is an overriding concern, with the rights of
capitalists having succeeded the rights of monarchs. Nowhere is this more apparent than in the relationship between business owners and workers, where
capitalists attempt to break laws that are intended to protect conditions of labor and ensure people are adequately compensated. She notes the irony that
while state and federal laws have been enacted, for example, to require over-
time payments, by politicians seeking to appeal to ordinary people, the owners
of businesses then negotiate to end worker strikes by pushing the strikers to
accept compromises that undo the effects of such legislation. Meanwhile, in
Albany and Washington, sit "representatives" who have been voted in by workers, but the workers themselves are never the legislators. Moreover, the wealth
of those who have succeeded in the business world was never attained because
they toiled more assiduously than the rest of the population, which for Woodhull is another aspect of society's failure to reward people equally, in propor-
tion to what they have done. In turn, the rich are presently taxed at an unequal
rate, paying the same flat percentage that everyone else pays, perpetuating their wealth, a situation that considerations of equity ought not permit to

continue (Woodhull [1872d] 2010). Given the desirability of individual liberty and equality, it follows that the pursuit of happiness is also entailed and should be protected by government (Woodhull 1871f, 90–91).

As for Tucker (before he changed his mind after reading *The Ego and Its Own*, and became convinced by its author, the German anarchist, Max Stirner, of the weakness of explanations in terms of natural law), so also for Victoria, individual freedom is a part of natural law: it "is an inherent, natural, God-given right" (Woodhull 1872e, 3) that can be deduced using reason. There is a point in humankind's intellectual development at which a person becomes able to contemplate the significance of liberty and the need to overthrow slavish conditions, to move beyond merely elemental considerations of survival; in the case of the United States, the attainment of this state by many caused the enslavement of Africans to end (Woodhull 1871f, 229). For Woodhull at this point, the deity is "the God of humanity" (1872e, 3), and what it has ordained, as a religion of humanism, founded by a God who gave women and men free will, is the right of every woman or man to be her or himself and to make their own decisions, with the proviso, again like Tucker and Mill, that the exercise of this individuality must not prevent anyone else from doing likewise. Moreover, in a characteristically anarchist formulation, Victoria argues that people are able to divine what is right, and thus emancipating them from artificially imposed human laws and enabling them to make their own decisions with regard to social matters will not lead to most of the problems that critics of her beliefs fear. She writes:

> This is to have natural virtue. This is to have natural, in place of artificial purity. ... Now, this is the kind of virtue, purity, and morality that I would have established; it is the kind I advocate as the highest condition to which the race can rise.
> WOODHULL [1876c] 1890, 32–33

So, there is an exception to the prioritization of freedom. Since every human being has an innate knowledge of and desire for liberty, he or she is bound to resist and resent all claims of government. And while, as Victoria has insisted, within each person's individual sphere there should be no attempts to interfere with that absolute dominion, beyond that domain, where multiple or millions of persons may interact, the governing principle should instead be equality. This is the same dividing line that Andrews and Tucker had drawn in their writings, and Victoria was of course influenced by each of them; for Andrews ([1851] 1895, 36), the limit that it is not permissible to be cross is engendered by "the concurrent Sovereignty of all men," and for Tucker (1888, 5,

[1897] 2005, 62–63) by the principle of "equal liberty." For Victoria, considering this in a different context, the application of individual freedom to states in the form of the doctrine of states' rights is absurd, because this allows states to ignore or violate the rights of much of the community; moreover, since the Constitution allows them to do this, it is an area that begs rewriting. At the time of the American Revolution, it may have been the case that the United States had briefly an appropriately good government, but it is clear that this is no longer the case:

> They [the Founders] were hundreds of years in advance of the general people, ... and it may be seriously questioned whether they have had any representatives since, and whether they have any at present, who are actuated by any such patriotism as they were.
> WOODHULL 1871f, 119

Although in the future human beings may become more educated and be able to live with less government, accepting the boundaries imposed by deference to others' liberty, for the present, Woodhull argues, creating a stronger federal government with a standardized, more passive role for the states, is the best direction for constitutional reform (Woodhull 1871f, 117–127).

The need for government should not extend to imposing norms and standards of individual behavior, because that would cease to benefit the community as a whole. The right to individual freedom includes not only religious and political matters, but also social freedom where, as with the imposition of religious and political values on those who disagree with them, "the compulsory observance of an imposed standard is at war with the nature of the individual as well as with the general good" (Woodhull 1872e, 4). At other times in Woodhull's life, the humanism on display here would be replaced by traditionally spiritualist and Christian perspectives as she became more conservative and repudiated her prior beliefs; in Boston, in 1872, in her speech to the American Association of Spiritualists, however, she stated that her "idea and hope for modern Spiritualism is, that it shall become the Religion of Humanity" (Woodhull 1872e, 6). In the early and mid-1870s, her attitude toward Christian institutions is quite skeptical, contrasting the wealth of church denominations with the poverty of many children in cities like New York, and arguing that many followers of Jesus, if they should encounter him today, would consider him guilty of blasphemy (Woodhull [1873b] 2010, 158–160); of course, that is a view that would be shared by some Christians.

Individual freedom should also govern what people may read. The concept of obscenity, she maintained, prevents scientific medical knowledge being transmitted through the US mail, and Walt Whitman's poems led to the end of his working for the Department of the Interior. How long will it take, Woodhull asks, before Anthony Comstock bans medical and legal books, biological diagrams, Shakespeare, the Bible, and many other valuable intellectual resources? In contradistinction, she argues, nothing should ever be classified as obscene if it has a legitimate purpose, which would surely have been a frightening criterion for Comstock to contemplate, but is today a standard embraced by the US Supreme Court (Woodhull [1873d] 2010, 143–144).

The notion of free love, which she was perpetually bound to defend, redefine, or repudiate is, for her, rightfully included in this general categorization of liberty. Symbolically, the Declaration of Independence means that Americans have liberated themselves from the ancient traditions of slavery and legal marriage (Woodhull [1873d] 2010, 135–136):

> Free love means nothing more, and nothing less, in kind, than free worship, freedom of conscience, free trade, free thought, freedom of locomotion (without a passport system), free schools, free government, and the hundred other precious, special systems of social freedom, which the great heroes of thought have fought for.
>
> WOODHULL [1873d] 2010, 135

For Woodhull, religious, political, and social freedom would include a perpetual title to one's body that could never be surrendered to someone else, but could be willingly exchanged with another for a certain amount of time on an equal foundation on the basis of mutual affection. Within social freedom lies this category of sexual freedom, which she calls "the last to be claimed for man, in the long struggle for universal emancipation" (Woodhull [1873d] 2010, 146). Such ownership of oneself would mean that no woman could be forced to bear children, a provision that would seem to imply acceptance of the ability to terminate a pregnancy although she generally in practice opposed abortion. It also involved for Woodhull both approval of the availability of divorce, and ultimately the abolition of marriage, an oppressive institution that forced wives to succumb sexually to their husbands' abuse:

> The woman who yields herself unwillingly to her husband is just as impure in reality as is the prostitute who sells herself for money, since the wife does it for a home or because the law has said she must, and not because her nature commends it.
>
> WOODHULL 1874a, 11; WOODHULL 1873c, [1874d] 2010, 232, and [1894] 2010, 61 are similar

This hypocrisy extends also to married women who groom their daughters to make a so-called good marriage, ideally to a wealthy man, a despicable custom by which the pursuit of money trumps the role of love in the life of one's own daughter, while the "Christians" who attempt this are outraged at the prostitute who must sell her body to provide food for her child. Indeed, it is that contempt which some wives display toward those who are being paid to service their own husbands that undermines efforts to unite all women against the practice. The irony extends, also, Woodhull argues, to the effects of sex on prostitutes and on the married women who reluctantly engage in it; sexual activity is less offensive to the person who is paid to perform, and results in its provider encountering less repulsion, and being less damaged by the process over time. Woodhull points out, too, that one of the functions of marriage is to procure for men these sexual services that are too expensive for many of them to obtain from ladies of the night. In this original fashion, she identifies one of the drawbacks of allowing the sale of sexual services, which is that it leads to the creation of alternative legal relationships from which it is difficult to extricate oneself, one of whose purposes is not to form an affectionate union with a woman but something hidden and much more nefarious. Consequently, to achieve sexual freedom, she advocates abolition of both kinds of prostitution, the sale of sexual services and also formal marriage. However, if the prostitution that operates outside of marriage can not be eliminated, it should be legalized (Meade [1976] 2000, 66; Woodhull [1874d] 2010, 232–234, 247–249, 258).

Victoria notes that "four-fifths of the children who are born are unwelcomed" (Woodhull [1873e] 2010, 205), and elsewhere that half of all children are "undesired by their mothers" (Woodhull 1874a, 11), which suggests that those raised in such homes are more likely to become mentally ill or commit crimes, another reason for seeking to end women's exploitation within families. Ironically, she observes, in the animal world, females choose their partners and rape is rare, while among the supposedly most advanced species, "millions of poor, heart-broken, suffering women are compelled to minister to the lechery of insatiable husbands" (Woodhull [1874d] 2010, 218). For humans, the development of marriage as a part of societal progress was perhaps inevitable, but that does not mean that it remains the best way to organize relationships and childrearing in the modern world, where ideally every pregnancy should be planned, and the maternity period valued and considered a good justification for not having to work elsewhere at the same time (Woodhull [1873e] 2010, 204, 1874a, 11, [1874d] 2010, 256). Actually, marriage is an exceptionally flawed institution:

> There is nothing else but marriage that licenses a man to debauch a woman against her will. There is no sexual license except in marriage.
>
> WOODHULL [1873e] 2010, 207; WOODHULL [1874d] 2010, 218 and 238 are similar; see also HASDAY 2000, 1446

Children are vulnerable also because their futures depend on their fathers' ability to earn sufficient income to provide for them and to prepare them for adult life, but many men lack the skills or opportunities to be able to perform these tasks in a manner adequate for their societal importance (Woodhull [1873b] 2010, 158). In fact, for Victoria, the family as a means of raising children is "the most unscientific, unreasonable and stupid system that could possibly be invented" (Woodhull 1872e, 4), and it is clear to her from the example of her own life, "through sorrows, trials and sufferings," that she has discovered the urgent need to emancipate women from their oppression and second-class status (Woodhull 1874c, 9). This dependence on husbands has all but guaranteed that, except for a few highly motivated individuals, women will never be successful economically, and will lack the individual liberty and distinctiveness to which everyone is entitled (Woodhull [1873b] 2010, 156–157), since "they must marry and merge their identity and individuality in some man" (157). Meanwhile, the women who attempt to avoid marriage and to be independent and become successful by themselves, maybe deciding not to have children, face the prospect of "social death" (157), so it is not surprising that instead, many women choose to be "willing slaves" (157). Here, it should perhaps be noted that, today, enthusiastic and promising female college students often soon abandon the paths to their chosen professions, giving birth, and are then themselves abandoned by the fathers of their children, which leaves them struggling in poverty perhaps for the rest of their lives. The institution of marriage, and the social practices attendant upon it, remain a substantial barrier to equality for women. For Victoria ([1874d] 2010, 217), marriage is "the most terrible curse from which humanity now suffers."

In her speech, "Tried as by Fire," Victoria notes that the most important human relations involve matters of sexual freedom, and yet these receive the least attention, with the society in which she lived even forbidding their details to be transmitted to children, with the consequence that people became involved in relationships having left the information they need to function effectively unexplored, being influenced instead by social norms and fads, but without scientific knowledge that could assist them in making better decisions (Woodhull [1874d] 2010, 214–215). On the other hand, many thoughtful people have come to realize that the institution of marriage is a façade, and what prevents them from admitting this dissatisfaction is "dread of a falsely educated public opinion and a sham morality, which are based on the ideas of the past, but which no longer really represent the convictions of anybody" (215). Here, Victoria resembles Tolstoy (1889), whose narrator, Pozdnyshev, in the story, "The Kreutzer Sonata," condemns honeymoons as being "awkward, ashamed, repelled, sorry, and above all dull, intolerably dull!" (1889): marriage thus is a deception that men are reluctant to admit they fell for, and Victoria seems to share with Tolstoy a repugnance at the physicality and dirt of sex, while, like her, the Pozdnyshev character criticizes the role of mothers who promote the marriageability of their daughters:

> They know with what sort of bait to catch men for themselves and for their daughters. "You see it is only we men who don't know (because we don't wish to know) what women know very well, that the most exalted poetic love, as we call it, depends not on moral qualities but on physical nearness and on the coiffure, and the color and cut of the dress."
> TOLSTOY 1889

Not surprisingly, Anthony Comstock also attempted to ban "The Kreutzer Sonata" (Rabban 1997, 30).

Also problematic is the fact that men and others who oppose the acknowledgement of women's need for equality repeatedly erect scarecrows to prevent progressive ideas from spreading to the majority, a practice to which Victoria refers to as being "part of the contest between despotism and freedom" (Woodhull [1873e] 2010, 201). Thus individual liberty is resisted because it will lead to the end of the family, an institution that, despite its symbolic appeal, far from being beneficial to society, actually compels incompatible people to live together, and damages the children that result from the arrangement. Furthermore, as society has advanced and preempted many of the decisions that parents once exercised over their upbringing – for example, by requiring that they attend school – then presently it seems that the idea that children "belong" to their parents can also be challenged, especially if this opinion leads to negative consequences, which it does (Woodhull [1873e] 2010, 201–206).

It is often (but not always) clear that the marriage that Woodhull most opposes is the institution she has encountered all her life, legal marriage in which women are never equal, where the conditions of the relationship and the opportunities for childbearing are seldom ideal. Consequently she attempted to publish an article called "What I Do Not Oppose in Marriage," only part of which made it to the pages of the *Boston Investigator*, in which she wrote:

> I do believe in the sanctity of marriage, and it is because I so believe, that
> I have plead so earnestly as I have for woman's complete emancipation
> from legal marital thraldom.
>
> WOODHULL 1876a, 5

In her article, "The Impending Revolution," which was first presented as a
speech at New York City's Academy of Music, Woodhull presents an evolutionary theory of societal development consistent with the preceding analysis.
Throughout history, political power has passed from heads of families to tribal
leaders, to nations run by tyrants, and to class-based societies run by aristocra-
cies, all of which suppressed individuality and individual rights; these same
violations were then, in turn, replicated by capitalism:

> Having obtained freedom from the despotism of rulers and governments,
> the rule and despotism of individuals began to usurp the places made
> vacant by them. Where once the king or the emperor reigned, capital,
> reinforced by the power of public opinion and religious authorities, now
> sits and forges chains with which to fetter and bind the people.
>
> WOODHULL 1873d, 3

Unfortunately, she notes, while law might be expected to protect individual
liberty and the equality necessary to exercise it, in practice the legal system
serves big business and its shareholders, whose interests undermine and oblit-
erate those of ordinary people. Elsewhere, she comments, "Money here is king,
and judge and jury also" (Woodhull [1876d] 1890, 239). The ordinary workers
who actually produce the wealth that these capitalists enjoy, Victoria argues,
are not much better off than the slaves who until recently toiled across the
South, and their dissatisfaction with the set-up is no less, either (Woodhull
[1873b] 2010, 153, 1873d, 6, [1876d] 1890, 258):

> Every year the excess of the produced wealth of the country finds final
> lodgment in the pockets of these classes, and they grow richer at each
> succeeding harvest, while the laborers toil their lives away; and when all
> their strength and vigor have been transformed into wealth, which has
> been legally transferred to the capitalists, they are heavy with age, and as
> destitute as when they began their life of servitude. Did ever Southern
> slave have meaner end than this?
>
> WOODHULL 1873d, 4

Meanwhile, even though it is "unpleasant" to have to say this, in the case of
wives, the aggregate effect of marriage slavery is far greater, she argues, than for

those who were slaves due to their African origins, because there are so many more married women, and a higher percentage of them are cruelly mistreated and "polluted" sexually by their husbands (Woodhull [1873e] 2010, 209; [1874d] 2010, 219).

Like Mercy Otis Warren, the subject of Chapter One of this volume, Victoria C. Woodhull makes a distinction between what she views as the noble intentions of the Founders and of the Declaration of Independence, and what she sees as the inappropriateness of the US Constitution, which changed the United States for the worse. Again like Otis Warren, who criticized the avariciousness of some Americans once the Revolution had achieved success, Woodhull argues that the Founders made many sacrifices, but surely their goal could not have been to create a society based on the rule of money wherein only a small minority could prosper:

> They endured the hardships and privations of that war for independence for themselves and their posterity. Nothing less than this was the inspiration of those years of suffering, nothing less than this could have given them inspiration to gain their independence.
> WOODHULL [1876d] 1890, 237

Moreover, "unfortunately, all who came to the New World had not these hopes and anticipations; some there were who still desired the strong hand of the tyrant to sway" (Woodhull 1871f, 228). Then followed the US Constitution, a document that betrayed the American spirit, wherein, until the passage of the Fourteenth Amendment, men born in England undid the commitment to equality, creating a powerful president who rules much like the king the revolutionaries had recently fought to remove.

> So far as the Constitution is concerned, it is Dead Sea fruit. It is an old and musty English sermon to which we have prefixed a new and vital text, the text and sermon having no common ground or meaning.
> WOODHULL [1876d] 1890, 238

One of the virtues of this system of capitalism is often regarded as being its ability to reward entrepreneurship, but for Woodhull, the arbitrariness of who makes a profit and who does not is appalling. A person who buys a piece of land on which a railroad station is later built is lucky, she writes, and multiplies his or her wealth without having done any work to justify that transformation, and thus they should be viewed as having appropriated the wealth of the people. The American Anarchist, Lysander Spooner, bought land with such a motive in Ohio, hoping it would become the spot where travelers transferred between horses and canal boats, creating a settlement, but the venture floundered when the canal's route was redirected, and he lost his money; Spooner would probably have responded that the risk and his loss justified the provision of profit for more successful investors (Shone 2010, v). Another example that Victoria provided was that legacies give money to the children of a person who dies, which has not been earned by the persons who inherit, and should not be allowed, she writes (1873d, 5), because it violates the principle of equality to which everyone else is entitled. When she expressed this opinion in a speech, a report in the *New York Times* upbraided her for "exhibiting her fondness for scolding men of respectability" and "inflaming the unthinking hostility of the poor to the rich" ("A Lamp Without Oil" 1872; Woodhull 1872b, 9–10).

Eventually, however, she views the process as ending more satisfactorily, with the creation of a world government. And here the other side of her humanism becomes apparent. She argues that in future, society should utilize every one of its members. Presenting society as an organism that can be undermined if some of its members are damaged, she writes:

> [T]he human family is in reality one and indivisible, and that the interests of every member of it are best [served] when the best interests of all are maintained, and in which no single member can be left to suffer and the rest of the body be not affected by it!
>
> WOODHULL 1871a, 9

Despite her criticism of the US Constitution, and in the manner of Tocqueville, she sees the United States as being ahead of the development curve; for Victoria, this is because her country is a land of immigrants, and the interaction of people from all over the world is gradually producing a new humanity that reflects all the influences and cultures of its many origins. That assimilative process worldwide derives from several factors, including the existence of immigration patterns, as well as the commercial prowess of Britain, the increasing influence of Russia on its Asian neighbors, and the development of new technology such as the telegraph, which she saw as allowing ideas to be spread instantly around the world – much as many people today would view the Internet (Woodhull 1871f, 152). In a later work, *Humanitarian Government*, Victoria adds another criterion, the effect of evolution on human beings:

> The laws which may be beneficial for two or three generations may be totally inadequate for the fourth. I recognize the law of evolution in me and that no single thing remains stationary.
>
> WOODHULL 1890, 4

This last factor might bring to mind Maupassant's story, "Vain Beauty" (also known as "Useless Beauty"), about how women have outgrown the breeding animal function that God, it may be believed, has assigned them (Maupassant 1926).

In the future, having become "a heaven of retreat for such of them as sought greater freedom and better equality, in which individuality could expand without coming in contact and being dwarfed by personal government" (Woodhull 1871f, 80), the United States should be expected to expand into a worldwide entity, for whereas the English have spread around the globe their Englishness, the United States will disseminate libertarian and multicultural values which will be more accepted by peoples around the world, eventually creating the need for a single language and a world government:

> All will be born free and entitled to the inalienable rights of life, liberty and the pursuit of happiness in self-chosen paths, which alone is perfect equality.
> WOODHULL 1871f, 84

That is not to say that the United States is presently an appropriate model of government, a fact to which the calamity of the recent Civil War attests; it is just the best system so far, founded by great minds, who recognized the importance of these virtues enshrined in the Declaration of Independence, and, in writing a new document, Americans should continue to be guided by them (Woodhull 1871f, 78–84, 228, [1876d] 1890, 238). While her admiration for the Declaration may reflect Victoria's upbringing and the heterodoxical teachings of Stephen Pearl Andrews, the reference above to "self-chosen paths" is a characteristically anarchist stipulation, although in a number of places, she cites "anarchy" as something to avoid; perhaps it is appropriate to note here again that, as indicated in the Introduction to the present book, although people sometimes confuse "anarchy" with "anarchism," no serious anarchist thinker has ever advocated anarchy or the complete abolition of government – just, like Victoria at this point in her life and Tucker throughout his, more personal liberty and a lot less government.

For the integration of polities to take place and the formation of what she refers to at times as the United States of the World to develop, the world of commerce must be transformed so that it no longer serves only as the means to pursue selfish personal goals, but becomes a medium for "the exchange of intellectual, moral, social and religious products also, and its application thereby becomes common to all the interests of humanity" (Woodhull 1871f, 199). This economic merging would then become the springboard for political unity, and modern social sciences such as political economy and sociology the means to understand the process (198–200).

Reflecting on some of the prejudices of her era, she suggests that the turmoil of this interaction will eventually raise the condition of black people to the level of whites (Woodhull 1873d, 2), a view that was also articulated by Mercy Otis Warren; in fact, Victoria argues that this process will end when "the Negro will ultimately be entirely lost in the white races" (Woodhull 1871f, 111). She is mindful of the fact that social change comes quickly in the United States:

> The blacks were cattle in 1860; a negro now sits in Jeff Davis's seat in the United States Senate.
>
> WOODHULL 1870a, 8, 1871f, 19

Moreover, she felt, a similar swift alteration in the status of women was now possible. But, if capitalism was to continue, the principle of equality should guarantee the right to work, and if necessary a government job, as well as wage rates that make it possible for everyone to live an adequate life. Current social organization, however, views the person who steals a loaf of bread to survive as being a criminal (Woodhull [1873b] 2010, 159–160). Her repudiation of the only alternatives available to a significant minority of people – "Beg, steal or starve?" (160), each of which results in societal sanction of the person making the choice, seems if anything to have even greater application to the contemporary United States than it did when she was speaking. Persons released from jail, theoretically having repaid their debt to society, often find themselves without access to money, clothing, transportation, or health care, and recent changes in the law make them effectively unable to obtain any job due to their prison records, which may also render them ineligible for government food or housing assistance. So, what should they do? If they beg, panhandling and vagrancy laws, and attendant police scrutiny of them as they stand on a public street (where sitting down or sleeping may now no longer be allowed) seem guaranteed to put an end to that option, while not eating or eating too little can last only so long. Consequently, society should not be too surprised to find out that the "recidivism" rate is quite high. Woodhull's argument, which is compatible with the anarchist viewpoint that most crime is social, and rarely a personal defect of individuals who make bad choices, is difficult to refute. She continues:

> A "States Prison Bird" has little chance in your social system. He can practice only those things for a living which continually return him.
>
> WOODHULL [1873b] 2010, 161

A society that guaranteed the right to work and survive and be happy to all its members would likely find crime rates would decline. For example, many laws exist to punish debtors who have experienced difficulty in paying their bills. The government's solution is often to humiliate the borrower, as it is those who have committed crimes, using the court system to achieve this, although, Victoria notes, fortunately few persons are now jailed for debt. However, if there existed no formal means for going after those who owed money, the only potential damage to a person who refused to pay would be to his or her reputation, a system that might ironically be more effective because people seek to protect their good names. Even if that were not the case, the costs of legal enforcement, which due to the high prices associated with attorneys and courts, often exceed that of the debt, could certainly be saved (Woodhull 1871f, 236–237). Later in life, Victoria would move away from this perspective; as with many other issues, she became more reactionary, now seeing criminals as being persons of differing characters, with whom different strategies would be effective in curing them, a more traditional approach that blamed them for their psychological conditions, physiology, or bad choices (Woodhull 1890, 29–40):

> In the humanitarian Government of the future, when our legislators have a thorough knowledge of psychology and pathology, our criminal courts will be presided over by a council of scientists who will examine into the nature and cause of the malady, whether the patient is curable or incurable, the effects of the environment and whether association with others of the same type by the power of suggestion would not intensify the malady instead of acting as a corrective.
>
> WOODHULL 1890, 31

At the People's Convention gathering of May 10, 1872 in Apollo Hall, located at the junction of Broadway and 28th Street in Manhattan, the day after Susan B. Anthony, anxious at the attention Woodhull was receiving, had turned off the lights at the nearby National Woman Suffrage Association (NWSA) meeting at Steinway Hall in order to end Victoria's speech, a new party formed, clustered around Victoria, who would speak at its evening session, even as the NWSA continued its own proceedings in the original location. Briefly called the People's Party, the new body was immediately, at the pressing of Stephen Pearl Andrews, rechristened, changing to the Equal Rights Party, the name of an existing abolitionist grouping with which he had been associated. The *New York Herald* described the event as a meeting of "the radical wing of the female shriekers," and alleging that most of the women attendees "were more homely in the face than as many nutmeg graters" ("A Piebald Presidency" 1872, 1; Carpenter 2010a, xiii; Johnston 1967, 145; Marberry 1967, 86; Meade [1976] 2000, 111–112; "The National Woman Suffrage Association at Steinway Hall" 1872).

Clearly threatened by what had transpired at Apollo Hall, the *Herald* reporter's tirade continued:

> A long series of resolutions were then read with such catch words as 'humanity,' and 'progress,' 'freedom,' 'the female sex,' 'down-trodden woman,' 'social life,' 'masculine tyranny,' and so on.
>
> 'A Piebald Presidency' 1872, 1

An entirely different perspective could be found in Woodhull's letter of acceptance of her ensuing presidential nomination, where she pointed to what she saw as the significance of her candidacy:

> The joint assemblage of all the reformers, of all schools, for the first time in the history of the great transition which human society is undergoing, blended and fused into the same spirit, coming to agree to stand upon the same platform of ideas and measures, and nominating by an outburst of inspiration a woman known to be representative of the most advanced and unmitigated radicalism, and because she was so known: and a negro, one of the boldest of the champions and defenders of human rights, a representative man and a representative woman of the two oppressed and repressed classes.
>
> WOODHULL 1872c, 8

Operating inside the new party and within this wide circle of radical interests – feminist, spiritualist, labor, Marxist, former abolitionist, etc. that surrounded it, were attracted to it, or supported it ideologically, Victoria and Tennie with Andrews (and perhaps Commodore Vanderbilt) through the stimulus of the *Weekly* were able to create a lobby (to which the *Weekly* referred as a "campaign club") known as the Victoria League, which would nominate Woodhull for president and then seek to gain for her candidacy and its uncompromising platform, which included the vote for women and government control of utilities and of some major industries, the formal support of the Equal Rights Party, which was accomplished in the late spring of 1872. Local Victoria clubs were formed and a button announcing "Victoria C. Woodhull for President" was manufactured, although to a large extent the League was what in modern terms would be termed an Astroturf group, with campaign muscle that extended way beyond its actual membership numbers, though almost no chance of electoral success (Brough 1980, 209, 213; Johnston 1967, 146–147; MacPherson 2014, 166; Meade [1976] 2000, 113, 117–118; Sachs [1928] 1978, 118, 122, 157, 206; Stinchcombe 2000, 11–12, 14; Tilton 1871, 28; "The Victoria League" 1872).

The endorsement of the Equal Rights Party demonstrated both the strengths and the weaknesses of such an arrangement. On the one hand, Victoria herself appears to have written the letter that was used to nominate her at the convention, a sign of her political skills. On the other hand, the amateurishness of the proceedings led to Frederick Douglass being nominated as her vice presidential running mate, without his knowledge and without ever receiving his permission or even an acknowledgement that the decision had been made. Some other men from minority backgrounds were considered, as was Theodore Tilton (Carpenter 2010a, xix–xx; Meade ([1976] 2000, 114). The *New York Herald* mocked the choice of Douglass with its story headlined "A Piebald Presidency," emphasizing that Woodhull was "white" and her running mate was "black," making an oblique reference to the use of selective breeding ("A Piebald Presidency" 1872, 1).

One important item included in the Equal Rights Party's platform was the desire to transfer control of policy away from Congress to the voting public via the use of referenda. For Victoria, the proper role for the national legislature would be to serve as "working committees," marking up potential legislation that the actual government, the people, would evaluate and decide whether or not to approve. The advantage of this change would be that the interests of ordinary people would replace the power of money and moneylenders, monopolies, railroad owners, and other corporations who currently exercised their rule from behind that apparent vehicle of democratic government, Congress. Ordinary people would include women, who would be added to the "impartial suffrage" of men called for by Douglass (1867) and the manifesto of her Liberal Republican presidential opponent, Horace Greeley. Woodhull wrote to the editor of the *New York Daily Tribune* to point out that "impartial suffrage" should "mean equal suffrage for all citizens" (Woodhull 1872a, 9). Hopefully, this would be a substantial change:

> The people no longer require rings, lobbies and cliques to attend to their business, and in adopting the *referendum* as one of the demanded reforms they propose to wipe them out of existence.
>
> WOODHULL 1872c, 9

In England, Victoria launched a new publication that to some extent reflected her changed attitudes, motives, and circumstances, as well as her wealth, although commentators have had quite diverse positions as to the extent of its differences with *Woodhull & Claflin's Weekly*. Called *The Humanitarian*, it lasted for nine years, from 1892 to 1901, and was coedited by her daughter, Zula Maud, rather than by Tennie. Robinson speaks of its "progressive agenda" (2010, 1) and notes that it allowed a range of women "to comment on and participate in a variety of sociopolitical activities, not just those traditionally considered either feminine or feminist" (27). For Stinchcombe (2000, 22), *The Humanitarian* "was as bold as" its predecessor, "although it avoided attacks on individuals." Similarly, for MacPherson (2014, 279), the new magazine "was even more forward-thinking" than the *Weekly*, "calling cigarettes lethal to one's health." However, while it anticipated a modern viewpoint with respect to tobacco, that same perspective also reflected a retreat from Victoria's early 1870s extreme commitment to individual liberties, a change that Tucker, for example, would come to deplore. MacPherson mentions *The Humanitarian*'s "new emphasis on theology" (279), although it is worth noting that, in the later years of the *Weekly*, she had started writing and including much more scriptural content.

On the other hand, while arguing that, with the appearance of the new journal, Woodhull had revealed herself to have finally grown up, with "a personality that at fifty-four began to be convincing" Sachs ([1928] 1978, 347) also criticizes *The Humanitarian* precisely for its self-absorption, as well as because "for with all its faults the *Weekly* crackled with the fire that never dates, while *The Humanitarian* limped in the limits of its time" (347–348). Sharing the criticism and the metaphor, Meade ([1976] 2000, 161) commented that "[t]he new journal dealt with social issues but lacked the fire that had made the *Weekly* so memorable." An article in the *British Medical Journal* took aim at Victoria's growing interest in eugenics and her desire to develop "methods by which unworthy individuals may be excluded from breeding" and the prevention of birth defects. The piece understandably questioned whether or not such policies should be seen as examples of "humanitarian government" ("Literary Intelligence" 1893, 975), although today, it might be argued that the use of therapy, sterilization, contraception, abortion, and ultrasound to achieve the same goals are benevolent.

It may seem surprising that, for a time, such an individualistic person as Victoria C. Woodhull, the pioneering female stockbroker, would soon and contemporaneously become an advocate of Marxism and even be an active participant in a section of the International Workingmen's Association (IWA) (also known as the First International), the organization founded in 1864 in England with the involvement of Karl Marx, who would give its Inaugural Address and soon become its leader, although, as Collins (1962, 402–403) notes, Marx's attendance at this first meeting was fortuitous due to his presence in London and his atypical decision to participate; on the other hand, Felix (1983, 25) points out that "[h]e had honestly earned the opportunity that came so carelessly," because his writings and revolutionary experience at that point had prepared him to lead the fight. Nonetheless, the IWA would self-destruct in 1876 for reasons hardly unconnected to its ties to Woodhull and her cohorts. In fact, it was predictable that this local group, Section 12, which met at the *Weekly*'s headquarters, would advocate views too radical to be tolerated by Karl Marx and many of his allies, that their section would be expelled from the IWA, and that she would later move away from such ideas, rounding on Marx (MacPherson 2014, 139; Messer-Kruse 1998, 1; Stern 1968, 114). An article by "Ramshorn," printed in the *Weekly* in 1876 would carp at the demise of the IWA, calling Marx a "demagogue," and arguing that he and his allies were responsible for that sad end, "not the armies, not the police, not the prisons of the combined kings, priests and plutocrats!" (Ramshorn 1876, 2).

Less than five years earlier, the situation was entirely different. In the December 30, 1871 edition of *Woodhull & Claflin's Weekly*, Victoria and Tennie became the first US publishers of a version of Marx's *Communist Manifesto*, which they titled "German Communism – Manifesto of the German Communist Party" (1871), accompanied by an introduction possibly written by Andrews, called "The "Internationale" Initiative" (1871) which described Marx somewhat pompously as "the world-famous leader of the "New Socialism"" ("The "Internationale" Initiative"1871, 3). The stockbroker sisters' apparent turn to the left seems to have been prompted by news of the crushing of the Paris Commune described in Chapter Two of the present work, the seventy-two or seventy-three day long (sources differ) revolutionary government much praised by but not really helped by Marx, which had taken control of the city on March 18, 1871 in defiance of the new Third Republic, and promptly held new elections; this news from France also made some Americans aware for the first time of the existence of Marx. The goals of the Communards, who were to some extent influenced by the ideas of the First International, who rejected the authority of the national government, and who were soon slaughtered by its army, were, with the *Weekly* being a notable exception, generally misrepresented by the press in the United States, their actions likened to the worst excesses of the French Revolution's period of Terror when people were guillotined simply for being aristocrats (Bernstein 1951, 150–151; Felix 1983, 34; Foner 1972, 4; Katz 1994, 393–396; MacPherson 2014, 138–139, 140; Marberry 1967, 54; Meade [1976] 2000, 65; Messer-Kruse 1998, 106; Stern 1968, 116). As Bernstein notes:

> All in all the *Weekly* helped to counteract the confusion and hysteria which the press generated among Americans.
>
> BERNSTEIN 1951, 152

While there may be some truth to Sachs' ([1928] 1978, 153) statement that "[a]s Victoria's fortunes waned, her interest in Communism waxed," the reasons for Woodhull joining up with the IWA clearly had their root in Andrews' earlier involvement with an organization known as the "New Democracy," an open-minded New York-based reformist group that started in 1868 and included members from a range of different professions, including one-time police officer William West, who would write many articles printed on the first page of the Weekly that charted the progress of the IWA in the US along with its eventual disagreements with more hardline and ideologically constrained factions, including Marx himself. West, like the sisters, admired "the slaughtered heroes of the Paris Commune" (West 1871, 3), and was involved in an attempt to honor the memory of those killed with a march in New York City that police authorities did not allow to take place. In some ways, New Democracy was much more far-reaching than its more Marxist counterparts, especially in the diversity of its membership, its advocacy of equal rights for women including the right to vote, and its commitment to civil liberties – in other words, to what Glickstein (1998) refers as its "disposition to recognize, and tolerate different paths to radical progress." Andrews' wife, Esther Andrews, a medical doctor, was also a key player in the New Democracy leadership. Eventually, the group would become transformed into two units, New York Sections 9 and 12 of the IWA, where its more genuinely tolerant views, including broadmindedness in considering different policy perspectives and openness to having membership from different alignments, would increasingly lead to conflict with other, far more dogmatic IWA factions, as would its commitment to the independence of each group, as well as the perspective of West (1871, 3) that "each section is responsible for the integrity of its own members." Alexander (1953, 283) refers to Section 12 as a splinter group: unlike most other US-based affiliates, which contained mostly immigrants and held meetings in German, French, Czech, or another foreign language, Sections 9 and 12 included many persons born in the US; they transacted their activities in English, and became known as the "Yankee International." West, Stephen Pearl Andrews, Tennie, and Victoria became members of Section 12. Due to their ownership of the Weekly, where all the employees were members of Section 12, Victoria and Tennie exercised a powerful influence over the activities of that group, and also increasingly over Section 9. Nevertheless, as conflict between the Yankee and other sections intensified in 1872, the sisters and their cohorts argued that even though the Weekly was written and published by Section 12 members (who also met at the Weekly's offices), it was a newspaper that was free to discuss independently issues that the IWA would have preferred to keep between members or not talk about at all (Bernstein 1951, 147; Johnston 1967, 121; MacPherson 2014, 139; Marberry 1967, 53; Messer-Kruse 1998, 1, 43, 74, 106, 110, 141; "Remarks" 1872, 3–4; Stern 1968, 114). As Messer-Kruse observes:

> The diversity of individuals attracted to the IWA flew in the face of the strategy that Marx and his German American cohorts had hammered out for America. Marx had called for organizing a coalition of German and Irish workers who would together radicalize the American proletariat. ... Much to the chagrin of the IWA's class conscious German American leaders, it instead found itself deluged with Yankee radicals who shared a distrust of coercive authority in any guise.
> MESSER-KRUSE 1998, 2

In fact, as a news report in the *Weekly* insisted, the members of Section 12 were confident of their own abilities to determine which policies were needed in the US:

> We (*Americans*) may be supposed to understand our own political status, at least quite as well as our fellow citizens of other nationalities residing beyond the seas.
> "Remarks" 1872, 4

In the United States, the leader of the opposition to Woodhull and Section 12 was a German-speaking music teacher named Friedrich Sorge, a former revolutionary who had been sentenced to death in Germany and who would in 1872 become the general secretary of the worldwide IWA. A few years earlier, when his local group, Section 1, had affiliated with the IWA, he expressed the desire to expand interest in the movement among English-speaking Americans; however, by late 1872, Hoboken, New Jersey-based Sorge's rather different New York faction had reversed course and, that December, it expelled all the English-speakers. Earlier in the year, in September, at the IWA's Fifth General Congress, which assembled in The Hague, Marx had called for the Section 12 to be ousted from the organization, citing Woodhull's interest in spiritualism, capitalist investment experience, support for women's rights, and, of course, her perpetual vulnerability, being associated with the movement for free love, and the expulsion took place following a vote of 49-0, with eight or nine abstentions (sources differ). The section itself, meanwhile, was faulted for being too "bourgeois" and not having enough "workers" among their membership (Barry [1872] 1958, 267, 289; DeLeon 1978, 73; Gerth 1958, 177–178, fn 2, 199; MacPherson 2014, 175–176;

Messer-Kruse 1998, 2–3, 75, 91, 127, 128–129, 183). Marx complained about Section 12's "talk of personal liberty, social liberty (free love), dress regulation, women's franchise, universal language, etc." (Marx, quoted by Gerth 1958, 194–195), all serious issues from many perspectives, but he viewed discussing them as a betrayal of the needs of the proletariat. West tried valiantly to justify the perspective of the Yankees, arguing:

> Sexual equality is the first step in the true path of liberty. While women are enslaved, men will never be free.
>
> WEST, quoted by BARRY [1872] 1958, 266

This clash had always been likely to occur, because Woodhull had rejected a class conscious approach, doubting the prospect of a "Labor" party prevailing in the United States precisely because she thought that, by "sectionalizing itself at the very outset" (Woodhull 1871f, 146), it would be inadequate at representing diverse interests, would provoke business-owners, and would rehash the conflicts concerning slavery. This flushing of the Yankees, meanwhile, David DeLeon (1978, 102–103) points out, was the process by which Sorge emerged as the head "of an essentially German-American movement," a key event in "[t]he sad history of American Marxism." Still, the document released by the sisters and other leaders of the Yankee sections that called for the exclusion of "aliens" from their own organization, notwithstanding the many immigrants who were their own participants was hardly an inspirational rejoinder (Marberry 1967, 53). Alexander (1953, 283, 308–309) suggests that throughout the subsequent history of socialism in the United States (including within the Socialist Party), there have been many such calls to Americanize the movement, of which Victoria and Tennie's was just the first. Ironically, he argues, all such cleansed factions have remained oriented toward European, rather than American issues. However, it seems unlikely that the feminist and social question concerns addressed by Woodhull and Claflin have any more or less applicability wherever in the world they are addressed – and, of course, nowhere have they been satisfactorily resolved.

In the light of Victoria C. Woodhull's own repudiation and denial of the views she clearly had held during the early and mid-1870s, and the dubiousness that surrounds the authorship of much of her intellectual output, it is perhaps understandable that so many authors have focused much more on her activities and reputation, rather than on her political philosophy. Nonetheless, in those few years of her heyday, when she appeared before Congress and first ran for president, when she was prioritizing the needs of labor, and extemporizing profoundly on the sad experiences and restricted opportunities of women, as she came to understand the inherent weakness of Marxism as a means for liberating the majority of people from the slavery we still in many respects enjoy (and which is commonly thought to be and falsely presented by political scientists as a system of democracy), when she was helping pioneer an alternative leftism rooted in actual experience, and one that retains in its many libertarian elements an opportunity to free people from the bondage of institutionalized religion, crony capitalism, ignorance in general, and marriage in particular, and to allow each individual as far as possible to live their own lives unpressured and unintimidated, without being exploited, sold, tricked, or raped, as they themselves see fit – during those years, she was a thinker of considerable merit, and her ideas remain just as valuable for us today.

ILLUSTRATION 4   Tennie C. Claflin, unknown photographer. Photo, undated.

CHAPTER 4

The Seductiveness of Tennie C. Claflin and of Her Ideas

The younger sister of Victoria C. Woodhull, Tennie C. Claflin (c. 1845–1923) has received nothing like the attention given to Victoria, a situation that has been remedied only occasionally with the publication of works that consider the lives of the two sisters together, most notably James Brough's *The Vixens: A Biography of Victoria and Tennessee Claflin,* and Myra MacPherson's recent book, *The Scarlet Sisters: Sex Suffrage and Scandal in the Gilded Age.* However, little attempt has been made to probe Tennie's political ideas, which is the task attempted in this chapter. Claflin's works, some of which exist as speeches of which published copies were made, and others as articles that appeared in the sisters' *Woodhull & Claflin's Weekly* and/or were collected in books, are well worth exploring, and represent a valid contribution to political theory and to the history of first wave feminism[1] that has so far been minimized. In MacPherson's generally excellent work, she claims:

> In this book, for the first time, Tennie is given the attention she deserves, and has been resurrected from a footnote in her sister's life. She played a far larger role than biographers intent solely on Woodhull have portrayed. Contemporary papers gave her more coverage than Victoria before her older sister's drive for the presidency and fame during the Beecher scandal.
>
> MACPHERSON 2014, XXV

While it certainly is good to look specifically at Tennie, which is why in the present book she has her own chapter, MacPherson, in claiming "first time" status forgets about Brough's *The Vixens,* though it is included in her bibliography (2014, 329); moreover, no one has really reduced Tennie to a footnote – that is an exaggeration and, in fairness to all the other authors who have centered their attention on Victoria, they were writing books about Victoria, so naturally her life would be what they prioritized. The real omission, considering the

---

1 First wave feminism usually refers in the United States to ideas protesting women's second-class status that often grew out of abolitionist sentiments (though some thought such as that of Abigail Adams is of older provenance), and continues until approximately 1960, a point at which scholars often consider second wave feminism to have begun.

literature as a whole, lies in the focus upon the biographies (and the once scandalous aspects of their lives) to the exclusion of assessing their political ideas.

Named by her parents Tennessee Celeste Claflin, a designation she used at times, particularly in its shortened form of Tennessee C. Claflin, she mostly preferred to be known as Tennie C. Claflin. Which was the original name and which the adopted appellation has been presented by some authors the other way round, as for example, by Morrissey (1910, 229), who writes of "Lady Cook, who was Miss Tennie C. Claflin, commonly called "Tennessee" Claflin by the newspapers," by Smith (1927, 293), who speaks of "Tennie, who in later life turned her first name and middle initial into the more euphonious Tennessee," and by Marbury (1967, 4) who informs his readers that "They were sisters and their names were Victoria C. Woodhull and Tennie Celeste Claflin, the latter preferring to be known as Tennessee, a compounding of Tennie C." However, as Johnson notes, what really happened was that Tennessee started signing her name Tennie, and when she ordered business cards, she decided to use "Mrs. Tennie C. Claflin" (Johnson 1956; Johnston 1967, 55; Meade [1976] 2000, 44).

Tennie C. Claflin was married twice and, in between, is generally believed to have had a long relationship with the entrepreneur Commodore Cornelius Vanderbilt. The first marriage, when she was living in Illinois, and working in her "infirmary" on Wabash Avenue in Chicago, was very brief. The husband's first name was John and, among her biographers, Sachs, Havelin, Marberry, Johnson, and Johnston refer to his last name as being Bartels, with Gabriel spelling it Bortels and, probably erroneously, a Memphis, Tennessee newspaper of the era, the *Public Ledger*, spelling it Bartin and saying he was a faro banker ("Facts and Fancies" 1872). Tennie and her father soon realized that being married would interfere with her medicine selling activities, as a part of which she was being promoted as "Miss Tennessee The Wonderful Child" and, to get John to go away, they may have paid him as much as $20,000; however, the couple did not divorce, an argument that she may have used to avoid marrying Vanderbilt when his wife, Sophia, died. Years later, in England, when her second husband was not thought to be going to live much longer, the couple participated in a remarriage ceremony with a new contract vetted by attorneys to forestall any attempts to challenge his will (without success); however, the concern that Claflin's marriage was bigamous, in the light of its predecessor embarked upon long ago in Illinois with John, was never addressed in the document or raised by others, who probably had no inkling that it had occurred (Gabriel 1998, 45; Havelin 2007, 27; Johnson 1956; Johnston 1967, 33; Marberry 1967, 269, 299; Sachs [1928] 1978, 39; Underhill 1995, 302).

The relationship with Commodore Vanderbilt seems to have begun when he was seventy-five, approximately half a century older than Tennie. She acted as a medium for him, a man whose spiritualist beliefs pressed him to seek advice prior to making important decisions, and she also performed the laying of hands massage technique upon him, explaining that as a system of magnetic healing; it replaced therapy from another quack that had involved electric shock treatment, so it was instantly a more pleasant regimen for him to endure, and Tennie was no doubt a more attractive administrator of the therapy. Although for a time he denied even knowing who she was, he came to refer to her as his "little sparrow" and, at times, she sat her on his knee, while, reportedly, on other occasions, she slept in his bed in his house at 10 Washington Place in Manhattan (Clews 1886, 445–446; Gabriel 1998, 34; Havelin 2007, 27; Hoyt 1962, 186–187; Johnston 1967, 46; Meade [1976] 2000, 39–40; Smith 1927, 295–302; "Woodhull, Claflin & Co.: The Petticoat Financiers in Another Flutter" 1870; Underhill 1995, 7, 46).

A decade and a half later, Tennie was living in England, a transatlantic move with her sister, Victoria, that, as explained in the previous chapter, had almost certainly been financed by the recently deceased Cornelius Vanderbilt's heir. Tennie also served as a medium to Francis Cook, who wished to communicate with his late wife. As Johnston (1967, 275) observes, the wife's advice, given from the grave was, not too surprisingly, that Cook should consider marrying his spiritual assistant. Like Vanderbilt, Cook was a very wealthy man. His company, Cook & Co. was an importer of fashionable silk clothing from India, and his home in London, Doughty House, contained paintings by great masters. Later, he would be knighted by Queen Victoria of England, and would become Sir Francis Cook, which meant that Tennie, when she married him in 1885, became known as Lady Cook. The King of Portugal also bestowed a title, that of Visconde de Montserrate, upon her husband, who owned an estate near Lisbon (Brough 1980, 273–274; Havelin 2007, 85; Meade [1976] 2000, 158; Sachs [1928] 1978, 320, 322).

If Francis Cook was taken advantage of to some extent by Tennie, he was by no means a foolish person. His second wife apparently replaced an earlier lover, an older woman called Mrs. Holland, who had been a housekeeper working in the same house as Cook and his first wife, and who had later lived with him as a couple. In 1893, claiming he had promised to marry her, Mrs. Holland filed suit for seduction and breach of promise but, in court, Sir Francis prevailed; he admitted the affair, but said he had not promised marriage. The jury found for him, although he had to pay the court costs, which he could easily afford to do. Despite the commotion surrounding the remarriage process, her husband did not leave his fortune to Tennie, just a very substantial income, a decision that suggests his faculties remained intact (MacPherson 2014, 272; Sachs [1928] 1978, 375, 382).

When Tennie was seventeen, she was "treating" cancer in a converted hotel, the Fox River House, in Ottawa, Illinois rented by her father, Reuben "Buck"

Claflin, and advertising the success of her "cures" in the local newspaper, the *Free Trader*, claiming that their "salve" would cure cancer in no more than two days. Then, something went wrong. In a letter published in the same paper, a former patient named Rebecca Howe disputed the claims, denying that she had written a statement Tennie had used to advertise them. Realizing that she was actually near death, Howe complained that the result of Tennessee's treatments had been "extreme pain, and an aggravation of all the symptoms, and I have grown worse every day" (Howe 1864, 2). This response led to an investigation into the activities of the Claflins' "hospital"; after Howe then succumbed to her illness, Tennie was indicted by a grand jury for manslaughter, for using a dubious substance to "treat" her patient, and she and her family promptly left town, leaving the other victims who had cancer to fend for themselves. Underhill (1995, 32) reveals Tennie's defense that her cancer treatment had been a placebo, but this remains an unsettling aspect of her earlier years, for giving cancer patients placebos will surely result in their deaths, which would appear to make it manslaughter. A quarter of a century later, when Tennie was living in England, the lawsuit was reactivated, a development that was reported in English newspapers, and which caused Tennie to avoid Illinois on a subsequent trip to the United States (Johnston 1967, 32, 73; Marberry 1967, 266–268, 270, 281–282; Townley 1948, 8–9).

Tennie's sister, Victoria, was the first woman to run for president, but a less well-known event is that, around the same time, in 1871, Tennie ran, as an independent candidate, for the US House of Representatives. At that time, New York's Eighth Congressional District contained a significant number of voters of German origin. Her candidacy was supported by many of the brokerage and business people she worked with on Wall Street, some local politicians, and US Senator George Eliphaz Spencer, a Republican and former Union army colonel. Like her mother, Roxanna Hummel Claflin, Tennie, who with Victoria was presently one of the first two female stockbrokers, could speak German, and her friend, Stephen Pearl Andrews, also fluent in the language, helped her develop a speech that was attended by many members of the German-American Progressive Society on August 11, at Irving Hall on East 38th Street in Manhattan. Emphasizing both her ancestry and the fact that she was born in the United States, Tennie stressed the argument that Victoria and other contemporary feminists were using at the time, that passage of the Fourteenth Amendment had made it clear that women were citizens and therefore eligible to vote, even though it was quite likely that, even if she were selected to represent the district in the US House, some men would resist seating her. Responding to the criticism that women might not be able to handle political decision-making, Claflin suggested that the voters perform an experiment in choosing a woman to represent them since, if she failed, they could always elect someone else to replace her. Moreover, she argued, if voters were concerned about corruption, a woman would be a superior choice, because they were naturally more honest than men. Tennie also made clear her objection to policies of alcohol prohibition, arguing that drinking beer or attending church services were equally choices that every law-abiding citizen should have the freedom to make, an argument she will have anticipated would be popular with the audience, which it was (Darwin 1919, 21–23; MacPherson 2014, 153–154; "Tennie and the Germans: Bankers and German Citizens Endorsing Claflin" 1871, 1). Characteristically enthusiastic, she exaggerated the significance of the occasion, though she was, after all, only the second woman ever to run for Congress:

> Perhaps I am the first woman who has ever presented herself before an appreciative public, in this or in any other country, with words of such significant import.
>
> "Tennie and the Germans: Bankers and German Citizens Endorsing Claflin" 1871, 1

Another distinguishing aspect of Clafin's life was her brief stewardship of the colonelcy of the New York National Guard's 61st Regiment. After the killing of James "Jim" Fisk, Jr., a railroad entrepreneur and the colonel of the 9th Regiment, a well-known unit which comprised white soldiers, she volunteered to be the replacement for Fisk, conceding in a letter proposing this appointment that her "communication will, at first sight, occasion incredulity as to my intentions" ("Tennie Claflin Wants to be a Joan d'Arc – Asking for the Colonelcy of the Ninth," 1). Surprisingly, an article in the *New York Times* supported her application with the argument that Tennie was no more unqualified to lead the unit than Fisk had been when he assumed the job, while another piece in the same newspaper noted sarcastically that, if selected, she would be able to supply the militiamen with copies of her paper, *Woodhull and Claflin's Weekly*. When she was not chosen for the position, she accepted the colonelcy of the 85th regiment, a new African-American unit that was poorly equipped. During the brief period of her service, she attended drills dressed in a standout outfit of her design, intending to use her own money to obtain uniforms and other supplies for the men, although she quickly resigned and that did not occur ("Col. Fisk's Successor" 1872, 7; Darwin 1919, 21–24; Johnston 1967, 148–149; MacPherson 2014, 156, 158; Marberry 1967, 92–93; Messer-Kruse 1998, 202, 204; "Two Wonderful Women" 1872, 10).

As with Tennie's sister, Victoria, there are issues of authenticity. Tennie's most cogent and important work, *Constitutional Equality: A Right of Woman*, which appeared at the height of the sisters' intellectual output, like much of Victoria's contemporary writings and speech content may have been penned partly or wholly by Stephen Pearl Andrews (MacPherson 2014, 147). As discussed in Chapter Three, there is no way to know to what extent that is actually the case, although the subject matter of *Constitutional Equality* is largely about women being second class citizens and the abysmal way that women had heretofore been treated by men in general and by their husbands in particular, and this was an area that Tennie (and Victoria) knew a lot about, of which they had personally experienced a great deal, and which, throughout their long lives, they were passionately concerned to rectify. Whether or not in this chapter we are at times discussing the writings of Tennie C. Claflin or of "Tennie C. Claflin," the material in question is identified with her and bore her name, she agreed with it, and she claimed to be responsible for it. Somewhat paradoxically, Marberry (1967, 285) lists Claflin's major published works and comments that, "None of these are readable by any standards." That opinion seems to the present author to border on the truly ridiculous, for Tennie addresses in a serious manner a number of different concerns that relate to women's rights and political philosophy with some originality and skill, as well as relevance to contemporary concerns, and it is a shame that so few people are knowledgeable about her intellectual output. In the remainder of this chapter, her most significant ideas will be outlined in an attempt, it is hoped, to begin to redress the balance.

1   Appearance

Among her male contemporaries, Tennie was often depicted in terms of her physical features. For instance, in his book, *Twenty-Eight Years in Wall Street*, financier Henry Clews reveals his own perspective, the view that Tennie was not attractive to many men, a statement that certainly clashes with what others have recorded. Clews (1886, 439) writes that "she was plain in every sense of the word, excepting in face, which certainly was quite pretty," claiming that she had little effect on males in general until she was introduced to her eventual second husband, Sir Francis Cook Such an account fails to explain her various encounters and successes as a fortune-teller, seller of patent medicine, clairvoyant, orator, colonel of a military unit, and arguably also as a prostitute. For Matthew Smith, more typically, speaking of Tennie and her sister Victoria:

> The ladies are rather attractive in their appearance, with a bold, resolute, and manish [sic] air. They dress in the highest style of Broadway promenaders.
>
> SMITH 1871, 274

Smith (274) describes Tennie as being ambitious and optimistic, an avid conversationalist. Morrissey (1910, 231) writes of "Miss Claflin, a young woman with beautiful eyes and complexion, and a charming manner with a touch of timidity in it that was exceedingly alluring, but rather odd, I thought, in a Wall Street broker." When she visited Eastern Iowa, a journalist with the Dubuque *Times* commented on some ambiguities related to her gender and manner:

> A clear, full, hazel eye lights up a rather finely cut face, and gives it an expression half intellectual, half roguish. While engaged in conversation her manner is light and cheery, and her eyes sparkle with electric flashes that tell of the indomitable pluck, the nervous force and mental power that are behind that seemingly boyish face.
>
> Quoted in CLAFLIN 1874a, 11

Speaking of a rival reporter, the editor at the Dubuque *Telegraph*, he notes that "Tennie, so fresh, so plump, so charming, so entertaining in his lonely office, was too much for the sedate old man who runs that establishment" (quoted in Claflin 1874a, 11). Meanwhile, a correspondent for yet another Dubuque paper, the *Daily Herald*, similarly impressed, noted that, "Her tongue is endless. She dresses plainly but jauntily, and has what some novelists would call a distinguished appearance on the street" (quoted in Claflin 1874a, 11). For Sutton (1874, 506–507), what stood out about the "saucy and piquante" Tennie was her curvaceous physique, original but tasteful costume, and seductive conversation that made her attractive to men. Leon Oliver (1873, 56), a popular historian of the Beecher-Tilton scandal (which is described in Chapter Three), wrote that to look at Tennie, "one would think her whole physical structure was inlaid with a thousand sensitive spiral springs." She bobbed around and she wandered around too:

> [S]he has since her girlhood been much around the world, and has mingled largely and freely with men of the world, she will say and do the most *outre* [sic] things, but with an air of the most childlike and unsophisticated innocence.
>
> OLIVER 1873, 58

When Tennie was in Utah, the *Salt Lake Herald* called her "the best talker in petticoats we ever had the pleasure of listening to," and proclaimed that "[a]fter a few minutes' conversation with her a man would pawn anything he could borrow and subscribe for the *Weekly*" (quoted in Claflin 1874b, 7). When she visited Omaha, a reporter reflected that, "She is a brilliant, rapid and entertaining conversationalist, never at a loss for the right words in the right place" ("Tennie C. Claflin" 1874). For Arthur Smith (1927, 293), "Tennie had what our film experts term "IT"; she was dainty in figure, peppy in her speech and attractive to look at. She specialized in men of mature years." Hoyt (1962, 185) compared Victoria to Hera, the jealous and manipulative Greek goddess of marriage and women, claiming that "Victoria wanted to be a wife to every man she met. Her sister, Tennessee, ran her a close second." He paints Tennie also as "a luscious, slightly bucktoothed twenty-two" year-old (186). Also comparing the merits of the two sisters, in her Portland, Oregon-based weekly newspaper, *The New Northwest*, women's rights campaigner Abigail Scott Duniway reported, along with some skepticism about Tennie's character, that:

> She [Tennie] is not so beautiful and refined as her sister, gives unmistakable evidence of Irish origin and "lops" from one side to the other very much as she walks, somewhat like a corpulent Jewess; but she is pleasant and amiable, and if I could believe her pure in morals, I should really like her.
>
> DUNIWAY 1872

Among modern biographers, Johnston (1967, 33) notes that, when the Claflin family was living in Cincinnati, "Tennessee, almost twenty, was delightfully pretty, and with every flick of her skirt, every wink of her eye, she deepened neighborhood suspicions. And a number of strange men did call at the house after dark." Underhill (1995, 34) comments that Tennie was "endowed with the same exceptional beauty and sensuality as Victoria," perhaps explaining some of the more divergent evaluations with her note that "[h]er unusual combination of physical – even animal – allure was enhanced by her facade as a proper lady" (1995, 46); Underhill also mentions that, in her own publicity materials, Tennie described herself as "[b]eautiful, bright-eyed, blond, young, sprightly and smart" (1995, 7). Referring to a campaign speech that she gave in Manhattan on August 11th, 1871, an occasion at which Clews was present, a reporter wrote:

> Her hair, which she wears short, hung loose and bushy about her forehead and temples. She wore no jewellery or ornaments. As soon as the applause had subsided, she proceeded to speak in a clear, strong voice, using the German language.
>
> DARWIN 1919, 22; "Tennie and the Germans: Bankers and German Citizens Endorsing Claflin" 1871, 1

In J.E.P. Doyle's book, *Plymouth Church and its Pastor; or Henry Ward Beecher and his Accusers*, the author reveals that he has spent considerable time pondering the matter of Tennie's appearance:

> Tennie is about twenty-nine years of age, is quite handsome, compared with the other sisters, and is rather below medium height, and while she is not stout, she has a plump, well-rounded form, and in both form and features singularly free from anything approximating to angularities; her complexion is light, almost to paleness, and her skin is fair as that of an infant; hair, light brown, worn short, and inclined to curl; eyes blue, sparkling, and very expressive. When engaged in conversation upon any topic which interests her, she is all animation; talking not only with her tongue, but with eyes, face, hands, and *all over*; and one would think her whole physical structure was inlaid with a thousand sensitive spiral springs.
> DOYLE 1875, 435

For her part, Tennie was well aware of the contradictions involved in the way that women tended to their appearance. For example, ladies dressed provocatively to some extent, but demurely in other respects. Cleavage may be fashionable, causing women to expose a substantial portion of their breasts, while the same women might always cover their legs in long skirts unsuitable for the world of business or for walking outside (Claflin 1871a, 90, 92–94; MacPherson 2014, 101):

> Ladies who would affect to blush when subjects are spoken of which are of the greatest interest to humanity generally, and who would hide their faces behind their handkerchiefs to cover the blushes they would have it supposed were there, appear at balls and receptions and at the opera, with the most perfect self-assurance, virtually naked to the waists.
> CLAFLIN 1871a, 90

Clearly, for Claflin, the solution lay in allowing women to wear what they wished, taking into account the nature of the activities in which they engaged, rather than being obliged to appear in clothing imposed by fashion or to impress men. She also criticized the negative aspects of women spending time and money on their appearance:

> Walk up Broadway and count the windows wherein are exposed for sale huge, vile bunches of hair, tortured into all conceivable, unnatural shapes, to transform the natural beauty of the head to a hideous affected thing.
> CLAFLIN 1871a, 23

For Tennie, one of the problems with the pursuit of fashion is that money spent in this way could leave children without provision for their basic needs, while men benefit more from the attention given to them instead, as women dress to impress them; additionally, the practice and goals of prostitution are furthered by the attention customarily given to women's appearance (1871a, 24–25, 144):

> Calves, hips and breasts are padded to make the form more deceptively voluptuous, and thereby to appeal with more direct force to the passions of men.
>
> CLAFLIN 1871a, 24

In a later essay, Tennie argued that contemporary fashions in England allowed women to show their arms and backs completely, and she wondered if it was appropriate for seventeen year-olds in this way "to expose their budding charms to the critical eyes of bold and observant men" (Claflin 1897, 22, 1898a, 14). Characteristically, her concern here was governed by a specific under-standing of modesty, whereby she notes that wearing shorter skirts was re-spectable and harmless, but using the way one dressed in some other manner to attract the attention of the opposite sex was not (1897, 21–22, 1898a, 13–15). Furthermore, because of females' inferior role in society, all that many younger women could do to survive was to find a suitable husband, and perhaps that goal would come to dominate their activities, with an emphasis on decorating their bodies in a dishonest way calculated to make them seem attractive to potential husbands eclipsing more serious elements of their personalities. Such reliance on hairpieces, make-up, and corsetry, she contended, was just as much a betrayal of a person's character as it would be to tell a bald-faced lie (Claflin 1871a, 55). Of course, the attempts of women's rights advocates such as Tennie and her sister, Amelia Bloomer, Elizabeth Cady Stanton and her cousin, Elizabeth Smith Miller, to wear modernized clothing suitable for doing physi-cal work, such as shorter skirts, which Tennie and her sister Victoria had sport-ed, was often greeted by others with horror as a retreat from appropriateness and femininity (Kesselman 1991, 496–501; Riegel 1963, 391–394; Strassel 2012, 38–40).

2   Marriage, Equality, and Social Change

Tennie's concern for women's rights is illustrated by an oft-described incident that took place at a swanky restaurant popular with businesspeople in downtown Manhattan called *Delmonico's*, to which she and her parents would go for dinner during the time she was working as a stockbroker. One day, Tennie and Victoria entered *Delmonico's*, which was located at the junction of Fourteenth Street and Fifth Avenue, and ordered tomato soup, but the waiter would not bring their order. It was after seven o'clock in the evening, and it turned out that the restaurant did not serve women in the evening unless they were accompanied by a man. After confrontations with the waiter and the owner, a Mr. Delmonico, Tennie went outside to where their coach was waiting and told its driver to come inside and join them, this time successfully ordering the meal (Darwin 1919, 26, 28; Havelin 2007, 34–35; Johnston 1967, 73–74; MacPherson 2014, 146; Meade [1976] 2000, 57–59; Sachs [1928] 1978, 63). Darwin comments:

> That incident proved the beginning of the breakdown of the unwritten social law that deemed a woman an outcast and a pariah, who sought to take an evening meal in a restaurant unaccompanied by a man.
>
> DARWIN 1919, 26, 28

Surprisingly, a few years later, Victoria, who did not always tell the truth, claimed in *Woodhull and Claflin's Weekly* that "Indeed, I never was in Delmonico's in my life" (Woodhull 1875a, 6).

In the nineteenth century, many states employed torts of seduction to prevent women from being taken advantage of by men who had obtained sexual favors from them in return for promises of marriage that did not later transpire, damaging the woman's reputation. These torts made it possible for compensation to be paid; not only could the women whose chastity had been violated sue, but so could their fathers. Later, at the urging of first wave feminists, these torts were repealed or no longer enforced; the argument that was made then was that allowing seduction torts implied that women were foolish, emotionally vulnerable, and unable to make responsible decisions. In theory, such civil lawsuits could still be implemented in some states today. In North Carolina, for example, in 2001, Nora Kantor, a student at Duke University, filed a seduction claim against a male student and his Sigma Alpha Epsilon fraternity, arguing that her boyfriend, James Thompson, had "wrongfully seduced and debauched her ... through persuasion, deception, enticement and artifice." After both students had been drinking for a number of hours and then went to a Christmas party at the fraternity house, they had sex, a development that Kantor, who had been a virgin, later regretted. Eventually, the suit was settled (Ballentine 2015; Cohan 2014, 45–46; Grossman 2003, 16–18).

In an article published in *Woodhull & Claflin's Weekly*, Tennie C. Claflin addressed the issue of seduction, ostensibly in response to a letter that had been sent to the newspaper by a man called "W. Boqua." Since Tennie had elsewhere used the strategy of submitting her own query to her publication, signed by someone called "Mary Bowles," and then "replying" to it (Johnston 1967, 137), it is quite possible that "W. Boqua" was in fact Tennie herself. Nevertheless, regardless of whomever the true author happened to be, the response is a work of some sophistication and present-day relevance. Boqua suggests that seduction might be "a deception practiced on a woman, resulting in her fall from "virtue,'" and asks Tennie to determine to what degree the man and the woman who are involved might be to blame (Claflin 1872c, 10).

Immediately, Tennie finds fault in three respects with the way that the question is framed. Firstly, she disputes the assumption that women are "weaklings and ninnies, and that they have no opinion, no character, no power of self-defense" (Claflin 1872c, 10). Moreover, she claims, if women protest that they have been taken advantage of, they add to the perception that they are fragile and irresolute, and easy targets for more sophisticated males. Secondly, she argues that men are also quite capable of being seduced by women; in reality, she thinks, women are the more proficient at seduction, and may in fact be the aggressors ninety percent of the time. In another article, she writes:

> No man will have the hardihood to deny that one woman of average looks, grace and manner can seduce, overcome and lead in forbidden paths fifty men, to every woman that any one of the fifty men can subordinate to his passions.
>
> CLAFLIN 1872a, 2

This is hardly surprising, she continues, since society is organized in a way that obliges women to find a husband, because it is almost impossible for them to support themselves independently, with women who decide not to marry also being victimized by social shame. Together these realities prompt her to argue for passage of a gender-neutral law, temporarily anyway, because it is unfortunate that a minority of women, denied the opportunity to become educated, remain "weak and silly and simple, and ... are taken advantage of by designing men" (11). Eventually, she argues, while it is true that seduction is often spoken of in the context of intentionally taking advantage of the other party, in what she calls "its bad sense, as the exertion of this charm unduly and adversely to the real wish and the true interests of the party affected by it" (11), Tennie does not believe that legal sanctions should apply even in such cases. Thirdly, Tennie makes the case that seduction is not generally something offensive at all: it "is simply sexual charm – the delight which one sex feels in contact with the other" (10), a natural catalyst for romance and an ongoing part of many relationships, which is not to say that women and men alike should wish to embrace it irresponsibly and without an appropriate level of caution.

In later works, Tennie will argue that "Although, as we believe, the woman occasionally seduces, it is more frequently the man" (Claflin 1898b, 82, 1922, 14). But in the 1870s, she wrote that for women to portray themselves as spoiled by the practice of seduction was ironic since they are in the main the seducers, but this is mere "cunning" and "sharp practice" on their part (Claflin 1872c, 10, 1898a, 125), Tennie writes, because we live in an unnatural and fundamentally deceptive society that benefits men:

> The depressed and oppressed woman is made to be hypocritical and friv-
> olous and in every way false to the higher nature of womanhood, false to
> her duties in life, and false to the true relations which she should hold to
> men.
>
> CLAFLIN 1872C, 11

Thus, almost all young women are devoted to seeking a good match, attempting to find the wealthiest husband because "[t]here is no distinction for women except to marry" (Claflin 1872b, 12). The leadership of society is dominated by men: religious institutions have men as priests and even angels are mostly men, while all types of government, even though they differ in other respects, are presided over by males, with women subservient and portrayed as the weaker sex. Consequently, it is not surprising that, "a large majority of women are content to forever remain "putty women," to be moulded to suit the tastes of men" (Claflin 1871a, 51). But consideration of equal rights and justice, Claflin argues, proceeding not from any notion of feminine weakness or need for kindness in response to that debility, seems to require that this situation be changed, in government, civil society, and faith organizations alike. Consequently, if we look at examples of the ways in which women are treated differently – at virginity, marriage, or prostitution, for example, we can identify the culture's fundamental unfairness to women. If virginity is important, Tennie writes, then preserving it should be equally important to men as it is for women. If having a child out of wedlock is to be an embarrassment, then the shame should also be shared by the father. Currently, prostitutes in New York City, she points out, are preyed upon by the police, who demand favors in return for not arresting them, thereby violating the very laws that threaten the livelihood of the women, but failing to protect them from the violence they encounter at the hands of some of their customers; if the streetwalkers try to go to court in an attempt to obtain justice, the nature of their profession will mean they are not taken seriously. Even if they cease to work as prostitutes, and move into respectable society, their reputations may follow them and perpetuate the injustice that women face, while the dalliances of men are accepted (Claflin 1872a, 2; a similar, later version appears in Darwin 1919, 32–36, 38). This inequity demands to be reformed:

> While this state of things exists, there can be no peace and no permanent improvement. Women must *come up*, or men must *come down*. Our mission is but commenced; the battle is opened. We ask no quarter and take no prisoners.
>
> CLAFLIN 1872a, 2; DARWIN 1919, 36 is similar

Today, Tennie's argument will probably not strike many readers as being especially outrageous, but the piece in question, "Beginning of the Battle," led to her and other *Weekly* employees being arrested, though not convicted, for obscenity (Darwin 1919, 31–32). As MacPherson (2014, 94) comments, the topic of prostitution was a dangerous one for Tennie, whom it exposed on two fronts: opponents of her and Victoria's ideas portrayed them as having themselves once been prostitutes, an accusation that may have been true, and forthright defenses of women's rights concerning sexuality in the Comstock age were often repressed using laws that ostensibly targeted obscenity, as happened here. Later in life, when she was living in England, she wrote somewhat more negatively that "Prostitution has no redeeming feature; it is a foul, and unmitigated, and unnatural evil" (Claflin 1898b, 81, 1922, 13); what may not have been apparent to her readers was that she saw exploitative marriages that violated women's rights as a kind of prostitution too. Elsewhere, she calls paid prostitution "a profanation of the human body," but explains it as "a survival of those remote times when men were governed by fierce, bestial passions rather than by moderation and reason" (Claflin 1898b, 29). It was clear in her much earlier book, *Constitutional Equality: A Right of Woman*, that she saw the denial of women's rights as the key to the existence of prostitution for money. She asks why most of its practitioners are female and not men, answering that women are limited by social rules that make it difficult for them to earn money in other ways (Claflin 1871a, 48).

On March 29, 1872, Tennie gave a speech at the Academy of Music in New York, entitled "The Ethics of Sexual Equality"; it was published a few days later in *Woodhull & Claflin's Weekly*. With much skepticism, the *New York Herald* reported that she had addressed the largely male audience "with a biblical plainness" ("Tennie's Tirade" 1872, 5). On this occasion, she emphasized a perspective she shared with her sister, Victoria, and many spiritualists, that some so-called moral problems related to sexuality and child-bearing should instead be seen as disorders of physical health. Whereas natural laws are accepted as legitimate regulators of most other human activities, it is strange, she writes, that in this area instead, civic laws attempt to regulate people's behavior. This can never work, because human beings will always want to do what is natural. Logically, sexual behavior should be investigated and explained scientifically, but unfortunately, when people attempt to do this, they "are at once branded as revolutionists, who desire to demoralize society by their immoral teachings, or who desire to excuse their own lives by advocating rules of conduct conforming to them" (Claflin 1872b, 11). In reality, at present, since there are no scientific rules governing this area of people's lives, Tennie concluded, they should be able to experiment, since there is no objective basis for favoring one practice over another (Claflin 1872b; "Free Love and Politics: The Multitude that Besieged the Academy Last Night" 1872, 1; MacPherson 2014, 159–160).

Applying her rationale to one of the sub-areas of the behaviors she is addressing, Claflin argues that marriage is either an inevitable, natural institution, or it is a societal construct. In the former case, then it should be allowed to function in the way it is intended, in accordance with natural laws, and any human-made rules should not contradict what is ordained by Nature. If, on the other hand, marriage is not a natural institution, then its rules should be the ones that sensibly fit with the purposes for which people have created it, rather than as "a custom which the self-styled conservators of morality impose upon society" (Claflin 1872b, 11). Unfortunately, in society at present, whatever strategy is employed to overcome the consequences of a bad marriage, moralistic condemnation imposes the price of "a standing reproach upon, and a permanent indictment against American women" (Claflin 1872b, 12). On the other hand, if women remain with a husband that they no longer like, they find themselves trading sex for financial security, which is also a humiliating circumstance, and one they are unlikely to admit that they have settled for. For Claflin, this is itself a form of prostitution: "Public prostitution is but nothing compared to that practiced under the cloak of marriage" (Claflin 1871a, 16). Moreover, she argues, if marriage is entered into for any reason other than love and mutual self-respect – for example, for lust, or vanity, or financial well being – then, like Mary Wollstonecraft, she considers it to be not true marriage, but "legal prostitution" (Claflin 1898a, 105, 1898b, 58). She compares marriage contracts to implements of slavery, because whenever women seek to advance their liberty, something in the contract or the laws that uphold it will prohibit what is desired. She argues that if the institution of legal marriage were abolished (although, she says, most couples would decide to stay together), the people who were unhappy would be able to enjoy their freedom once more, and the basis for adultery, bigamy, and other transgressions would be substantially lessened. Liberalization of marriage laws, so that people could end relationships easily, would also have the effect of making people less likely to rush into any ceremony when they had doubts about the partner, because they would know that in the event of things not going well, the mate would be able to leave (Claflin 1871a, 114–117). In the society in which she lived, Tennie laments that liberty is a gendered concept, with "free woman" being a term of criticism – "a free woman is a contemptible being; a drab, a harlot, what you will" (Claflin 1871c, 13), whereas to be a free man is considered desirable, a release from negative restraints.

For Claflin, marriage was ordained and is rationalized using religious arguments, but a modern society needs to base its traditions on science. Furthermore, the nature of religious arguments is that they are intended to apply forever, and do not anticipate social change. However, considering the matter logically reveals that the marriage institution is bound to develop as human beings become more and more sophisticated. In fact, the permanency of relationships is surely something that was not always the case, occurring only at a point on society's evolutionary scale, and, Tennie notes, consideration of contemporary practices among some Native Americans in California and aborigines in Australia reveals that they still engage in less formalized ties (Claflin 1898a, 80–82). Here, Tennie's argument resembles the evolutionist ideas of William Graham Sumner ([1940] 1971, 83), particularly in the conviction that, at the time of writing, some aborigines and Native Americans lie at a lower point on the evolutionary ladder, and it is apparent from the sources that she cites that she has some familiarity with contemporary anthropology.

Thus, Claflin continues, marriage customs have already changed in many ways through the centuries, with some societies ceasing their practices of capturing brides from rival ethnicities or paying dowries. Today, she argues, more change is needed, and one area where this is certainly necessary is in that of selecting a partner:

> [A]t this period of human evolution we require more rational processes of mating – processes which will promote truth and honesty between the sexes prior to marriage, and thus prevent unpleasant developments.
>
> CLAFLIN 1898a, 117

For example, women should be able to propose marriage to men, not least because they are better able to identify suitable partners (Claflin 1898a, 91–94, 117–121).

Considering the tradition of monogamy as expressed through the contract of marriage, Tennie notes that spouses are expected to promise to cherish, love, and serve each other for the rest of their lives, a period of time entirely in the future where it is impossible to say with any certainty what will take place and thus to guarantee that the promise will be kept. Furthermore, when people become married, they are often happy, but this condition seldom lasts for a long time:

> I believe that a large proportion of married people will agree with me that, as compared to what they anticipated, marriage is a stupendous failure – a gigantic fraud. But they don't realize this until the blow is struck – until the deed is done – from which, twist it as they may, there is no escape.
>
> CLAFLIN 1872b, 12

The marriage "experiment" is the most important contract of most people's lives, but they lack the knowledge to understand what they are getting themselves into: "people are required to shut their eyes, or be blindfolded, and walk straight in, in the most complete and blissful ignorance of what the results are to be" (Claflin 1872b, 12). Although it takes a number of years to get to know another person well enough to be able to truly assess their character, teenagers become married with the consent of their parents in almost complete ignorance of the person with whom they are suddenly expected to spend the rest of their lives. Social pressure makes matters worse, with engagement trapping people into situations from which it is difficult to admit, once more information about one's fiancé is acquired, that one wishes to back out of the betrothal agreement (Claflin 1898a, 143). For Tennie, consequently, the solution to the problems incurred by married women is to give all women from the age of eighteen the opportunity to earn money and be as independent and educated as men; then, they should consider giving up their liberty and becoming married only if they are sure that they are in love. Only when these circumstances are achieved will the institution of marriage comport with what natural law allows (Claflin 1871a, 42–43, 74).

Tennie's dislike of abortion has its roots in her belief that children have rights from conception (Claflin 1871a, 123), and she also criticized the feeling, experienced by some women who discovered they were pregnant, that having a child would be a negative factor in their lives:

> The practice of abortion is one which spreads damnation world-wide. Not so much in those cases where it is accomplished, but in those much more numerous cases where it is desired, attempted, but not reached. As soon as a woman becomes conscious that she is pregnant and a desire comes up in her heart to shirk the duties it involves, that moment the foetal life is the unloved, the unwished child.
>
> CLAFLIN 1871a, 144

That being said, she was also a realistic supporter of abortion choice, who, in her characteristically anarchist approach, saw it as an inevitable consequence of modern social *mores*, which might occasion the death of the woman at the hands of the incompetent abortionist. But, she asks, "Who really wants that there should be no opportunity to secure an abortion under *peculiarly trying circumstances*?" (Claflin 1871b, 1898b, 102; see also Carpenter 2010a, xxi–xxii; and MacPherson 2014, 107). Many women had no realistic choice but to terminate their pregnancy, and for that reason, Tennie writes, doing so should always be legal. Cayleff (2016, 77) also sees Tennie's position being moderate in this way, in the sense that she did not really approve of the practice, pointing out that "Claflin took an antiabortion stance, arguing that birth control should prevent conception." Much later, Tennie would illustrate her disdain for the fact that abortion needed to be tolerated:

> Can nothing be done to prevent the countless abortions and the numerous stillborn? Are we, who claim to be a humane and just people a Christian people to sit calmly with folded hands while these tens of thousands of innocents perish daily before our eyes, and thousands of pure maidens become the foul and loathsome creatures that infest our streets and contaminate our youth?
>
> CLAFLIN 1898b, 80, 1922, 12

When she was older, Claflin attacked the concept of illegitimacy, arguing that it was a subjective category, the existence of which served to benefit men (Claflin 1898b, 81–82, 1922, 12–13; Reekie 1998, 4). She notes a study that showed that illegitimate babies in England were four times more likely to die in their first year of life, perhaps because of neglect caused by being unwanted, but in some cases because they were strangled or otherwise deliberately killed (Claflin 1898b, 75, 1922, 7). Yet, many couples live normal, respectable lives except for the fact that they have no marriage certificate, which unfairly means that their offspring will be permanently disadvantaged and tainted by a "so-called social evil," a situation that Tennie argues should be remedied (Claflin 1898b, 71, 81–82, 1922, 4, 13).

> The laws for the discouragement of illegitimacy are peculiarly harsh, and appear to have been made rather with a view to the preservation of clerical emoluments than to the reformation, or the amelioration, of the unfortunate and ignorant.
>
> CLAFLIN 1898b, 77, 1922, 9

Tennie points out how unfair it is that an illegitimate person has no right to inherit their father's wealth or even to use that parent's last name. To some extent, a solution would be, she continues, to confer the status of legitimacy on children whose parents later decide to marry, while making the father of a child pay for the cost of bearing a child and giving birth would also improve the situation. If the mothers did not wish to keep their baby, they should be able to hand it over to the state (Claflin 1898b, 78, 84, 1922, 10, 15)

Late in life, Tennie would lecture audiences about the purity of "true marriages," and she used the example of the birth of Jesus as described in the New Testament to portray the dignity of the nuclear family where husbands and wives celebrated the birth of a child that resulted from their loving relationship. Even if they lack money, women in traditional, affectionate monogamous relationships will always be better off than those who engage in prostitution or adultery. Unlike the formal legal and ceremonial aspects of the practice, which for her are irrelevant to its success, true marriage "is a natural and spontaneous union of ideas, aims, and sympathies" (Claflin 1897, 30, 1898a, 21). Opposing any other versions of marriage, relationships, and sexuality, she warned against fornication, citing the Bible's teachings. However, for Tennie, a spiritualist-influence persisted as she claimed:

> The true Trinity, then, is the father and mother, both equal and both responsible to complete the Trinity, the child.
>
> CLAFLIN 1912, 2

Citing specific Catholic teachings, Tennie blames the long history of gender discrimination on what she describes as the widespread delusion that women are liars. Similarly, celibacy has been lionized as a virtue, and women, being identified in the minds of many with procreation, have been portrayed as offenders. She derides Christians in general for emphasizing this apparent sinfulness that many believe is rooted in sex and childbearing. Because mothers have been tarnished and intimidated in this way for generations, the most truly sacred things can not even be explained properly to children, who must learn how they came into the world from their cohorts because their own parents are unwilling to give them the scientific answer. She is sure that if women were more forthright with their sons, and explained sexual matters in a loving way, this would make it less likely that they would grow up to have a disparaging view of females or to act in a disreputable way with them; prostitution and human trafficking would diminish (Claflin 1912, 3, 1920, 6). Unfortunately, she argues, the consistent message of the Bible of women's usefulness to the world has in modern society been transformed into prudery:

> I once observed some young women arriving unexpectedly in a gallery upon a group of nude statues. They gave one good look, then screamed, and fled as if pursued by satyrs.
> CLAFLIN 1912, 7; CLAFLIN 1897, 20 and CLAFLIN 1898a, 13 are very similar

Being pure, Tennie continues, requires no fake modesty, which in fact derives from the prurient minds of those who are ashamed of their bodies, and which undermines women's ability to contribute to and improve society. In fact, she views prudery as being an affectation, a close-minded attitude subscribed to by those who have never really assessed the consequences of their own situations (Claflin 1897, 66–67, 1898a, 53–54):

> The prurient mock-modesty which is horrified by the sight of a naked child or a nude statue or picture is a reproach to our weakmindedness and to our defective moral training. If we were not so nice as we are, our ideas would not be so nasty.... For it is not *what* we see, but *how* we see.
> CLAFLIN 1897, 70, 1898a, 56–57

For Claflin, like her sister Victoria, the fundamental social problem is the oppression of women throughout human history, and its solution is the granting of equal rights, including identical access to education that affords the opportunity to study with, and compete with males; women also require the right to work in any occupation, as well as the franchise, and the same liberties – such as, she writes, the ability to walk around outside unescorted, or to start a conversation with a man. Although the sisters grew more conservative as they aged, this viewpoint never changed, rooted as it was in their personal experiences (Claflin 1897, 26–30, 1898a, 17–22). At the beginning of *Constitutional Equality: A Right of Woman*, she notes that, even when girls are born, "the daughter is mourned over by the fond mother, because she is not a son who may rise to honor and fame" (Claflin 1871a, 1). The best route for avoiding the disadvantage bestowed upon females at birth is to be beautiful, because therein lies the main chance for their success. Unlike boys, girls are not encouraged to become educated or to develop their brains, to enrich society with new ideas, inventions, or solutions to problems; meanwhile, their parents teach them that this inferiority is a desirable condition for them, that it is one of femininity (Claflin 1871a, 1–3). Tennie traces this prevailing opinion that women are inferior to men to interpretations by Christian and Islamic theologians, and notes that even in classical Greek societies, the same outlook also limited women's access to true citizenship; here, she speaks of "Corinth, where she [woman] enjoyed the highest freedom then known" as being no real exception to the practice (Claflin 1897, 27, 1898a, 19), perhaps mistaking for a moment Corinth for Sparta. Without this equality of freedom, women will continue to be manipulated into marriage contracts and other societal positions where they will be forever unhappy, as the imagined rectification of a correspondingly unsatisfactory prior existence:

> And thus, longing to be a wife and mother, she must wither in her virginity unless chance direct an offer, or an alternative presents itself. She is sought in marriage, so-called, by a man for whom she has no regard, who is in no way qualified to make her happy, but whose means are equal to her rank. He may have run through a long career of vice, and be physically and mentally enervated and diseased.
> CLAFLIN 1897, 29, 1898a, 20

If caring, loving family relationships were widespread, Claflin believes that other problems would be lessened. She notes that presently some mothers kill their children, and she attributes this at least partly to the reality of inadequate conditions and marriages, and to unwanted pregnancies. Having a child every year wears women out. She writes, "We want children neither born nor bred in ignorance" (Claflin 1912, 5). Unfortunately, Tennie writes, while loyalty is a virtue that will strengthen a true marriage, many women tend to stay faithful to their husbands even when they are trapped in much less satisfactory circumstances. Instead, they need to stand up for their right to have improved relationships or none at all. Citing Queen Gorgo of Sparta, she claims that the greater equality enjoyed by the women of her city was an important factor in the might of the Spartan army, for it comprised strong men who were raised by strong women (Claflin 1897, 9, 46, 57–58, 73, 1898b, 96, 1912, 1–12, 1920, 16–17).

In realty, however, Claflin argues in her essay, "The Ideal Woman," many mothers find themselves enduring lives that are substandard; in England at the time she is writing, she claims there are three million such women who have been unable to adequately raise their progeny – to breastfeed them, for instance, or more generally, to bring them up with intelligence and tenderness; natural mothers almost always provide the best company for children, Tennie maintains, and the educational and civilizing process should begin soon after they are born. Despite the importance of marriage and reproduction to the human race, many women remain ignorant of the proper, scientific knowledge that would enable them to succeed in that goal, and they may have become married for reasons that have nothing to do with being a part of a successful family or the development of healthy offspring. For many women with affluent husbands, who rely upon servants and governesses to do domestic work, their marital function consists mainly of creating children (Claflin 1871a, 15, 1897, 7–10, 51, 1920, 10):

> Overlooking or ignoring all the natural capacities and inclinations of the mind, they are and have been trained specially for the matrimonial market, and it can be called nothing else. Nor has their training looked to any point beyond the mere fact of marriage – just as though in that point existence ceased. How many know aught of the duties, cares, responsibilities, trials, sufferings, that fall to her after reaching what should really be considered the beginning of her actual, individual life?
>
> CLAFLIN 1871a, 4

Moreover, the widely believed and much revered absurdity that males are better than females, and thus more deserving of education, and more capable of succeeding in a professional career, leads to inadequate social outcomes because "how many daughters are superior to the sons, and how many women are there whose learning and abilities would adorn any office and any position"? (Claflin 1897, 31, 1898a, 22). When women have been allowed to work in an occupation, they have shown that they can do the tasks successfully, even as opponents of the change, some of them touting a religious perspective, have tried to deny the achievement. Mary Wollstonecraft had suggested in *A Vindication of the Rights of Woman* back in 1792 that women should be able to vote and to become physicians, but even now such ideas had scarcely been realized (Claflin 1898a, 104–105). Tennie believes that, in some respects, women are more skilled than men – for instance, she writes that women are more perceptive and inventive, capacities that would aid them in the areas of social life from which they have been excluded. Instead, however, deprived of the opportunity to stretch their talents and engage in serious study or succeed in the workplace, some affluent women content themselves with more trivial matters such as the latest fashions (Claflin 1871a, 79, 1897, 33–34, 1898a, 24). Within marriage, wives find that their individuality is sacrificed to the needs and personality of their husbands as they submit themselves to another's dominance. Tennie defines individuality in a way that almost every nineteenth-century marriage – with that of John Stuart Mill and Harriet Taylor Mill, whose book, *The Subjection of Women* (1869), she cites, being an exception (Claflin 1897, 62, 1898a, 49) – would necessarily fail to preserve the individuality of the wife:

> To become individualized presupposes being independent, self-reliant and self-supporting. This is individuality. All individuals, therefore, must have a direct interest in the rules and regulations under which they shall be compelled to be self-reliant.
>
> CLAFLIN 1871a, 59

It may not be obvious to everyone, she thinks, but, in this way, the conditions experienced by married women resemble those of the multiple wives of Mormons in Utah or members of harems in Turkey: like them, women in more common forms of marriage elsewhere have no control over their lives. Yet, it is clear that women and men have equal capacities for intellectual and moral development, and equal ability to make decisions, and that the gender-based differences observed at present in regard to these faculties are developed socially by the differing ways in which boys and girls are raised, with males being given the skills of privilege, allowing them to be independent, while females must learn capacities that make them subservient for the rest of their lives to men. Even as some women discover that this is the case, that they have been educated for an unsatisfying dependence (Claflin 1871a, 6, 8–11, 30, 52), they continue to urge their daughters to work toward the same inferior status, to do "little else than eat, drink, sleep and flirt, and prepare for the marriage market" (Claflin 1871a, 14):

> Music, French and drawing are excellent in their places, but they will scarcely help you maintain political equality, and thus it is with the greater part of female education.
>
> CLAFLIN 1871a, 12

But the age of dignity for women is at hand. Tennie argues that the political agenda of equal rights and liberties must be achieved as soon as possible and this must include educating the sexes based on their identical capacities for learning, rather than the way that society and religion have mandated up to this point. This should also involve women having respect for themselves as women, learning practical skills and striving to be independent and able to support themselves, as well as holding men and women equally responsible for any sexual dalliances, rather than the present situation under which women are held to a higher moral standard (Claflin 1871a, 6–7, 12, 37, 1897, 10). For her, this is a process of societal development by which women and civilization will gradually improve and become better able to function in a rational manner:

> But as Paganism gave way to Christianity, so the mystical theology of nineteen centuries is rapidly vanishing under the fierce light of modern scientific research.
>
> CLAFLIN 1897, 8, 1898a, 2

For Tennie, the goal of equal rights regardless of gender should be effected also in those areas where men are at a disadvantage. She points out examples of contemporary unfairness with respect to the financial support that a husband is required to pay for his separated wife, and the situation that, while a man might be held to account by a court for abandoning his wife, a woman was generally free to "frequent public houses, and neglect her children, and the husband has neither remedy nor power to prevent her" (Claflin 1898a, 147). In fact, the assumption is that men have an obligation to financially support their families, whereas their wives do not. Thus her solution is to make a marriage a civil contract for a certain number of years, setting out the obligations of the participants and allowing separation to be achieved with comparative ease. In the event of divorce, provision for children should take into account the relative wealth of the partners involved (Claflin 1898a, 146–149).

Like Mercy Otis Warren, the thinker discussed in Chapter One, Tennie finds a cautionary tale in the decline of the Roman Empire amid the signs of modern social change. Unlike the modifications she believes are necessary, she notes that "[t]he Romans were the English of ancient times; the English are modern Romans" (Claflin 1897, 18, 1898a, 11). In England, where she now lives, modesty, honor, and duty are being replaced by a culture of self-absorption and self-gratification. In praise of a modesty that she argues means pureness of heart, and is not the same thing as prudery or chastity or concealing one's body, she argues that reason and dignity should prevail over women's degradation (1897, 18–23, 1898a, 11–15):

> We hope the day will soon come when every girl will be a member of a great Union of Unmarried Women, pledged to refuse an offer of marriage from any man who is not an advocate of their emancipation.
>
> CLAFLIN 1897, 91, 1898a, 74

To accomplish this would necessitate a radical reconfiguration of social norms, for selecting husbands on the basis of their opinions and their compatibility with the needs of women would also mean that some wives would have agreed to forgo the financial benefits proffered by a wealthy but otherwise less compatible match.

3   Poverty

Despite the success and affluence that Tennie enjoyed throughout her life, she remained familiar with the difficulties that poverty imposed on the majority of citizens, and perhaps this would have endeared her to her constituents if she had been elected to Congress. In an article called "Aid for the Poor," she embarked upon a number of proposals to lessen the pain of the disadvantaged. She identifies inadequate compensation, competition from a steady supply of immigrants, and a lack of safety standards as causes that make life difficult for ordinary people. As a solution to some of the consequences, she suggests that poor people should be able to purchase food and medicines at a lower price. Tennie's suggestion resembles to some extent modern attempts to make life more tolerable for the working poor, such as the SNAP/food stamp program in the United States, the Cook Islands' pricing caps on the retail sales of staples such as instant coffee, or Greece's one-time two-tier system of controlled restaurant pricing for Greeks and "tourists."

Market forces ensure that customers who buy in bulk will pay a lower overall price, which she notes benefits the wealthy and imposes the worst detriment on those who have the smallest salary; stores thus achieve their highest rate of return from purchasers least able to satisfy their own basic needs. Additionally, being poor often obliges customers to buy the least satisfactory products. Similarly, impoverished persons, lacking access to sources of credit available to the more affluent, may be obliged to resort to pawnbrokers, where loans on their property will attract a usurious rate of interest.

Describing an aspect of being poor and the way it multiplies exponentially the negative effects of predatory lending, she anticipates the drawbacks of contemporary payday loans. Tennie writes:

> Thousands of the poor pledge things one week and take them out the next. But if they redeem them on the same day, they must pay a month's interest, so that frequently it amounts to 100 or 200 per cent. per year. It was proved a few days ago that a poor woman had agreed to pay on a bill

of sale 35 per cent., and had actually paid 150 per cent. Even so, the Judge
could not help her, because the law allowed it.
    CLAFLIN 1897, 95, 1898a, 78

As a solution, she suggests local governments make lower interest loans available to poor people, whom she believes will mostly be willing to repay them as
requested (Claflin 1897, 92–97, 1897, 75–79).

In her writings, Tennie C. Claflin reveals much originality amid her constant
concern for the needs and rights of the disadvantaged, in particular presenting
a sophisticated analysis of how women are systematically oppressed, which
she expresses in a serious, detailed, and intellectually challenging way. It is a
shame that to the extent that she is remembered today, as in the era when she
was alive, the focus is mainly directed at her more trivial attainments, such as
her romantic life, the way she looked, and her eventual considerable wealth.

ILLUSTRATION 5   Lois Waisbrooker, unknown photographer.
PHOTO, UNDATED, THAT SHE MAILED TO HER DAUGHTER (MARIA
HAWKINS) AROUND 1900. WIKIMEDIA COMMONS.

CHAPTER 5

Lois Waisbrooker: Anarchist Opponent of Marriage

For many decades following her death, Lois Waisbrooker (1826–1909) – the name adopted by Adeline Eliza Nichols – was, as Pam McAllister (1985, 1) points out, "a long-buried, long-forgotten woman." Despite the challenges imposed by the impoverished circumstances of both her parents and her own life as an adult, she has become recognized in recent years as a worthy intellectual contributor to anarchist and feminist theories alike and as a particularly cogent critic of the institution of marriage, a woman who dabbled in the spirit world, lambasting organized religion, and opposing oppression in many different forms, a crusader who yearned for a world free of coercion in which partnerships between men and women would be based on love and equality, to the greater benefit of society.

A survivor of two unsuccessful marriages herself (to George Fuller at the age of seventeen and then to Isaac Snell), into both of which undertakings she had been cajoled by her father, a laborer called Grandison Nichols, Waisbrooker promoted her ideas through a number of different media, including personal correspondence, speeches to spiritualist conferences, and the publications that she edited, which included: *Foundation Principles*, in which Waisbrooker's response to a letter writer that he should be able to divorce his wife with whom he had not lived for some years and marry his mistress led to a charge of obscenity that was eventually dismissed by a Kansas court; *Our Age*, a Battle Creek, Michigan-based periodical, copies of which have not survived; *Clothed with the Sun*, which she published during the years that she was a resident of the anarchist colony at Home, Washington; and for a time, Moses Harman's *Lucifer, the Light Bearer*, a free-love bastion for which she also penned many articles, as did many persons of similar views, including Voltairine de Cleyre and Dora Forster. She contributed pieces to a number of other journals, including *Woodhull and Claflin's Weekly*, the organ of sisters and fellow free-love advocates Victoria C. Woodhull and Tennie C. Claflin, the subjects of earlier chapters. Waisbrooker also wrote short books and pamphlets in which she presented many of her political ideas, some of which took the form of novellas, one of the best-known of which is called *Helen Harlow's Vow*, which illustrated the many problems faced by women of the day and suggested solutions to their predicaments (Dawson 1897, 56; Hayden 2010, 115, 2013, 39; Malin 1964, 121, 130–131; Passet 2003, 47, 114, 2004, 148, fn 22, 2006, 231, 232; Willburn 2006, 72;

Wood 2008, 38). She wrote poems and essays, too, some of which were published in her collection, *Mayweed Blossoms* (Waisbrooker 1871).

Waisbrooker moved about, living in several states during her lifetime, including New York, Ohio, Michigan, Iowa, Kansas, Washington, and lastly California, where it was that she died at her son, A.B. Fuller's home in Antioch (Hayden 2013, 40; LeWarne 1975, 189; Malin 1964, 131; McAllister 1985, 46). She was born in Catharine, New York, growing up in Ohio, where her mother, Caroline Reed Nichols, whom Lois calls "a quiet, retiring woman," fell victim to tuberculosis when she was 36 (Passet 2003, 113, 2006, 230; Waisbrooker 1906). In *Mayweed Blossoms*, Waisbrooker (1871) talks of a sister who died as an infant. In her poem, "The Emblem," she imagines speaking to her mother (who is also by the time of the book's publication, deceased) about that child as follows:

> Then, mother, while you're gazing upon some tiny cloud,
> And thinking of the dear one they covered with a shroud,
> Remember that the dew-drop, on which you loved to gaze,
> Has been attracted upward; is sparkling in the blaze
> Of heaven's eternal sunlight; is dwelling in a home
> Where sin can never reach it, and sorrow never come.
> WAISBROOKER 1871, 140

In her essay, "Twenty Years Afterward," Waisbrooker writes of having a brother and of an unspecified number of sisters, who are now "scattered and far away" (Waisbrooker 1871, 149; 1871, 46 is similar). Many of the details of her childhood are unknown.

As an adult, Waisbrooker continued to experience poverty, being forced to give up her children for adoption, and working as a household maid before acquiring some advanced education and becoming a teacher of African-American students in Ohio (Braude 1989, 137; Malin 1964, 117; Marsh 1981, 53, 125; McAllister 1985, 37; Passet 2003, 114). She wrote about this experience in *Suffrage for Woman: The Reasons Why*:

> At the age of twenty-six I resolved to add to my little stock of education that I might be able to teach instead of working in other people's kitchens; for, be it remembered, I was the same as a childless widow, as poverty and broken health had forced me to give my darlings to the keeping of others. In carrying out this my determination, I came in contact with intellectual culture such as I had before known nothing of.
> WAISBROOKER 1868, 12

Feminist publications of the time were constantly subject to censorship and prosecution for advocating "obscenity" in violation of the 1873 Comstock Act, the brainchild of campaigner Anthony Comstock, which sought to eliminate the public discussion of contraception, skepticism about marriage, and the fact that husbands maintained an immunity from prosecution if they sexually assaulted their wives. For example, when the *Lucifer* editor, Moses Harman, published a contribution (known as the Markland letter), which was about marital rape, and which contained the word "penis," he was charged with obscenity. As Harmon defended himself against this charge, Waisbrooker deputized as editor of the publication, where she protested against Comstock's activities by reprinting material from a US Department of Agriculture volume, its *Special Report on Diseases of the Horse*, which discussed horses' penises, a subject that, in view of Harman's prosecution, clearly would not have been allowed if the male anatomy in question had been human. In this incident, which is known as the Horse Penis Affair, Waisbrooker argued that the agriculture secretary should also be prosecuted (Garrison 1978, 537; Hedrick 1997, 12; McAllister 1985, 40; Sears 1977, 229; Stoehr 1979a, 383–384; Willburn 2006, 74).

From 1891 to 1892, Lois Waisbrooker lived in the Home, Washington anarchist colony, during which time she encountered her third prosecution for obscenity. Waisbrooker started her monthly publication, *Clothed With the Sun*, a subscription to which was fifty cents a year, while living in San Francisco, and then, when she relocated, she continued to issue it, notwithstanding the financial limitations that afflicted each of her enterprises. Moses Harman had included an article in *Lucifer* that asked its subscribers to consider buying some of Lois' publications so that she would be able to move to Home, and eliminate some of the hardship caused by having to pay rent in the Bay Area (Harman 1900). This was not the first time that Harman made such a plea on her behalf. In 1897, Lois had, in a state of despair, written to the editor as follows:

> I seem to be in that stage of life that comes to many people of my age, when it is for a time a question of going down or going on. If I can have two or three months free from anxiety as to the means of living, I feel, and all signs indicate, that I shall rally and do good work, perhaps the best of my life; otherwise, it is a doubtful question.
>
> WAISBROOKER, quoted in HARMAN 1897

In response, Harman also suggested that readers purchase some of her books, this time recommending *Helen Harlow's Vow*.

A year into her colony residency, she would find herself involved in a Comstock Act-induced federal court legal battle over the purported obscenity of an article that she had included in *Clothed*. Hal Sears (1977, 233) points out that the prosecution was "part of the official harassment of the anarchist community of Home, Washington" that commenced following the assassination of President McKinley by an alleged anarchist. (LeWarne 1975, 184, 195; Marsh 1981, 118; Maurice 2004; McAllister 1985, 44; McLaren 1992, 533, fn 29; Passet 2003, 121–122, 2006, 243–244, Wadland 2014, 28).

The offensive item that Lois had included in the December 1901 number was called "The Awful Fate of a Fallen Woman," in which Waisbrooker had argued that there was nothing wrong in a having a romantic relationship outside the bounds of marriage. The Home postmaster, Mattie D. Penhallow, also a resident of the anarchist colony, was prosecuted too, in her case for having allowed a copy of the questionable "lewd, lascivious, and obscene" edition of Waisbrooker's publication to go out in the mail to someone (actually tricky postal inspector Confucius Wayland) who had claimed to be a subscriber who had not received it, but who was really attempting to entrap her into breaking the law. Discussing the coming trial in a later issue of *Clothed*, Lois was upbeat:

> I could forgive Mr. Wayland for causing my arrest had he let her [Penhallow] alone. Yes, it wo'd be a pleasure to stand up before that or any other court, and, conscious of my integrity of purpose, defend the cause of purity and love against the obscene minds that see only impurity in sex.
>
> WAISBROOKER 1902, 1

More cautious, individualist anarchist James F. Morton, Jr. commented as follows:

> Poor of purse, and in feeble health, at 76 years of age, she is to be dragged before a judicial tribunal, to answer the charge of upholding the cause of womanhood.
>
> MORTON 1902

In fact, during the July 1902 court hearing, Waisbrooker fainted, and was unable to be present for the verdict. Penhallow was acquitted by the jury. Lois was convicted of obscenity, but the judge, John J. DeHaven, who was unconvinced that what she had done was illegal, responded by imposing only a symbolic $100 fine, the minimum punishment available – the maximum penalty was five years in jail and her bond had been $300 (Koenig 2004, 209; LeWarne 1972,

165, 1975, 184; Maurice 2004; McAllister 1985, 44; Sears 1977, 233–234; Verity 1902; Wadland 2014, 46–47).

This was not the first time that the Home residents had been snared in a politically motivated trial for obscenity. Prosecution of another publication that was produced in the colony, *Discontent: Mother of Progress*, a paper for which Morton wrote, had come to trial earlier in the year, and the charges were similar. In January 1902, an article by James W. Adams had appeared in *Discontent* that promoted the idea of free love and criticized monogamy. In that case, however, the judge, C.H. Hanford, determined that the article was not obscene and directed the jury to return a verdict of not guilty (Maurice 2004; Morgan 1955, 109; Verity 1902).

Founded as an anarchist commune where there would be few rules, and residents would be able to immerse themselves in their own cabins and own projects and hopefully avoid many of the conflicts that plagued other similar colonies such as the Glennis project near Tacoma, Washington and Albert K. Owen's Credit Foncier of Sinaloa in Topolobampo, Mexico, Home was set up in 1896 so that, true to anarchist goals, its leaders would have little power and decisions would be made unanimously (Koenig 2004, 202–203; LeWarne 1972, 157; Slosson 1903; Youmans 1899). As Koenig (2004, 200) points out, the princi-ples that Home appeared to exemplify, particularly as they were projected in the pages of the publications that emanated from some of its residents, made the commune seem exciting and interesting, and this is why important people of similar persuasion, including Alexander Berkman, Emma Goldman, Moses Harman, and Margaret Sanger, came to see the work that was being pioneered there (Maurice 2004; Morgan 1955, 111). Although ultimately, the colony lasted for only a quarter of a century, it can be viewed as a successful experiment. For instance, Koenig comments:

> For a time Home served as the most successful example of anarchism that the United States ever witnessed. With collective individualism as the basis for its social organization, Home suggested a very different face of anarchism than that of destruction, violence, and chaos which was typically ascribed to anarchism in popular thought. That anarchists did not succeed in founding the basis for a new world order does not negate the significance of its residents' efforts.
>
> KOENIG 2004, 218

However, challenged in the ways that any anarchist enterprise might be, Wad-land (2014, xi) points out that, being "a community valuing liberty above all else and resolutely averse to coercion in any form, Home was in conflict with itself from the beginning."

1   Waisbrooker's Feminism

For Lois Waisbrooker (1896, 35), the key to satisfactory relationships between
men and women can lie only in the gift of complete freedom to both sexes, and
particularly to women, who have until (and since) the time when she is writing
been kept in a state of subjection that, like many other nineteenth century
feminists, she considered akin to slavery. Liberty for women would require that
they never be used by men, and always enjoy the right to choose a partner and
to determine the nature and length of their commitment, employing "her sex
functions only at the promptings of her love" (Waisbrooker 1890a, 81). With
this liberation would come equal participation in any relationship, including
sexual activity and childbearing roles, and the ability to decide whether or not
to have a child (Hayden 2012, 194–195; Passet 2003, 8, 65; Waisbrooker 1896, 24,
1907, 3, 26). Sadly, however, Waisbrooker points out that we live in a world
whose progress toward these accomplishments is obviously puny, with women
necessarily subjected to the rule of men, an arrangement mandated by Christian teaching (1896, 153), because "so long as the church rules sex she rules everything" (1896, 221). This causes society to be "unbalanced" (1907, 4), for
example leading to the consequence that a woman has no choice but to serve
as her husband's "sex slave" (1907, 11) in a society where it is quite legal for men
to rape their wives under a legal doctrine of "once consent, always consent"
(1896, 224). She "must submit to his embrace no matter how repulsive he has
made himself" (1907, 11). Furthermore, the institution of marriage, which legal-
izes, promotes, and perpetuates this gender imbalance, contributes to the tendency of men to view their wives as inferior sex objects rather than as partners
(Passet 2003, 71). The pursuit of money and property is not unaffected by this
unusual structure of human society that has hitherto robbed women of opportunity, since we live in a world where undesirable marriages, prostitution,
and abortion become profitable choices in the minds of the disadvantaged,
even though they are in reality morally unsound. In the manner of Mercy Otis
Warren, who was discussed in Chapter One, and who warned of the dangers of
mounting acquisitiveness as the United States progressed, contrasting it with
the values of New England society up until that point, Waisbrooker takes aim
also at the pursuit of wealth that now has a far greater influence:

> Woman must be free to use her sex functions only at the promptings of her
> love, and then the material of which the throne of the money god is built
> and sustained will no longer be manufactured. Sex life will nevermore
> flow forth at the beck of Wealth, of the money which tempts Poverty.

> Thus Acquisitiveness will no longer rule, but take its place as the ser-
> vant of Love – and Love worketh no ill to its neighbor.
>
> WAISBROOKER 1890a, 81

When that happens, the influence of Christian teaching will also have been allayed:

> There is the idea of what God wants – what God commands. Humanity
> has been laid at the feet of a supposed personality, and has hitherto been
> a perpetual sacrifice. If society is to be reconstructed upon the basis of
> life, creative life as existing in ourselves, must be recognized as of para-
> mount importance, and if life is first, it follows as a logical sequence that
> all else must yield to life's needs.
>
> WAISBROOKER 1896, 161

Here, Waisbrooker's humanism is characteristically anarchist, and it resembles also Feuerbach's position in *The Essence of Christianity* that human beings have projected their highest virtues, the greatest achievement of their own species, onto an imagined but actually non-existent deity, thus devaluing their own significance and distorting society so that it functions in an inadequate and unfair way (Feuerbach 1854, 29–30). For Lois, the critique applies not only to Christianity – for instance, she points out that "Theosophy does not solve the problem of Humanity" (Waisbrooker 1896, 64).

When women are obliged to work as prostitutes, the societal lack of balance described by Waisbrooker also involves an ironic tendency in the way that the institution of marriage is viewed (Braude 1989, 121–122):

> Women prostitute their bodies nightly to legal brutes called "husband,"
> and *thinking* themselves virtuous, shrink from the very touch of the gar-
> ments of the more-womanly woman who is prostituted illegally – forced
> thereto by the accursed edict of respectability.
>
> WAISBROOKER 1890a, 79

As Hayden (2013, 130) notes, for Lois, this norm is doubly flawed, because many women who become prostitutes have no other way to obtain adequate income and are not objectively morally reprehensible, whereas women who choose the more socially acceptable option of marriage may be in reality committing themselves to a way of life that is humiliating. In addition to inflicting psycho-logical and physical damage on women, the institution of marriage is an

unsatisfactory institution for the raising of children, yet society does everything it can to prevent amelioration of the condition of wives:

> [B]roken health and diseased, discordant children are the legitimate
> fruits of these legal prostitutions – evils fully as terrible as those that arise
> from illegal prostitution .... Why then is it that when a portion of us try to
> put this theory into practice by giving woman the control of her own per-
> son and demanding that the wealth of the world shall be so used that she
> shall not be pressed, either directly or indirectly, into giving herself from
> the money plane; or, in other words, for a support – why is it when we
> demand this that the spasms of Respectability are so terrible?
>
> WAISBROOKER 1890a, 79

Respectability also requires women to think of themselves as being without
sexual desire, or at least to pose as if that were the case, a stance that Braude
(1989, 138) observes reflects further the societal disparity between men and
women; for Waisbrooker, men are too motivated by passion, while women
have been forced to restrain their feelings.

For Lois, the need to reform the characteristics of relationships between
men and women, and to eliminate the institution of marriage, is supported by
arguments that are scientific, Darwinian, and, to a greater or lesser extent,
compatible with contemporary theories of eugenics (Gomel 2007, 753; Hayden
2010, 111, 116). She relies additionally on the belief that women are in some respects superior to men, a tactic that McAllister (1985, 6) notes was also employed by Elizabeth Cady Stanton, the topic of Chapter Seven. For example,
Cady Stanton also believed that women were better able than men to control
their romantic impulses. For Lois, women are more advanced morally, and the
roots of this difference lie in the capacity of women to bear children and the
various practices necessary for childbirth and childrearing (Davis 2008, 171;
McAllister 1985, 6). Here, Waisbrooker resembles contemporary libertarian
feminists such as Camille Paglia, Christina Hoff Sommers (2000), and other
libertarian "equity feminists" who, by emphasizing the "biological mission" of
women, deny that males and females will ever live exactly similar lives. For
Lois, men's physical contribution to the creation of a child is very limited, symbolically as well as biologically – sperm "needs a microscope to distinguish it
from the surrounding mass" (Waisbrooker 1868, 16; Waisbrooker 1896, 12 is
similar) – and although "[p]arentage is an incident to man" (1868, 16), it constitutes an important part of the lives and labor of women, so activities in this
area of human activity should be regulated by the person who is mainly
involved.

A logical connection between Waisbrooker's view of marriage and the eugenics movement lies in the belief that, if women free themselves from the norms of current relationships and lifestyles, the rules of which are determined by men's sexual interests and their need to be dominant, as well as from the approbation of society, laws, and religious institutions that constantly reinforce the imagined propriety of such limiting circumstances, then women, once liberated from these constraints, and able to choose partners based on their own interests, values, and needs, may wish to raise "superior" offspring, and may act in ways that ensure that outcome. For Waisbrooker, however, the children to be raised in that new world and their wishes and requirements must not be allowed to be a new constraining master that again governs women (Hayden 2012, 182, 194–195, 199–200):

> Woman must have both economic and sex freedom. And she must turn her attention to herself, to the rounding out of her own nature, not for the sake of a possible child, but for her own sake. Then she will need to take no anxious thought for the coming one, for nature, true to the law of life producing like, will reproduce in her child that which she has loved to cultivate in herself.
>
> WAISBROOKER 1903, 18

As indicated in the passage quoted above, Waisbrooker appeals also to Nature and to natural law. Here again, women's reproductive and nurturing capacities pertain to her political goal as she asks whether these important functions, necessary for the survival of the species, could possibly be intended to be executed by a second-rate person: "to me it is self evident that Nature, not being a fool, would not put her highest work, that upon which the greatest unfoldment of the race depends, into the keeping of an inferior" (Waisbrooker 1896, 11). Moreover, among other, "lesser" species, the subordination of the female is not to be witnessed, so, given the assumption that humans are the most developed creatures, Waisbrooker points out that it is likely that women's present predicament is a violation of Nature (Hayden 2010, 119). Rectification of society's unnatural imbalance, a change that women enjoy Nature's authorization to bring into effect, will benefit themselves and their progeny alike. Resembling Kropotkin (1904, 73–74) in condemning the exhaustion felt by the losers in an unfair set-up, Waisbrooker suggests that, if the changes she advocates are adopted, women "will not as now, be weary and worn, for all things will contribute to her work" (Waisbrooker 1896, 25), while children will be raised in circumstances that facilitate their development. Currently, however, Christian traditions and society's laws and norms each violate natural law by failing to protect women from their husbands' unwanted sexual activity, and denying to each woman "a natural, an inherent right to herself" (Waisbrooker 1910, 26). She argues, consequently, that the perpetuation of male dominance among humans threatens ultimately to put an end to civilization (Hayden 2010, 121; Waisbrooker 1868, 33, 1896, 27–28, 1903, 21, 23).

2   Waisbrooker's Anarchism

Lois Waisbrooker may be considered a subscriber to anarchism in at least ten different respects. Firstly, her response to the hanging of the Haymarket Martyrs, which is generally regarded today as an instance of judicial slaying, made her see how similar her own beliefs were to those of the Chicago anarchists, a realization that came to attract other thinkers, including Voltairine de Cleyre, to anarchist formulations (Passet 2006, 237). Secondly, her belief that women aged eighteen and older should receive a salary from the state in order to relieve the pressure on women to marry and rely on the husband for financial support is essentially anarchist, because meeting people's basic needs is central to anarchism (McAllister 1985, 39). Thirdly, to the extent that she was a supporter of contemporary eugenics proposals, it is clear that what she believed in was what Sears (1977, 120) calls "anarchistic eugenics." That is, the belief that the conditions under which women lived would have an effect upon the fetus, and that women who enjoyed more liberated circumstances would give birth to hardier babies (Sears 1977, 121). She wrote:

> [M]any children are, so to speak, "born damned," born to be cursed all through life because of inherited tendencies, the result of what the mother had to contend with during gestation.
>
>   WAISBROOKER 1903, 24–25

Despite the metaphysical aspects of the way in which Lois sometimes understood and explained such beliefs, it should be noted that the idea in general is consonant with many anarchists' notions that human beings possess innate knowledge of virtue (Shone 2013, chap. 10), and with recent medical research about the effects unhappy mothers bestow on their fetuses (Velasquez-Manoff 2015; Wang 2012; Ward 2007). Some passages are entirely compatible with modern thinking. For example, Waisbrooker writes that, "excessive physical labor imposed upon the mother will deteriorate the child either in mind or body; perhaps in both" (Waisbrooker 1868, 29). Additionally:

A woman's nerves sustain a similar relation to the child in the womb that the lens does to the sensitized plate in the camera box; they are to receive and transmit impressions, and whatever is thus stamped upon the child in embrio [sic] is very likely to come out in life's developing process.

WAISBROOKER 1903, 9

However, with regard to the desire of some of her contemporaries to prevent "inferior" persons from giving birth to children, Lois made it clear near the end of her life that she thought such proposals were impractical and should not be imposed by law, even though she also made it clear that she did not consider everyone suitable to become a parent. In fact, in 1907, before a meeting of the Social Science League of Chicago, she cautioned delegates to reject eugenics, claiming that enlightened methods of child-rearing would be able to achieve the same goal (Passet 2003, 170, 219, fn 51; Sears 1977, 244; Waisbrooker 1907, 24, 25, 59).

Fourthly, Waisbrooker was fundamentally committed to the rejection of authority, a pledge that strengthened as she aged, and which was firmly in place by the time she took up residence in the Home, Washington anarchist colony in 1891 (Malin 1964, 132). For example, she wrote:

Society has been built upon the idea of authority – the idea that the ruling power has the right to command us arbitrarily, upon the idea that the powers that be are ordained of God – upon the law of authority instead of the law of love, consequently the crystallized idea rules; it is too strong for our sense of justice. This will, must continue till the law of love becomes strong enough to break in pieces the institutions formed on the basis of the old.

WAISBROOKER 1896, 38

For Lois, the desire of wealthy elites in the United States to obscure more accurate understandings of sexuality and the way in which women were oppressed by contemporary societal institutions – criticisms which, if widely promoted, might ultimately lead to a diminution in their own power – explains why reformers such as herself were under attack for publishing articles that discussed contraception, elucidated how bodies worked, decried marital rape, or opposed marriage (Waisbrooker 1896, 64). Similarly, she pointed out that writers who identified the exploitative character of contemporary capitalism and the deleterious effects it inflicted upon the working poor would be routinely vilified in order to preserve the public ignorance that allowed the ill-treatment to continue (Waisbrooker 1890a, 112). "Where," she asked, "are the healthy, happyfying conditions of tenement houses, cellars, garrets and the unceasing struggle to raise the rent to keep from being turned into the street" (Waisbrooker 1895, 7)? In this war of words, excessive individualism, which she identifies as "[s]elf-aggrandizement," a masculine virtue, as well as patriotism, have each enjoyed the benefits of cultural prioritization, while more egalitarian and feminine aspects of human existence have been obscured (Waisbrooker [1893] 1985, 55). In this view that there are contradictory developmental human traditions, she resembles Kropotkin ([1927] 1970), although the originality of Lois' formulation lies in identifying the individualistic strand as being a male characteristic. Of course, Engels had conceived of the family in this way, writing that "he is the bourgeois and the wife represents the proletariat" (Engels 1884). For Waisbrooker (1895, 1–2), like Engels, it is clear that within marriage, too, the present economic system benefits men and disadvantages women.

A fifth reason why Waisbrooker may be seen as an anarchist thinker lies in her understanding of the world of work, where she notes, again resembling Kropotkin, the redirection of the benefits that technological innovation might be expected to bring to ordinary men and women, "the honest toiler" who "is but the serf" (Waisbrooker 1890a, 68), which instead has actually enabled an expansion of exploitation by capitalism:

> Invention fails, for the telegraph, the railroad and all the grand achievements of mechanical art, the result of brain-work, intended to lessen the labor of the poor while bringing them greater returns – these, all these, have been confiscated to this money king and are being used to fill the coffers of the rich. The poor gain nothing.
> WAISBROOKER 1890a, 67

Waisbrooker is also a characteristically anarchist thinker in a sixth respect, the way that, like Luigi Galleani, Johann Most, Lucy Parsons, Lysander Spooner, Benjamin Tucker, and other anarchists who saw little value in voting and rejected the use of elections as a criterion for determining that a polity was democratic, she sees voting as actually being a way that elites and governments fool citizens into believing that political participation is prized. In the case of Waisbrooker, this position signifies an evolution in her ideas, moving away from being an advocate of women's suffrage to doubting that women's rights could actually be achieved through accomplishment of this goal. Her 1868 work, *Suffrage for Woman: The Reasons Why*, was a suffragist polemic, but even by 1875, considerable skepticism had surfaced in her mind and she was writing as follows:

> Suffrage for woman I believed was a legitimate right; and yet I had come to see that even a right may be exercised under such false conditions as to render it a curse.
>
> WAISBROOKER 1875, 4

In fact, from her perspective, the ability of women to vote in Colorado and Wyoming only solidified the reaction against more meaningful change by creating the appearance that it had already taken place: "I see in woman's suffrage only an extension of the rule of force" (Waisbrooker 1897b). Possibly, Lois writes, voting can be the means of emancipating women and poor people from their deplorable circumstances, but, if it does not work, then she warns that violent revolution will become inevitable. Moreover, while peaceful change is certainly preferable, the future of civilization demands a radical reordering of society and it is better that that change happen through violence than the world remain in its current state (Waisbrooker 1875, 6, 1907, 14). Here again, she takes a position similar to that of anarchist Lucy Parsons (2004), the wife of Albert Parsons who was one of the executed Haymarket Martyrs, though she is more willing than Lucy to accept the possibility that voting might lead to peaceful change.

Why, as her life went on, did Waisbrooker change her views about voting, moving from a feminist commitment to women's right to suffrage on to a more anarchist skepticism about the ability of elections to bring about social change? In *Suffrage for Woman: The Reasons Why*, she had expressed the view that, since men but not women enjoyed the right to vote, men might use that privilege to advance the raw advantages that men tend to possess. With the support of male voters, the benefits of men's typically superior physical strength could become prioritized in more ways, while what she saw as women's differing achievements and needs, their greater interest in childrearing and creating a nurturing home environment, their less warlike nature, their compassion, and their moral superiority, might be even further disfavored without the ability to influence social development through the franchise. Only by including women's diverging perspectives could voting reasonably be said to constitute representation (Waisbrooker 1868, 5, 6, 14, 22, 25). Soon, however, Lois Waisbrooker came to realize that voting can only work as a tool of democracy if the society in question desires to be a democracy. It is interesting to note here that Margaret Marsh's (1981, 59) discussion of *Suffrage for Woman* cites what she says is Lois' commitment to "diversity in the same sphere, and not the separation that indicates separate spheres," to which Marsh refers as "a refusal to believe that men and women should have different spheres of influence." Such an interpretation is difficult to reconcile with what Waisbrooker actually wrote.

There is a seventh reason why Waisbrooker may be considered an anarchist thinker, and that lies in her skepticism concerning organized religion and her tendency toward anticlericalism. As Willburn (2006, 75–76) notes, "At a base level, finding the church and the government to be evil, Waisbrooker defined her beliefs as anti-Christian." Nevertheless, when she was younger, she does seem to have been very religious in a traditional sense. In many of the verses in her collection of poems and essays called *Mayweed Blossoms*, Waisbrooker (1871) reveals her Christian faith. For example, in her poem, "Morning Clouds," she declares:

> God rules, and with unerring hand
> Arranges all below,
> Permits the wrong a while to stand,
> That by its overthrow
> The world may learn that he is just,
> Though patient with presuming dust,
> And truth the lovelier be seen,
> Contrasted with the works of sin.
> WAISBROOKER 1871, 72

On the other hand, she long opposed the teachings of mainstream religion and that skepticism seems to have existed contemporaneously at this point. In a prose piece titled "Sanctification," Waisbrooker writes of "the world of anxiety, the absolute mental torture that a false theology inflicted upon me" (Waisbrooker 1871, 55). At the age of fourteen, she designated herself a Christian convert, but her association with the dogmas of organized religion lasted for but a few months (56). Later in the same collection, in "Twenty Years Afterward," Waisbrooker recalls returning to her childhood home, where she could readily apprehend a dichotomy between her brief spell of religiosity and her true nature:

> Yonder stood the old log barn, where I used to go to pray to the God they told me of, who didn't like bad girls; but he didn't seem inclined to answer my prayers by making me good, for, judging by the standard of those about me, I grew no better all the time.
> WAISBROOKER 1871, 150

For Waisbrooker, organized religion, and in particular the Christianity with which she was most familiar, posits conditions for moral existence that are in violation of Nature, particularly where sexuality and women's rights are concerned. In fact, the power of religion is built to a considerable extent on the ability to issue proclamations about how people should conduct their relationships and sexual activity (Waisbrooker 1896, 52, 1907, 30), and this is not rendered any more credible by the fact that the existence of God remains doubtful:

> Now, howl, ye slaves of church and state! Surely, there is nothing so cruel, so infernal, as is the idea that we must sacrifice health and even life to the supposed commands of some supposed God and to statutes founded on such supposed commands.
>
> WAISBROOKER 1905

Furthermore, the unnaturalness of these edicts has a negative effect on the quality of people's lives: McAllister (1985, 8) observes that Lois viewed them as "distorting the naturally positive, joyful experience of sex," and Braude (1989, 138) comments that "Waisbrooker insisted that the true woman had sexual feelings and that her purity was compromised by society's insistence that she deny them." Certainly, for Waisbrooker (1907, 57), there was no validity to the identification of purity with sexual abstinence, so long as the activity that was engaged in was mutually consensual. Unfortunately, the prominence of religious institutions and traditions and their influence has had the effect of preventing people from asking the questions that they really need to ask. It is as if exposure to the claims of Christianity has numbed the brains of people who should be able to see through its limited capacity to explain reality or serve human beings:

> If a chicken is once tamed, no matter how much it is beaten it will never get wild again, will never have sense enough to be afraid of you. ... no matter how many disappointments, the praying ones never get any sense into their heads. They'll keep praying to their Jesus, no matter what the result.
>
> WAISBROOKER 1896, 50

In contradistinction to the beliefs of Christians, she comments:

> It matters not what any God is supposed to have commanded, nor what Moses, Paul, or any, or all other men may say or think, not until woman has such freedom, not till society recognizes her right to herself as the evolver of human life shall we as a race actualize the ideal of the ages.
>
> WAISBROOKER 1896, 12

In particular, for Waisbrooker, women need to inquire whether their dominance by husbands and by religious doctrine is compatible with the task that
Nature has ordained for them, which is to give birth to and raise the next generation (Waisbrooker 1890a, 96, 1903, 35, 1910, 27). Here again, as noted earlier,
the parallel between Waisbrooker's ideas and the "biological destiny" arguments of modern "pro-men" libertarian feminists such as Camille Paglia (1991)
are quite apparent.

There is an eighth reason why Waisbrooker may be considered an anarchist
thinker, her belief that crime is social. Denying that a major determinant of
criminality is the perpetrator's intention, she argues that the circumstances of
disadvantaged people put pressure on them to such an extent that they have
no choice sometimes but to break the law. Part of the answer to this predicament lies in the liberation of women so that they can raise their children, all of
whom in the future will have been born because they were wanted, under improved conditions that will allow their progeny to prosper (Waisbrooker 1875,
3, 1896, 17). The view that criminal behavior has its roots in malformations of
society is a common anarchist viewpoint. For example, Josiah Warren wrote in
Equitable Commerce:

> To what purpose, O legislators, do ye say "thou shalt not steal"? To what
> ends are all your horrid inventions of punishment? Stealing still goes
> on, and ye repeat "thou shall not steal," and still punish, even though
> you said at first that punishment was a remedy! Ye have no remedy, but
> only inflict tenfold more evils by your abortive attempts to overcome
> effects without consulting causes, or opening your eyes and ears to
> explanations.
>
> WARREN 1852, 38, 2011, 66

Waisbrooker's skepticism about law presents a ninth reason for considering
her to be an anarchist. For her, the very intransigence of human-made law,
which is often believed to constitute its strength, makes it inferior to the wisdom of people's own judgements, especially when they discern where natural law stands on a matter (Waisbrooker 1896, 19, 40). In fact, "no amount of
legality can prevent or cover up the consequences of the violations of nature's law" (40). Like Lois, other anarchists have expressed this view that
natural law is superior to man-made law, while others have preferred the prioritization of societal norms; in the case of Benjamin Tucker, he moved from
arguments based in natural law to ones in terms of customs enforced by contract. Moreover, for Waisbrooker, in typical anarchist fashion, "Morality must
be measured by conditions, by needs and not by set rules" (Waisbrooker
1896, 216).

3   Free Love

A tenth and final reason for considering Waisbrooker to be an anarchist thinker lies in her opposition to marriage and her advocacy of free love. Wendy
Hayden explains:

> Anarchists were drawn to free love since they rejected government in-
> volvement in personal relationships. Anarchism matched well with free-
> love philosophy in its denunciation of government control and focus on
> individualism. Many free-love feminists identified as anarchists, such as
> Waisbrooker, Lizzie Holmes, and Voltairine de Cleyre.
>
> HAYDEN 2013, 47

Indeed, Benjamin Tucker opposed marriage and was never married, and in his
publication, *Liberty*, for which Waisbrooker wrote some articles, he included
many debates between anarchists about how best to advance individual freedom at the expense of formal romantic affiliations. Voltairine de Cleyre, like
Tucker, participated serially in a number of relationships, and she refused after
giving birth to a child to take on the role of mother and did not visit her son
until he was seventeen; she wrote an essay titled "Those Who Marry Do Ill."
Lizzie Holmes, however, lived more conventionally, marrying twice; her second husband, William "Will" Holmes worked together with her on her anarchist pursuits.

At the heart of the prosecutions of Waisbrooker and the other Home residents lies the question of what "free love" might represent and whether it is a
goal that is morally uplifting and a desirable outcome toward which humanity
should direct itself, or whether it is evil, an assault on established traditions
and the Christian morality that undergirds them, and something that government, and in particular the United States federal government, should have
wished to root out. For Lois, opposition to the institution of marriage has its
origins in both her feminist and her anarchist beliefs, and it is perhaps the
most distinct aspect of her philosophical thought.

As noted in Chapter Three, at the center of the concept of free love is not, as
has sometimes been supposed, a commitment to sexual profligacy or an abandonment of decency. Far from it, for free love advocates such as Lois Waisbrooker desired to place relationships on a higher moral plain. Garrison comments:

> But these defiant libertarians of the late Victorian period were not liber-
> tines. "Free love" rarely meant absolute sexual freedom to its advocates,
> but simply that there should be no legal restrictions on sexual behavior.
>
> GARRISON 1978, 537

Waisbrooker explained the distinction as follows:

> No, we are far from advocating recklessness in this direction. There is too
> much of that now. What we want is the knowledge that will give us genu-
> ine purity. We are tired of the counterfeit.
> WAISBROOKER 1890a, 118

In fact, Waisbrooker opposed the spreading of the doctrine of free love using
individual correspondence because she feared that men would assume that
the women involved in the movement were morally lax (Passet 2003, 159). At
the same time, she rejected the double standard whereby men's sexual dalliances were tolerated or at least kept quiet, while women's indiscretions were
considered a blight on their character. Passet writes:

> Many of the didactic novels and polemic tracts Waisbrooker wrote after
> 1868 portray young women victimized by the sexual double standard,
> and employ frank language to describe woman's sexual enslavement in
> marriage.
> PASSET 2006, 234

In particular, as indicated above, Waisbrooker was repelled by the unjustifiable
power husbands could exercise over their wives, being legally free even to rape
them as a consequence of marriage. Unsurprisingly, she wished for women to
always have the ability to say no to sex, but she wanted also to be able to say yes
without incurring societal, legal, or religious censure; what mattered was how
the participants, including the woman, felt (Battan 2004, 604). Thus, with
respect to the number of partners a woman might have, Waisbrooker sounds
remarkably tolerant by the standards of existing societal *mores*. Hayden notes
that "She championed the right of a woman to practice promiscuity because
"she should have the right to bring one or a dozen men to her home if she
wanted them," believing few women would choose to do so" (Hayden 2013, 21;
Waisbrooker 1898a).

That is not to say that, given the ability of women to make free choices on
the basis of their preferences, the advocates of free love in the late nineteenth
and early twentieth centuries had an open mind about all sexual practices. An
opponent of abortion, Waisbrooker also condemned masturbation and oral
sex, and criticized the use of contraception under most circumstances, regarding it as appropriate only in emergency situations; as was noted earlier, however, she also disputed the value of sexual abstinence (Hayden 2013, 200;

Waisbrooker 1895, 10–11, 1897a, 1904). Lois gives an account of the son of a friend whom she describes as having "contracted the habit of self-abuse," an activity that Waisbrooker, in common with others of her generation, believed was damaging to his health. For a while, he worked as a spiritualist medium, which Waisbrooker assumed caused the unisexual activity to end, although when he ceased his spiritualist activities, he began to masturbate again (Waisbrooker 1896, 61). On the other hand, she presents a differing hierarchy of vice when considering the alternatives of masturbation and intercourse using a condom:

> [W]ere I thirty instead of seventy ... I would seek self-relief before I would enter into a sex relation with a man and scientific appliances between.
> WAISBROOKER 1897c

With respect to oral sex, she wrote a letter to *Lucifer the Light Bearer* in which she told of a husband who "did not care to enforce his claim in the natural way, [and] forced her to relieve him by making a 'sucker' of her and she would vomit with the disgust and nausea thus caused" (Gordon [1974] 2007, 78; Hasday 2000, 1449–1450; Waisbrooker 1890b). In fact, it was only when she was 48 years old that Lois discovered the existence of fellatio. In another letter, she wrote, "I shall never forget the horror I felt when I first learned ... that such a thing was possible. For years I could never bring myself to put the diabolical perversion into words" (Sears 1977, 225).

In correspondence with her negative views concerning some sexual practices, she also believed that there was a "correct" use for people's romantic and physical prowess:

> Many are accepting the thought that the creative power of men and women is evolving to a higher plane where sex intercourse will be more of brain and soul than of the body, and a few are beginning to see what the writer [Lois] has all along maintained, that to be a soul and brain association the bodily organs need not be left out.
> WAISBROOKER 1896, 122–123

McAllister sums up Lois Waisbrooker's views about relationships and childbearing as follows:

> Waisbrooker believed that she had her finger on the pulse of the world's misery: If only people would cease their contempt of sex which, because

we think it is so, is degrading, and instead would honor its positive creative power, sex would become nothing less than the vehicle for the re-
demption of the human race.

MCALLISTER 1985, 10

Here, it becomes necessary to ask whether this strand of her thought constitutes a form of sexual correctness, and whether it is any less narrow-minded
than the proscriptions advocated by the Christians Lois tended to despise, and
thus is perhaps scarcely compatible with individualistic anarchism. Moreover,
there seems to be an inconsistency in Waisbrooker's desire to use women's
ability to withhold sex from men in order to improve their position in society
(Passet 2003, 162), while also arguing that there is a higher, non-carnal but "regenerative" form of sex that is more satisfying potentially for women and men
alike, its regenerative character residing "in the union of souls, of astral as well
as physical bodies in the sex act" (Waisbrooker 1895, 16). When she writes, characteristically, that the improvement of women in this respect "does not come
from obedience to our stereotyped morality, but from the action of nature's law
transferring the materially creative element of sex into psychic or soul life"
(Waisbrooker 1896, 126), it can be argued that she may be replacing one "stereotyped morality" with another, even if the replacement is less oppressive. As
regards the choice of "regeneration" as a name for the higher form, Lois writes
that "we find in common use among religionists the word "regeneration," and,
knowing that something cannot rest on nothing, we infer that it has a meaning
rooted in truth; and as generation is a tangible physical fact why should not
regeneration be also?" (Waisbrooker 1890a, 16). Unhappily, her argument here
is not very logical, for while regeneration has a meaning, so does "boogeyman."
However, the fact that a word has a meaning does not mean that what it de-
notes exists. For Waisbrooker, many Christian teachings made quasi-historical
claims and thus they had a meaning that was understandable to many believers, but nevertheless she denied they were rational. In fact, whole religions
may rest on nothing empirical at all, on "faith" or fear or confusion. As well as
relying on this unsatisfactory approach to naming what she was writing about,
she also failed to define exactly its characteristics. Hayden (2013, 160) comments that "[f]or ... Waisbrooker, regeneration occurred in a spiritualist sense –
the conquering of death – or in an unspecified utopian sense."

Waisbrooker conceptualized this higher, reproductive instinct as being
present only in women, while men had a stronger drive toward baser, more
physical behavior (Gordon 1973, 8; McLaren 1992, 533; Marsh 1981, 78). But did
this formulation include more than the conventional distinction between
physical pleasure-seeking and romantic attraction that is often used to separate

the approaches of men and women, and which was also used by Waisbrooker herself? Hayden does not think Lois is able to overcome this criticism:

> What exactly [Juliet] Severance [a medical doctor and fellow-feminist] and Waisbrooker advocated when they celebrated the virtues of a higher purpose to sex seems unclear.
>
> HAYDEN 2013, 68

Given Lois' Victorian understandings of, and limited knowledge about some sexual matters, as well as the difficulties attendant upon writing candidly in the age of Comstock, she may not have been able to articulate all the finer aspects of that which she desired. Certainly, at times, she lacked the legal ability to send out her writings to subscribers or even, if she used the US mail, to disclose where it would be possible to obtain them (Waisbrooker 1898a, 1902). Indeed, in an article called "The Rainstorm Duck," she lamented the capacity of the federal government to monitor and suppress the opinions of those with whom it disagreed, and would surely have been horrified to observe the extent to which this power has expanded in the present day:

> Are our letters then subject to supervision? Will they next try to supervise our thoughts?
>
> WAISBROOKER 1898a

However, despite the gaps in her scientific expertise, and notwithstanding the resistance to her pioneering ideas that she invariably encountered, the attention she gave to the need to allow only consent-based relationships is particularly praiseworthy.

Hayden (2013, 142) points out that embryology was used by Lois to dignify her conceptualization of a superior form of sex: "the sex act had to be positioned in a scientific perspective as a step in the process of reproduction and a step in the process of evolution." Yet, despite the directives of Christian doctrines that, ironically, Waisbrooker loathed, human beings mostly do not engage in sexual behavior for reproduction, and often use contraception in order to prevent it from happening. So Waisbrooker is outlining a template for a higher form of sexual activity that excludes the main motivations for the behavior. However, she believes that, in a more commonsense and egalitarian society, her perceptions will become more acceptable to others: "when the young are taught to look beyond more physical pleasure, then they will expect this awakening and prepare for it" (Waisbrooker 1896, 126–127). In such a world, "intercourse will be more of brain and soul than of the body" (1896, 122), unlike today, where the interlacing of mental and physical faculties in a less uplifting way "cannot fail to affect the brain to its injury" (Waisbrooker 1890a, 21). Additionally, victims' mental health can be damaged by rape, prostitution, or sexually transmitted diseases, each of which are, Lois writes, promoted by sexual misunderstanding and, in consequence, inflicted recklessly. Waisbrooker's ultimate higher purpose here is to seek a more equitable, meaningful, and enjoyable life for women.

4   Spiritualism

As previously indicated, Lois Waisbrooker's life and philosophy were influenced also by spiritualism (communication between the living and the dead, typically employing the services of a medium) and Dianism (the belief in and practice of a supposedly higher form of sexual activity that involved the exchange of "magnetism" rather than body fluids, which might be undertaken with a partner either living or resident in the spirit world), although at different times she expressed greater and lesser degrees of interest in these more supernatural approaches to knowledge, essentially rejecting them when she was old (Barrow 1986, 139; Malin 1964, 118; Waisbrooker 1896, 104, 105; Willburn 2006, 77). The intention of the present chapter has been to deemphasize this aspect of her thought and to focus on the anarchist and feminist strands, emphasizing her rejection of marriage, since spiritualism remains unproven and incompatible with scientific knowledge. One justification for that approach relies on Waisbrooker's own view of the value of spiritualism that it should be invoked based on its usefulness to her overall political and philosophical principles. For example, she wrote:

> In the first place, I deny that mediumship, enlightened or otherwise, is the hope of Humanity. The principles of justice between man and man, and between man and woman, truth, love and liberty, an intelligent understanding of the laws of our own being – these are what we need, and if mediumship comes to our aid in the application of these, well.
>
>   WAISBROOKER 1900

Nonetheless, it should be noted that Lois' career as a spiritualist medium conferred some facility upon her desire to influence others. In some ways, it served functionally as a means to an end. Passet (2006, 232) argues that spiritualism "empowered women to reject externally imposed laws and social codes of behavior." Furthermore, as Barrow (1986, 139, 140, 277) notes, it is much easier to become an expert in this type of "discipline" than in more traditional under-takings such as medicine or engineering, and the criteria that define its achievements are relatively opaque. Additionally, it is a category of belief sys-tem associated with low status and marginalized groups, particularly in the case of women (Barrow 1986, 139; Lewis [1971] 1989, 12). Lewis ([1971] 1989, 26) refers to these types of phenomena as "women's possession cults," arguing that spiritualism surfaced in Somalia, for example, because men dominate society there and women are not allowed to enter mosques (68). Interestingly, Lewis points out that men generally accept the development of such cults, viewing them as an outlet for women's intellectual development (79). In the United States, Braude comments:

> Spiritualism helped a crucial generation of American women find their voice. It produced both the first large group of female religious leaders and the first sizable group of American women to speak in public. Wheth-er one views the medium's voice as inspired by an external intelligence or by some remote region of her own mind, the trance state liberated it. ... More women stepped beyond conventional female roles because of Spir-itualism than they would have without it.
>
> BRAUDE 1989, 201

Willburn (2006, 65, 73) argues that through the paraphernalia of spiritualism, Waisbrooker's belief in the power of Nature took on an original character that came to represent the power of natural law, capable of overruling any prognos-tication of empiricism, and thus even the record of human history became subjective and malleable. In other words:

> Lois Waisbrooker, a sympathetic medium, completely redefined natural selection.
>
> WILLBURN 2006, 70

5   No to Marriage

From Waisbrooker's perspective, immersed in free love, feminist, and anar-chist understandings, the existence of formal, legal marriage was ultimately untenable and needed to be replaced as a social convention. Partly this was because, regardless of the attraction of any romantic imagery infused into a relationship, it was never possible to obviate the fundamentals of economic exploitation that underlay the practice:

> In marriage, no matter how little or how much love there may be the legal
> basis is a financial one. The woman pledges her sex and the man pledges
> support. ... If legal marriage is not a financial transaction, I don't know
> what is.
>
> WAISBROOKER 1907, 15

This inefficient and humiliating system, which, among other deficiencies, relies upon oppression and denies the free expression of sexuality, does not ultimately guarantee the eventual survival of human beings (Waisbrooker 1907,
58–59). Thus the key to Waisbrooker's political philosophy is surely her rejection of marriage as a failed institution that oppresses women:

> Let woman get the idea fully fixed that there is no help for the race under
> this system of force which man has formulated, a system which is held
> together by external pressure instead of a centralizing attraction.
>
> WAISBROOKER 1898c

Instead, what Waisbrooker sought was "an entire reconstruction of society,"
by which she meant movement away from the pursuit of selfishness and in
favor of much more morally upright, altruistic behavior (Waisbrooker 1896,
11–12, 15). Such a reordering would embody an anarchist perspective:

> If all men were Anarchists no woman would ever be intruded upon. An-
> archists believe in freedom, believe in the right to rule one's self, but not
> to rule others. ... They recognize mutuality as the only sanction for sex
> association.
>
> WAISBROOKER 1898b

Such a transition could not, she argued, be achieved through voting, which
would never be able to overcome "evils which are inherent in the system"
(Waisbrooker 1903, 30). Yet, when less passive remedies produced the necessary societal change, and women were finally liberated from the control of
men – including the financial support of men – then, taking advantage of their
ability to nurture succeeding generations, a new species of human being would
arise, personified by males and females alike, one that would finally be in accord with Nature's intentions.

ILLUSTRATION 6   Itō Noe, unknown photographer.
PHOTO, BETWEEN 1910 AND 1923. WIKIMEDIA COMMONS.

CHAPTER 6

Itō Noe, Japanese Anarchist Follower of Emma Goldman

Itō, Noe (1895–1923), as she is known in Japan, with her family name being given first, was born in a fishing village in Fukuoka Prefecture on Kyushu, the third largest island of Japan, located in the southwest of the country. At fourteen, she enrolled at the Ueno Girls' School (*Ueno jogakkō*) in Tokyo, and at eighteen, she ran away from her parents' home after becoming trapped in a brief arranged marriage to a local man, Suematsu Fukutarō. Later, she would reflect on the events of that time:

> The agreement was made in circumstances in no way different from those common in most such cases: based on the needs of my parents, and to me essentially a humiliation. Of course, I was unable to be submissive as was the wish of my parents. I fled, more or less blindly and straight ahead, out of the boundaries set by a situation that baffled and dumbfounded me. Because of that, my parents and everyone else concerned lost their standing with others. The man selected as my partner and his parents also lost face.
>
> ITŌ NOE in "Jiyū ishi ni yoru kekkon no hametsu" ("The destruction of marriage by free will"), quoted by FILLER 2009, 72

Returning to Tokyo, she rapidly became a member of *Seitō-sha* (The Bluestocking Society) and started a paid position working for that group's radical magazine, *Seitō*, soon becoming its editor, where she changed its focus. She began a relationship with her high school English teacher, Tsuji Jun, the couple having two sons, Makoto and Ryūji, together and eventually marrying. Her translation of the ideas of Emma Goldman (or more likely, according to Tsuji, her husband's translation, with which Noe later admitted she had had help) attracted the interest of the anarchist Ōsugi Sakae (1885–1923), with whom Itō became romantically involved, and with whom she had five more children. Itō's writings promoted much greater liberty and autonomy for women, focused on social problems, and rejected the class-based domination of her culture. Despite her brief life, these ideals were also well reflected in her own strikingly revolutionary mode of living, her relationships being the main focus of her fiction writing. An historical novel about her life, *Beauty in Disarray*, was written by Harumi Setouchi (now known as Jakucho Setouchi) and has been translated into English (Setouchi 1993). Although the present author is not proficient in the Japanese language, there now exist today sufficient translated materials about Itō Noe that it is possible to include a chapter here about her ideas, one of the purposes of which is to identify, for readers beyond Japan who will quite likely never have heard of her, Noe's life and perspective as a feminist and anarchist defender of freedom, as well as the similarities between her thinking and that of many of the women discussed in other chapters. The author is grateful to the work of Jan Bardsley, Mikiso Hane, and Lori Sue Shube for translations used in composing this chapter (Bardsley 2007, 120, 122–126, 2008, 213–214; Filler 2009, 57, 60–61, 65; Goldstein and Ninomiya 1993, 12; Hane 2003, 248; Large 1977, 443; Reich and Fukuda 1976, 285; Stanley 1982, 92–93).

In abandoning her husband after a few days of marriage, Itō began to carve out a path for herself based on individual liberty, an approach that ran completely counter to the teachings of Japan's traditionalist society. In a letter she sent to her cousin, Kimi, ultimately rejecting her family's negative accounts of her behavior in terms of selfishness, loss of face, and failure to conform to norms of filial piety, she explained:

> I have my own rationale. And I believe it is the true explanation for my actions. I believe that in all things a particular person's thoughts can be understood only by that person, and by no one else.
>
> ITŌ [1914d] 2003, 248

In another piece, she commented:

> A person without self-awareness has to spend her whole life following the will of others. She is fixed in a most disadvantageous position ... if my teachers had had a distinctive self-awareness, I would not have behaved so stupidly, since I would have been taught to seek self-awareness.
>
> ITŌ [1913a] 2003, 258

Later in life, shortly before she was murdered, she made the connection between individualism and anarchism as follows:

> When I was young and widely entranced by ideas poured into me by others, I was unaware for my propensity for individualism. But when I awakened to this quality, my life view became highly intense. My thoughts and beliefs as an anarchist are deeply rooted in this characteristic.
>
> ITŌ [1923c] 2003, 290

1   Anarchism

Like Margaret Sanger and other radical thinkers of the early twentieth century, Noe and the other *Seitō-sha* members are often considered New Women. Within the context of Japanese society, this meant that they rebelled against the deferential "good wife, wise mother" role model that relegated them to second class citizenship and forced them to put their husbands' beliefs and needs ahead of their own. Many more conservative contemporaries viewed the New Woman (*atarashii onna*) approach, which threatened male dominance, as being controversial. In her article, "The New Woman's Road" (also translated as "The Path of the New Woman" by Bardsley (2007, 131–133)), Itō ([1913b] 2003, 252–253) formally addressed the goals of her perspective, arguing that women should seek leadership opportunities and not be restrained from doing this because of traditional norms, laws, and government-promoted ideology. In fact, the creation of groups like *Seitō-sha* and publications like *Seitō* constituted typical New Woman approaches to strengthening opportunities for women to advance. Because *Seitō-sha* sought the development of individual freedom among women, the faction was compatible with the contemporary Japanese naturalist movement that, in the first decade of the twentieth century, sought personal development among men (Lowy 2007, 1–2, 6, 8–9, 11–12, 58, 87–88, 148, fn 21). Whether or not the *Seitō-sha* had originally seen themselves as New Women is debatable (Neuss 1971, 142–143). Bardsley (2012, 8) points out that "The Bluestockings had not set out to be New Women; it was the media that initially gave them this title." Similarly, in an article in *Seitō*, Noe conceded that the connection might have been made most muscularly by the press. She wrote:

> It is true that they made us new women. ... The press first sensationalized, and then denied, the existence of the New Woman, and although we tired of the fuss and withdrew, we were not so fragile as to be elated or bruised according to what the newspapers wrote.
>
> ITŌ [1914c] 2003, 255

As in the case of Victoria C. Woodhull, the originality of whom was discussed in Chapter Three, one of the issues that impacts serious analysis of Itō Noe's work is the question of whether or not she was an active translator of Goldman, and of other feminist and anarchist thinkers, or whether, notwithstanding the fact that articles appearing in *Seitō* were claimed to have been translated by her, she was not proficient enough in other languages to have accomplished this, and so was mostly relying on the work of her partners, a detail which was usually not revealed. The translation of "The Tragedy of Woman's Liberation," an essay by Emma Goldman from *Anarchism and Other Essays* (Goldman

[1910] 1917) appeared under Noe's name, but scholars believe that it was actually translated by Tsuji Jun (Filler 2009, 72–74; Large 1977, 444). While Stanley (1982, 93–94) comments that it was "Itō's translation [which] appeared," more recent writers have disputed this. Bardsley comments:

> Itō Noe presents the most unusual experience of translation because she did not actually translate at all. It was her former girls' school English teacher and new husband Tsuji Jun who translated the texts published in *Seitō* under Noe's name.
>
> BARDSLEY 2008, 212; see also BARDSLEY 2007, 17

Even so, it is perhaps more significant that Itō was profoundly influenced by reading Goldman, and that her own life and plans for the future were forever changed by the encounter with Western anarchism. Diggs (1998, 99) for example notes that "[l]ike other radicals of the time, Itō Noe was most influenced by none other than Emma Goldman," and Bardsley (2008, 214) points out that the title of a story that Noe wrote about her breakup with Tsuji called "Beggar's Honor" (*Kojiki no meiyo*) came from Emma's writings.

Indeed, Goldman's defense of individuality in "The Tragedy of Woman's Liberation," and her commitment to self-assertion as the means for attaining true equality with men, rather than what she designated superficial landmarks such as winning the right to vote, could hardly have failed to impress Itō who, in her short life, had already put some of the theory into practice. Similarly, Noe, who was often accompanied at work by her small children, appreciated Goldman's argument ([1910] 1917, 219–223) that being able to be employed outside the home has had the opposite effect, trapping women into a life where they are controlled at work, following which they must then put in a second shift when they return:

> Our highly praised independence is, after all, but a slow process of dulling and stifling woman's nature, her love instinct, and her mother instinct.
>
> GOLDMAN [1910] 1917, 223

Bardsley points out that in "Beggar's Honor," Noe found the inspiration for overcoming this predicament lay in Emma's words:

> Frustrated with her inability to balance work, motherhood, and the pursuit of a meaningful personal life, the lead character Toshiko is in despair until she remembers how bravely Emma Goldman led her life.
>
> BARDSLEY 2008, 214

Meanwhile, the general unsuitability of men to be a true friend and supporter of their partners, Goldman continues, notwithstanding women's
contemporary so-called emancipation, further exacerbated by the social control exerted by gossips, mothers, moralists, and other would-be guardians of
female respectability, has so far ensured that the attainment of true liberation
and individuality is a hope yet to be achieved (Goldman [1910] 1917, 226–229).
Ironically, despite the attraction of these sentiments to Noe, some commentators such as Filler (2009, 58–59) note that Itō's writings are nevertheless much
influenced by the intellectual concerns of the men in her life.

When "On The Tragedy of Woman's Emancipation," appeared in *Seitō*, Itō
wrote in a personal introduction:

> [B]ased on my own experience, I have realized that the nature of love has
> become entirely separate from so-called marriage, and through [Gold-
> man's] writings, I am even more sure.
>
>   ITŌ [1914a] 1996, 32

As she became more involved with running *Seitō*, more translations of Goldman soon followed (Sievers 1983, 181–182). Bardsley comments:

> Goldman had shown her that women's liberation was more than a simple
> matter of changing one's hairstyle or clothing, drinking alcohol, or flirting
> with some taboo, as the public seemed to think. Real liberation was a pio-
> neering act of self-discovery.
>
>   BARDSLEY 2008, 214

Goldman (1918), who had written, "Long live the Boylsheviki! May their flames
spread over the world and redeem humanity from its bondage!" quickly grew
disenchanted with what she had earlier seen as a positive revolution in Russia
due to her firsthand experience during the first months of Lenin's rule following her deportation there, and she learned to distinguish from Marxist practice the more positive aspects of her own anarchism. However, her admirer,
Itō Noe, did not need to undergo that harrowing experience and fortunate
eventual desperate escape to apprize the falsity of communist dictatorship.
She wrote:

> The capitalists used their financial resources to gain power. In order to
> seize that power, the ambitious communists are seeking to use the work-
> ing class as a shield in confronting the capitalists. Their movement is de-
> signed not to liberate the workers but to arouse the workers for their own

interests. The workers will still be kept at the bottom of the ladder by the
power wielders. This is for the benefit not of the workers, but of these
ambitious leaders.

ITŌ [1923a] 2003, 288–289

The influence of Kropotkin, who voluntarily returned to Russia only to become dismayed at the direction that the revolution was taking under the
policies of Lenin and Trotsky, is also apparent, both in the case of Noe as
well as for the other major anarchist thinkers in Japan in this era. The presence of unemployment and its consequence, starvation, as a very prevalent
aspect of capitalist society caused her to rail against what she saw as a violation of "the right to life." In doing so, she embraced values that are compatible with the anarchist concern to satisfy all people's basic needs, and the
current interest in establishing universal basic income (UBI), long advocated
by left-libertarians:

> The right to life! The most important and the most essential business in
> life is to honor the right to life. We must not engage in such a pathetic act
> as to beg others to grant us what is inherently ours, the right to life. What
> must we do to ensure that we can live in a state in which no one starves,
> everyone is granted a fair share, and no one violates the rights of
> others?
>
> ITŌ [1923b] 2003, 286

Ōsugi Sakae, the partner with whom Itō would spend the last few years of her
life, is regarded as one of the most important anarchists in Japanese history.
Marshall writes:

> Labeled a "pioneer of freedom" and "the shogun of anarchism," he was
> admired by some of his fellow Japanese before and by many more after
> World War II for his rebellion against an overbearing state and an oppres-
> sive society.
>
> MARSHALL 1992, xi

While Ōsugi benefited to a considerable extent from Itō's participation in the
work they did together, he also expected her to agree with his own point of
view, which was often starkly individualistic, albeit consistent with anarchist
thinking (Stanley 1982, ix, 169). Even as a child, he resisted the exercise of power at his expense. For example, when a second or third grade teacher named
Saitō punished him, he fought back:

I was even locked in the pitch-dark storeroom. ... When I was kept there too long I would get bored and sometimes just emptied my bowels in the middle of the floor.

ŌSUGI [1930] 1992, 13

Stanley comments:

Ōsugi Sakae's primary concern as an anarchist was with how the individual should live. In fact, although he is labeled an anarchist and was well-versed in anarchist ideas, his relevance to his own era as well as to the present might best be seen in terms of individualism rather than anarchism. The student of Ōsugi's ideas quickly notes that his life and many of his writings ultimately deal with individualism rather than with anarchism; put another way, anarchism provided a philosophical basis to support the rebellious, nonconformist style in which he wished to live.

STANLEY 1982, 167

However, Ōsugi's commitment to individualism was hardly a style unique to himself. Individualistic anarchism is a major subgenre that includes Max Stirner, whose main work, *The Ego and Its Own*, was translated by Ōsugi into Japanese (Filler 2009, 66; Large 1977, 442). In Boston and New York City, at the same time as Noe and Ōsugi were active, individualist anarchists congregated around Benjamin R. Tucker and his journal, *Liberty*, exploring many of the issues considered important by them; Tucker was heavily influenced by Stirner, and also had his book translated from the original German. Other important devotees of individualist anarchism include Lysander Spooner, John Henry Mackay, and Hakim Bey. Later, Stanley explains his argument in a somewhat contradictory way, writing:

Ōsugi's anarchism attempted to accomplish the liberation of the individual through two avenues: the individual's own efforts toward expansion of the creative self and the organized action of individuals united in labor unions. Incorporating the extreme individualist and collectivist wings of anarchist theory, his thought seems internally inconsistent; yet his goal remained steady while his means varied between individual and collective action, depending on circumstances. Although he at times appears to have been primarily an individualist, he was an individualist well within the anarchist tradition.

STANLEY 1982, 170

After Ōsugi translated Kropotkin's "Appeal to the Young" into Japanese, he was imprisoned for the first time ("Anarchists Assassinated by Japanese Government" 1923, 60), the first of many attempts by authorities to stifle his intellectual output. Then, as Stanley (1982, 48–49) notes, while Ōsugi was in jail, he read both Kropotkin's *The Conquest of Bread* and *Mutual Aid*, and he later translated *Mutual Aid*. With respect to his second point in the quoted passage above, that Ōsugi was influenced by the two extremes of anarchist thinking, by Kropotkin's collectivist anarchism (or anarcho-communism) as well as the nonconformist sort mentioned above, this does not seem to be a particularly unusual perspective and nor is it necessarily "internally inconsistent." After all, Kropotkin (1924, 28), though he disliked antisocial egotism and the excesses of entrepreneurship, was also supportive of other kinds of individual freedom, including meaningful temporary seclusion in order to read, learn, and reflect, the absence of which for many poorer persons in a capitalist society was, he thought, a major negative influence on the development of humankind. Furthermore, Stirner, despite his aggressive commitment to an extremely individualistic form of anarchism nevertheless sought ways to assist the individual's quality of life through the use of pragmatically cooperative behavior. Thus, he (Stirner [1907] 2005, 275) encouraged collaborative (though still self-interested) deeds in securing access to bakery products that it would be impractical for each person to make, advocating the creation of "associations of egoists" who could "multiply the individual's means" (258).

Certainly, Kropotkin's thinking and in particular the concept of mutual aid appealed to more radical elements of Japanese society at this time when the repression and hierarchy that had characterized the Meiji era began to be challenged at the beginning of the Taishō period, which commenced in 1912, when Crown Prince Yoshihito became emperor, adopting the name Taishō. Ōsugi's contemporary, Kōtoku Shusui (1871–1911), often regarded as the other major anarchist of that time period, was also heavily influenced by Kropotkin, whom he also translated and with whom he corresponded. Like Noe and Ōsugi, Kōtoku would be killed for his beliefs, being executed in an event known as the Great Treason Affair. While Kōtoku was imprisoned during his prosecution for treason, Ōsugi was in the same jail, and the two talked quietly with each other, scared that they would be overheard, which made it difficult for the partially deaf Kōtoku to catch everything his fellow-anarchist was saying. In fact, due to his deafness, the first time Ōsugi encountered Kōtoku there, Kōtoku had walked past him without responding to his attempts to start a conversation (Konishi 2007, 126–127; Large 1977, 441; Ōsugi [1923] 2002, 153, 163; Plotkin 1990, 1–4, 21; Stanley 1982, x, 46; Szpilman 1998, 103–104).

The Great Treason Affair (also known as the High Treason Incident) was a reaction to the social change going on at the time, an attempt to partially retard it by eliminating anarchist thought. Twenty-one anarchist thinkers and sympathizers, the feminist Kanno Suga (or Sugako) (1881–1911), who had founded a magazine with Kōtoku, and four Buddhist monks were arrested following the discovery of bomb-making equipment that it was claimed might be used by the dissidents to kill the Emperor. Following a flawed trial, eleven persons, including Kōtoku and Kanno were promptly hanged and most of the rest, though initially sentenced to die, received life imprisonment. Documents relating to the affair were filed in the Ministry of Foreign Affairs under the name "The Case of the Conspiracy of the Socialist, Kōtoku Denjirō [his legal name], and Twenty-Five Others" (*"Shakaishugisha Kōtoku Denjirō hoka nijūgomei no inbō ikken"*), although it is highly unlikely that many of the putative connections between the persons convicted existed at all, but it is quite possible that Kōtoku was seen as the most dangerous of the twenty-six, as suggested by the title (Ōsugi [1930] 1992, 153; Plotkin 1990, 5–6; Susumu 2013, 27). As Tanaka notes, anarchists of the time regarded, and scholars today view the affair as an act of unnecessary repression:

> Western anarchists quickly realized the Japanese government had fabricated the 'high treason incident' so as to suppress local anarchists and socialists. They sensed the similarity of the high treason incident to the contemporary series of executions or 'judicial murders' of anarchists in the West, of which the best-known cases were the Haymarket Affair in the US in 1887 and Francisco Ferrer's execution in Spain in 1909.
>
> TANAKA 2013, 80–81[1]

In addition to Kōtoku, Ōsugi, and Itō (whose inclusion is admittedly somewhat problematic due the translation issue discussed above), the other major Japanese anarchist of the time was Takamure Itsue (1894–1964), whose significance has been welcomed mainly since her death, partly because of past government efforts to suppress anarchist and feminist thought. She is remembered for embarking upon the Shikoku Pilgrimage, a walking tour of Buddhist temples on the island of Shikoku, by herself, without the protection of a man, which was unusual for the era and gained her public attention. However, despite her focus upon the need to improve the quality of women's lives, her support for Japanese expansion into other Asian nations is rather uncharacteristic of anarchist thinking in general. Notwithstanding that point, the fact that in some sources, Kōtoku and Ōsugi are viewed as the pioneer anarchists of

---

1   Francisco Ferrer y Guardia was the founder of the Escuela Moderna in Barcelona, where anarchist principles and pupil-centered learning offended government and Catholic Church sensitivities, leading to his execution for supposedly teaching students to be terrorists.

their time and place, but Noe and Takamure are not mentioned in that context, seems to indicate the presence of gender bias (Konishi 2007, 129). Itō is sometimes explained as becoming an anarchist because Ōsugi was one – for example, Filler (2009, 61–62) says that "Now firmly in the anarchist camp, Noe worked with Ōsugi as a publishing partner," even though it was actually by lauding the writings of Emma Goldman that she first attracted his attention (Bardsley 2008, 214); Reich and Fukuda (1976, 285) point out that "Emma Goldman's ideology had a significant influence on her." Additionally, Tsuzuki summarizes his article about Kōtoku and Ōsugi in the following way:

> The following is an attempt to trace the lives of two prominent Anarchists, Kotoku and Osugi, and thereby to present a brief account of Japanese Anarchism during the Meiji-Taisho.
> TSUZUKI 1966, 30

While it is of course perfectly reasonable to decide to write about Kōtoku and Ōsugi, the manner in which that choice is described above seems to suggest that Japanese Anarchism can still be elucidated without reference to Noe and Takamure. Tsuzuki (1966, 40) mentions Itō in his paper, but only in connection with her involvement with Ōsugi. But, as Komatsu and Nanta (2002, 51–52) point out, there were many other thinkers participating in anarchist circles in Japan: "Les anarchistes ne se résument pas à Kōtoku, Ōsugi et Ishikawa Sanshirō" (Komatsu and Nanta 2002, 52) [The anarchists are not summed up by Kōtoku, Ōsugi and Ishikawa Sanshirō]. The ideas of Kōtoku, Itō, and Ōsugi appealed, among others, to Chinese students who were present in Tokyo at the time. Ōsugi, the founder of the Japan Esperanto Association, opened an Esperanto school, using the classes to promote anarchist ideas, regarding both subjects as internationalist in scope and thus preferable to the Japanese traditions that found it necessary to repress his beliefs (Konishi 2013, 102, 104).

Following the 7.9-magnitude Great Kantō Earthquake of September 1, 1923, and the fires and the tsunami that followed it, Japan's government declared martial law, incorrectly promoting the idea that anarchists, socialists, and/or people of Korean ethnicity were the ones responsible for the devastation caused in the Tokyo-Yokohama area. Some Japanese citizens, including members of the military, the police, and right-wing groups, hearing the rumors that enemies of Japan possessed bombs and were poisoning the wells, responded to the propaganda by setting up roadblocks and attacking those they believed belonged to the delineated groups, slaughtering at least 6,000, as well as a few hundred ethnic Japanese persons who were incorrectly believed to be Korean. Ryang notes:

An eyewitness described how the mob lined up children in front of parents and cut their throats; they then nailed parents to the wall by their wrists and ankles and tortured them to death.

RYANG 2007, 3

Among the victims of the panic were Noe, Ōsugi, and Tachibana Munekazu, Ōsugi's Portland, Oregon-born six year-old nephew (some sources say he was seven), who were all murdered by the police. Inspired by the atmosphere that promoted vigilante vengeance, or possibly directly ordered by the government to do so, though he denied this, Captain Masahiko Amakasu, the commander of the Kajimachi Gendarmerie Corps, had once like Ōsugi been a student at the Nagoya district Cadet School; perhaps he was aware of Ōsugi's activities there, where Sakae experimented sexually and was then expelled for fighting, even though he had resisted the temptation to draw his knife while the other student, who was also expelled, stabbed Ōsugi in the neck, shoulder, and arm.

Amakasu later admitted that he arrested the three, imprisoned them, and finally killed them, an assistant, Sergeant Mori Keijirō, being the one who murdered the boy when Amakasu was unable to force himself to do it. The bodies were thrown down a well and secreted with trash. In his courtroom testimony, Amakasu said that he strangled Noe by tying a cord around her neck, an action she tried to resist, scratching him, so it took ten minutes for her to die. Sentenced to ten years' imprisonment for the killings, Amakasu was released after serving three years, in 1926; Mori received three years ("Anarchists Assassinated by Japanese Government" 1923, 60; Coutts 2012, 338; Crump 1998; Hane 2003, 291–292; Humphreys 1995, 56–59; Filler 2009, 62; Lu 2004, 139, 225; Meyer 2014, 91–93; Mitchell 1992, 45–49; Ōsugi [1930] 1992, 4, 60, 82–83; Stanley 1982, 23–25, 159–160; Tsuzuki 1966, 42). Notwithstanding Masahiko's conviction, it is clear that between the two world wars in Japan, as Pelletier comments, radicals were not entitled to due process:

Les militants sont souvent jetés en prison, où ils sont maltraités et où ils finissent parfois par mourir. Les forces policières bénéficient d'un climat et d'une certaine impunité qui les poussent à franchir le cadre légal. Pour justifier son crime, Amakasu Masahiko, le capitaine qui commanda l'expédition punitive contre la famille Osugi et qui étrangla Sakae de ses propres mains, déclara ainsi avoir agi « au service du pays ». (Pelletier 2002, 95) [The militants were often flung in prison, where they were ill-treated and where they sometimes ended up dead. The police authorities benefited from an atmosphere and a certain impunity that made it possible for them to go beyond the legal limits. To justify his crime, Amakasu

Masahiko, the captain who commanded the punitive expedition against the Ōsugi family and who strangled Sakae with his own hands, thus claimed he was operating "in the service of the country."]

Like other problematic issues in Japanese history, such as the fate of the comfort women, who were forced to work as sex slaves during World War II, discussion of the lynchings that followed the 1923 earthquake also remains challenging. In 2013, the board of education in Yokohama recalled a textbook and ordered teachers to confiscate students' copies of it because it stated that, "the military, the police and vigilante groups persecuted and massacred Koreans" ("Yokohama Recalls Texts Describing 1923 'Massacre' of Koreans" 2013). In 2017, Tokyo governor Yuriko Koike caused controversy when she discontinued the long-time practice of the metropolitan government to send its condolences for the killings to a ceremony held each year on the anniversary of the earthquake ("Tokyo Gov. Skips Eulogy to Koreans Massacred after 1923 Quake" 2017).

2   Free Love

Like most of the other women discussed in the present book – in particular, Victoria C. Woodhull, her sister, Tennie C. Claflin, Lois Waisbrooker, Elizabeth Cady Stanton, Margaret Sanger, and Rose Pesotta – Itō was concerned about females' ability to decide whom they would marry, the need to achieve equality within relationships, and the right of women to determine when to end a partnership. These worries, which became of significance during the brief time period in which she lived, were simultaneously criticisms of the social norms and laws that governed their lives. In Itō's case, the conservatism of Japanese society and of the Meiji Civil Code, which granted males more significant autonomy in sexual matters, was necessarily the subject of her attack, which often came in the form of fictional pieces that were loosely modeled on her brief association with Suematsu Fukutarō, as well as on her far more substantial relationships with Tsuji and Ōsugi. During her time as the editor of *Seitō*, she was able to make these interests the central focus of the magazine. For instance, she argued in *Seitō* that women and men should be viewed as having equal rights to determine whether or not to engage in a sexual encounter. However, like other feminist anarchists of the era, she was troubled by the question of abortion because she viewed fetuses, which had the potential to become children, as persons who would wish to exercise autonomy in their own lives (Filler 2009, 65–66; Lowy 2007, 58; Stanley 1982, 188–189, fn 14). She wrote:

First of all, I feel that abortion is extremely unnatural. Whether the embryo will develop or not is unknowable. But it is a fact that life has begun to bud. No one can know what destiny surrounds this life that has been conceived. Then to kill this life for one's own convenience is an insult to nature, regardless of the excuses that are presented.

BARDSLEY 2007, 61–62; ITŌ [1915] 2003, 268

For Noe, marriage as currently constituted in Japan was fundamentally flawed. She criticized arranged marriages and the practice of women seeking out a man who would be able to support them well financially because such practices were no way to create a partnership based on mutual affection:

I cannot help but regard marriage as a stupid practice. At least I cannot be satisfied with the laws of marriage as it currently exists. If people become more self-aware, they are not likely to be satisfied with foolish marital laws implemented by others.

ITŌ [1913a] 2003, 259

For Itō, mutual empathy between committed partners is a vastly superior basis for relationships because it promotes freedom and happiness, rather than the contemporary system of ownership of a wife like a piece of property by a man, which deprives the woman of liberty and meaning, and is thus inhumane and inconsistent with nature (Itō [1913a] 2003, 260). If love is the basis for a relationship, then, she notes, the contemporary practice of expecting chastity on the part of unmarried women (but not men) is unnecessary since loving partnerships by their very nature will make such proscriptions unnecessary. Furthermore, like Tennie C. Claflin and Lois Waisbrooker, the subjects of previous chapters, she points out that viewing women who remarry or practice serial monogamy more critically than similarly situated males is unfair:

If chastity is not necessary for men, neither should it be necessary for women. If chastity is required of women, the same should be required of men.

ITŌ [1915] 2003, 265

Sievers notes that it was hard for Itō to conceal her contempt for anyone who believed the rules should differ based on a person's gender:

Women who wanted to proclaim their chastity, sweetly accepting the double standard, should be prepared for Itō's anger.

SIEVERS 1983, 187

Similarly, although women have been brainwashed into thinking that virginity, like chastity, is something to be prized, they should realize that, in a society where relationships were conducted on the basis of love, perpetuating one's virginity would not matter (Itō [1915] 2003, 265–267; Shube 1996, 19–20).

At the time when the Bluestockings (*Seitōsha*) founded their new journal, *Seitō*, in 1911, taking its name from the eighteenth-century English Blue Stockings Society feminist literary discussion group, the current rage in Japanese society was the New Woman. By the next year, three thousand copies were being distributed, but the magazine would continue only until 1916, when it closed at least partly for financial reasons, but also because of events in Noe's life. Stanley comments:

> Itō claimed that she had in mind no particular rules or regulations for the magazine, no set policy, and no doctrine, yet her own name and her anarchist opinions came to be synonymous with *Seitō*. When her affair with Ōsugi led her to leave Tsuji's home and left her with a besmirched reputation, *Seitō* suffered too: no one was willing to take it over, and the last issue appeared in February 1916.
>
> STANLEY 1982, 93

Moreover, the lack of editorial guidance itself became the basis for criticism that Itō felt was substantial enough for her to need to try and refute it in the pages of the magazine, which she did (Bardsley 2007, 6; Coutts 2006, 171; Reich and Fukuda 1976, 286 Suzuki 2010, 29).

Among the founders and financiers of the *Seitō* project were the poet Yosano Akiko, one of whose works was included in the first issue, and Hiratsuka Raichō, who became the first editor, serving until 1915, when Noe took over. These leaders were aware of the activities of New Women elsewhere in the world; for example, they were familiar with the doings of Margaret Sanger, the topic of Chapter Eight, and had read some of her writings. Sanger's commitment to birth control attracted both support and disagreement among the *Seitō* community, who tended to be college educated and to come from affluent families, with Raichō expressing concern about the ways its spread might change society. Similarly, Noe defended legalized prostitution, while others, such as Yamakawa (née Aoyama) Kikue, who took the opposite position in the pages of *Seitō* in 1915, disagreed; Itō ([1916a] 2003, 269–270) pointed out that in the absence of radical social change, some poor women needed to sell their bodies to survive (Bardsley 2007, 128–131; Shube 1996, 22–23). Like Sanger and Goldman, the *Seitō* principals were devotees of Henrik Ibsen and his play, *A Doll's House*, which they translated and published in their journal. Goldman saw *A Doll's House* as being illustrative of her own perspective to relationships:

> Is there anything more degrading to woman than to live with a stranger, and bear him children? Yet, the lie of the marriage institution decrees that she shall continue to do so, and the social conception of duty insists that for the sake of that lie she need be nothing else than a plaything, a doll, a nonentity.
>
> When *Nora* [italicized sic] closes behind her the door of her doll's house, she opens wide the gate of life for woman, and proclaims the revolutionary message that only perfect freedom and communion make a true bond between man and woman, meeting in the open, without lies, without shame, free from the bondage of duty.
>
> GOLDMAN 1914C, 24–25

The play, which had been widely performed in the United States, was first staged in Japan in 1911, with Matsui Sumako playing the lead role of Nora. Kabuki playwright and college professor Tsubouchi Shōyō had translated the play the previous year, and lectured on the need to take seriously the New Woman, a phrase that had possibly not previously been uttered before in Japan, and to give women equal rights. His Literary Society now performed the play at their own auditorium, its success causing it then to be moved to the Imperial Theater. Since *Seitōsha* and *Seitō* debuted around the same time, in September 1911, its members acquired the nickname of the "Japanese Noras." The next year, *Seitō* would include an extensive discussion about the heroine of *A Doll's House* (Bardsley 2007, 1, 3, 119, 2008, 206, 207; Coutts 2006, 170, 172; Filler 2009, 61; Goldstein and Ninomiya 1993, 8–9; Lowy 2007, 8–9, 21–22; Molony, Theiss, and Choi 2016, 229–230; Reich and Fukuda 1976, 281, 284, 285, 286–287; Takeuchi-Demirci 2010, 262; Wu 2002, 64). Sato argues that it was likely the appeal of the Nora character that was rendered in the production that most connected with the audience:

> The acclaim that actress Matsui Sumako received for her rendering of Nora in Shimamura Hōgetsu's 1911 Japanese production of the play stemmed more from the emotional response generated by Nora's boldness in female audiences than in Matsui's artistic talents.
>
> SATO 2003, 15

Similarly to the English Bluestockings, *Seitō-sha* and *Seitō* were originally conceived as literary projects, but the Japanese women quickly expanded their

energies into political matters, something that the original group had steadfastly refused to do, but which Noe, from the beginning in her writing, and then
later as editor, was always committed to achieving. Perhaps for this reason, or
alternatively because of the threat that the Japanese Bluestocking participants
represented to those of more traditionalist perspectives, their name came also
to symbolize a type of woman whose behavior was eccentric or inappropriate.
To some extent, the process that was going on at the time was a quite common
one of generational change, as Noe warned at the time:

> We are not saying that we want the older people to think just like us. We
> only request the older generation not to exert unjust, arrogant pressure
> on young people. We ask that they become more tolerant.
>
> ITŌ [1914b] 2003, 263

Seitō's discussions of sexuality were very controversial, since, as Wu (2002, 81)
points out, they represented a direct challenge to patriarchy, in particular to
the extent that they alluded to *Seitō-sha's* interest in or practice of bisexualism,
a stance that at the time many viewed as outrageous. In fact, in 1912 Hiratsuka
openly conducted and wrote about a relationship for a while with another
Seitō-sha activist called Kōkichi Otake, who wore men's clothes and who was
referred to by Raichō as "my boy." In 1911, the double suicide of two high school
students who doubted that their relationship could be tolerated beyond their
sheltered educational environment brought the discussion of lesbian attraction to the attention of the wider public, but it was generally explained as a
distorted and dangerous form of otherwise legitimate same-sex friendship. It
was not easy for most Japanese people at that time to accept alternative sexual
behavior on the part of females (Bardsley 2012, 8; "Japan's First Feminist Magazine was a 1910s Phenomenon" 2018; Molony, Theiss, and Choi 2016, 231–233;
Rupp 2009, 171; Suzuki 2010, 24–25, 30–31).

In Japanese society, women were encouraged to conform to a "good wife,
wise mother" role, refraining from many of the activities that were condoned
only in the case of men. Yet, in addition to engaging in lesbian sexual activity,
some of the *Seitō-sha* had visited a geisha, a profession also viewed in some
quarters as a questionable role for a lady, and they had drunk in bars. Ironically,
the hiring of greater numbers of female elementary school teachers in 1908 to
accommodate an expansion of the education system was criticized by Itō because their teaching would likely emphasize traditional expectations of how
women ought to behave (Bardsley 2012, 1, 7; Endo 2008, 88; Filler 2009, 66; Lowy
2007, 10; Wu 2002, 64–65, 71–72, 81). Unsurprisingly, the attention that *Seitō's*

more risqué activities received among its readership and in society in general meant that the government began to look at its editors with some critical objective, seeing them as being purveyors of "subversive ideas"; meanwhile, the magazine's content, influenced by Itō's and Raichō's fascination with Goldman and other anarchists, became increasingly radicalized (Bardsley 2008, 207, 209, 212, 222).

Seitō folded in February 1916, after 52 issues, but the sense of scandal that some people attached to Noe's activities was hardly dissipated by what was going on in her personal life at the time. Since the previous December, she had been involved in an open and to some extent openly publicized four person liaison in virtue of which Ōsugi was engaging in sexual relations with Noe, his wife Hori Yasuko, and another *Seitō* contributor, Kamichika Ichiko. On a theoretical level, this activity was explained by its protagonists as being an instance of "free love." As discussed in earlier chapters of the present book in connection with the ideas of Victoria C. Woodhull and Lois Waisbrooker, the concept of free love is readily open to misinterpretation, and defenders of the practice become obliged to respond that they simply want people (and in particular, women), to be able to decide whether and with whom to start or end a relationship. The four person variant in which Noe was a participant for approximately one year, and about which each of them discoursed in print, was inherently likely to draw criticism from those skeptical about the suitability of free love for making improvements in social norms. However, Ōsugi had long identified free love as being integral to the attainment of individual liberty, and he and Yasuko had written an essay back in 1906 called "Our Idea of Free Love," which defended both it and its corollary, the ability to obtain a divorce (Bardsley 2007, 4, 263; Large 1977, 442–443; Suzuki 2010, 92). Noe had also written strongly in favor of the practice:

> Love is to be completely free. They maintain their distinctive selves and carry on their distinctive lives, and at the same time they sustain relations and live their lives together. In this manner, they each maintain their rights as individuals and respect each other's rights. In this relationship, there must be mutual sympathy and understanding.
>
> ITŌ [1913a] 2003, 259

From Ōsugi's perspective, the atypical variant of free love upon which they were embarked could only work if the participants followed a particular regimen, living separately and being self-supporting, and accepting the liberty of each of the others to manage their own romantic relationships, an arrangement that he viewed as addressing the need to give women sexual freedom, in the manner advocated by Emma Goldman. Unfortunately, this is not what actually occurred, since none of the three women were able to curb their feelings of jealousy that were engendered by the process, and Yasuko remained financially dependent on her husband. Thus, Ōsugi's interactions with the three women were often problematic, and his notoriety in Japan to some extent derives from the fact that one of them, Kamichika, in November 1916, resentful that he had now taken a third lover with whom he was living (Itō), followed him to a hotel in Hayama where they were having a romantic interlude; after her rival departed, she stabbed him several times in the neck. Ichiko received four years in jail for attempted murder, ending the free love experiment. Up until this point, Itō had hesitated to commit herself fully to Ōsugi as long as he was sexually involved with the other two. Yasuko filed for divorce a month after the stabbing, and from this point onward, and for the remaining years of their lives, Ōsugi and Noe continued their partnership alone, living in a manner they still believed consistent with Goldman's ideas, naming one of their children Ema, and with Itō even dressing in a way that made her look like her idol. For Hiratsuka Raichō, just as she had exercised skepticism about the freer lifestyles that would accompany the availability of contraception, the stabbing made her decide to reject free love as a way to live, and although she continued to be in favor of liberal divorce laws, she foresaw them, like free love, as facilitating the breakup of many formal relationships (Bardsley 2007, 126–127; Filler 2009, 61; Frederick 2017, 57–58; Large 1977, 444–450; Marcus 1993, 730–731; Marshall 1992, xi–xii; Stanley 1982, 91, 95–96, 98–99; Suzuki 2010, 92; Tsuzuki 1966, 40).

The month before *Seitō* closed down, aware that the open-minded approach to content that Noe had instigated when she took over as editor had not necessarily led to inspirational material being published, nor for most prominent women to have wanted to participate in writing articles for the periodical, she confessed:

> This magazine has no other value than to serve as a seedbed. The meaning of the magazine's existence should become clear to those who remain curious about where the seedling that grows from the magazine will be transplanted and how it will grow.
>
> ITŌ [1916b] 2003, 262; also translated as "Anti-Manifesto: To All of You, My Readers" by BARDSLEY (2007, 271–272)

However, the magazine had produced many significant developments. Sievers comments:

The Bluestockings were not Japan's first feminists, or probably even Japan's first literary feminists, but they became, almost in spite of themselves, the shapers of Taishō feminism.

SIEVERS 1983, 187

As Bardsley (2008, 207) reports, the tree of feminist thought in Japan that proceeded from the roots that Itō and *Seitō-sha* nourished had by the 1970s grown much stronger, and the agenda of women's liberation had now become a serious influence on society's norms.

ILLUSTRATION 7   Drawing of Elizabeth Cady Stanton, art located at the Frederick Douglass
home in Washington, D.C.

CHAPTER 7

The Radicalism of Elizabeth Cady Stanton

Among some scholars of feminism and political philosophy, it is not hard to find the view that Elizabeth Cady Stanton was a first-rate intellectual. Thomas (2016, 1) calls her "the principal feminist thinker, leader, and "radical conscience" of the nineteenth-century woman's rights movement," while Griffith (1984, 165) notes that she "was the women's movement's major thinker during this period." Unfortunately, as Barnes points out, many people today have still not heard about her life and work:

> I wondered why she was so unknown. I asked many friends, male female, all college educated and whom I considered intelligent and relatively well read, if they had heard of her. Some had a vague recollection she had something to do with getting women the right to vote, but most replied, "Elizabeth Cady who?" None knew of the 1848 Seneca Convention or the Declaration of Sentiments; none knew about the National Woman Suffrage Association or the proposed 16th Amendment to grant women the right to vote first presented to Congress in 1878. None knew about *The Woman's Bible* or Stanton's great essay "The Solitude of Self."
>
> BARNES 1999, 22

A related question concerns why her work has not been included in classes and books presenting the history of political theory. The answer for Davis (2008, 223) is that, since she was "a major figure in the history of American ideas," she has been unfairly left out of the catalog, and that this error should be fixed (1, 223). What, then, explains the curious omission? For Ginzburg (2009, 3, 11, 77), it is Stanton's radicalism that has caused not only her eclipse from the history of American thinkers but also a lessening of her presence in feminist accounts of their own movement, despite her centrality to feminism as a system of beliefs. For Banner (1980, 70), it is Stanton's focus that deemed the exclusion, for her "central concerns – the behavior of men and women, marriage, family – had always been peripheral to the main emphasis of the Western philosophical tradition." For DuBois (1975, 257), it is partly the fact that Elizabeth left no adherents who could remind future generations of her influence. As indicated in the introduction to the present volume, if Banner is correct, this suggests that such traditional categorizations, notwithstanding the development of Women's Studies departments in universities, remain significantly unreformed, and retain a selection bias that confers a continuing ideological misrepresentation of the subject, itself disadvantaging women by underreporting their experience. Yet, when Stanton died, Josephine K. Henry, one of the founders of the Kentucky Equal Rights Association, compared her to Washington and Lincoln, and wrote:

> Elizabeth Cady Stanton is one of the majestic figures of modern times, and her strong character, her mental and moral influence, and the achievements of her great and noble life are positive forces, that are powerful factors in developing national and individual life.
>
> HENRY 1902, 1

Elizabeth Cady Stanton (1815–1902) grew up in Johnstown, New York, in a socially important, and arguably the most notable family in the town, one that employed black servants. Her father, Daniel Cady, was a prominent attorney and sometime judge who had been a member of the state Assembly as well as the US House of Representatives. Her mother, Margaret Livingston Cady, was related to the old money of families who enjoyed much influence in the region. Educated for five years at the local Johnstown Academy, but unable to accompany the boys with whom she was taught to Union College in Schenectady, Elizabeth instead continued her studies at the Troy Female Seminary in Troy, New York, where she was able to receive some more training in academic subjects. She was also taught Classical Greek by a family friend, the Rev. Simon Hosack (Banner 1980, 1, 12; Burgan 2005, 17; Gornick 2005, 17; Griffith 1984, 3, 15; Lutz 1940, 3, 6–7, 8, 10; Stanton [1898] 1971, 33).

She married her husband, Henry Brewster Stanton, in 1840 when she was 25, and they stayed together until Henry died in 1887, although they had gradually become estranged and did not spend much time with one another. Elizabeth's cousin was the abolitionist presidential candidate, Gerrit Smith, and she met her future husband at his house in Peterboro, New York, a town named after Gerrit's father. Elizabeth and Henry had seven children. Following a few years spent in Boston, where her husband practiced law, the couple moved to Seneca Falls, New York in 1847 (Lutz 1940, 13, 18, 37, 40).

Elizabeth Cady Stanton gave many speeches and wrote many articles, identifying herself on some of the latter with her initials or alternatively as "Sun Flower" (Lutz 1940, 56–60). Today, at least to the extent that her writing is remembered today, scholars often refer to her critical analysis of religious text, *The Woman's Bible*; her autobiography, *Eighty Years and More*; or her philosophical essay, "The Solitude of Self." In addition to her own account of her life, which was to some extent based on her memories of events, Stanton has been profiled in several works by other authors, the earliest of which is Alma Lutz'

THE RADICALISM OF ELIZABETH CADY STANTON

pioneering *Created Equal: A Biography of Elizabeth Cady Stanton, 1815–1902* (1940). More recent biographies include Elisabeth Griffith's *In Her Own Right: The Life of Elizabeth Cady Stanton* (1984), Michael Burgan's *Elizabeth Cady Stanton: Social Reformer* (2005), Sue Davis' *The Political Thought of Elizabeth Cady Stanton: Women's Rights and the American Political Traditions* (2008), Lori D. Ginzburg's *Elizabeth Cady Stanton: An American Life* (2009), and Tracy A. Thomas' *Elizabeth Cady Stanton and the Feminist Foundations of Family Law* (2016).

Elizabeth Cady Stanton's political life began at the Anti-Slavery Convention that took place in London, England in June, 1840. The fact that Henry was scheduled to be attending it as a delegate made her reconsider her earlier decision to call off the couple's engagement; instead, in the light of her sudden realization that Henry's presence on another continent would separate them for a while, they were married, and traveled to the event together. It was at this point that Stanton came to see an upsetting situation in common with many of the women who campaigned to end slavery, that their own rights were far from equal to those of their husbands and other men. In fact the issue of securing the franchise first for either women or for African-American men would develop into a problem on many levels, including for Stanton herself. As was often the case, interpretation of Christian teachings was believed by some of the organizers of the convention to prevent women from speaking in public, so, although she attended the meetings, she and other women such as fellow-feminist Lucretia Mott, even if they were among the official delegates, found themselves screened from the proceedings behind a curtain, sitting at the back of the hall and prohibited from talking. The Stantons had already met many of the women representatives because they were staying at the same hotel, one that was owned by an abolitionist. Later, Elizabeth would describe the actions of the great majority of those attending who wished to separate the women in this way as follows:

> [I]t was really pitiful to hear narrow-minded bigots, pretending to be teachers and leaders of men, so cruelly remanding their own mothers, with the rest of womankind, to absolute subjection to the ordinary masculine type of humanity.
>
> STANTON [1898] 1971, 81

Conscientiously, other attendees who were unhappy with the gender segregation, including William Lloyd Garrison and Wendell Phillips, attempted to end it. Phillips introduced a motion to seat the women and, when it was defeated, Garrison sat behind the curtain with them in protest. Henry Stanton spoke eloquently in favor of them being seated, but two delegates later claimed that he also voted against the motion (Ginzberg 2009, 36; Griffith 1984, 36; Lutz 1940, 26–30; Squire 1911, 67–68; Stanton [1898] 1971, 71; Wolff 1989, 636).

One issue that has concerned many interpreters of Elizabeth Cady Stanton is the extent to which she was a serious opponent of slavery. For Lori Ginzberg and Elisabeth Griffith, in their biographies of Stanton, the argument is made that the latter was only ever a token abolitionist, and was much more concerned about the problem of women's rights, seeing in black men another category of males who would share the desire to maintain hegemony over their wives (Ginzberg 2009, 46–47; Griffith 1984, 111; Sneider 2010, 16). Similarly, Sue Davis (2008, 44) comments that Stanton did not really become an antislavery activist because "her primary concern was always women's rights." However, this position is difficult to reconcile with things that Stanton wrote, such as in "The Slave's Appeal," in which Stanton writes, from the perspective of a Southern slave:

> Lose justice, speak the truth, do the right ever and always, though like the martyr John Brown – the slave's Christ – you give yourself a living sacrifice. Bow down neither to cotton or gold; to union, constitution or law; to false judges or fawning priests; but in thy brother man behold thy God."
> STANTON [1860b] 1994, 693

With reference to the servants who lived in the Cady family household as Elizabeth was growing up, there is some confusion as to their status, their names, and how many of them there were. Stansell (2007, 35–36), for example, mentions a Peter Tiebout, to whom he refers as a slave; slavery continued in New York state until 1827. Other sources spell the last name as Teabout, and many writers including Stanton herself give only the first names of three persons to whom they identify as servants – Abraham, Peter, and Joseph. In her autobiography, she speaks favorably of them, describing in detail Peter's preparation of Christmas dinner, the games the children would play with the servants, their music-making, and Peter's penchant for attending Johnstown court proceedings. Though he made wreaths for the local Episcopal church, he was obliged to seat himself at services in the "negro pew." In protest, Elizabeth and her sisters had joined him in his segregated space near the door. For Banner (1980, 6), this positive experience with black servants and the discrimination that they faced "predisposed her toward her later abolitionism." The way that Stanton describes Cady family life makes it difficult to believe she lacked a commitment to equality for African-Americans (Stanton [1898] 1971, 5–6, 14–17).

Consequently, it is surprising that many commentators have portrayed Elizabeth Cady Stanton as being a racist. For instance, Sneider (2010, 16) writes that "Stanton's racism is well-documented," and Giesberg (2011, 562) comments that Stanton's "post-1865 pursuit of white-only suffrage ... was not the result of a sudden change of heart but rather a consistent set of beliefs." Gornick (2005, 49), meanwhile concludes as follows: "When at peace with herself – that is, hopeful – she spoke like a philosopher; when demoralized, a racist and an elitist." Gornick (102–103) points out that Stanton used the derogatory word "Sambo" to refer to black people, and contends that she was similarly intolerant of Irish immigrants. However, when she was living in Seneca Falls, Stanton often provided assistance to neighbors originally from Ireland, and some of them sought her out when in trouble. Although it is obviously an offensive term today, the use of the name "Sambo" lived on across the United States into the 1980s, popularized by the existence of the chain of Sambo's family restaurants; one of these restaurants, the flagship unit, located near the beach in Santa Barbara, remains open today, and vacationers eat pancakes there, gazing unbothered in the direction of the Pacific Ocean. Similarly, those who have criticized Stanton's use of the word "Saxon" to describe the white majority (see, for example, Davis 2008, 146) seem to have missed the point that "Anglo-Saxon" is still widely used, and that Saxon and Anglo-Saxon often quite routinely and innocently refer to ethnic origins in Saxony and England; Anglo-Saxon is also a language that remains a topic of study in universities. The usage of insulting and quasi-insulting words and statements is not necessarily an accurate indication as to a person's attitude, especially if the significance of the words uttered decades or even centuries ago has changed.

Indeed, making the argument that Stanton became more racist with time is to ignore or downplay the fact that her reason for being skeptical about giving the vote to black men was that she was mainly concerned to secure it for women. Moreover, she viewed black men as a subsector of male culture, one that had no particular reason to be sympathetic to the needs or rights of women. Neither was she sure that recent immigrants, including people who could not read or those who were not fluent in English had the capacity to make intelligent choices at the ballot box. Unfortunately, she phrased her apprehension in terms that would not be appropriate today when she expressed her unwillingness to "better stand aside and see 'Sambo' walk into the kingdom first." In the nineteenth century, voters lacked the ability to research candidates' positions and backgrounds, and ballots were generally not available in languages other than English. Here, again, it seems anachronistic to accuse Stanton of prejudice against the foreign-born when she was mostly motivated by a justifiable concern that women who had grown up and been educated in the United States were being denied a reasonable equality. "So we say to-day," Stanton (1868n, 213) wrote in *The Revolution*, "educated women first, ignorant men afterward." A few months later, in a response to a reader named Marcus M. "Brick" Pomeroy, the editor of the *La Crosse Democrat* newspaper, she would make her true position crystal clear:

If this nation is not ready to admit its virtuous, educated, tax-paying women to the polls, then we say the fewer men the better. ... But when Mr. Pomeroy says that black men are not as well qualified to make laws as white men, we cannot agree with him. We have an idea that [abolitionist] Robert Purvis, Frederick Douglass, and [abolitionist] Charles Lenox Remond, could make as good laws as the ship-loads of ignorant white riff raff from foreign lands that are every day landing on our shores. In fact they could have made better laws for their own race in the south than Jeff. Davis, Lee, [Confederate Vice President Alexander H.] Stephens or [Confederate Secretary of State Robert Augustus] Toombs.

STANTON 1868a, 373

Thus for Davis to refer to Stanton's "inegalitarian, undemocratic arguments" (2008, 2) and to her "Anglo-Saxonism" (2008, 209), and for Stansell (2007, 32), who designates her as "a one-time abolitionist," to speak of Stanton's "episodic outbursts after the Civil War of xenophobic and racial language [that] still disturb, exasperate, and anger" is to miss the point that it is unlikely that a person will be able to understand the issues involved in a vote choice if he or she can not read, or can not read in the language in which information is presented. Additionally, at that time, non-citizens were allowed to vote in some states, a factor that would tend to exacerbate the problems outlined above. Consequently, and notwithstanding the actual racist barriers to African-Americans' and other minorities' right to vote in the United States, which continue to this day through the imposition of racially motivated "voter ID" requirements, Stanton's advocacy of an English literacy test for voting was a reasonable response to the potential challenges that she identified. If a commentator today were to point out that there are a substantial number of Americans who have never in their lives read a book from cover to cover, it would presumably be viewed as a contribution to a debate about literacy and citizenship, rather than an attempt to discriminate against a disadvantaged group (Davis 2008, 210; Ginzberg 2009, 121–122; Newman 1999, 5, 63; Parker 1971, xii–xiii; Woloch 1996, 221).

Stanton's argument, although clearly vulnerable to dispute, as is her proposed solution, is essentially of a different kind:

Some of you who have no capital can see the injustice which the laborer suffers; some of you who have no slaves, can see the cruelty of his oppression; but who of you appreciate the galling humiliation, the refinements of degradation, to which women (the mothers, wives, sisters, and daughters of freemen) are subject, in this last half of the nineteenth century? How many of you have ever read even the laws concerning them that

now disgrace your statute-books? In cruelty and tyranny, they are not sur-
passed by any slaveholding code in the Southern States; in fact they are
worse, by just so far as woman, from her social position, refinement, and
education, is on a more equal ground with the oppressor.

STANTON [1860a] 2007, 171–172

Stanton's key point is that, because women enjoy a few advantages and in
some areas share responsibility for decision-making with men, their position
in society is all the more puzzling, all the more oppressive, and all the more
galling. In some respects, she writes, women are not treated contemptuously
and brutally like slaves, but in a number of other ways they very clearly are. To
outline this is not to criticize slaves, former slaves, or black people; it is to
emphasize the urgent need for women's rights. It is not, as Davis (2008, 145)
contends, to utilize "ascriptive racial themes, pointing to white women's
superiority to black men and immigrants." As Davis (225) herself later points
out, "racism was a thoroughly entrenched, long-standing tradition in the
nineteenth century."

Elizabeth Cady Stanton was also cognizant of how pervasive and unusual
race-consciousness tended to be in the United States. When in England in 1840,
she reports that she "found none of that prejudice against color ... which is so
inveterate among the American people," although somewhat characteristically, in a manner that would not be acceptable today, she recalls that she dined
with "a gentleman from Jamaica" who was "as black as the ace of spades" (Stanton [1898] 1971, 87). Alexis de Tocqueville and Gustave de Beaumont, visiting a
theater in Philadelphia in the early 1830s, were astounded that a woman "of
perfect whiteness" (Beaumont [1835] 1958, 5) was seated in the mixed-race
"mulatto" section. That a theater would have three sections based on race –
white, black, and mulatto – was strange enough to the French noblemen, but
even more astounding was the fact that a man sitting next to Beaumont was
able to offer a detailed explanation for her seat location by specifying the woman's ancestry. Stanton's awareness of this unique type of peculiarity and cruelty
in American racism was not limited to her childhood experiences with the
Cady household servants, but continued into adulthood, and it enriched her
determination to institute reform. For example, as a Sunday school teacher
when she was in her twenties, when she encountered Johnstown residents
who did not want the black children to participate in activities that were conducted in public, she insisted on bringing them with the rest of the class in a
march through the streets, and when they were barred from a local church at
the end of the procession, she took them to the family residence instead (Stanton [1898] 1971, 111–112).

Today, Elizabeth Cady Stanton is best remembered for organizing the convention of July 19–20, 1848 that was held at the Wesleyan Chapel in Seneca Falls, New York, and the document that was drafted as a result of that meeting, the Declaration of Sentiments, which was initially titled the Declaration of Principles and Resolutions. Other women who worked with her on this project included Lucretia Mott, who had been with her at the London Anti-Slavery Convention; the latter's sister, Martha C. Wright; Jane Hunt, at whose home the decision to hold the convention was made; and Mary Jane McClintock, at whose house the Declaration was compiled. Approximately three hundred persons attended the gathering, some of them being men, including Frederick Douglass but not Stanton's husband, who saw the demand for votes for women as ridiculous; many of those present, including Mott, Wright, Hunt, and McClintock, were or had been Quakers (Ginzberg 2009, 57; Griffith 1984, 55; Harper 1915, 731; Lutz 1940, 44, 45; Thomas 2016, 7). As Stanton ([1898] 1971, 148–149) recalled, "The house was crowded at every session, the speaking good, and a religious earnestness dignified all the proceedings." While this is a significant and noble achievement in itself, and is often viewed as the overture that began the women's rights movement in the United States (though similar musical strains had been heard long before), any deliberate focus on these specific accomplishments, the virtue of which nowadays seems self-evident, obscures all the many, generally more radical contributions that Stanton also made (Minister 2013, 13). Thus an important function of the present chapter is to point out the necessity of reconsidering Stanton as a substantial thinker of the first rank. Sadly, as Thomas (2016, 1–2) suggests, "the Declaration of Sentiments, demanding women's right to vote ... is generally all that history has remembered of Stanton."

The structure of the Declaration of Sentiments was modeled upon that of the Declaration of Independence, a stratagem by which Stanton was able to link women's quest for equality and a better life to the same urges felt by the Americans who yearned to be free from colonial status and the rule of the English king, thereby expanding the reach of theories of individual rights so that they specifically included women (Davis 2008, 21, 51; Gornick 2005, 39; Thomas 2016, 66). However, while Banner (1980, 41) may be correct that attaching women's desire for equal liberty to a document written by Thomas Jefferson "was a brilliant propagandistic stroke," the fact remains that other words of Jefferson (1816) – for instance, his comment that "were our state a pure democracy, ... there would yet be excluded from their deliberations ... women; who, to prevent depravation of morals, and ambiguity of issue, could not mix promiscuously in the public meetings of men" – could be used to show his agreement with the segregation and silencing behind a curtain of Stanton and the other women at the 1840 conference.

However, it is Susan B. Anthony, not Elizabeth Cady Stanton, whose head is etched on the dollar coin, and whose activities are far more often evoked than those of her friend and ally. In 1869 and 1870, Anthony came to see Stanton's attempts to address other issues, such as the problems caused by excessive drinking, the need to liberalize divorce law, and designing clothing for women that would make it easier for them to work outside the home, as undermining what was most important to her, which was to obtain the vote. Consequently, with this divergence, the friends moved apart. Anthony no longer stayed at Stanton's house, and Stanton refused to contribute to paying off the debt incurred by the failure of their newspaper, *The Revolution*, even though it is clear that she had the resources to have been able to do this. Additionally, as the 1870s rolled on, Stanton was much more supportive of the ideas, and apologetic about the antics of Victoria C. Woodhull, while, as indicated in Chapter Three of the present volume, Anthony was jealous and fearful of Victoria's sudden rise to prominence (Banner 1980, 105; Burgan 2005, 78–79; Griffith 1984, 149, 152, 162). Stanton could see that presenting Woodhull as a "loose woman" would to some extent become a tactic designed to undermine feminism. In a letter to Lucretia Mott, she complained that "[t]his is one of man's most effective engines, for our division, and subjugation" (Hasday 2000, 1445, fn 238; Stanton 1872a). For Stanton, the goal was to have a single standard of morality for men and women alike, and criticizing Woodhull for her sexual activity while saying nothing about men who behaved in a similar way was wrong (Harper 1898, vol. I, 379; Sachs [1928] 1978, 79). Furthermore, the glaring double standard on matters of sexual propriety oftentimes meant that women would find themselves in difficult situations where they had no reasonable options, and where they could not even explain their behavior. Presently, because of these pseudo-moral constraints, only women could reasonably be expected to empathize with those who found themselves in trouble. In a speech to the New York Legislature in 1854, Stanton pointedly emphasized this perspective:

> Shall an erring woman be dragged before a bar of grim-visaged judges, lawyers, and jurors, there to be grossly questioned in public on subjects which women scarce breathe in secret to one another? Shall the most sacred relations of life be called up and rudely scanned by men who, by their own admission, are so coarse that women could not meet them even at the polls without contamination? and yet shall she find there no woman's face or voice to pity and defend? Shall the frenzied mother, who,

to save herself and child from exposure and disgrace, ended the life that had but just begun, be dragged before such a tribunal to answer for her crime? How can man enter into the feelings of that mother?

STANTON [1854] 2007, 158–159

What Stanton had in mind was cases like what would later happen to Hester Vaughn (some sources spell her last name as Vaughan), a scandal about which she wrote in *The Revolution*. Hester was an immigrant from England (different sources give her age as eighteen or twenty) who was assumed to have murdered her baby after it was born, although the death might have been caused by the cold conditions, disease, or an accidental injury. Assigned an attorney who did not consult with her before the trial, and not being allowed to testify, she was found guilty of murder and sentenced to be hanged. Previously the victim of a bigamous husband, Hester was a domestic servant likely impregnated by her employer in a Philadelphia home who, in the light of the sexual double standard, must have felt shame and embarrassment for her condition, while the father of the child faced no sanction. For Stanton, even if Hester had deliberately killed the newborn, the mother, "poor and friendless," a "trembling captive, pale, hopeless, deserted" (Stanton 1868d, 312; see also 1868e, 360–361), was entitled to sympathetic consideration of her actions, and the absence of women on the jury guaranteed that this would not be possible. Eventually, following the uproar caused by Elizabeth and her allies, Hester Vaughn received a pardon from Pennsylvania Governor John W. Geary and was forcibly repatriated to England at Stanton's and Anthony's expense, this being the governor's condition for granting clemency, and eventually she returned to her father's house (Banner 1980, 106–107; Griffith 1984, 159; Kirk 1869, 35; Lutz 1940, 162–163; Stanton 1869a, 195; Thomas 2016, 181–185).

By the end of the century, Elizabeth would become dejected because Anthony was now viewed as the leader of the new National American Woman Suffrage Association (NAWSA), which had itself moved in the direction of moderation, while she, who had had the courage to question whether or not marriage was a good institution and had challenged the teachings of the Bible, proclaiming them sexist, was seen as being far too radical. In fact, her publication of *The Woman's Bible* had prompted a formal rejection of her ideas concerning religion at the NAWSA meeting of 1896, a resolution that suggested her viewpoint was intolerant (Burgan 2005, 93; DuBois 1992, 191–192; Griffith 1984, xv; Hogan and Hogan 2003, 431; Mace 2009, 10; Woloch 1996, 222). Even though Elizabeth Cady Stanton was the first female to run for Congress, in the Eighth District of New York, standing in 1866 as an independent and advocating suffrage for women (Burgan 2005, 69; Lutz 1940, 140, 141); even though she had founded the National Woman Suffrage Association (NWSA) with Anthony in 1869 – it would later merge with the American Woman Suffrage Association (AWSA) in 1890 to form the NAWSA – Stanton's fate was to become dimly identified with the convention at Seneca Falls that Anthony had not attended, while, as DuBois (1992, 191) notes, Susan was now made into "a suffrage saint"; thus, Elizabeth has become "a relatively shadowy figure in the history of American feminism" (DuBois 1975, 257). Unfortunately, allowing this denouement to develop has meant that women's rights have to some extent been telescoped into an argument about voting, a familiar oversimplification that is frequently to be found in the modern priorities of academic political science, but one that is to undervalue all the other many aspects of democracy, including those which address the quality of life experienced by the disadvantaged. Furthermore, Parker (1971, v) is surely correct that unlike Stanton, Anthony, the person now lionized as the feminist leader of the era, was not a scholar. The eradication of much of Elizabeth Cady Stanton's thought from the knowledge base is thus a blow both to feminism and to its intellectual content.

Stanton's early experience as a member of the Presbyterian Girls' Club was one of several warnings she encountered that, in view of her gender, she could not expect to be treated equally to men, and her humiliation helped propel her toward a feminist perspective that would strengthen throughout her long and varied life. She and her fellow teenage members of the club raised money from bake sales and other fundraising activities so that a poor man would be able to train for the ministry and assemble a professional wardrobe. When he graduated, they invited him to give a sermon to his sponsors and the rest of their congregation. In his speech, much to Elizabeth's chagrin, the newly qualified minister rebuffed them with Scripture, reading out I Timothy, 2:12, which says: "But I suffer not a woman to teach, nor to usurp authority over the man, but to be in silence" (Lutz 1940, 11–12; Stevenson-Moessner (1994, 673) misidentifies the verse as 21). Many years later, Stanton would appear to reflect upon this experience as follows:

> Now, to my mind, there is nothing commendable in the action of young women who go about begging funds to educate young men for the ministry, while they and the majority of their sex are too poor to educate themselves, and if able, are still denied admittance into some of the leading institutions of learning throughout our land.
>
> STANTON [1895] 1999, part II, 125

An important element of Stanton's thought is the idea that women had not been allowed to fulfill the potential that they necessarily possessed. Partly, this was because it was men who wrote the rules that governed society and government; in such an environment, females could hardly expect to prosper or to fare equally well. Instead, these rules had forced women to devote much of their time to frivolous pursuits, such as fine-tuning their appearance and clothing, or amusing children, which made it as difficult as possible for them to compete in other areas of human activity. Similarly, having men pay for women when they ventured outside the home to the theater or to a restaurant perpetuated the marginalization within thought processes that meant women as well as their partners had come to accept this inefficient situation (Lutz 1940, 58, 59; Stanton [1851] 1991, 114–116, [1888] 1992, 212). With respect to this perspective, some commentators have pointed out an apparent influence of, or at any rate a familiarity with and similarity to the opinions of Mary Wollstonecraft; Stanton had read Wollstonecraft's *A Vindication of the Rights of Women* (1792), she serialized it in *The Revolution*, and she discussed the book with Lucretia Mott at the conference they attended in London in 1840, later making a visit to Wollstonecraft's grave in Bournemouth, England (Botting and Carey 2004, 716, 719; Gornick 2005, 9; Stanton [1898] 1971, 427). Wollstonecraft had written in a manner similar to Stanton:

> The passions of men have thus placed women on thrones, and, till mankind become more reasonable, it is to be feared that women will avail themselves of the power which they attain with the least exertion, and which is the most indisputable.
>
> WOLLSTONECRAFT [1792] 2008, 65

Moreover, the pursuit of gender-specific lifestyles had made it even more complicated to try and achieve social change when wives were more and more routinely attached to what DuBois (1975, 257–258) calls "the conservative habits of mind to which domesticity had trained them." About this state of affairs, Stanton, like Wollstonecraft, assigns some of the blame to her own gender:

> We do not blame man for his injustice to woman, no more than our baby for upsetting the inkstand on a valuable manuscript, they are alike ignorant of what they have done. So long as woman supposed herself made for no higher purpose than to be the toy or drudge of man, how could man possibly know any better himself?"
>
> STANTON [1868k] 2000, 178; THOMAS 2016, 108

To some extent, this situation gave women an eventual tactical advantage, for they were presently disadvantaged in access to education, and thus it might well follow, she allowed, that women were the academically weaker sex.

Similarly, it was often the case that women were physically weaker than men because they had been denied much opportunity to exercise and participate in many types of employment; clothing norms and requirements exacerbated this disadvantage even further. For Stanton, who found the Bloomer costume advocated by other feminists, notwithstanding its utility, unattractive, the solution lay in having men and women dress in similar ways, while giving women equal access to education, exercise, and the ballot, which, by opening up their minds and extending the range of their experiences, would allow them to gradually shuck off the appeal of home comforts that presently constrained them:

> Give woman freedom of thought, a liberal scientific culture, and you strike a blow at old church establishments, with their dogmas and traditions, their fears and superstitions.
> STANTON 1869g, 104

However, until they had been given an opportunity to draw level with men, a process that Stanton feared might take a century before equality was achieved, it would be unfair to consider women truly any less intelligent or educationally accomplished or less able to take on various kinds of employment as men (Minister 2013, 13–14; Stanton [1848] 1992, 29, 1869g, 41, [1892] 2001, 22–23). When they did catch up, she wrote, they would have "large brains and large waists" (Stanton 1869d, 185). One related problem, however, that needed to be instantly addressed, was about access: women who donated endowments or paid taxes were contributing to college education from which, in many cases, they were barred on the grounds of their gender from accessing: for example, "Lafayette College, which the daughters of Pennsylvania are forbidden to enter" (Stanton 1870a, 274). More generally, sales taxes victimized females because a woman who may not be allowed to own property "is taxed on all she eats and drinks and wears" (Stanton 1869f, 281). Presently, females could not go to medical school and become physicians, and they were tried in courts even though they were not allowed to become attorneys (Stanton [1848] 1992, 29, 1868j, 152, 1868o, 120).

As Stanton admitted the weaknesses of disadvantage imposed upon women by lack of access to education, she also emphasized that fairness would require questions of equal rights to be decided as such – as rights rather than as matters of presently existing intellectual skill. White males, the persons who exercised most of the power in society, differed in many respects from one another, but they were assumed to possess (and be endowed with) the same rights, and therefore those same rights should be the basis for determining what accrued to women. Speaking at the NWSA's convention in 1878, she stressed the US

Constitution's commitment to equal rights for each of its citizens, which would include voting and much more (DuBois 1987, 862; Offen 1989, 200). She longed for a day when women and girls were no longer "slaves to the needle" (Stanton [1851] 1991, 116), when each individual would take care of his or her own chores, which would include men and boys making their own clothes and doing their own sewing. While there were some differences between men and women, she doubted that, when scientifically investigated, they would amount to much, despite the "mysterious twaddle" (Stanton [1855] 1991, 130) employed to stress how different gender roles needed to be (129–130).

1   The Bible as a Weapon Used against Women

Most scholars who write about Cady Stanton, even though they often refer to the outrage that greeted the publication of both parts of *The Woman's Bible*, say little about the feminist ideas that it contains. This is a shame because its main author considered it the centerpiece of her intellectual contributions to feminist thought (Gornick 2005, 19). In the present chapter, an enumeration of that much skipped-over wisdom will be attempted. As noted earlier, Stanton became largely eclipsed from the history of the women's rights movement because she was perceived by many of the women in the NAWSA and by other organizations and chroniclers as being too radical. Partly, this was because she favored liberalization of divorce laws and partly it was because she evinced a healthy skepticism about the institution of marriage. Both of these positions threatened the teachings of, and were opposed by, mainstream factions of the Christian church. But Stanton did not stop at these apparent heresies. In addition, with the assistance of a number of other women – a "revising committee" of twenty-five women, fifteen of whom provided comments that were included in the book (Mace 2009, 10; Stevenson-Moessner 1994, 685) – she conducted an analysis of the Bible in which she pointed out the many ways in which she thought women were discriminated against, underrepresented or excluded by its teachings, and forced by cultural custom mandated by theology to stay silent when they wished to speak; using irony to critique an account in Genesis, she quipped, "As the wives made no reply, it shows that they had already learned that discreet silence is the only security for domestic happiness" (Stanton [1895] 1999, part I, 30). While she found that only about ten percent of the document contained problematic passages of that sort, her critique nonetheless amounted to a severe criticism of a source much revered by many persons, some of whom are not particularly religious. Unlike her colleague, Susan B. Anthony, and many other feminists who were loath to criticize religious teachings, Stanton realized that to fail to do what she attempted in *The Woman's Bible* would ultimately also be to fail to undo the damage that society has inflicted on women (Stanton [1895] 1999, part I, 5, 11). Unfortunately, many women, including many of her allies, were psychologically unable to contemplate challenging the religious teachings subjugating their brains, and thus, as Mace (2009, 9) points out, Elizabeth felt that they were victims of "women's participation in their own oppression":

> So perverted is the religious element in her nature, that with faith and works she is the chief support of the church and clergy; the very powers that make her emancipation impossible."
>
> STANTON [1895] 1999, part I, 8

Thus women in New York State in 1848 had prayed not to be given the right to own property, although Stanton ([1895] 1999, part I, 108) points out that eventually many came to enjoy its exercise; ultimately, common sense would prevail.

For Stanton, the Bible was an instrument of women's subjection, spreading the belief that she was not only the inferior gender, bound eternally to be the dependent of men, but also, via the legend of Eve, the dishonest sex that had betrayed and undermined the moral integrity of humankind. Furthermore, officers of the church found it easy to claim that whatever policies and beliefs they favored, including the subordination of women, were somehow mandated by God, an omnipotent being who could apparently make even the incompatible animals on Noah's Ark, predator and prey alike, behave amicably toward one another (Stanton [1895] 1999, part I, 7, 36, 40). Thus Christianity, which prevents women from occupying leadership positions within its organizations, is "a strictly masculine religion, that places the sex at a disadvantage in all life's emergencies" (Stanton [1895] 1999, part I, 74). Even motherhood could be criminalized (part II, 184). Such a contemptuous attitude toward women displayed by religious leaders sends a message to men lower down the social hierarchy that the domination of women is acceptable (part I, 76). Likewise, in their treatment of witches, Christians had demonstrated a hatred of women that they justified by reference to the Bible, although curiously their aversion to the practice of black magic had seldom applied to wizards and its other male enthusiasts (Stanton [1895] 1999, part I, 93–94). Similarly, the preservation of marriage and resistance to allowing divorce forces women to live with their husbands long after their unsuitability has become apparent (part I, 137). Yet, strangely for Stanton, Christianity itself alone remains insulated from justifiable criticism, while those who expect to be able to lobby and hold legislatures to account give religion a pass, which allows sermonizing to validate wrongdoing even after laws have been changed to guarantee women's civil rights. Unchanging, unamenable to improvement, spiritual thought preserves its wrongful teachings, never responding to developments in society (part I, 10, 13, 131).

The Woman's Bible was released in two volumes, published in 1895 and 1898, although Stanton had been planning the work since at least a decade earlier; she had discussed the project in detail with her daughter Harriot in the summer of 1886, but at that time found little additional support among her friends. One person who was enthusiastic about the project at that juncture was Frances Lord, an English writer and theosophist, who advertised in a freethought publication for assistants who might help overturn women's "Bible bondage," thereby causing considerable offense (Kern 2001, 93, 100; Thomas 2016, 223). Originally, the plan was to conduct the analysis in Greek and Hebrew, the languages in which the Bible had been written, as well as English, but this blueprint was abandoned, partly because many theologians, including those with competency in ancient languages, were reluctant to participate in an activity that they considered, or might be considered by others, to be anticlerical, which, of course, is how the finished product strikes some contemporary readers: Banner (1980, 161), for example, says that "Cady Stanton reserved the full force of her anticlericalism for her Woman's Bible." In *The Woman's Bible* itself, Elizabeth skips somewhat glibly over her eventual decision about languages, commenting:

> As the position of woman in all religions is the same, it does not need a knowledge of Greek, Hebrew or the works of scholars to show that the Bible degrades the Mothers of the Race.
>
> STANTON [1895] 1999, part II, 8

Ginzburg notes that Stanton, earlier, "[w]ith a rare twinge of humility ... acknowledged that she lacked some of the skills for the work – she especially needed women scholars of Hebrew and Greek" (Ginzberg 2009, 173). Perhaps, in fairness to Stanton's subsequent viewpoint, it should be pointed out that the original texts in Hebrew and Greek often have little influence on the practice and teachings of born-again Protestantism in the United States, neither today in the sermons of televised preachers as they tearfully beg impoverished viewers for some of their hard-earned money, nor in Elizabeth's time to the claims of itinerant preachers shouting that non-believers will go to Hell. It is hard to believe that Jim and Tammy Faye Bakker developed their televangelism inspired by a deep, scholarly familiarity with classical languages. The vernacular

Bible, to be found even in motel rooms, is generally the basis for prognostications that devalue and denigrate the majority of the population, women, and it is quite easy to see, as Elizabeth Cady Stanton gradually came to do, that once any psychological ceiling of intimidation and unlearning that childhood exposure to its fantasies had erected was lifted, it could look to be far from an inspirational document. Purchasing a number of used copies, the authors of *The Woman's Bible* cut out the passages they found questionable or offensive in their attitudes or non-attitudes toward women, and pasted them into scrapbooks (Davis 2008, 189; Gornick 2005, 121; Lutz 1940, 295, 296–297; Mace 2009, 5, 9–11; Thomas 2016, 223).

In analyzing the Bible's narratives, Elizabeth Cady Stanton, who, notwithstanding the efforts of those who assisted her, wrote most of the commentary found in *The Woman's Bible* herself, relies on reason to explain some of its accounts of the paranormal in Jewish history. For example, she concludes that "[w]hoever wrote The Revelation was evidently the victim of a terrible and extravagant imagination and of visions which make the blood curdle" (Stanton [1895] 1999, part II, 179). The employment of reason was important to her, and she (part II, 57) notes that in the Bible's account of King David, he "was ruled entirely by his passions. Reason had no sway over him," whereas women have on occasion been able to moderate the excesses of men through "the development of self-respect and independence in woman, and a higher idea of individual conscience and judgment in religion and in government" (57). In this spirit, she considers the curses inflicted upon Adam, Cain, and the daughters of Eve as being hallucinations, pointing out that, far from being burdens, being obliged to work and the experience of motherhood would anyway be seen by many persons as belonging with the positive aspects of human existence. Neither should the female characters to be found in the scriptures be viewed as role models for modern women, but rather as examples of how they should *not* behave. In fact, she believed, these accounts were inappropriate for impressionable teenagers to read and should be censored to avoid their message corrupting their minds. Ironically, the stories and explanations found in the Bible had not been intended for the modern people upon whom today their quasi-teachings were inflicted, but for our superstitious and illiterate forefathers, whose limitations made them incapable of reason. For Stanton, this religious literature has validity only as an account of history, and not as religious guidance, nor as counseling about how contemporary women are to be treated (Kern 2007, 99; Stanton [1895] 1999, part I, 30, 39, 53, 60–61, 71, 72–73, 78, part II, 184). Rejecting a religion that promotes both sycophancy and infanticide at the expense of compassion and common sense, she ridiculed the "loving fathers in the Old Testament, like Jephthah and Abraham," who "thought to make themselves specially pleasing to the Lord by sacrificing their children to Him as burnt offerings" (Stanton [1895] 1999, part II, 24). Similarly, Stanton criticized the tradition of arranged marriages whereby love and courtship and the woman's wishes were sacrificed so that brides' fathers could sell their daughters for a profit, even if they spent more time arranging the sale of their camels or farm animals. For women, scripture endorsed self-sacrifice, which Stanton rejects in favor of the pursuit of self-improvement (Stanton [1895] 1999, part II, 53, 131).

Although Stanton herself relied on reason and science in analyzing the Bible, she noted that its own accounts, to which she referred as "myths," despite the fact that "they are claimed to have been written by God," were clearly "at variance with all natural laws" (Stanton [1895] 1999, part II, 12). Thus, to believe in them would require the suspension of all logic:

> It seems that the Lord was so well pleased with Joshua's refined military tactics that he suspended the laws of the vast solar system to vindicate the superior prowess of one small tribe on the small planet called the earth. ... There are no events recorded in secular history that strain the faith of the reader to such a degree as the feats of Joshua.
>
> STANTON [1895] 1999, part II, 13

Rationality would require the ending of religious restrictions on what men and women could do on a Sunday. People needed an opportunity to escape from the drudgery of their work, and yet parks, music, and playing sports were off-limits to them at the instigation of "religious bigots" (Stanton [1895] 1999, part II, 135). On the other hand, women's labor in their households enjoyed no Sabbath remission, as they continued to make meals, do laundry, and take care of children (part I, 82).

For Stanton, the Bible was an error-prone tome that, rather than providing a sourcebook for how men and women should behave, misrepresented the nature of women, insulted them, and provided examples of societal roles intended to maintain their oppression. During the 1870s, she had been a lyceum speaker, traveling the United States, staying in shabby hotels, and giving speeches that at the time were considered a form of adult education. Unlike some of her Social Gospel colleagues, Stanton did not advance the value of religion as she discoursed on a range of political and family issues (Ginzberg 2009, 143; Hogan and Hogan 2003, 415–419; Lutz 1940, 194). As Hogan and Hogan comment, discussing an attribute of this twelve-year phase of her life:

> In the first of many jabs at organized religion, Stanton pronounced conventional missionary work worthless in elevating the "moral status" of

the working class, and she scolded the churches for wasting money on "useless statutes of marble and bronze." If only half of the money "now invested in monuments and cathedrals" were used to build "comfortable homes" for the working class, Stanton concluded, "we should take a long step toward the solution of the vexed questions of temperance, capital and labor, and the education of the masses." For Stanton, the lesson was simple: "Cleanliness is next to godliness. It is not easy to raise men's spiritual nature, when ragged, filthy, and hungry."

HOGAN and HOGAN 2003, 422

As Setzer points out with respect to *The Woman's Bible*:

In placing Nature over the Word of God, rationalism over religion, reason over revelation, the commentary creates the impression that attributing divine authorship or even inspiration to the Bible is an idea that belongs to a less enlightened age, away from which society is rapidly evolving.

SETZER 2011, 73

If humans (i.e., men), rather than God had composed the errors, it would seem to some commentators that Stanton's task is to rewrite the Bible, turning it into an equal opportunity document. Thus Wolff (1989, 629–630) views the work of the compilers of *The Woman's Bible* as an "avowedly political undertaking" (629) that sought to rectify the spiritual faults of men and construct an authentic version of Christianity's teachings. Similarly Kern (2007, 94) denies the secular orientation to which Stanton adjusted, arguing that she "was deeply immersed in theological ideas" and "acknowledged the fundamental importance of religion to women." However, these perspectives do not tally accurately with how Stanton herself viewed the project, especially in the later years of her life when she was engaged in conducting it, an era in which she had come to see religion as a type of delusion and replaced its role in her life with the use of reason (Davis 2008, 5, 179–180). Rather, by this time, it is clear from the comments that she made in *The Woman's Bible* and in her other writings and activities that she was determined to emphasize the folly of Christian teachings as a whole. At the NWSA annual convention of 1885, for instance, she had proposed resolutions, which were subsequently revised – Stanton ([1898] 1971, 382) says "sugar-coated" by her cohorts – and then voted down anyway, her original motion being "impeaching the Christian theology – as well as all other forms of religion, for their degrading teachings in regard to woman" (Setzer 2011, 75; Stanton [1898] 1971, 381). Gornick comments:

The more she [Stanton] had read in the Bible the more persuaded she had become that women must be freed of religion before suffrage could do them any good.

GORNICK 2005, 124

Even earlier in her life, rejecting Christian proselytizers, and even theology itself, Stanton wrote:

Let the missionary spirit of the Christian world begin with the heathen of their own country, town, neighborhood, with the high duties of this life, which they know and understand, instead of that which is to come, of which they know nothing. Let them give more thought to their outward conditions, their bodies, instead of cultivating such undue anxieties about their souls.

STANTON [1868] 1975, 262

Later, she would deny that religious teachings could be of any benefit in rectifying the problems caused by women's subordination and suppression:

It is not to any form of religion that we are to look for woman's advancement, but to material civilization, to commerce, science, art, invention, to the discovery of the art of printing, and the general dissemination of knowledge.

STANTON [1885] 2007, 244

In John Stuart Mill, Stanton found an ally, another author criticized for trying to stir up women to rebel, a rebuff that Stanton, like Mill, gladly embraced. She praised him because she saw that Mill had a similar aim to herself, which was at least to put wives on an equal footing with their husbands, even if such a project was tantamount to revolution. Additionally, she praised his argument in *On Liberty* that it is easier to identify despotism when there is a single dictator than when many persons – for example, if just the men, possess the vote but women do not (Stanton 1868i, 392, 1869c, 120, [1895] 1999, part II, 7). On the other hand, as a Quaker, part of a denomination that employed a more enlightened understanding of woman's role, Susan B. Anthony would not take part in the project of *The Woman's Bible*, and became alarmed when she encountered the horrified reaction that it caused, particularly from clergy, some of whom viewed the publication as Satanic for separating the Bible's teachings from their imagined creator; its publication thus exacerbated the growing disagreement between the two feminist thinkers, while other critics thought that women had no right to be participating in theological discussions (Banner 1980, 75, 171; Burgan 2005, 92–93; Ginzberg 2009, 175; Gornick 2005, 60; Lutz 1940, 296, 299; Stanton [1895] 1999, part I, 11).

2   Marriage and Divorce

Elizabeth Cady Stanton's view that women were oppressed by society and therefore unable to attain the skills and mental development that were their due extended also to her understanding of the institution of marriage. She wrote:

> Our present laws, our religious teachings, our social customs in reference to the whole question of marriage and divorce are most degrading to woman.
>
> STANTON [1856] 1991, 191

Husbands misjudged their own wives, seeing them as possessing mainly proficiencies that could be utilized in the domestic environment to which they typically found themselves confined, "forgetting that the poor, cribbed slave would be transformed in freedom, and in her native dignity develop powers that he never dreamt she possessed" (Stanton 1872c, 7). While religion preserved the belief that couples should stay together regardless of most problems that existed within a marriage, including abusive and drunken husbands from whom wives wished to escape, Stanton saw the difficulty of obtaining a divorce as an offense against both the use of the reason she applied to all societal conventions, and also to the liberty to which women, just as much as men, were entitled. Speaking at the Tenth National Woman's Rights Convention, which was held at the Cooper Institute in New York City on May 10th and 11th, 1860, she emphasized the folly of divorce laws that permitted a woman to allege impotence in order to end a marriage, but deemed unhappiness, cruelty, desertion, addiction, or incompatibility to be insufficient. To raise this issue, which would generally be portrayed by her opponents as extreme, and often as violating scriptural teachings, was always a risk to the emancipation of women agenda as a whole, but it was a concern that Stanton was determined to bring to public attention (Ginzberg 2009, 100; Gornick 2005, 62, 65; Thomas 2016, 125).

In her belief that husbands and wives should be equal partners who continued to enjoy and consent to their relationship (Davis 2008, 80–81), Stanton seems, to many modern interpreters of her ideas, to have been influenced at least to some extent by her own forty-six-year long marriage to her husband,

Henry Stanton. For Lutz (1940, 265), her original biographer, the partnership remained rewarding through the years, and she portrays Henry's death in 1887 as leaving Elizabeth, who was presently living in England while he had remained at home, as "bravely adjusting herself to life without Henry. Their affection for each other had been deep and true" (Lutz 1940, 265), and, moreover, "no personal bitterness influenced her or distorted her views" (111). For Thomas (2016, 76), however, "Stanton's own marriage failed to live up to her theoretical ideal of the true partnership. ... The two lived most of their years physically apart, in a de facto separation." Similarly, Banner (1980, 34) writes of Henry that "[t]he once doting lover had become staid and indifferent, absorbed in his career and his interests outside the home." That perspective is echoed by Griffith (1984, 189), who notes that Elizabeth's "respect for him [Henry] as a principled and heroic agent diminished"; however, she also adds that, since her husband was not violent, an alcoholic, or an adulterer, she had no reason to become divorced – she just gradually moved away from him. This would seem to be a reason why many such relationships persist legally even when compatibility and common interest has ebbed.

Regardless of the degree to which her personal experience influenced her desire to liberalize divorce laws, it seems clear that Stanton viewed a break up in some situations as a moral responsibility, one that in conditions of legitimate gender equality might be accepted by both parents as being in their own interest, as well as that of any minor progeny. Divorce was particularly necessary when violent or drunken husbands threatened other members of the family, but in other circumstances, separation need not be seen as primarily a legal matter (Thomas 2016, 109). She wrote:

> If divorce were made respectable and recognized by society as a duty as well as a right, reasonable men and women could arrange all the preliminaries, often even the division of property and guardianship of children, quite as satisfactorily as it could be done in the courts. Where the mother is capable of training the children, a sensible father would leave them to her care, rather than place them in the hands of a stranger. But where divorce is not respectable, men who have no paternal feeling will often hold the child, not so much for its good, or his own affection, as to punish the wife for disgracing him.
>
> STANTON [1890] 2007, 260

Stanton long connected excessive drinking by husbands with the campaign for women's rights. Her first experience leading an interest group came in 1852 when she and Susan B. Anthony were involved in setting up the New York State

Woman's Temperance Society, an organization that quickly amassed a membership of five hundred who eagerly chose Elizabeth as its president. In virtue of her new standing, she was able to promote the argument that alcohol-related problems were one of the ways that women were oppressed within marriage. Previously, she had been involved with another group, the Daughters of Temperance, and she had spoken at its annual meeting earlier in the year. However, as she had found at the London Anti-Slavery Conference, the roles that women could assume within the association were limited, as Protestant ministers dominated its management. Even within the newer grouping, where some of her fellow members preferred to focus mainly on drunkenness as a problem in itself, Stanton's support for liberalizing divorce laws was controversial, and prevented her reelection as its president as religious interests were reasserted (Banner 1980, 54; Davis 2008, 86–88; Griffith 1984, 76–77; Woloch 1996, 132). Certainly, no one could have mistaken Stanton's emphasis as being mainly about alcohol when she spoke to the New York State Legislature in 1860:

> [A]lone in the darkness and solitude and gloom of night, she has trembled on her own threshold awaiting the return of a husband from his midnight revels ... when, stepping from her chamber, she has beheld her royal monarch, her lord and master – her legal representative – the protector of her property, her home, her children, and her person, down on his hands and knees slowly crawling up the stairs[.] Behold him in her chamber – in her bed! The fairy tale of "Beauty and the Beast" is far too often realized in life.
>
> STANTON [1860a] 2007, 174

Like other first wave feminists, Elizabeth Cady Stanton opposed breach of promise torts that allowed female fiancées to sue for compensation if the men to whom they were promised did not eventually marry them, viewing such laws as humiliating (Thomas 2016, 105). She also rejected the practice, still often subscribed to today, of women adopting their husband's last name when they wed, or in Stanton's words ([1895] 1999, part I, 73), "as she changes masters, and she has so little self-respect that she does not see the insult of the custom." She notes how remarriage consequently imposes more of a burden upon women than it does to men because this custom tends to obscure their identity when their names change, and who they were at one point is disassociated from whom they become later in life; through these sexist naming traditions, female spouses become not only a facet of their husband's identity, which is derogatory in itself, but the coherence of their own life stories is imperiled, as people lose touch with them and what they have stood for and achieved. It should perhaps be added here, that the perpetuation of the habit makes it more difficult today to google lost female friends, because they have become someone else appellation-wise, while men have not. Somewhat whimsically, she notes too that, in the early days of the American Revolution, it was tea, a beverage mainly enjoyed by the women of the time, that was dumped in Boston harbor. Would men, she asks, have been such avid revolutionists if required to sacrifice tobacco or alcohol? Underlying the humor, the point here is that people tend to advance their own interests without considering those of others; in this case, as with naming traditions, men's interests have tended to determine and perpetuate cultural practices (Stanton [1895] 1999, part I, 84).

3   Self-Sovereignty and the Solitude of Self

For many scholars of Elizabeth Cady Stanton, it is not *The Woman's Bible* that is the jewel among her writings, but rather it is "The Solitude of Self." Originally a speech that she gave on January 17, 1892 before the Judiciary Committee of the US House of Representatives, it was soon repeated at the annual meeting of the NAWSA, and then published as a short monograph. For Griffith (1984, 203), "The Solitude of Self" is "a definitive statement of her feminist ideology," showing her commitment to total independence for each woman, in every sphere of social existence. Each of us, Stanton argues, discovers at some time in our life that we are completely alone and, recognizing our condition of "self-dependence" (Stanton [1892] 2001, 3), find that we must solve our own problems and, if we are able, rely on our own inner resources to dig ourselves out of trouble. The spirit of the American Revolution recognized this fundamental fact, and it follows, she argues, that to be able to discharge the responsibilities that the character and culture of the United States expects, including the pursuit of happiness, women must possess every faculty and opportunity that is available to men, because each person is unique and possesses thoughts, feelings and experiences that are never shared with anyone else, and therefore must find their own way to fulfilment (Engbers 2007, 323, 324, 327; Gornick 2005, 7; Stanton [1892] 2001, 1–2, 4, 6–7, 9–10, 14–15, 29; Wolff 1989, 643–644).

While for some commentators, "The Solitude of Self" is a piece of philosophy, for others such as Thomas (2016, 239), it evokes the emotions described in Betty Friedan's much later work, *The Feminine Mystique*, because it also senses and describes the despondency felt by women who lack the opportunity to put their education into practice or compete with men in the workplace. It can also be understood as portraying the loneliness felt by all individuals, including women trapped at home, as "an existential declaration of people's utter isolation" (Ginzberg 2009, 170). But it seems clear that Stanton's purpose is to argue that, in the light of this separation of individuals with respect to many facets of their lives, all persons, including women, must possess the capacities needed to address the many problems they will encounter in their lives. Thus Griffith (1984, 204) explains, "[h]er tone was tragic; her argument, existential; her case, powerful. Alternatively, Flexner and Fitzpatrick (1996, 224) refer to *"The Solitude of Self"* as "a "working" statement rather than a reflective philosophical essay, written to serve an immediate, practical purpose," and Lutz (1940, 289) characterizes it as a speech she had been fine-tuning for a long time: "Original, philosophical, basic, it was the culmination of all the pleas that she had made before Congressional committees for the past twenty years." Offen (1989, 199) comments that it "is not only individualist but can be read as a transcendentalist or even an existentialist philosophical tract. It contains virtually no acknowledgment of society or relationships; its main concern is with the soul and with consciousness," Gornick (2005, 6) agrees that, for Stanton, "Connection was an ideal; the exception, not the rule, in the human condition," and Smith (2007, 68) deems the work "relentlessly suspicious of community." However, Davis sees it as an example of an extreme individualism, with Stanton being heavily influenced by William Graham Sumner and his Social Darwinist work, *What Social Classes Owe to Each Other.* Such a view seems exaggerated, as does her portrayal of Sumner, who was not, as she characterizes him, an extreme advocate of *laissez-faire* (Davis 2008, 215). Notwithstanding the many differences between the ways in which different authors explain this quite concise cogitation by Stanton, the present author's opinion is that its very brevity alone is a justification for not seeing it as her finest achievement, whereas *The Woman's Bible* contains many grounds for considering it be a great work, which is part of the reason why so many people, dogmatic Christians and more pragmatic feminists alike, sought to have its magnificent analysis suppressed. Fortunately, today, readers are permitted to appraise the value of both works together.

It is clear from *"The Solitude of Self"* and from a number of other speeches and writings that Stanton is advocating self-sovereignty, for women as well as men, which she defines as follows:

> Nothing adds such dignity to character as the recognition of one's self-sovereignty; the right to an equal place everywhere conceded, a place earned by personal merit.
>
> STANTON [1892] 2001, 19

Unfortunately, however, some commentators have discussed Stanton's ideas in a way that distorts this concept, which clearly has application to all aspects of society and is committed to equality for women in every one of them. For example, Davis writes:

> One of her goals [Stanton's] for women was what she called "self-sovereignty," or control of their own sexual lives. Women – not their husbands should have the power to determine how often they would engage in sex. Or, as she explained, "the mother of mankind" should have the prerogative to "set the bounds to his indulgence."
>
> DAVIS 2008, 170

There seems to be no textual basis for limiting Stanton's concept of self-sovereignty to matters of sex and marriage, and to do so is to ignore the nineteenth-century author's own demarcation. Davis' citation is to a letter that Stanton wrote to Susan B. Anthony on March 1, 1853, and it concerns some of the problems encountered by women in unhappy marriages, but it does not anywhere employ the word "self-sufficiency" (Stanton [1853] 1992, 55–56).

In similar fashion, DuBois redefines what Stanton means by self-sovereignty:

> In [Victoria C.] Woodhull's writings and speeches, "self-sovereignty" remained relatively abstract, but in Stanton's accomplished hands it turned into a much more concrete program for women's sexual rights. In addition to her advocacy of divorce law liberalization, Stanton came to imagine that women might have rights with respect to their maternity. To describe such rights – which in the 1870s had no name but which would later be called "birth control" and, even later, "reproductive rights" Stanton used the term "self sovereignty."
>
> DuBois 1987, 856–857

Meanwhile, Thomas writes:

> The "sovereign right to her own person," as Stanton articulated it, was a wife's cognizable right to counter the husband's common law conjugal right. It was a right of sexual refusal and abstinence.
>
> THOMAS 2016, 159

Unfortunately, Thomas gives no citations for this interpretation or its rephrasing.

Obviously, Stanton's own understanding of the concept as "the right to an equal place everywhere conceded" entails the liberty of women to determine how many children to have, when to have sex, whether or not to remain married, whether or not to marry, and many other aspects implied by Davis and DuBois. Stanton was seriously concerned about these aspects and expressed them frequently and articulately. But her classification did not indicate just reproductive freedom: she meant that she wanted women to exercise every right that existed and was available to men. She stated in her 1854 address to the New York state legislature that "the rights of every human being are the same and identical" (quoted by Gornick 2005, 52). As Ginzberg (2009, 12) points out when she describes Stanton's definition, she "believed devoutly in the power of the individual to make, remake, and save herself." What scholarly point is served by limiting the application of this useful term to relationships?

In fact, at times, Elizabeth Cady Stanton applied her commitment to equal rights for all to poor people, including the impoverished in Ireland, whom she encountered when she visited there:

> Is it right that millions should suffer with hunger while the few feast to satiety, that the multitudes should be left in ignorance while the few by superior intelligence outwit and oppress them, that the many should be clothed in rags, while the few shine in the garments the poor have woven, in the jewels they have dug from mines of wealth?
>
> STANTON [1868] 1975, 261

Like many others of her time, she was committed to addressing the social question, the deplorable conditions under which the vast majority of the population was obliged to eke out an existence. The elimination of this reality from the concerns of the political system, sanctioned by religious authorities, actually served the interests of a small minority while children starved. But this was not a natural condition; Stanton argued that it would be possible to eliminate poverty from a just society. At present, the elite profited from a society that history had made unnatural, as they owed the luxury they enjoyed to forefathers who had cheated everyone else, and today their descendants, who had inherited their wealth, employed the majority at wages that were unfair as well as inadequate. For that reason, she supported organized labor and others who sought to institute an eight-hour working day (DuBois 1975, 259; Stanton [1868] 1975, 263, 1872b, 4, 1889). She wrote:

> You who boast that in this land all men are free, look for a moment at the laborer's lot. He rises early to a scanty breakfast, with his wife and children

in poverty and rags, and with his dinner in hand goes forth to daily toil. He works till the twilight hour, when, worn and weary, to his prison home he comes to lose himself again in sleep; and thus he works and lives, living but to work, his higher nature, thought, hope, ambition, all chained to earth by the stern necessities of bodily want.

STANTON 1868b, 264

In Ireland, where she had felt obliged to hand out pennies to the destitute, she saw no difference in the cause of this suffering, and she wrote, "I rejected the idea that it [poverty] was a necessary link in human experience – that it always had been and always must be" (Stanton [1898] 1971, 104). However, she also qualified this by pointing to the oppression of the Irish people by the English, a variant on the theme of an elite that obtained its wealth unjustly, and which today uses the power of its wealth to inflict misery on the majority (105–106). She compared the condition of the people of Ireland to that of slaves in the American South:

When the masses in any country can neither read nor write, are taxed to support a government in which they have no voice, a church in which they have no faith, and are compelled for their daily bread to till the lands they can never own, it needs no argument to prove such people slaves.

STANTON 1868g, 137

Insincere in their commitment to devolve power to Ireland, the British elite had profited from the sexual scandal that had weakened the Irish leader Charles Stewart Parnell, allowing the independence issue to be delayed. Having committed adultery, Stanton believed, should not be a disqualification for a political leadership position; on this matter, she displayed the same tolerance that she had earlier applied to the activities of Victoria C. Woodhull, and she conferred it also on the Liberal Party Member of Parliament, Sir Charles Dilke, who also supported Home Rule for Ireland, and whose career was similarly damaged by allegations of sexual impropriety (Holton 1994, 1126; Messer-Kruse 1998, 38; Stanton [1898] 1971, 422–423).

Indeed, Stanton could not see a significant difference between loving wedlock and an excerpt of the much criticized "free love" advocated and practiced by Woodhull, who, as discussed in Chapter Three, was eventually forced to deny she had ever favored it. If people consciously chose whatever relationship they happened to practice, whether or not it lay within the bounds of a marriage contract, then Stanton felt it was equally of worth. This was because:

It is indeed of the essence of freedom that it does not attempt to pre-
scribe what the result shall be, trusting to the laws of Nature and to the
enlightenment, good conscience, and culture, or good taste of the parties
to be affected by it.

STANTON [1870b] 1975, 266–267

In fact, Stanton's libertarian viewpoint was itself sometimes considered to be
one of free love, not only because of her tolerance of others' sexual arrangements, but because she embraced an agenda of marriage and divorce reform.
Her apparent radicalism in the 1860s and 1870s helped delay the merger of the
NWSA with its rival, the AWSA, until 1890 (Davis 2008, 165, 168; Gordon 1999,
39). It was with respect to this specific issue that Stanton expressed her admiration for Mary Wollstonecraft as follows:

If I mistake not, the true free lovers are among the most virtuous of wom-
en and men. The true nobility and virtue of Mary [Wollstonecraft] compelled her admission with the most aristocratic and most moral circles in
England despite her rejection and while she rejected all allegiance to the
marriage institution and lived or had lived openly as the mistress of the
man of her choice. Freedom is demanded at this day by the most enlightened and the most virtuous, and not by the vicious.

STANTON [1870b] 1975, 267

Indeed, as Thomas points out, Stanton was not converted to this position by
Woodhull's sudden splash onto the women's rights scene, but rather already
held a consistent set of views that conditioned her respect for the free love
stance:

Stanton shared many similar positions with the free lovers that preceded
her affiliation with and support of Victoria Woodhull. Like the free lovers,
Stanton early in her advocacy espoused the foundational premises of individual sovereignty, self-ownership, and the oppressive nature of marriage for women. She supported many of the same specific positions on
no-fault divorce, voluntary motherhood, marriage as a contract, and the
necessity of divorce so women could leave abusive marriages.

THOMAS 2016, 91

Among those campaigning for an eight-hour day were the Chicago anarchists,
some of whom would be executed as part of the Haymarket Tragedy. Many of
Stanton's more radical ideas were compatible with what people of the era who

considered themselves to be anarchists were saying. She had been persuaded by her cousin, Gerrit Smith, to be as radical as possible in order to attract more notice and perhaps obtain the vote for women through her own notoriety, which, with the advantage of hindsight may appear to have been Woodhull's tactic; in that respect, the Bloomer costume that was adopted by those around her gained public attention as it drew attention to the way that women's clothing made it difficult for them to work outside the home (Galpin 1935, 324; Stanton 1871, 5). Stanton's attempt to critique the Bible as a sexist document certainly struck many people of the time as being extreme. In London, she met Peter Kropotkin, who had been imprisoned for his beliefs, and together they discussed the plight of prisoners in Russia and their cruel treatment at the hands of the Tsar (Stanton [1898] 1971, 409). For Russians and Americans alike, she advocated a liberalization of conditions and a greater respect for human rights in the hope "that the ideas of virtue, religion, honor, justice, taught in the pulpit, school-house, at the fireside, will crystalize, in another generation, in the statutes and constitutions of the State" (Stanton 1872b, 3). In this manner she urged the creation of "a true republic" (3), one based on equality for all, in which all laws, state and federal, would be subject to approval by voters. Thus, like most anarchists, she supported a policy of land reform, although she felt that the wealthy landowners who constituted many members of Congress would be unlikely to pass legislation that would allow each family a piece of property on which they could build a home:

> But when the righteous indignation of the people shall at last scourge these money-changers all out of the capital, and exalt labor, honesty, and education in their place, then may we hope for legislation that will ensure to the poor man a spot on this green earth he may call his own.
> STANTON 1868f, 200

Just as Elizabeth Cady Stanton shared the concern of the Chicago anarchists Albert and Lucy Parsons about the numbers of hours the poor were forced to work, so she also had the same opinions as they did about criminal justice, believing, like many anarchists, that crime was social (Stanton [1868h] 1990, 240). Convinced that many crimes could be attributed to lack of resources and to frustration at the hands of the great wealth divide, she argued in favor of penal reform to make it possible for those imprisoned eventually to be reintegrated into society:

> It is these grave inequalities that rouse all evil passions, envy, jealousy, hatred and malice that culminate in lying, theft, arson, murder and war.

When we behold how many suffer that the few may shine, the instinct of every generous soul must rebel.

STANTON 1872a

She also criticized the way in which jails were set up, advocating that, instead of being incarcerated with little to do, in filthy conditions that caused depression, prisoners should be allowed to take classes, work outdoors, and grow fresh vegetables and fruit in adjacent gardens (Stanton 1868m, 40–41). She took particular exception to the imprisonment of those not yet convicted of a crime in New York's the Tombs prison and other insanitary facilities, drawing attention to the unfairness of bail requirements:

And here are men and women against whom no crime has been, or will be, proved. A rich man can get bail, if arrested for a crime, and go at large until the day of his trial, but not so with the poor man; he is seized, imprisoned, and his family left to the tender mercies of the world.

STANTON 1869e, 9

Such unfairness caused New Jersey in 2017 to abolish most bail, but in most locations even today, poor people accused and imprisoned while they wait for trial often plead guilty in order to be released. As far as capital punishment was concerned, she was vehemently opposed, viewing murderers as another group of sick individuals who, in the environment of a humane prison, might eventually be cured. Outrageous punishments had been instituted at the hands of men, but eventually, more reasonable opinions would prevail, she argued: "There will be no gallows, no dangerous nor needless cruelty in solitude when mothers awaken the land" (Stanton [1868h] 1990, 240; 1868m, 40 is similar; see also 1869b, 200).

As Banner (1980, 172–173) points out, members of Elizabeth Cady Stanton's family have said that once a range of infirmities started to undermine her ability to continue on meaningfully, she ended her life with a drug overdose, assisted in her suicide by a female doctor. With this final defiant act, she paid homage to many of the qualities that distinguish her still today as a first-rate intellectual and role model for women, and perhaps the most gifted feminist thinker the United States has produced so far. In her manner of dying, she demonstrated her disdain for her old enemy, religious teaching, at the same time emphasizing her own self-sovereignty, her love of liberty, and her commitment to the application of reason to the problems of human existence.

ILLUSTRATION 8   Margaret Sanger, by Underwood & Underwood

CHAPTER 8

Margaret Sanger: The Scientist of Human Salvation

Margaret "Maggie" Louisa Sanger née Higgins (1879–1966) was born poor in Corning, New York, the upstate factory town home of the Corning Glass Works, the sixth of eleven surviving children, to a Catholic mother, Anne Purcell Higgins, who would die of tuberculosis when she was 47, 48, or 50, according to different sources. Her father was Michael Hennessy Higgins, a long-haired, County Cork, Ireland-born freethinker who had emigrated to Canada as a child and later volunteered for the New York Cavalry during the Civil War, before eventually arriving in Corning where he worked for low pay as a graveyard stonemason; he died when he was 80. Sanger's experiences growing up provided an explanatory introduction to the social problems that would occupy her professional life as a nurse and then as an eminent and much excoriated advocate of family planning. Intending to study medicine at Cornell University, she spent two years at Claverack College and Hudson River Institute, a boarding school in the Catskills. Instead of going on to Cornell, she started working as a nurse at White Plains Hospital in New York (Baker 2011, 9–11, 22–23; Blustain 2012, 4; Chesler [1992] 2007, 22–25; Gray 1979, 13–14; Reed 2003, 11; Sanger [1926] 2003, 9–10, 1931, 4–5, 23, [1938] 1999, 11–13; Tipton 1997, 339).

Early in 1912, textile workers in Lawrence, Massachusetts, a city with many immigrants, went on strike to fight against a 3.5% wage cut, the consequence of the state legislature reducing working hours, and many radical organizers, including some associated with the Industrial Workers of the World (iww), also known as the Wobblies, including Carlo Tresca, Elizabeth Gurley Flynn, and William Dudley "Big Bill" Haywood, arrived in the city to assist the strikers in what has become known as the Bread and Roses Strike. One of the big events of the dispute, which had propaganda value for the activists, was the relocation of many of the children of the textile workers, a move initially resisted by the employers and the police, who made arrests and attacked some of the parents with clubs at the station from which they were departing for Grand Central Station in New York. Haywood, who knew Sanger, had invited her, as a nurse, to come and assist the effort with the children, which she did. Eventually the strikers succeeded in avoiding the pay cuts, and the strategy of removing the children influenced opinion, contributing to the pressure that led to passage of federal child labor legislation in 1916 and 1918. Data from the medical examinations of the children that Sanger performed provided more information to her about the miserable conditions under which many people lived. Not only did some of the children suffer from contagious diseases, but all were undernourished, and most lacked enough clothing to keep warm (Baker 2011, 58–59; Baskin 1976, ii–iv; Capello 2014; Deland 1912; Gray 1979, 49–52; Reed 2003, 26–27; Robbins 2012, 96–97, 98; Sanger 1931, 78–79). Some, Sanger ([1938] 1999, 82) discovered, "had never seen a toothbrush."

Events in Lawrence received widespread media attention, much of it sympathetic to the workers, and eventually the public concern sparked a US House Rules Committee investigation, at which Margaret Sanger gave testimony, where she stated that both the parents and the offspring of the strikers had revealed that the children, approximately two hundred of whom had been moved temporarily to New York City, typically in Lawrence only ate meat once a week, saying that "the condition of those children was the most horrible that I have ever seen" (US House of Representatives 1912, 227). A committee member from Illinois, Republican US Rep. William Warfield Wilson, suggested a theory that he said he had heard from others, that the youngsters may have removed or else selected tattered clothing to wear in order to give the impression that their poverty was more adverse than it really was, an insinuation that Sanger calmly discouraged (Sanger [1938] 1999, 82–83; US House of Representatives 1912, 232–233).

Working as a nurse in Manhattan later the same year, Sanger became even more aware of the damage inflicted upon family life by poverty, encountering firsthand the consequences of botched abortions and widespread ignorance about contraception on New York's Lower East Side. She wrote:

> Pregnancy was a chronic condition among the women of this class. Suggestions as to what to do for a girl who was 'in trouble' or a married woman who was 'caught' passed from mouth to mouth – herb teas, turpentine, steaming, rolling downstairs, inserting slippery elm, knitting needles, shoe-hooks.
>
> SANGER [1938] 1999, 88–89

As she cared for Sadie Sachs, a victim of her own attempt to end her unwanted pregnancy, Sanger witnessed a conversation between Sachs and her physician about the need to avoid becoming pregnant again, an eventuality that the doctor warned would lead to the patient's death. When Sachs responded that she did not know how she could manage this, he suggested that her husband, truck driver Jake Sachs, might sleep outside the home in order to avoid sexual contact. Later, Sanger would comment on the inadequacy of such strictures:

> Why continue to send home women to whom pregnancy is a grave danger with the futile advice: 'Now don't get this way again!' They are sent

back to husbands who have generations of passion and passion's claim to outlet. They are sent back without being given information as to how to prevent the dangerous pregnancy and are expected, presumably, to depend for their safety upon the husband's continence. The wife and husband are thrown together to bring about once more the same condition. Back comes the patient again in a few months to be aborted and told once more not to do it again.

SANGER 1920b, 200

The next time that Sanger visited the Sachs' tenement dwelling, three months later, Sadie was in a coma, and she soon died (Baker 2011, 49–50; Baskin 1976, v–vi; Gray 1979, 53–55; Sanger 1931, 51–54, [1938] 1999, 89–92). Later, in 1919, when she gave some lectures in Elizabeth City, North Carolina, advocating the use of birth control, she encountered considerable resistance to her ideas from female physicians who practiced there. One of them suggested a different solution for any woman who was unhappy about being repeatedly impregnated: she should leave her husband (Sanger 1919b, 8). Ellen Chesler, writing in her biography of Sanger, *Woman of Valor*, where she often portrays Margaret as being dishonest and disingenuous, suggests that the oft-told Sachs anecdote may not have been literally true:

Sadie Sachs may have existed in fact or may have emerged as an imaginative, dramatic composite of Margaret's experience, but the presence of maternal mortality and morbidity in the urban ghetto she confronted is indisputable.

CHESLER [1992] 2007, 63

Sadie Sachs – assuming she did exist – had appealed to Sanger to explain the mysteries of contraception to her, but, as Lehfeldt (1967, 253) points out, most people in the United States, including herself and other members of the medical profession were not well-informed, and it was only while she was in Europe the next year that she was able to fill the many gaps in her knowledge; meanwhile, distribution of printed materials explaining how contraceptives worked was generally illegal and viewed by the federal government as being a form of obscenity.

After she attacked the legal situation head-on by discussing contraception in her journal, *Woman Rebel*, she was charged with violating the anti-obscenity Comstock Act, and the Post Office barred distribution of that issue. Almost singlehandedly, Sanger had set up, run, written for, edited, promoted, and financed the *Woman Rebel* from her own home, the first, eight-page, publication appearing in March 1914, and including, on its third page, brief excerpts from prominent anarchists: Emma Goldman compared being married without having the ability to control pregnancy with slavery, and a piece by Voltairine de Cleyre praised the ability to strike, arguing that violence was implicit in various forms of direct action. Emma helped distribute some of the copies, and asked her to mail more to Minneapolis, Los Angeles, and Denver, so that she could distribute them at places she was planning to speak. For many women, including even Sanger's sisters, venting such topics, subjects then not often discussed in polite society, and more specifically, her agenda for addressing them, were thought to indicate mental illness. At this point in her life, she could not afford an attorney, and she decided to go to Europe for a while. Following the indictment, she took a train to Montréal, traveling on to England on an ocean liner, the R.M.S. *Virginian*, under the name Bertha Watson. Before she left, she produced a pamphlet called "Family Limitation," which provided the information that people like Sadie Sachs had wanted to know; a fellow-IWW member, Bill Shatoff, printed a hundred thousand copies for her. Although Margaret now left the country, her German-born Jewish architect first husband, William "Bill" Sanger, was then indicted by Anthony Comstock in a sting operation in which Bill gave a copy of the 16-page booklet, in fact the only copy that he would distribute, to an undercover operative, who turned out to be Charles J. Bamberger of the New York Society for the Suppression of Vice; eventually, Bill would refuse to pay a $150 fine and served thirty days in jail. Other radicals, including Goldman and Elizabeth Gurley Flynn, made sure that this publication was widely distributed. In England, Margaret arrived in Liverpool without documents to indicate her citizenship but was allowed to enter the country; she spent some of her time meeting with the Liverpool Fabians and later, in London, studying in the British Museum and meeting there with the pioneer sexologist and physician, Havelock Ellis, while also engaging in an affair with Spanish anarchist Lorenzo Portet, a colleague of Francisco Ferrer of the Modern School in Barcelona on whose philosophy the anarchist-run New York/Stelton, New Jersey Ferrer School was based; like Sanger, Portet suffered from tuberculosis, from which he would die in 1917. Margaret and Bill would divorce in 1921 (Avrich 1980, 85; Baskin 1976, i, viii, xi, xii; Baker 2011, 35, 80, 90–91, 126; Blustain 2012, 3; Buckman 1944, 421; Chesler [1992] 2007, 108–109; Cullen-DuPont 1999, 3; Goldman 1914a, 1914b; Gray 1979, 78, 87–94, 109; Jensen 1981, 549; Lerner 1971, 242–243; Reed 2003, 56, 69; Sanger 1931, 85–88, 96–102, [1938] 1999, 110–125, 176, 178, 258; [William] Sanger 1915; Stone 2017; Woloch 1996, 270).

This was a difficult time for her, because her daughter, Peggy, had contracted pneumonia and died in hospital in New York, and she took a long time to recover from that devastating blow. When she returned to the United States shortly before, sailing from Bordeaux, France, she turned down an offer from prominent attorney Clarence Darrow to represent her. Then, fortunately, the three charges against her, with which the prosecutor, H. Snowden Marshall, had not wished to proceed, partly on account of the effect that the death of Peggy had had on her mother, were dismissed with an *nolle prosequi* order being filed in the US District Court on February 18, 1916. Now she was free to push ahead with the establishment of her first clinic, one which would provide contraceptive advice for women. It opened in October 1916 in the Brownsville area of Brooklyn, a disadvantaged community of people of Jewish and Italian origin, and leaflets that were made to advertise its services were printed in Italian and Yiddish as well as English. Within a few days, the Brownsville clinic was raided by police and closed down, with Sanger and her sister, Ethel Byrne, and another person involved with its set-up, Fania Mindell, the New York theater set designer and active feminist, each receiving short jail sentences (Avrich 1980, 260; Baskin 1976, xiii, xiv–xv; Marshall 1916; Sanger 1931, 139–140, 153–160, [1938] 1999, 179–187, 215–217). However, the eventual decision in Margaret's case created a loophole when New York Court of Appeals Judge Frederick E. Crane determined, in *New York v. Sanger* (1918), that physicians were not covered by the state's ban on contraceptive distribution, and nor were pharmacists and others involved in filling a patient's prescription. This then allowed Sanger to open a new clinic under the titular leadership of Dr. Hannah Mayer Stone, although it did not prevent more attempts to close down her facilities on other pretexts. Later, in *United States v. One Package* (1936) (also known as *United States of America v. One Package of Japanese Pessaries*), which concerned approximately one hundred and twenty diaphragms that had been ordered by Dr. Stone that were seized by the US Customs Bureau, eventually the Second Circuit Court of Appeals, in an opinion by Judge Augustus Hand, ruled that information about birth control was not necessarily obscene (Buckman 1944, 421; Capo 2004, 30–31; Goldstein 1917, 8; Gray 1979, 357–366; Sanger 1918b, 3–4, 1931, 126–128, [1938] 1999, 220–223, 227, 292, [1960] 2003, 81–85; "The People of the State of New York, Respondent, vs. Margaret H. Sanger, Appellant" 1920, 3; "Tracing *One Package* – The Case that Legalized Birth Control" 2011).

In February 1917, the *Woman Rebel* was succeeded by *Birth Control Review*, a publication that Sanger ([1938] 1999, 252) hoped would be educational rather than polemical. As the years went by, she quickly moved in a less radical direction, to some extent for pragmatic reasons, to the extent that she stopped criticizing marriage as an institution, and focusing more explicitly on the potential benefits for society from making contraceptives and information about them be freely available. Allied with the medical community, she came to undermine the rationale for her original clinic by endorsing the requirement that contraceptives should be distributed only by physicians, which of course also fit nicely with the decision in *New York v. Sanger* (1918). Two years after *Birth Control Review* began, she was using it as a forum to argue against allowing just anyone to give advice about or dispense contraception. This, she stressed, was not because she believed it would be immoral to permit this, but rather she thought that, in order to try and guarantee that whatever information was provided was scientifically accurate, restricting the role to nurses, doctors, and midwives was advisable (Sanger 1919c, 8). Gradually, the intelligence of her arguments persuaded less radical women to move away from the formulations of religious leaders and see birth control as something that was in their interest and worthy of support (Baker 2011, 147; Hodgson and Watkins 1997, 475–476; Jensen 1981, 554; Johnson 1977, 64; Kett 1978, 645; Woloch 1996, 255).

Sanger did not restrict her advocacy of contraception to the United States, but was active in encouraging other nations she understood as having excessive birthrates, including Japan, China, India, and Russia, to implement family planning. In the case of Japan, she met the Baroness Ishimoto Shizue (whose name following remarriage would become Katō Shidzue) in 1920 when the latter was living in New York City and studying there with her first husband, Baron Ishimoto Keikichi. Although Katō, who in 1922 founded the Japanese Birth Control Study Society, which was based in Tokyo, and who would come to occupy a similar role promoting contraception in Japan to Sanger's in the United States and be referred to as "Japan's Margaret Sanger," it was only during her residency in New York that she had discovered what birth control was. She would share the experience that Sanger had in the United States, of opening clinics and having the government close them down; later, following her successful advocacy of giving women the vote, she would serve in both houses of Japan's Diet. In 1922, she translated Sanger's new book, *The Pivot of Civilization* into Japanese and arranged to have it published, and she invited Sanger to Japan. The latter was surprised to find out that Japan's authorities had blacklisted her from obtaining a visa due to her "dangerous thoughts," which its police were legally empowered to suppress; she was eventually admitted into the country following a tense period during which she languished on the racially segregated ship, the *Taiyo Maru*, in port while her entry was negotiated, with Sanger agreeing not to give public lectures about contraception. The copies of "Family Limitation" she had brought with her were seized by Customs, but the visa furor worked to her benefit because it meant that her visit received additional press attention (Bardsley 2008, 210; Blacker 2002; Frühstück 2003, 130; Gray 1979, 185–186; "News from Japan: A Letter from Baroness Ishimoto" 1923, 7; Pearce 2010; Sanger [1922a] 2003, 140–144, 1931, 238–246, [1938] 1999, 317–322, [1956] 2003, 263; Takeuchi-Demirci 2010, 257, 264; Tipton 1997, 339, 345–347).

Another of Margaret Sanger's achievements was her planning and organization of the World Population Conference that was held in Geneva in August 1927. Sanger worked on the conference with her long-time collaborator and correspondent, Edith How-Martyn, a British suffragette who had once been imprisoned for protesting in the House of Commons, and who later emigrated to Australia where she continued her campaign for women's rights. Great effort was expended in designating the gathering as an opportunity for scientific inquiry, rather than as an piece of political activism, and the use of "world population" in the event's title was designed to achieve that effect, as was Sanger's decision not to stir up resistance by personally addressing the conference. Crafting this different theme had the effect of emphasizing the fact that the globe's resources are limited, an additional issue clearly allied with her more typical arena of operation, the need for access to and knowledge about contraceptives. She had long argued that famines and hunger around the world were caused by overpopulation, whose effects had been exacerbated by the First World War. One of the outcomes of the conference was the realization that nations had optimal population levels that were significantly lower than the number of residents that they were able to support (Bashford 2007, 175–176, 179, 196; Guttmacher 1967, 252; Huxley 1928, 84; "Margaret Sanger and Edith How-Martyn: An Intimate Correspondence" 1993, Sanger 1920a, 3).

In 1921, Margaret Sanger founded the American Birth Control League (ABCL), which would eventually become the Planned Parenthood Federation of America (PPFA), adopting its new name in 1942. She was also involved in funding research into oral contraception in the early 1950s, getting the PPFA to give a grant of $2,100 to Gregory Goodwin Pincus, a Catholic doctor who was researching the possibility of creating such a pill along with obstetrician John Rock and biologist M. C. (Min Chueh) Chang. Sanger also persuaded Katharine McCormick, the wealthy philanthropist, to massively increase the financial support for the project (Baker 2011, 292–298; Cullen-DuPont 1999, 6; "Dr. Pincus, Developer of Birth-Control Pill, Dies" 1967; Eig 2014; Johnson 1977, 63; Lehfeldt 1967, 254; Sanger [1938] 1999, 300).

In poor health during her later years, Margaret Sanger, a tuberculosis victim for much of her life who also suffered from gallbladder disease, coronary artery disease, and other ailments, lived in Tucson, Arizona with her second husband, wealthy Cape Town, South Africa-born 3-in-One Oil entrepreneur J. Noah Slee, to whom she was married from 1922 until 1943, when Noah died (Sanger 1931, 296–297). In Tucson, the clean air was beneficial to Margaret's health, but, against the advice of her doctors, she continued to travel and promote the use of contraception around the world until she died in 1966. Today, from the perspective of political philosophy, considering her as a contributor to feminist and anarchist thought, her most significant works are *Women and the New Race* and *The Pivot of Civilization* (Sanger 1920b, 1922d); in the early 1920s, these works together sold more than half a million copies (Chesler [1992] 2007, 198). Her two autobiographies were *My Fight for Birth Control* and *Margaret Sanger: An Autobiography* (Sanger 1931, [1938] 1999); the latter was also published by Dover Publications as *The Autobiography of Margaret Sanger*.

1   Sanger's Anarchist Influences

During the time of Margaret Sanger's involvement with the Wobblies, both she and her first husband were members of the Socialist Party. However, she also interacted with anarchist thinkers whose ideas had found some respectability in the years running up to the United States' entry into the First World War. In particular, she was influenced by Emma Goldman, who was viewed with great reverence by many radicals in Greenwich Village and other liberal sections of New York City. Gray (1979, 40) remarks that, "Margaret undoubtedly received her first concrete ideas on the subject [birth control] from Emma." Paul Avrich, the great chronicler of the history of anarchism, notes that "Margaret Sanger and her architect husband William were then confirmed anarchists," and that Goldman was "her chief ideological mentor during this period" (Avrich 1980, 85). Sanger sent her three children to the anarchists' New York and later Stelton, New Jersey-based Ferrer School with which Goldman and her former lover, Alexander Berkman were involved; it relocated away from the city to Stelton as authorities led by J. Edgar Hoover cracked down on anarchists as part of their "Red Scare." Goldman and Sanger shared the view that every child should be wanted, demanding the liberation of women from the slavery of unwanted pregnancy. Like other radicals involved with the Ferrer School, they were both admirers of Henrik Ibsen, whose 1879 play, *A Doll's House*, which had been widely staged in the United States, asked serious questions about the institution of marriage and women's role within it. The selection of former Columbia University faculty member, Bayard Boyesen to be the school's director appears to have been influenced by the fact that his father was Hjalmar Hjorth Boyesen, a leading Ibsen scholar. Sanger also spoke and held meetings at the school, and when she was in Spain in 1915, she sent posters that once had hung in the first Ferrer School in Barcelona to her colleagues in Stelton (Avrich 1980, 76, 85, 141, 241; Baskin 1976, vi; Gray 1979, 40, 58; Takeuchi-Demirci 2010, 259).

Sanger and Goldman wanted to make contraception and other sexual matters part of the ongoing campaign to give women the vote. However, many more moderate feminist allies were reluctant to take that extra, even more controversial step (Hodgson and Watkins 1997, 474–475; Tobin-Schlesinger 1997, 67; Woloch 1996, 226). For Goldman (1916, 469), governments' ability to fight wars hinged upon having a working class that was unable to control pregnancy, and consequently a willing cadre of men from whom soldiers could be pressured to volunteer, hostilities being then "eulogized by political charlatans and upheld by public hysteria." In her journal, *Mother Earth*, she expressed some agreement with the well-known writings of Thomas "Robert" Malthus, which stressed the dangers of overpopulation, but Goldman explained the problem not in terms of the planet having limited resources, but rather in a more political sense that increasingly a small minority of rich people were monopolizing the reserves that were available (468). One of the most negative consequences of this was that the health and improvement of the human race was now compromised by "indiscriminate and incessant breeding on the part of the overworked and underfed masses" (469). Fortunately, Goldman argues, society has now reached a point at which women can finally dispute their status as compulsory breeders of soldiers for the war machine and advocate restricting birth to children who will survive, will be healthy, are wanted, and have been created by loving partners. In all cases, she suggests, women should rest their bodies for three to five years before having another child. Some men, she continues, have also become aware of the fact that they work too much, striving to feed a large family, and living lives that afford little opportunity to do anything more than work hard and sleep; meanwhile, the women in their lives are similarly exhausted as they struggle to take care of their many children. Thus the quest for legal contraception forms a part of a campaign for social change that will emancipate women from the rhetoric of preachers and others who attribute the desire to reduce the number of gestations to moral laxity, puffery that is widely and pompously expressed even as back street abortionists quietly and dangerously provide the only realistic solution to forced pregnancy (Goldman 1916).

For Margaret Sanger, as for Goldman, war and other forms of social problem, such as the lack of adequate housing and access to medical treatment, were interconnected with population control and the need for women to be able to determine how many children they would have. If there were less people in the world, she argued in an article in *Birth Control Review*, there would be less people living in overcrowded conditions, and this would mean less of them would be forced to emigrate to other countries, not because they wanted to, but because they were desperate to escape poverty. In turn, the reduction in the numbers of immigrants frantically seeking to survive would be of benefit to labor unions and their goal to improve the standard of living of their members. Similarly, the actions of desperate women unable to cope with another child, who resorted to abortion or infanticide, along with the deaths of children ill-cared for, would each be lessened if all women throughout the world had access to contraception (Sanger 1921a, 4).

Again, like Goldman, Sanger sees the second decade of the twentieth century as being the time when women can finally visualize themselves and their role in society in a different way, overcoming the arguments of political and religious leaders that had hitherto rationalized their subservience. Up until this point, most women had assumed, as most men did, that women were naturally weak, placid, and inferior. Even as they campaigned for equal property rights and the ability to vote, they were not asking for concessions that would revolutionize society, and their relationships to their husbands would remain substantially the same. Finally, there was much greater potential in the new "free motherhood" (Sanger 1921c, 7), the ability of women to say no to childbearing, and to contribute to a global movement for peace to an extent that diplomacy had failed to achieve, because by having fewer children, they could deprive the military of some of the soldiers that it needed to fight wars. Moreover, by changing the nature of their relationships, they could become completely different people, at long last able to achieve their true potential (Sanger 1920b, 1–2, 1921a, 4, 1921c, 7). Sanger saw this moment as signifying an important transformation of society in the direction of the improvement of human beings. As such, it would inevitably be resisted by conservative forces who always attempt to halt the progress of civilization. Typically, she argued, such critics would ignore the scientific value of contraceptives or of the positive changes that would be achieved by their widespread use, but would rather attack people who sought the improvement of humankind. Likely, they would engage in defamation of those who spoke in favor of women's rights:

> They realize that the splendid youthful vitality of this movement is a symbol of the growing power of science, human intelligence, enlightenment and liberty. Crush this, and the clock of human progress will be set back; human society will stagger through centuries of darkening obscurity into new dark ages, for upon the ruins of civilization, upon lies and deceit and ignorance these sinister influences flourish.
> SANGER 1922b, 241

Perceptively here, she saw the manner in which her own life work would be attacked by reactionary Catholic and born again Christian opponents up to the present day, those who would portray her as a sex addict, a racist, or a lunatic, and in the process tell lies about her motives and background. Yet the present situation was one of chaos, of chronic overpopulation, wherein women unthinkingly or reluctantly gave birth not only to their offspring, but to the expanded tenements and shantytowns, prison populations, and mental health problems that were caused by overcrowding and poverty (Sanger 1920b, 4). Meanwhile, lack of access to or knowledge about contraception endangered women's health and lives because many of them were forced to turn to illegal abortion as a remedy for unwanted pregnancy as they endured stress and embarrassment, and some mothers killed their children after they were born. By making abortion illegal and offering religion-based condemnations of the practice, society missed the fundamental point that abortion could never be ended without open access to contraception, a policy that, if implemented, would do much to reduce the numbers of terminations (Sanger 1918a, 3–4, 1920b, 26–27, 76–77, 121–122):

> This problem comes home with peculiar force to the people of America. Do we want the millions of abortions performed annually to be multiplied? Do we want the precious, tender qualities of womanhood, so much needed for our racial development, to perish in these sordid, abnormal experiences? Or, do we wish to permit woman to find her way to fundamental freedom through safe, unobjectionable, scientific means? We have our choice. Upon our answer to these questions depends in a tremendous degree the character and the capabilities of the future American race.
>
> SANGER 1920b, 29

Like Emma Goldman, Sanger argued that women should have absolute freedom to control whether or not to have children and, if they did give birth, restrict the number of children they had. Meanwhile, she argued that children had a right to be born to loving parents who wanted to be their parents and would take care of their health. Consequently, access to contraception was a right that every individual in the world, male and female, should possess; this implies that birth control should be available to the poor for free (Sanger 1922c, 12). Again like Emma, she advocated a rest period between pregnancies, saying that women needed two or three years' respite before going through the childbearing experience again (Sanger 1919a, 4, 1920b, 87).

Like Elizabeth Cady Stanton, the subject of the previous chapter, Sanger was a critic of excessive drinking and in particular of the effect that male drunkenness had on wives and female partners. Discussing prostitution in New York City, she pointed out also that this was a line of work that almost necessitated alcohol consumption to some degree in order to be able to deal with the men and the situations that practitioners would encounter. Even though most women, including most prostitutes, are moderate drinkers, she points out that drinking affects the way that females in general behave when they are with men, changing their characters, making them more open to engagement in sexual activity and less able to think rationally at the same time, but paradoxically perhaps undermining their enjoyment of what transpires (Sanger 1914, 44). On the other hand, one of her achievements, radical for its day, but accepted by many today, was her desire to distinguish between sex designed to produce children and that engaged in solely for pleasure. Recognizing that among her friends and acquaintances, many had already mentally performed the decoupling, she sought in the new society she wanted to create an acceptance of sexual activity for its own sake, for fun. This, of course, brought her into even more conflict with the teachings of the Catholic Church and other conservative religious thinkers who had long maintained, and often still do, that intercourse is only allowable as an attempt to become pregnant (Blustain 2012, 4). For example, in recent times, when he was Texas solicitor general, Republican US Sen. Ted Cruz actively opposed allowing the sale of sex toys in Texas on the grounds that their purpose was enjoyment rather than to try to have a baby (Corn 2016). Woloch (1996, 272) notes that, as contraception gradually became more socially acceptable in the United States, Sanger's separation of sexuality from the need to procreate became increasingly tenable, because the dangers of unprotected intercourse, including accidental pregnancy and transmission of sexually transmitted diseases (STDs) were, at least for educated women, greatly reduced. Additionally, the feminist agenda to change the nature of marriage by increasing the power of wives was also emboldened. But Sanger also sought an emboldening of a different sort. She saw that an increase in the incidence of non-procreative sex and greater tolerance of this change could translate into an improvement in women's enjoyment of the practice. This she understood in terms of an increasing extension of women's rights, whereby most sexual activity would not take place so as to become pregnant, but it would also not be undertaken just to gratify the male partner. Rather, it should be a positive aspect of being a female (Sanger 1922d, 211–212):

> In increasing and differentiating her love demands, woman must elevate sex into another sphere, whereby it may subserve and enhance the possibility of individual and human expression. Man will gain in this no less than woman; for in the age-old enslavement of woman he has enslaved himself; and in the liberation of womankind, all of humanity will experience the joys of a new and fuller freedom.
>
> SANGER 1922d, 212

It was true, she argued, that many aspects of human existence, such as the sexual instinct, were influenced by Nature, but it was also the case that men and women possessed the capacity to change these influences, and convert or divert Nature to the benefit of humankind (Sanger 1922d, 226). For Sanger, the Catholic Church's separation of these two possible purposes of sexual activity, childbearing and gratification, had had a fundamentally negative effect upon society as a whole, causing conflict, and had been bound to fail, because the instinct toward sexual activity cannot possibly be controlled by doctrine but must, as it has always done, creep into many different aspects of human life, some of the incursions causing social problems and the spread of disease; to brainwash women into believing their natural impulses are disgusting and sinful is a form of oppression (Sanger 1922d, 204–205).

Like Goldman, she opposed the First World War, referring to it as "the fiendish internecine strife of the militarists in Europe" (Sanger 1917, 5). It was an issue that the anarchists found divisive, Peter Kropotkin, for example, being in favor of the conflict. In no uncertain terms, however, Margaret wrote as follows:

> I knew what I thought about the war; it was so outrageous I would not be mixed up in it. I still believe it was not only a dreadful thing in itself – a slaughter and a waste of human life – but, even more disastrous, it exterminated those who ought now to be ruling our national destinies according to the pre-War liberality of thought in which they had been reared.
>
> SANGER [1938] 1999, 253

In the early years of the century, for example, Goldman's ideas had become fashionable but, by the time of the First World War, she was a major target for deportation because of them, although admittedly, for some members of the federal government, including J. Edward Hoover, the desire to rid the country of Goldman went back at least to 1908 when the citizenship of her ex-husband, Jacob Kersner, had been revoked as a cynical precursor to making Emma herself deportable (Drinnon 1961, 113–118). Eventually, however, Sanger too would come to distance herself from Emma, notwithstanding the many influences that are so apparent. She wrote, surely somewhat disingenuously:

> She was never happy until people had arrived [intellectually] at her own doorstep and accepted the dogma she had woven for herself.... Though I disliked both her ideas and her methods I admired her; she was really like a spring house-cleaning to the sloppy thinking of the average American.
>
> SANGER [1938] 1999, 72

Chesler ([1992] 2007, 58) confirms this perspective when she writes of "Emma Goldman, whose brash manners Margaret never forgave, even as she absorbed her forceful doctrines of radicalism and feminism." Later, Chesler writes:

> Margaret continued to popularize Emma's claim for the revolutionary potential of women's control over their own bodies but never admitted any debt to her. She would deliberately disparage Goldman in her own memoirs and lie outright about their association in a 1935 letter to a new supporter of birth control.
>
> CHESLER [1992] 2007, 87

As Margaret Sanger's arguments in favor of birth control came to be viewed more favorably by different segments of society, their association with causes advanced by socialists, anarchists, and the IWW became unnecessary, and actually threatened their increased acceptance due to the growing unpopularity of many radical groups following the First World War, with the perception that there was a "Red Menace" abroad, along with the activities of those in the US government who were manipulating the development of that dislike. Furthermore, it became apparent to Sanger that she had many mainstream supporters, including others in the medical profession, and also, problematically, because she agreed with them about some issues but not others, the eugenics movement. While she encountered difficulties in forming alliances with some leaders of the women's rights movement, she found many eugenicists wanted to be her collaborator (Hodgson and Watkins 1997, 473). In an article about Sanger, Joan M. Jensen (1981, 549) notes that by 1920, when a tenth edition of *Family Limitation* appeared, the new version of the pamphlet lacked some of its stridency in the light of the nation's apparent move away from tolerance of the left. She was at her most radical during the second decade of the twentieth century, and from the viewpoint of the present author, at her best during this time, when she most openly advocated opposition to war, religion, and custom, while advancing the cause of some of those most oppressed by tradition: women and the poor.

In the case of anarchism, even though she had moved toward the mainstream, she retained her appreciation for the significance of its perspectives, many of her own activities remaining compatible with its philosophy. In *Margaret Sanger: An Autobiography*, she wrote:

> You could either belong to a group that believed civilization was to be saved by the vote and by protective legislation, or go further to the left

and believe with the anarchists in the integrity of the individual, and that it was possible to develop human character to the point where laws and police were unnecessary.

SANGER [1938] 1999, 69

She maintained an encouraging perspective about Alexander Berkman, who had been released in 1906 from a workhouse stay that followed thirteen years' imprisonment in the Western Penitentiary of Pennsylvania for attempting to kill industrialist Henry Clay Frick. She had spent hours chatting with Berkman about politics, often in Russian restaurants in Manhattan, and he had been a visitor to her home. Later, he was deported with Emma Goldman as part of the Red Scare. She recalled him endearingly, with a similar appreciation of his creed (Gray 1979, 39):

His emergence had stirred anarchism up again, and particularly its credo of pure individualism – to stand on your own and be yourself, never to have one person dictate to another, even parent to child.

SANGER [1938] 1999, 72

2   Not A Marxist

In the case of Marxism, Sanger made her rejection of its doctrines clear, even explaining away her early Socialist Party membership, during which she had opened letters to writer Upton Sinclair and others with the salutation, "Dear Comrade":

My own personal feelings drew me towards the individualist, anarchist philosophy, and I read Kropotkin, Bakunin, and Fourier, but it seemed to me necessary to approach the ideal by way of Socialism; as long as the earning of food, clothing, and shelter was on a competitive basis, man could never develop any true independence.

SANGER [1938] 1999, 75

Of course, the half of the sentence above that follows the semicolon is not only Sanger's rationalization for joining the Socialists, but it is also Peter Kropotkin's argument for providing for everybody's basic needs. In her first autobiography, *My Fight for Birth Control*, she described the ideological atmosphere in New York in the first years of the twentieth century as follows:

> Almost without realizing it, you became a comrade or fellow worker, like
> the primitive Christian, a member of a secret order. The martyr, it has
> been well said, creates the faith. Well, there were martyrs aplenty in those
> days – men and women who had served sentences in prison for their be-
> liefs and who were honored accordingly. One had hardly any social stand-
> ing at all in radical circles unless one had worked for wages, or brushed
> up against the police, or had served at least a few days in jail.
>
> SANGER 1931, 77

Rejecting the economic determinism assumed by many Marxists, Sanger
pointed out in her book, *The Pivot of Civilization*, that earlier thinkers had failed
to account for the role of sexuality, an instinctual capacity, in shaping social
norms and institutions, and thus in acting as an oppressor of men and women
alike. While making it clear that, like her Marxist allies, she was in favor of improving the condition of ordinary workers, she denied that their exploitation
by capitalists could alone account for the extensive misery present in the world
(Sanger 1922d, 1, 7). In fact, she continued, the need for access to birth control
was the most important factor with the potential to improve the human condition. Yet, embarrassment about discussing sexual matters, and in particular,
about the instinct that propelled individuals toward sexual activity, caused
policymakers to steer around the edges, focusing on the effects of the problem
such as the increase in the population or of immigrants or of the poverty rate,
but without addressing their biological cause (Sanger 1922d, 126–127):

> Political palliatives will be mocked by actuality. Economic nostrums are
> blown willy-nilly in the unending battle of human instincts.
>
> SANGER 1922d, 127

The focus on economic factors had led many Marxists to believe that poor
workers might benefit from having larger families because the increasing diminution of their circumstances would cause them to realize a social revolution
was inevitable; thus they championed the opposite solution to what was
needed (Sanger 1922d, 9–10). She argued that even Marx himself, in his theories, which demonstrated a "superficial, emotional and religious character,"
and thus imposed a "deleterious effect upon the life of reason" (167), had not
overcome the intellectual assumptions of mainstream classical economics,
and had shared many of his followers' dislike of Malthus, whom he designated
a class enemy because he had advocated birth control. In *Capital*, Marx had
failed to explain how birth control might fit into a complete analysis of

capitalism, or why he thought its use was not a policy that should be promoted. Partly, this was because Marx's "historical" analysis of capitalism was not truly historical, but rather was a polemic that created only the imaginary proletariat of his dreams, the reality being that the working class was "an inert, docile, irresponsible and submissive class, progressively incapable of effective and aggressive organization" (138). For Sanger, this error was a failure to account adequately for human nature and its biological influences, although many Marxists might protest that there is no such thing as human nature (Sanger 1922d, 103, 138, 147–148). Ironically, she claimed, by locating the blame for the deplorable condition of the working class on the rich capitalists, Marx had absolved poor people from accountability for their problems, as using contraception and having less children would have been of considerable benefit to them (Sanger 1922d, 153–154). But at least, unlike the various pillars of contemporary society, including the mainstream media, religious organizations, and the education system, and notwithstanding the fact that Marxist analysis and its revolutionary emotionalism were lacking, at least its advocates knew which side they were on, poor people, which was correct (Sanger 1922d, 11, 167–168).

3   Not a Racist

The use of birth control to reduce the number of pregnancies among the poor was a policy advocated by Margaret Sanger, a commitment shared by many in the eugenics movement who wanted to "improve" the human race by refining its gene pool. However, although they coincided on this agenda to some extent, and each party was glad to enjoy the support of the other, Sanger was not a eugenicist (or eugenist), and did not share their belief in racial superiority, though opponents of Sanger, of contraception, and of common sense have often attempted to claim that this was the case. In fact, she mocked the eugenicists' suggestion of "race suicide." What she wanted was for the underprivileged to have an improved standard of living in which any children who were born could be taken care of adequately and would have the opportunity to live an enjoyable life; she wanted to reduce the incidence of abortion and for women to be able to control their bodies so that they could have equal rights and live comparable lives to those of men. These were the reasons why she was such a strong advocate of contraception (Hodgson and Watkins 1997, 477–478). In a speech written to address a eugenics conference, she cautioned:

> They [eugenicists] affirm that heredity is everything and environment
> nothing, yet forget that it is precisely those who are most universally
> subject to bad environment who procreate most copiously, most reck-
> lessly, and most disastrously.
>
> SANGER [1921b] 2003, 155

As Valenza (1985, 44) points out, the significant successes of the eugenics
movement can be seen in the numbers of states which passed compulsory
sterilization laws affecting the mentally challenged, while its proponents
were actually in two minds about the desirability of contraception, because
they wanted the more ethnically pure to have as many children as possible,
replacing the potential progeny of those whom they considered inferior. In
Women and the New Race, Sanger made the separation between their perspectives clear. In response to the eugenists' claim that affluent, sophisticated
women would be best able to have children, Sanger wrote that having a larger
family would lessen the wealth of such women, make them more agitated as
they lived their daily lives, and take time away from them, time that could be
used more creatively for other pursuits, but which must now be devoted to
childrearing. The physical toll exacted from giving birth more frequently
would undermine the acquisition of the very sophisticated talents believed
by the eugenists to distinguish affluent mothers. Accomplishing such a make-
over, she argued, would be immoral, a movement backwards toward a less
sophisticated era. Fortunately, she continued, well-to-do women, some of
whom had already experienced their own liberation from the oppression of
compulsory childbirth, would be unwilling to compromise their hard-won
success (Chesler [1992] 2007, 196; Sanger 1920b, 67–71, 1922d, 104, 140, 180; Valenza 1985, 45). Instead, women would seek to transform themselves in a
different direction:

> We expect her to demolish old systems of morals, a degenerate prudery,
> Dark-Age religious concepts, laws that enslave women by denying them
> the knowledge of their bodies, and information as to contraceptives.
> These must go to the scrapheap of vicious, cast-off things.
>
> SANGER 1920b, 70–71

In response to the desire of some eugenists to impose sterilization on career
criminals, Sanger ([1921b] 2003, 156, 1922d, 184–185) advised caution, stressing
the need for more scientific research to determine the causes of crime. Additionally, in *The Pivot of Civilization*, she asks why local offenders are viewed so
much more negatively than those who cause destruction on a much larger
scale while wearing a soldier's uniform:

Might not some with equal cogency proscribe army contractors and their accomplices, the newspaper patriots? The crimes of the prison population are petty offenses by comparison, and the significance we attach to them is a survival of other days. Felonies may be great events, locally, but they do not induce catastrophies [sic]. The proclivities of the warmakers are infinitely more dangerous than those of the aberrant beings whom from time to time the law may dub as criminal.

SANGER 1922d, 185

With respect to race, and Sanger's desire to give black women the ability to limit the number of pregnancies they had, there has been much misinformation printed, alleging that she wanted to reduce the number of African-Americans. This is not true. As Reed points out:

[W]riters Angela Davis and Dinesh D'Souza, among others, have spread the lie that Sanger was a racist and by implication that contraception and birth control lead to race suicide. This is an unfortunate insinuation, insulting to black women – and all women – who may not want more children than they can care for.

REED 2003, 223

Similarly, Baker writes:

By distorting Sanger's views, by attaching the label "racist" to her name, and by, in the most ridiculous, hateful version of her demonization picturing her as the woman who inspired Adolf Hitler, critics of reproductive rights seek to challenge not just legal abortion but access to contraception.

BAKER 2011, 3–4

Additionally, Katz comments:

The conflation of birth control with Nazi extermination policies is a strategy regularly employed by prominent right-wingers such as Pat Buchanan, the Rev. Pat Robertson, and other of the more extreme abortion foes, a group better known for their race-baiting than their concern for protecting the rights of minorities.

KATZ 1994, 43

Rather, in seeking to give women control over their biological functions, and increase their power over other aspects of their lives, Margaret Sanger was grounding a radical new system of morality, superior to the rantings of the eugenicists who wanted to intensify racial hierarchy, and to the goals of the men who had written the dogmas of Christianity, whose aspirations lay in continuing to enforce a gendered hierarchy.

4   Birth Control and a New Morality

Like Elizabeth Cady Stanton, Sanger was familiar with the ideas of John Stuart Mill and identified strongly with his perspective. Like Mill, she credits the development of improved technology with the potential to improve the quality of life. However, she also cautions that a better way to improve the economic status of workers would be to limit the number of people in the labor market, forcing businesses to pay higher wages and raise the standard of living (Sanger 1920b, 145). In expounding that view, she does not account for the role of demand in creating employment opportunities, assuming that the number of jobs is fixed, not realizing that having a greater number of consumers will add to demand and create additional work. Additionally, she approves of Mill's agreement with Malthus, that overpopulation is a cause of war, and that, in the more perfect society that she seeks, many marriages, along with the ensuing children, should perhaps best be avoided (Sanger 1920b, 159, [1938] 1999, 125).

Sanger was often unfairly criticized for her ideas and for the manner in which she lived her life. Even the name "birth control" was faulted as meaning something other than the use of contraception, the implication being that in using that term she was promoting sexual profligacy or, as noted above, wanted to kill African-American babies. That is not to say that she did not intend the term to indicate a radical societal transformation, including the emancipation of women, who by its successes were now freed to determine the extent to which they might engage in relationships or give birth. By being empowered to make such choices, she argued, women would improve their self-knowledge and personal development, which would indicate an improvement in the human race – that is, in the sense of its day to day existence, not of its genetic characteristics (Sanger 1922d, 12, 16–17, 24–25):

> The very idea of Birth Control resurrected the spirit of the witch-hunters of Salem. Could they have usurped the power, they would have burned us at the stake. Lacking that power, they used the weapon of suppression, and invoked medieval statutes to send us to jail.
>
> SANGER 1922d, 14

Sanger felt that the lack of sophistication applied to childbearing in the absence of access to contraceptives necessarily meant that there would be many more physically or mentally damaged individuals being born, and it was surely not beneficial to society as a whole to sit by while the defects they possessed were transmitted to succeeding generations. Similarly, the practice of many poor people, who decided to have several or even a dozen children, "the chance consequences of the blind play of uncontrolled instinct" (1922d, 53), mired them in hardship from which they could never expect to escape, contributing also to the weakness of the whole community. In addition, fear of becoming pregnant, with no realistic way to address that fear, could be physically damaging as well as mentally challenging. She agrees with William Graham Sumner that it is surprising that a government which interferes with individual freedom in so many other ways makes an exception when it comes to the ability of people to irresponsibly give birth when they have syphilis, or if they do not possess adequate resources with which to take care of the children. Like Sumner, she sees what passes for empathy in this regard, by allowing and forgiving those who engage in reckless breeding, as a species of sentimentality, or as Sumner and Sanger express it, "sentimentalism," which works to the detriment of society, one aspect of which is an unnecessarily high rate of infant mortality, and another being the legions of children who are raised inadequately by their irresponsible parents (Sanger 1919a, 4, 1922d, 25, 53, 97, 245–246, 273; Sumner 1914, 32). Statistics such as those obtained from the medical reports generated by military recruitment in the First World War demonstrate the overall weakness of the population at the time, over a million of its potential draftees being rejected for health reasons, while a quarter of those considered for service were found to be illiterate (Sanger 1922d, 55–56).

The widespread utilization of birth control would enhance the human race by extending the wise and considerate practice of "voluntary restriction" (Sanger 1922d, 73), lessening the numbers of children being born, which in turn would make more Americans come to appraise their offspring as a valuable commodity who should not be forced to work until they are fully grown, or be allowed to perish as a draftee in pursuit of some cynical political goal. This would exemplify a new approach to morality, one that prioritized the making of intelligent and responsible choices, rather than seeking to scare people with tales of the horrific consequences that might accrue to those engaging in sinfulness or acquiring disease, a morality that instead would center itself around the needs of women (Sanger 1920b, 167, 227, 1922d, 73, 74, 79, 97, 144, 207). Yet this sensible transformation is perforce resisted by those in government and by persons claiming religious authority, who disdain scientific knowledge and practices in favor of "the miseries, diseases, and social evils they perpetuate or intensify by enforcing the primitive taboos of aboriginal customs, traditions, and outworn laws" (Sanger 1922d, 144). Sanger's criticism is such a vital attack on the way that Christianity has operated for centuries, with its habit of threatening "sinners" with future or even actual punishments if they fail to comply with its doctrines, that it is unsurprising that the Catholic Church would come to see her as a major enemy. The Church's political influence soon became a vehicle for undermining her life's work:

> Priests denounced me in churches and warned those who came to hear me of hell fire and the Devil! Few politicians, though they have sworn to uphold the Constitution, dare jeopardize their future as office holders by incurring the displeasure of the clerical authorities who often control the vote of their adherents.
>
> SANGER 1931, 200

For Margaret, the Catholic Church was viewed with similar disdain, as a major opponent. Because of the denomination's great age, it had itself been able to draw many of the lines of demarcation that most occasioned and symbolized women's oppression. For example, she lambasted the Church for definitionally categorizing sex outside marriage as immorality, yet considering any abuse of women by their husbands, including the imposition of pregnancy upon them due to a reckless desire to instantly achieve orgasm, as being socially acceptable. Where, she asked, was the Church's concern for the unlucky children who would result from such imprudent conduct, many of whom were destined to spend their lives unwanted and unhappy? By opposing divorce, the male Catholic leaders had cemented women's role as the property of men, while resisting sex education was a way for them to obscure truthful scientific explanation that would aid emancipation (Sanger 1920b, 168–169). Today, such inhumane religious teachings were the whining voice of the past, desperately seeking to scupper "the rising flame of modern ideals, to reforge our chains when we have broken them, to arrest progress" (1920b, 188). Because of the dominance of such false notions, women had lived for centuries under the force of sexual repression, a permanent condition of ignorance and unhappiness, an unnatural state that retarded their development as human beings (1920b, 115–117). Thus, it would appear to be unsurprising that, in her profile of Margaret Sanger in the *New Yorker*, her contemporary, Helena Huntington Smith, was unable to comprehend anyone venturing beyond the dogmas of a religious upbringing, even if their father was an atheist:

[O]ne of her [Sanger's] parents was a Catholic. In view of her long and bitter duel with the Catholic Church over the alleged sinfulness of contraception, that circumstance is artistic, to say the least.

SMITH 1930

In an article first published in the *American Mercury* that was substantially reprinted in her *Birth Control Review*, Sanger emphasized the anthropological origins of the concept of morality. The more conservative and underdeveloped a society or tribe happened to be, the more it would stick to its own traditions and view whatever practices had developed as being morally correct while any attempt at innovation or movement toward a more scientific perspective would automatically be rejected; this was particularly the case in matters concerning sexuality (Sanger 1924a, 245):

In contrast with this tyranny of the primitive *mores* civilization has brought about the gradual extension of the sphere of individual liberty and of personal choice. It has substituted heterogeneity in behavior and thought for rigid and routine servility to custom.

SANGER 1924a, 245, 1924b, 232

This primitive resistance to common sense about sexual behavior masquerading as morality characterized the strategy of Anthony Comstock to silence progress, particularly his demonizing of the idea that sexual activity might be engaged in legitimately in any way except with the specific goal of achieving pregnancy. In the case of the Catholic priesthood, men obliged to engage in celibacy understandably embraced this code, believing that sex was sinful on the basis of hierarchical authority. The advocates of birth control, on the other hand, Sanger continued, seek only the ability of women to make their own decisions as a part of a more modern and extensive understanding of personal liberty and, unlike Comstock and the Catholic Church, have never imposed their perspective on anyone, but focused just on making possible a choice to limit childbirth, while allowing their opponents the freedom to disagree (1924a, 245–247).

Just as they are the ones who have the most to gain from the spread of birth control, women will benefit the most from the change in morality that she advocates. The older, religion-based codes, she observes, were scribed by men, and they reflected the perspectives of men; when women abided by their proscriptions, they lived their lives according to the needs and values of men. Today, presenting a characteristically anarchistic outlook, Sanger argues that, by subscribing to the new moral perspective, through "the exercise of self-guidance and intelligent self-direction" (1922d, 209) they can cast aside that domination. This is the revolutionary import promised by gaining access to contraception for, by saying no to randomly giving birth, women will greatly increase their power and thereby be able to change other aspects of society for the better (209–210). By removing women's ignorance about sexual matters, their new ability to participate equally in physical relations with their male partners will raise the quality of their lives as the current preoccupation with attaining gratification for the man is replaced by a mutually beneficial experience (Sanger 1920b, 110–111). While they have every right to subscribe to their own beliefs, Sanger (1922d, 196) stresses, the Catholic Church and other Christians of similar views should refrain from using the law to impose their anti-birth control agenda onto people who do not agree with their teachings. What is needed is a comprehensive program of education to empower women and men alike to break away from "the slavery of tradition," and see that they could be self-governing and live in a way that serves their own interests and those of the community as a whole (Sanger 1922d, 232). If successful, the new morality would also contribute to mental health, because the distinction between appropriate and inappropriate sexual activity, which is a conflict between instinctual desires and religious teachings, would disappear (238–239). Moreover, such a program would lessen the antagonism between the successful and the unsuccessful, the knowledgeable and the ignorant, and promote the spread of culture and science (266). More specifically, the development of individuality and self-realization among women has the potential to fundamentally change human beings, by bringing the intellectual power of all adults to bear on the problems that afflict everyone, including the rights of children to have a decent life. Humankind in general would benefit from the widespread implementation of birth control, which would reduce the pressures caused by overpopulation, including the excessive burdens imposed on the bodies of women by frequent pregnancy and on the criminal justice system caused by children who do not know how to behave because they have not been successfully raised (Sanger 1922d, 273, 1925, 164).

ILLUSTRATION 9   Mollie Steimer, unknown photographer
PHOTO, 1919. WIKIMEDIA COMMONS

CHAPTER 9

Forever an Anarchist: Mollie Steimer

Mollie Steimer (1897–1980) arrived in New York with her family of eight in 1913 at the age of fifteen and immediately started to work in a shirtwaist (a style of blouse or dress) factory. Her parents were poor, and Mollie had received little formal education. Dunaevtsy, her home, was a village in the Russian Empire that, in the decades before the Holocaust, had a majority Jewish population. Known also by its Yiddish name, Dinovitz, it is today located in Ukraine. She read the works of working class sympathizers such as August Bebel, the German social democrat author of *Woman and Socialism* (1879), who opposed the institution of marriage, and Sergei Stepniak (or Stepnyak-Kravchinsky), the Ukrainian revolutionary author of *Underground Russia* (Stepniak 1882), who, in St. Petersburg, assassinated the Russian police chief, General Nikolai Mezentsov. In *Underground Russia*, Stepniak describes leading anarchist Peter Kropotkin's account of his spectacular escape from Nicholas (Nikolaevsk) Military Hospital in St. Petersburg. Mollie also read the writings of explicitly anarchist thinkers, including Mikhail Bakunin, Emma Goldman, and Kropotkin, whose book, *The Conquest of Bread*, the title of which in Yiddish was *Broyt un Frayhayt*, was particularly influential. In the New York City area, where she at first lived with her parents in Elizabeth, New Jersey, she was soon involved with other young anarchists in the *Frayhayt* (Freedom) group which issued a Yiddish anarchist publication called *Der Shturm* (*The Storm*), which Steimer ([1930] 1983, 80) notes, rejected an article by fellow *Frayhayt* member Bernard Sernaker (another émigré anarchist from the Russia Empire, who worked at the Modern School in Stelton, New Jersey, and was eventually deported) about Kropotkin because, like Kropotkin himself, Sernaker supported the Allies against Germany in the First World War. *Der Shturm* was followed soon after by another paper, itself titled *Frayhayt* (Avrich 1988, 214; Crockett 2016; Marsh 1981, 32; Polenberg 1987, 18–22, 126; Stone 2004, 138–139). Steimer ([1930] 1983, 80) recalled that at the time, "All our members sincerely believed that the Revolution was around the corner."

1   Russia Attacked: Two Leaflets

In August 1918, Steimer's activities and those of four of her friends (Jacob "Jack" Abrams, Jacob Schwartz, Samuel Lipman, and Hyman Lachowsky, all radical

Jewish immigrants from the Russian Empire, and all anarchists but for Lipman, who was a socialist) soon became familiar to the majority of Americans when the newspapers of the time announced their arrest by two army sergeants working for military intelligence named Henry Barth and Thomas Jenkins. Schwartz had printed two different twelve inch by 4½ inch single-sided leaflets, one of them in English written by Lipman, and one in Yiddish written by Schwartz that criticized the deployment of marines by the United States to destabilize the newly-formed Soviet Union; the troops arrived in Vladivostok the same month. A dozen allies, including France, the United Kingdom, Canada, and Japan were also involved in the invasion. The Soviets had signed a peace treaty, the Treaty of Brest-Litovsk, with Germany, and President Woodrow Wilson was concerned that this would allow the Germans to strengthen their troops on their western front where Americans were among the opposing ranks. From a radical perspective, the deployment looked far more sinister. An editorial in the London, England-based anarchist periodical, *Freedom*, referred to the move as "making Russia safe for plutocracy" ("The Allies and Russia" 1918, 41). Another piece continued:

> This means that the British, French and American workers are going into Russia at the command of their Governments to refasten on the necks of the Russian workers those chains which they broke in the Revolution last year.
>
>   'To Get Rid of the Bolsheviks' 1918, 47

Mollie dropped some of the leaflets onto the street from the seventh floor restroom of the building in which she worked. She, along with Abrams and Schwartz and their wives, lived in an apartment at 5 E. 104th Street in Harlem, and their printing press, which was in the basement of another building, not far away on Madison Avenue, was immediately destroyed by authorities as though they had already been found guilty of the charges filed against them, and as though they possessed no First Amendment rights (Avrich 1988, 215–216; Belknap 1989, 249; Delaney and Rice, 1927, 98–99; Hagedorn 2007, 11; Isitt 2010, 1–4, 55–56; Levinson 2009, 48–49; Polenberg 1987, 23, 44, 122; Szajkowski 1971, 12; Stone 2004, 139, 205–206; "The Allies' Intervention Cant" 1919, 4–5).

Some of the defendants were beaten by police and all were held in the Tombs, the New York jail that was home to many other anarchists currently being viewed as enemies of the United States. Jacob Schwartz, who had a weak heart, died during the phase of jury selection, an event that Abrams, Emma Goldman ([1931] 1970, 666, 667), and others viewed as being the result of his violent mistreatment by the authorities, which Schwartz himself said included being beaten by blackjacks and a chair leg after the radicals refused to respond to questioning. His death occurred in Bellevue Hospital, and the cause of death was officially Spanish influenza, though he may also have had pneumonia (Avrich 1988, 216–217; Hagedorn 2007, 66–67; Healy 2013, 178–179; Polenberg 1987, 65, 88–91; Steimer [1930] 1983, 82; Szajkowski 1971, 10–11).

The two leaflets were not only written by different people, but they also addressed different audiences, and it was the one written in Yiddish that appeared to be the most problematic. In his monumental study of the trial, *Fighting Faiths: The Abrams Case, the Supreme Court, and Free Speech*, Richard Polenberg (1987) had the leaflet translated again, demonstrating that what it actually said was not nearly as damaging as had been believed (Belknap 1989, 250; Polenberg 1987, 49–55). The English language leaflet, titled "The Hypocrisy of the United States and her Allies," cast the new government of Russia as having created a "workers' republic," a characterization that would become ironic when the *Frayhayt* activists were eventually deported there and experienced the flaws and violent excesses of Lenin's dictatorship firsthand. Referring to President Woodrow Wilson as a "coward" and to his government as "the plutocratic gang in Washington," it identified capitalism as being the enemy of the people of the world, while enlightenment of the working class was the real enemy of those in power. The leaflet also made it clear, as Steimer would at the trial and Justice Oliver Wendell Holmes would in his well-known dissent during the US Supreme Court appeal, that the authors were not in any way siding with Germany, stressing that they also opposed the militarism of that nation's leaders – from their perspective, rather more sincerely than did the president. Dirck (2003, 108) argues that the *Frayhayt* group were not very efficient, for writing their arguments in Yiddish and throwing their propaganda out of a window were necessarily ineffective strategies. However, Jacob Schwarz's Yiddish version, which bore the title "Workers – Wake Up," was addressed more toward ordinary workers, and especially to the immigrants among them, people who may have invested in Liberty Bonds to help finance the war against Germany, but who now found themselves still supporting the government, although due to the secrecy of the deployment to Siberia, not knowing that they were enabling an attack on Russia. Its response to the situation was the characteristic anarchist remedy of a call for a general strike. Its tone was more hostile than that of the English flyer, referring to the leaders of the United States and the United Kingdom, the launchers of the deployments to Russia, as "His Majesty, Mr. Wilson, and the rest of the gang; dogs of all colors!" Here the issue of Americans and American residents being asked to finance the First World War effort struck a sour note once the new Russian government had become a target: "Workers in the ammunition factories, you are producing bullets, bayonets, cannon, to murder not only the Germans, but also your dearest, best, who are in Russia and are fighting for freedom." Both leaflets suggested vaguely a need to resist the new government policy, phraseology that might imply the use of violence, but the general strike was the only remedy specifically suggested by either of them. Steimer had been the group member who distributed most of the total of ten thousand leaflets (Avrich 1988, 215–216; Healy 2013, 3, 171–173, 198–199; Polenberg 1987, 49–55; Solomon 2010, 212; Stone 2004, 203, 205–206; Szajkowski 1971, 6–9).

In their October 1918 trial, which lasted for two weeks, the defendants were accused of having violated the recently passed Espionage Act of 1917, which outlawed the spread of false information about the United States' war with Germany and attempts to lessen enlistment in the military, a law which President Wilson had wanted to also include press censorship. The 1918 Amendments to the Espionage Act, which are often referred to as the Sedition Act of 1918, greatly increased the boundaries of speech that would be not be allowed during wartime, banning scornful and belittling criticism of the federal government and its war with Germany. Geoffrey Stone (2006, 35) argues that much of the president's motivation for these legal changes was designed to address perceptions among the public that the purpose of World War I was not to advance a legitimate interest, but rather to benefit war profiteers, and thus silencing critics became a desirable tactic. He notes that Wilson also set up the Committee on Public Information, the purpose of which was to create propaganda vilifying Germany and German culture. Truth would be stifled by limiting freedom of speech while the government's lies were freely propagated. Through the medium of their flyers, Steimer, Abrams, Lipman, and Lachowsky were found to have engaged in speech that brought the government into disrepute, a violation of the amended Espionage Act, and, even though they had been criticizing the deployment to Siberia, to have damaged the war effort against Germany. Steimer received a sentence of fifteen years' imprisonment, and the three men were given twenty years, which was the maximum penalty. Also indicted had been Gabriel Prober, a bookbinder friend who did not belong to *Frayhayt* and who was acquitted by the jury, and Hyman Rosansky, a hat maker who testified against the others and received only a three-year sentence ("Abrams, Jacob" 1991, 1–2; Avrich 1988, 216, 218; Delaney and Rice, 1927, 98–99; Goldman [1931b] 1970, 667; Hagedorn 2007, 68–69; "Net for Bolsheviki in East Side Raid" 1918, 414–415; Polenberg 1985, 405, 1987, 145–146).

The judge was an unlikely choice. US District Judge Henry DeLamar Clayton, Jr., a former congressman from Alabama, brought in to help lessen a backup in the court calendar, lacked the judicial experience to normally be put in charge of such an important First Amendment case, and he displayed what Belknap (1989, 249) describes as "a sometimes outrageous bias in favor of the prosecution." Polenberg's research has focused on other aspects that suggest the unsuitability of Clayton to be the trial's adjudicator. For instance, he explores Clayton's peculiar "Southern" sanctimoniously racist attitude toward black people as illustrated in the case of a defendant who appeared before him, Helen Johnson (or Helen Wilson), who had sold alcohol illegally. Explaining why he insisted on addressing Mrs. Johnson as "Helen," he commented at the trial:

> 'Down where I come from we do not call negroes "Mister" or "Mistress" – we call them by their first names,' he explained, 'not to belittle them' but because southerners understood blacks better than northerners.
>
> POLENBERG 1985, 400, 1987, 97

Notwithstanding the offensiveness of this paternalistic approach, Clayton boasted of his leniency in general toward African-American defendants (Delaney and Rice, 1927, 98; "Long Prison Terms for the Bolsheviki" 1918; Polenberg 1985, 399–400, 1987, 96–98).

Judge Clayton was also, Polenberg points out, an opponent of woman suffrage and favored the use of literacy tests to restrict the numbers of immigrant US citizens who could vote. He argued against naturalized citizens being allowed to criticize the United States, and the fact that his brother, Bertram Tracy Clayton, in honor of whom he wore a black armband, had been killed by a German bomb rendered him particularly hostile to Germans and their imagined sympathizers, another factor that may have influenced his ability to oversee the anarchists' trial. Certainly, as Polenberg has demonstrated, Clayton eschewed due process in a number of different ways, disparaging the accused and editorializing in a negative way throughout the trial, expressing his own nativist perspective and criticizing anarchism as a doctrine, all the time presenting the defendants as persons who were not Americans, as foreigners whom the law should treat differently. The judge argued with Mollie Steimer about the reasons why women married – it seems, to identify her views about women's rights as placing her as an outlier, beyond the limits of permissible political philosophy, as an advocate of sin and immorality – and he dismissed her characteristic disdain for people who enjoyed power. Steimer intelligently responded that women often marry to improve their financial circumstances and divorce because they do not really love their husbands; anyway, she also replied, Judge Clayton's questions were not pertinent to the subject matter of the case (Kennedy 1999, 81, 108; Hagedorn 2007, 67–68, 72; Healy 2013, 177; Polenberg 1985, 402, 404–406, 1987, 101, 130).

Avrich and Avrich (2012, 338) describe Steimer as having been "petite and apple-cheeked," yet "as energetic an activist as anyone in radical circles, possessing a ferocity that belied her delicate appearance." Healy (2013, 170) comments that she "did not exactly look like a dangerous anarchist. She was four foot nine, weighed ninety pounds, and had the round, soft features of a child." She understood the ways in which Judge Clayton had used her anarchism and feminism to craft an undignified and dangerous portrait of herself, but she also resisted the attempts of her supporters to try and apply the same approach in reverse. With respect to her defense attorney, Harry Weinberger, she rejected his personalization of her as "this little girl," a comparison made easier by her height and appearance, as a misguided or immature person entitled to forgiveness for an adolescent mistake. She refused even to answer his questions in court when he addressed her as "Mollie." Instead, as she explained in a letter to Agnes Smedley, a campaigner for Indian independence also arrested for violating the Espionage Act as well as for promoting contraception, who had shared a cell with her at the Tombs, Steimer wanted the case and its surrounding debate to address the important political and constitutional issues, to be confined to questions about the legitimacy of the deployment to Russia, the ways in which groups such as immigrants and anarchists enjoyed less validity in society and before the courts, and the limits to free speech (Hagedorn 2007, 12; Kennedy 1998, 121–124, 1999, xv, 35–38; MacKinnon and MacKinnon 1977, 531; Polenberg 1987, 127–128; Steimer N.d.; Stone 2004, 138). While her ideas had infuriated the trial judge and Tombs officials, Smedley praised her for standing up for some of the other prisoners:

> The girls in prison loved Mollie. She talked with them at great length, disagreeing with them and frankly criticising them if she thought best. At night she would talk gently to some girl who was trying to smother her sobs in the rough prison blankets.
>
> SMEDLEY 1977, 535

During the trial, Steimer tried to undo the damage that Clayton was doing to her reputation and to the reputation also of anarchism, which she went to pains to describe:

> By anarchism, I understand a new social order, where no group of people shall be governed by another group of people. Individual freedom shall prevail in the full sense of the word. Private ownership shall be abolished. Every person shall have an equal opportunity to develop himself well, both mentally and physically. We shall not have to struggle for our daily existence as we do now. No one shall live on the product of others.
>
> STEIMER, quoted by AVRICH 1988, 218; see also POLITICAL PRISONERS DEFENSE
> AND RELIEF 1919, 20

Weinberger focused on the constitutionality of the amended Espionage Act and the fact that the US was not at war with the Soviet Union. He argued that the deployment of troops there was illegal, with the consequence that the leaf-leteers had been performing a public service by drawing attention to the government's failings. He brought in expert witnesses who confirmed that the information about the deployment that was given on the flyers was true, which allowed him to make the argument that the defendants, who were "liberty-loving Russians" (Polenberg 1987, 134), were thus innocent of the charges in question. Under the older Sedition Act of 1798 (which had soon been repealed), truth would have been considered an adequate defense to such charges, and thus firm limits to the application of that legislation were established by the concept of "libel of the government." However, the fact that Weinberger's argument was not acceptable to the Court shows how much more extensive was the new law. At the trial, Weinberger contended that Russia was not an enemy of the US, but Judge Clayton responded that "the flowers that bloom in the spring, tra la, have nothing to do with the case" (Avrich 1988, 217; Goldman [1931b] 1970, 668). The choice of Weinberger to handle Steimer's case was inspired, because his prominence as a defender of anarchists and other radicals ensured that the media would pay attention to what was happening, even if the *New York Times* and other journalists of the era approved of Mollie's conviction; in its coverage, that newspaper, at times uncertain even about the participants' names, frequently described the anarchist defendants as being Bolsheviks ("Bolshevist Witness Curbed by Court" 1918; "Long Prison Terms for the Bolsheviki" 1918). After the trial, Weinberger was able to secure the release of the four on bail as they awaited his appeal of their convictions. Weinberger, an opponent of World War I and a supporter of Emma Goldman and Alexander Berkman's efforts to oppose the military draft, had represented them in an appeal of their conviction for obstructing the Selective Service Act of 1917, and it was Emma who suggested to Weinberger that he become involved in Mollie's case (Avrich 1988, 217–219; Hagedorn 2007, 11–12, 64–65, 370; Polenberg 1987, 76–79, 137, 163–164, 183; Szajkowski 1971, 10).

Weinberger appealed Judge Clayton's decision to the US Supreme Court. Two sympathetic organizations issued opinions in support of the defendants: "Is Opinion a Crime?", asked a publication of the League for the Amnesty of Political Prisoners, who included among their members M. Eleanor "Fitzi" Fitzgerald, an activist colleague of Goldman and Berkman, who had wanted to travel to Russia with them when they were deported; and "Sentenced to Twenty Years Prison," crafted by the Political Prisoners Defense and Relief Committee (1919), which contained *Frayhayt* supporters (Avrich 1988, 219).

Surprisingly in the light of other recent decisions, the Court revealed itself to be very divided. In the 7-2 decision in *Abrams v. United States* (1919), both sides accepted that Russia was not an enemy of the United States. However, for the majority, Justice John H. Clarke said that, because it had decided to interfere in the Russian Revolution, the US was by its action involving itself with the war against Germany. Consequently, undermining the operation against the communists in Russia would indirectly affect the war against Germany, so there was still a clear and present danger to the government, the criterion for not allowing speech, which Justice Oliver Wendell Holmes had adopted in *Schenck v. US* (1919). The defendants should have anticipated this, and should be assumed to have done so: they "must be held to have intended, and to be accountable for, the effects which their acts were likely to produce" (Clarke). Consequently, the convictions were upheld (Levinson 2009, 50; Rabban 1997, 345).

In dissent, Holmes (with Louis Brandeis concurring) for the first time argued that the need to protect the government against clear and present danger is more urgent during wartime. The dissent has prompted much discussion as to why Holmes switched sides at this point. Many commentators believe that it was because the First World War had ended when the decision was rendered. However, in his book, *The Legacy of Holmes and Brandeis*, Samuel J. Konefsky ([1956] 1974) argues that what Holmes started to do in this case was to look at freedom of speech from the perspective of the individual, rather than the state. Moreover, he had been discussing the decisions in recent freedom of speech cases with other eminent legal scholars such as Harvard law professor Zachariah Chafee, Jr. and Judge Learned Hand, responding to their criticisms in defense of liberty (Rabban 1997, 350, 353–354). Once the transformation is made, it becomes apparent, as Schauer (2005, 2164) notes, that "restrictions on speech are not, as Holmes noted in *Abrams*, "perfectly logical," but rather are, by and large, faintly ridiculous." Unsurprisingly, Holmes was then led to write:

> I believe the defendants had as much right to publish [these leaflets] as the Government has to publish the Constitution of the United States.

Additionally, Holmes argued that, even if his current interpretation of clear and present danger was incorrect, the offense that Steimer and her codefendants had committed was insignificant and ought only to be rewarded with a "nominal" punishment. Moreover, the ideology of the defendants, with which Holmes pointed out that he personally disagreed, should not have been a factor in the trial. All ideas, including "fighting faiths," he argued, should be rejected not by legislation, but by their own failure to convince in a market of possible positions, "by the free trade of ideas." Here, Holmes is close to classics in political theory such as John Milton's *Areopagitica* ([1644] 2011), in which he

asks, "[W]ho ever knew Truth put to the wors, in a free and open encounter?";
and J.S. Mill's argument in favor of a marketplace of ideas in *On Liberty* ([1859]
1956); as well as Justice William O. Douglas' later dissents in other US Supreme
Court First Amendment cases, including *Dennis v. United States* (1951), where
he wrote that "Communism has been so thoroughly exposed in this country
that it has been crippled as a political force. Free speech has destroyed it as an
effective political party" (Belknap 1989, 248; Delaney and Rice, 1927, 100). However, Holmes did not take his point about Judge Clayton's bias as far as Chafee
and explain it as a flaw that undermined the possibility of the legal process
being fair in its entirety:

> The author remains of the opinion that the judge during the trial, by
> bringing out the fact that the defendants were anarchists and by examin-
> ing them as to their anarchistic views, had created a prejudice against
> them which was not cured by his charge, and that taking the proceedings
> as a whole the jury certainly may have thought, and probably did think,
> that an intent to prevent intervention in Russia was a criminal intent un-
> der the indictments.
>
> CHAFEE 1921, 12

Chafee led a group of Harvard law professors that included Felix Frankfurter
which argued that the content of the leaflets was covered by the First Amendment's protection of speech. Citing the United Kingdom's tolerance of Kropotkin, who had been imprisoned in France and Russia for his beliefs, but allowed
to write and prosper in England despite his anarchist views – reprising an argument that had also been made by Harry Weinberger at the trial – ironically
Chafee did not mention that, notwithstanding the Bill of Rights, the anarchist
prince had no longer been allowed to enter the United States following the assassination of President William McKinley in 1901, allegedly by an anarchist,
Leon Czolgosz (Avrich 1988, 218–219; Hagedorn 2007, 67–68, 72, 74).

   Later, when Mollie was out on bail, she (though not the other three defendants) became active with a publication called the *Anarchist Soviet Bulletin*
(also sometimes translated as the *Soviet Anarchist Bulletin* and as the *Anarchist
Federated Commune Soviet*), in which the writer of an article titled "Anarchism
and Bolshevism" took pains to point out the difference between the two:

> [T]he fundamental difference between Anarchism and Bolshevism is
> nothing else but the difference between Centralization and Decentral-
> ization.
>
> *Anarchist Soviet Bulletin*, August 1919, quoted in POLENBERG 1987, 180

Steimer was soon arrested for being involved with publishing a pamphlet that called on people to "Arm Yourselves!" in response to what the leaflet described as police murders, and which was sent to local officials, including Sergeant James J. Gegan, the person in charge of the city's bomb squad who had directed a significant amount of surveillance activity at anyone considered radical or "Bolshevik." Mollie continued to engage in radical activities, being arrested eight times for various reasons; when incarcerated, she was sometimes placed away from other prisoners, and she used hunger strikes to pressure authorities to lessen the restrictions. Skeptically, a report in the *Evening World* noted that when Mollie made a court appearance, "[s]he looked as plump as an anarchist bomb" ("Mollie Steimer Gets Six Months in Workhouse" 1919, 18). When she was not in jail, she was constantly watched by the government. Polenberg (1987, 2) notes that Steimer's repeated imprisonment "only strengthened her belief in anarchism and her faith in its eventual triumph." Mollie's involvement with the *Anarchist Soviet Bulletin*, which J. Edgar Hoover and the General Intelligence Division (GID) of the Bureau of Investigation (BI), which would in 1935 be renamed the Federal Bureau of Investigation (FBI), had identified as a particularly dangerous publication, along with the fact that Mollie did not, despite the fifteen year sentence, appear repentant, caused Hoover to press for a deportation warrant for Steimer, as well as a charge of disorderly conduct for being involved with the paper, of which she was convicted and sentenced to six months' incarceration at the New York City Workhouse for Women on Blackwell's Island in the East River. The *Frayhayt* group had left copies of the *Anarchist Soviet Bulletin* in the New York Public Library hoping that people encountering it would read and distribute their perspective. While at the workhouse, locked in Cell 98, she clashed frequently with the superintendent, New York University law school graduate Mary M. Lilly, refusing to work, reading German anarchist Max Stirner's principal work, *The Ego and Its Own*, and loudly singing revolutionary songs (Avrich 1988, 219–220; Belknap 1989, 252; Goldman [1931b] 1970, 705; Hagedorn 2007, 370–371; Lowenthal 1950, 110–112; "Mollie Steimer is Held" 1919, 11; "Mollie Steimer Put in Jail as a Radical" 1919, 7; New York State Senate 1920, 911; Polenberg 1987, 165–166, 178–187, 291–300).

From the workhouse, following the Supreme Court decision upholding the convictions and sentences, she was moved in April 1920 to the Missouri State Penitentiary in Jefferson City, where Goldman had also been incarcerated, a typical destination for radical women convicted on federal charges. That was to be her home for a little more than a year. Abrams and Lipman saw deportation to Russia as their best option to escape their long-term imprisonment, but at first Steimer and Lachowsky resisted such a proposal. Mollie refused to sign any application that requested a pardon or to plead for deportation:

Since I am in the anarchist movement I constantly called upon the workers not to petition the Government officials. And if I were to do it now it would be indeed contrary to my convictions.

STEIMER 1920b, 310

She argued also that all human beings have a right to live wherever in the world they choose, but agreed not to seek to prevent Weinberger from acting on her behalf. As he pointed out at the time, the period after the end of the First World War did not signify an increased tolerance for those on the left who had criticized government:

Wilson and Gregory and Palmer are gone – but amnesty has not, and will not, come. Every country in the world has declared amnesty – except the United States. We are lagging behind kings and the despotisms of Europe. The spirit of Jefferson after the Alien and Sedition Laws, the magnanimity of Lincoln after the Civil War, are war casualties of the World War.

WEINBERGER 1921a, 40

Eventually, the sentences of all four were in fact commuted in return for deportation and the condition that they would never come back to the United States; it was agreed that they were to pay their own transportation costs, and the Political Prisoners Defense and Relief Committee provided the funds following a letter from Weinberger (1921b, 299) that was published in the *New Republic* asking readers to donate to that organization, noting that, having been imprisoned for the last two years, the deportees even lacked clothing; a later piece in the same magazine made a similar appeal ("The Week" 1921, 335). Weinberger had contacted the new Russian government, and it had informed him that it was willing to welcome the deportees (Avrich 1988, 220–221; Belknap 1989, 252; "Girl Won't Accept Deportation Offer" 1921, 10; Hagedorn 2007, 370–375, 433; "Mollie Steimer May be Freed to be Deported" 1920, 18; Polenberg 1987, 335–337; Stone 2004, 232–233; Szajkowski 1971, 25–26, 29).

2   Deported

On November 23, 1921, Steimer, Abrams, Lipman, and Lachowsky were handed copies of their conditional presidential pardons by immigration officials and then deported on the *S.S. Estonia* (sometimes written as *Esthonia*) to Russia via the port of Liepāja (also called Libau), in Western Latvia. Abrams' wife, Mary Abrams, went with them. Lipman would die a victim of Stalin, and Lachowsky would be killed in Minsk when the Germans invaded. Steimer and Jacob and

Mary Abrams would eventually settle in Mexico, having discovered that the Soviet Union, far from being a workers' paradise, was a ruthless dictatorship with the blood of many of its erstwhile supporters on its hands. Goldman, Berkman, and Kropotkin had quickly come to the same conclusion, and none of them were available to greet the *S.S. Estonia* passengers, Kropotkin having died, and Goldman and Berkman having departed the country determined to tell the rest of the world what was happening there; they were in Latvia at the same time as Steimer and the other new deportees, though the two groups did not meet (Avrich 1988, 222; "Conditional Pardons for Four Deportees" 1921, 17; "Deported Radicals Enter Soviet Russia" 1921, 1; Kohn 1994, 133–134; Levinson 2009, 54; Polenberg 1987, 341–345; Stone 2004, 233; Szajkowski 1971, 29). In a letter sent from Stockholm dated January 7, 1922, they reported the deaths of ten anarchists who had been executed the previous September, including two prominent activists, Fanny Baron and Lev Tchorny (also called Lev Turchaninoff) (Berkman and Goldman 1922, 4). Steimer would join them in this activity, the attempt to convince radicals in the West that the Soviet Union was not the utopia they often continued to believe that it was. She wrote:

> While the Communists are issuing long protests against the persecution of political prisoners (they mean only Communists) in 'capitalist' countries, they themselves are imposing savage sentences upon their opponents and are forcing many of our best comrades to die slowly in the jails and concentration camps, and hundreds of others to suffer the bitter pangs of hunger and the unbearable cold of northern Russia and Siberia.
>
> STEIMER 1925, 102; SZAJKOWSKI 1971, 31

Following the testimony of Berkman, Goldman, and Steimer, some groups began to listen. The Libertarian Group of Los Angeles, for instance created a pamphlet containing a letter that Mollie had sent from Russia, and printed ten thousand copies (Spivajc 1925, 8). While other leftist publications were excusing Lenin's crackdowns as a response to counterrevolutionary plots, *Freedom*, which kept in touch with Kropotkin when he was still alive, Goldman, and Berkman, pointed out that Lenin had at the Tenth Congress of the Russian Communist Party (held in Moscow from March 8–16, 1921) explained the motivation for crushing anarchism and other "expression of petty-bourgeois and anarchist wavering in practice," which might "actually weaken the consistency of the leading line of the Communist Party and help the class enemies of the proletarian revolution"; thus, he was entitled "to wage an unswerving and systematic struggle against these ideas" (Lenin [1921] 1965; see also Durham 1985, 206, 209; Rocker et al. 1924, 47; "The Persecutions in Russia" 1924, 39).

In Russia, where Samuel Lipman became reacquainted with his girlfriend, Ethel Bernstein, an earlier deportee on the *Buford*, Steimer soon became involved with Simon "Senya" (or Senia) Fleshin who would become her partner until he died, meeting him at the Museum of the Revolution in Petrograd. Like Mollie, he had emigrated to the United States from Ukraine, where he had been born in Kiev in 1894; in New York, he had worked for Goldman in the office of her publication, *Mother Earth*. Like Mollie also, he had viewed the Russian Revolution as a sign of progress and he had returned there voluntarily in 1917. In 1920, Mollie had written in a letter to her mother Fannie Steimer that "[a]t last our great hope, our beautiful ideal of international workers solidarity for the coming good of humanity, is coming true!" (Steimer 1920a; Szajkowski 1971, 16). Little more than a year later, she could tell firsthand that it was not true at all. When they met, Fleshin had already been imprisoned, and one of the groups that he worked for, the Nabat Confederation of Anarchist Organizations, which was created in Ukraine in 1918 by anarchists who had moved there to escape increasing Bolshevik hegemony in Russia, was closed down in 1920 as the communist government became stronger. By the end of 1922, having formed an organization to assist the anarchists who were locked up in Soviet jails, Mollie and Senya were arrested by the secret police, the Tcheka, for in this way loudly expressing their opinions and associating with other anarchists, and she again used her tactic of going on a hunger strike, which, along with support from visiting European labor union activists, who complained to Trotsky, soon led to their release, although they had in theory already been exiled for two years in Siberia as punishment. Visiting Moscow, one activist called Lucien Chevalier, the Secretary of the Unitarian Federation of Metal Workers of France, wrote to Trotsky, who had earlier refused to see him, pointing out in the letter, dated December 16, 1922, that Steimer had been imprisoned and removed from the United States, and had arrived in Russia with a positive attitude about that country:

> Her joy was great when she was told that she could see again the country where, thanks to the power of the proletariat, freedom had triumphed.
>
> CHEVALIER [1922] 1925, 103

Now, apparently, he noted Steimer was to be deported again. However, although Chevalier's irony was biting and such protests did have a temporary effect, Steimer and Fleshin were arrested again on July 9, 1923, and along with 39 other members of the Society to Help Anarchist Prisoners, charged with promoting anarchism, which was now a crime; they were given the option of being incarcerated for three years in a concentration camp in the Solovetsky Islands in Siberia, or of leaving the Soviet Union, Choosing the second option, they left by ship for Germany on September 27, where they met their correspondents, Goldman and Berkman in Berlin, from where Steimer continued her efforts on behalf of imprisoned anarchists in Russia. During their time in the alleged workers' paradise, she and Fleshin had been imprisoned, tortured, and watched carefully by the secret police (Avrich 1988, 222–223; Kohn 1994, 134; Marsh 1981, 38; Polenberg 1987, 353–357; Porter 2006, 64, fn 43; Rocker [1972] 1983, 23–24; "Soviet Deports Girl Anarchist" 1922, 1; Steimer 1925, 95; Stone 2004, 233; Szajkowski 1971, 31; Yelensky 1958, 31, fn 22). In a letter sent from Berlin in November 1923, Mollie emphasized the differences between anarchist theories and Bolshevism in practice as she had experienced it:

> Thousands of workers, students, men and women of high intellectual attainments, as well as undeveloped but intelligent peasants, are languishing today in Soviet prisons. The world is told they are counter-revolutionists and bandits. Though they are the most idealistic and revolutionary flower of Russia, they are charged with all sorts of false charges before the world, while their persecutors, the 'Communists' who exploit and terrorise the people, call themselves revolutionaries and the saviours of the oppressed.
>
> STEIMER 1924a, 2

She pointed out that anarchists and anyone else remotely critical of the regime were dispatched to jails and concentration camps by an administrative process, without there even being a trial:

> When I reached Russia at the end of 1921, I found that most of my Anarchist comrades were imprisoned, and those few who were out were so terrorised that they would not be together several at a time for fear that the Government will suspect them of having a meeting.
>
> STEIMER 1923, 58

Moreover, she argued in another piece, the myth of the Soviet Union as being a decent place to live was enforced not only by imprisonment, but by a state-wide system of censorship:

> No one can receive books, newspapers, or even a plain letter from his relatives without the control of the censor. This institution, which keeps the people in absolute ignorance of all news detrimental to the interests of the Bolsheviks, is now better organised and more strict than was the notorious 'Black Cabinet' under Tsar Nicholas II.
>
> STEIMER 1924b, 22

In Berlin, in 1929, Senya found work as a photographer in the studio of Sasha Stone, but the rise of Hitler and of unemployment there led to a decline in the portraiture business and Mollie attempted to obtain work as a nanny. At the time, Goldman responded that the couple should stay in Germany because they were likely better off there than they would be anywhere else, and they would lose money if they sold the photography business. In the period following the First World War, she noted, conditions in Germany had improved, and this would probably occur again (Goldman 1931a). Eventually, however, the absence of what Emma predicted might happen caused the couple to relocate to Paris in 1933, where, in turn, the German occupation led them to move to Mexico, where they remained for the rest of their lives. The couple continued to press the Russian government on behalf of imprisoned anarchists; for example, Mollie attempted to find out what had happened to Zenzl Mühsam, the partner of German anarchist Erich Mühsam, whom the Nazis had tortured to death at the Oranienburg concentration camp. Zenzl had traveled to the Soviet Union, where she hoped that she would be able to publish Erich's writings at the Maxim Gorki Institute. However, she was soon accused by authorities of being a Trotskyite, and in 1936 she "disappeared." She was incarcerated for many years, being allowed to return to what had become East Germany in 1955. In France in 1940, Mollie was also imprisoned, but managed to escape. It was only in Mexico, where they arrived at Veracruz on December 16, 1941 that she and Senya were able to become citizens; on arrival, they were met by Jacob Abrams, he and Mary having already moved to Mexico. Up to this point, Steimer and Fleshin had been traveling on Nansen passports, documents given by the League of Nations to some stateless persons such as themselves, former residents of a Russian Empire that no longer existed. For the next twenty years, Senya had a photography business in Mexico City, the couple retiring to Cuernavaca in 1963. Senya Fleshin died in Mexico City in 1981, a year after Mollie Steimer had succumbed following a heart attack in 1980 at her home in Cuernavaca, where she had been visited by other like-minded thinkers, including Clara Rothberg Larsen of the International Ladies' Garment Workers' Union (ILGWU), and by fellow-ILGWU leader, Rose Pesotta, the subject of the next chapter of the present work (Avrich 1988, 223–226; Goldman 1936; Polenberg 1987, 360–363; Steimer 1931a, 1931b, 1936a, 2, 1936b, 1936c, [1966] 1983, 67; Stone 2004, 233).

Mollie Steimer remained a committed anarchist throughout her adult life. In letters to Emma Goldman written in 1931, in which she encouraged Goldman to travel to Spain to participate in events there, she expressed the hope that increased popular interest in anarchism in that country would present an opportunity for the movement to lead a genuine revolutionary change in society:

> Spain is the only country where the Anarchists have organizations that
> count hundreds of thousands of members and are looked upon the peo-
> ple as *real fighting bodies* and not as dead corpses.
>
> STEIMER 1931C

Eagerly, she enthused about what was happening there as follows:

> But for this [to occur], the organization must now develope [sic] its ac-
> tivities as never before. They must open schools to teach its members not
> only the theory of Anarchism, but HOW TO WORK, TO ORGANIZE,
> TO CONTROL and REGULATE the means of life.
>
> STEIMER 1931b

The next year, when Goldman published her autobiography, *Living My Life*
(Goldman [1931b] 1970), Steimer lamented the fact that it was an autobiographical work, rather than a compendium of anarchist theories:

> Well, what I found is a most interesting document written by a great and
> splendid personality. A woman strong in mind and heart. A tremendous
> character and a passionate fighter for what she considers right. But I am
> sorry to note that there isn't even an explanation of the ideal to which the
> authores [sic] dedicated her life. Strange and disappointing to me.
>
> STEIMER 1932

For Steimer, anarchism always came first. At a time when she was briefly less
active, she apologized about her lack of involvement in a letter to Emmy Eckstein, who was the final partner of Alexander Berkman, and who would survive
him, discovering his body when he committed suicide in 1936 to escape constant pain (Wexler 1989, 193–194). Mollie wrote:

> I have a very guilty conscious [sic] indeed! For, although my thoughts – as
> well as my whole being – belong to the movement, yet I do very little for
> it of late, and this makes me very unhappy.
>
> STEIMER 1931d

Notwithstanding this ideological affiliation, though, the fact remains that Mollie Steimer was harshly treated for merely distributing political leaflets that
truthfully told citizens what their government was doing, which was invading
another nation with which the United States was not at war, an activity the
validity of which many Americans at the time as well as today would find

questionable. Because she was an anarchist, she was arrested, prosecuted, denied a fair trial by a biased judge, imprisoned, deported, and banned from ever returning to the United States. It is clear that she was denied her First Amendment right to voice her opinion, a protection that, if not aggressively enforced, renders it hardly realistic to claim that the country from which she was expelled is a democracy. In the same way, a nation that militarily attacks other countries with which it is not at war must always find its legitimacy and decency in question.

ILLUSTRATION 10   Rose Pesotta addresses the floor at the 1965 ILGWU convention. The *New York Times* published an obituary on December 8, 1965.

CHAPTER 10

Rose Pesotta, the Working Anarchist

Rose Pesotta (1896–1965) was born Rachelle (or Rakhel) Peisoty in the Jewish quarter of Derazhnya in the Ukraine, a technologically undeveloped area within the Russian Empire's Pale of Settlement, to which Russians referred to as Malo-Russya (Little Russia); her parents were Orthodox Jews who ran a grain store. Derazhnya, a market center for nearby farmers, had about 5,000 Jewish residents. The family identified as Ukrainians, speaking the language, and were familiar with Ukraine's history. Her mother, who became Masya Peisotaya, had married Rose's father, Isaack (or Izaak or Itsaak) Peisoty, when she was sixteen. Rose was one of eight children, and had three sisters, Esther, Marishka, and Hannah. When her sister Esther Peisotaya visited Odessa, she encountered electric lighting for the first time (Glass 2016, 221–222; Leeder 1993, 4, 5; Pesotta 1944, 9–11, 19, 31, 44). However, Pesotta (1958, 82) notes in the second of her two autobiographies, *Days of Our Lives* (1958), that "though we lived in a ghetto town, we had for the most part a happy childhood."

Residents of Derazhnya looked to the United States as a haven where they might achieve some success, escaping poverty and the ordinariness of their lives, if only they could scrape together enough money to buy a ticket for the ship across the Atlantic. Rose encountered a former resident, Israel Telpner, who had spent a few months working in New York and had returned with gold teeth, although she points out that not everyone who went there would succeed. On the other hand, many of the people in Derazhnya looked skeptically at their Russian rulers, and had no wish to provide soldiers to their government. During the rule of Emperor Nicholas (Nikolai) I (1825–1855), local Jewish boys had been kidnapped and trained for military service, returning to the Pale only when they were used up and no longer needed; Pesotta (1958, 12, 48) observes that many of these culturally alienated *Nikolaever soldaten* had trouble identifying their own families or even where they lived. Derazhnya was a spot on the exit route for many fugitives from the Russian Empire's authorities, a two-hour train ride to the Austrian border being a favored method of escape. Some wayfarers would stop in town for a while to try and earn some money before they continued the journey to safety (Pesotta 1958, 187).

Derazhnya lacked public schools, but there was a coeducational cheder, a religious elementary school, where Pesotta benefited from her interactions with teacher Rosalia Davidovna Tabachnik (Pesotta 1958, 104). But for Rose, already familiar with anarchist texts and demonstrating a feminist perceptiveness, the potential of Derazhnya was particularly limiting:

> [W]hen I become 17 I can see no future for myself except to marry some young man returned from his four years of military service and be a housewife. That is not enough .... In America things are different. A decent middle-class girl can work without disgrace.
>
> PESOTTA 1944, 12

Rose's younger sister, Marishka, overheard her parents say they were going to marry Rose to a specific soldier who had just returned from the army, whose family lived in a nearby street. It quickly became clear to her that her best chance to live the kind of life that she wanted lay in emigrating to the United States where paid work and greater independence would substantially expand her horizons (Kessler-Harris 1976, 7; Leeder 1993, 10–12; Pesotta 1958, 217–221):

> As the first star came into the sky, the answer that I sought flashed into my mind. My sister Esther! She had escaped the fate that now hung over me.
>
> PESOTTA 1958, 221

Esther Peisotaya had been the first member of the immediate family to follow the emigrant crowd; at Ellis Island, she encountered a quite common situation whereby her last name was casually changed, in her case to the Italian-sounding Pesotta, a fate that would also determine her sister's identity in the New World. Esther found a job at a factory manufacturing shirtwaists in New York, and in 1909–1910 was involved in the New York Shirtwaist Strike, also known as the Uprising of the 20,000, which was led by Ukrainian-born Clara Lemlich. Rose Peisotaya followed her sister to the United States in October and November 1913, a weeks-long journey accompanied by her father as far as the German border, traveling through Poland on the way, and then sailing second-class across the Atlantic from Antwerp, Belgium. Rose's mother was the daughter of her grandfather's first wife; his third wife, whom the family called Babushka, accompanied her, headed for Ohio, where her son had moved, but she stayed a few days with Rose and Esther in New York, where the traffic scared her, and she refused to ride in a train, which, Pesotta notes, was ironic because later Babushka would die after being knocked down on a Chicago street (Buhle 1988, 15; Leeder 1993, 13–14; Pesotta 1944, 12–13, 1958, 76, 246; Zimmer 2010, 114). Thus, Laslett (1993, 23) is not quite correct when he writes that Rose Pesotta "crossed the Atlantic alone at the age of seventeen." Naomi Shepherd (1993, 245) notes that Rose traveled "with her grandmother as chaperone (her parents feared the traffickers that waylaid single girls)," although, of course, Babushka had her own reasons for coming to the United States.

Rose found a job making blouses with another shirtwaist maker, Bloom and Millman on West Eighteenth Street, where another strike led to her involvement with Local 25 of the International Ladies' Garment Workers' Union (ILGWU), with her eventually becoming one of the union's national leaders (Buhle 1988, 15; Leeder 1993, 16). In 1920, her father was murdered by anti-Jewish opponents of the Bolsheviks affiliated with Symon Vasylyovych Petlura's army, who knocked on the door of his house, and when Isaack opened it, shot him down (Leeder 1993, 31; Pesotta 1944, 15). Petlura, who could not control the military who were conducting these pogroms, would later be assassinated in Paris by the Russian Jewish anarchist, Sholom Schwartzbard. Daniel Katz explains Isaack's murder incorrectly when he writes:

> Her [Pesotta's] distaste for communism was at least as personal as it was political because … Bolshevik sympathizers killed Pesotta's father in Russia.
>
> KATZ 2011, 89

Petlura's affiliates were not "Bolshevik sympathizers" – they would be much better described as fascists who hated the Bolsheviks: in *Bread Upon the Waters*, the first of her two autobiographies, Rose (1944, 15) records the event as follows, saying that "'General' Petlura's 'army' of hooligans, both anti-Bolshevik and anti-Semitic, sweeps into Derazhnia in the night like a swarm of rats." Furthermore, although this took place in the Russian Empire, it was in the Pale, in Ukraine, not really in Russia. Nonetheless, she was definitely not a supporter of communism.

By 1922, Pesotta was one of the successful applicants participating in the eight-week-long Summer School for Women Workers in Industry at Bryn Mawr College, taking a range of academic subjects, including labor history. Interviewed by the *New York Herald*, where she was described as "a Russian Jewess" who was a leader of the local dressmakers' union, Pesotta spoke of the value to society of factory work, while the story's author emphasized that some of the more radical graduates of the previous year's program had now improved their outlooks: "The radical ones toned down. They got to know something about the employer's side" (Coman 1922, 2; "School for Women Workers" 1922, 10). In *Bread Upon the Waters*, Pesotta described how the faculty and tutors – who, she notes, unlike some of her cohorts, had always been able to eat – and the students from the industrial class had benefited mutually from the interaction (Pesotta 1944, 16). For the next forty years, she would be involved in labor union politics while remaining an active anarchist who often came to the aid of those radicals who found themselves involved in the federal government's attempts to suppress their activity or deport them, her efforts often not being successful, or triumphing only after a large amount of time and effort. Bryn Mawr's Summer School, however, was a less long-lasting project. Notwithstanding the *Herald*'s attempt at a balanced portrayal of its philosophy and achievements, others at the college, including the trustees, were critical of sometimes violent union activity beyond the academic environment, and its eviction from campus in 1935 was soon followed by its demise in 1938 (Maguire 2009, 413). This was unfortunate, because, as Maria Tamboukou (2013, 524) argues, the Summer School phenomenon was "crucially important in opening up political spaces wherein human beings appeared to the world 'through words and deeds' and found freedom through making new beginnings." That was essentially also the model via which Pesotta plied her anarchism. Moreover, although Pesotta was already an ILGWU official when she spent a summer at Bryn Mawr, her responses in her interview answers with reporter Martha Coman displayed a preference for manual rather than organizational labor:

'I do not want to go out of the ranks of the people who produce,' Rose explained. 'It's just as fine to be a producer with your hands, actually to make things that the world uses and needs, as to be a doctor or a teacher.'
COMAN 1922, 2

In her biography of Pesotta, Elaine Leader interprets that attitude in a similar way:

Pesotta never had ambition to hold executive authority. In accord with anarchist ideology, she wanted to keep from becoming co-opted and from stepping far beyond the rank and file.
LEEDER 1993, 63

Rose Pesotta lived her life, therefore, as a working anarchist.

1   **Pesotta as an Anarchist Theorist**

One positive aspect of life in Derazhnya was that residents' skepticism concerning their Tsarist rulers allowed them to consider alternative ideas, and Pesotta's parents' house contained the writings of the anarchist Mikhail Bakunin, as well as those of another radical, the revolutionary socialist Alexander Herzen; as a teenager, she had already read these books. Near her new home in

Harlem, after she emigrated to New York, she continued her informal education at the local library, reading the great novelists who tried to address the
problems of the Russian Empire, many of whom were critical of Tsarism, and
some of whom, though desiring reform, would become critics of the Bolsheviks: she mentions Dostoevsky, Gogol, Gorky, Tolstoy, and Turgenev, as well as
Vladimir Andreyev, Mikhail Artsybashev, and Vladimir Korolenko (Buhle 1988,
15; Laslett 1993, 23; Leeder 1993, 8–9, 20, 22; Pesotta 1958, 247–248). Like Itō Noe,
Margaret Sanger, and Mollie Steimer, the subjects of prior chapters of the present volume, Pesotta was influenced by the leading anarchist, Emma Goldman.
In Rose's case, the interactions lasted for decades. However, the claim of Glass
(2016, 222) that "[a]fter hearing Emma Goldman speak at a meeting Pesotta
became an anarchist" seems unlikely, since she seems to have been an anarchist before she emigrated to the United States, as demonstrated not only by
what she had read, but also because she had been involved with radical groups
back in Derazhnya. Friends and acquaintances who had relocated to Western
Europe packaged the ideas of radicals and revolutionists and sent them to
what she calls her "democratic circle," at meetings of which Pesotta would read
out loud the dangerous ideas (Leeder 1989, 52, 1993, 10; Pesotta 1958, 218).

Rose Pesotta first encountered both Emma Goldman and the latter's former
lover and fellow-anarchist Alexander Berkman at a Madison Square Garden
meeting in Manhattan as, in May 1914, they rallied the audience to oppose the
institution of a military draft (Leeder 1993, 24; Pesotta 1944, 15). Pesotta had an
even more personal connection with anarchism and to the fate that awaited
Goldman and Berkman, deportation to Russia, because of her romantic relationship with a Russian sailor called Theodore Kushnarev, another anarchist
who would be joining them on the former army transport ship, the *Buford*,
which, on December 19, 1919, carried approximately 246 radicals (sources differ
slightly) to Finland, from where the journey continued to Russia by train. Like
Goldman and Berkman, Kushnarev was a prime target of Attorney General A.
Mitchell Palmer, J. Edgar Hoover, and the Bureau of Investigation (which later
would become the FBI) to be one of the passengers on that month-long "Red
Ark" voyage. It was at Ellis Island earlier that year, ironically not only the location where Rose had arrived as an immigrant to the United States, but also the
place where many of the anarchists were detained prior to being removed
from the country, that she first chatted with Goldman during her visit to see
her boyfriend. Eventually, Kushnarev would find a new partner in Russia, and
in 1925 he fell victim to typhoid (Cornell 2011, 197; Hassell 1991, 34–35; Leeder
1989, 53, 1993, iii, 25, 30, 108; Pesotta 1944, 15; Zimmer 2010, 350).

Rose would have a number of other relationships with men over the years, a
situation that Rasmussen describes in the following way:

After World War I, her anarchist boyfriend, an anti-war protester and draft resister, was among those deported to Russia in the 'Red Scare' of 1919. In the years that followed, Pesotta's affairs were many, reflecting her commitment to sexual freedom.

RASMUSSEN 2000

As suggested in Chapter Three, sexual freedom and free love are ambiguous phrases, and today, while Pesotta's relationship history seems anything but unusual, it does not necessarily display a commitment to free love. Leeder (1993, 126) comments that "Rose fell in love with married men a number of times throughout her life"; Kessler-Harris (1976, 22) says that "she sought solace in men"; and Orleck (2001, 242) notes that "Pesotta moved in and out of passionate and ultimately unsatisfying relations with radical men." One of them with whom she was very close was Harvard-educated anarchist supporter and union official Powers Hapgood, but, as Bussel (1999, 147) notes, unfortunately for Hapgood, who was quite open about the existence of the relationship, it was "a liaison that plunged both his marriage and his psyche into turmoil." In fact, Rose specifically repudiated the concept of free love when she discovered that Hapgood was not, after all, going to leave his wife, and she decided to stop sleeping with him (Bussel 1999, 148; Kessler-Harris 1976, 22; Phelan 2000, 1760; Shepherd 1993, 271–273).

Leeder (1989, 52) writes that "[o]ne of the most important people to influence Pesotta was Emma Goldman, who helped her reconcile the differences between the labor movement and the anarchist movement." During the last decade of Emma's life, when the friendship was at its strongest, Pesotta and Goldman's closeness would be reactivated in person on a number of occasions. They met in Montréal in 1934, when Emma was touring there. Then, at the end of 1937, Pesotta visited Europe, where she met Emma soon after arriving in France, at a Syndicalist conference held in Paris at the Maison de la Mutualité. She had been unable to join Goldman in Spain the previous year to become involved in the ongoing civil war there, which she had wanted to do, due to pressure from ILGWU president David Dubinsky. Now, in France, Emma, who had recently returned from viewing the conflict firsthand, was able to update her friend about the progress of the war (Leeder 1989, 54, 59; Pesotta 1944, 185; Zimmer 2010, 449–450). In January 1938, Pesotta continued on to London, where Goldman was now a resident, and, following her disingenuous marriage to James Colton, was able to live there permanently. Becoming well-acquainted for the first time, the friends spent a few days together, Pesotta finding it difficult to sleep or bathe due to the freezing temperatures in Emma's apartment, and they drank beer together at the Café Royal. They discovered that they shared an interest in preparing food for dinner guests though Rose noticed that Emma's unfortunate encounter soon after she was deported to the Soviet Union during its first years, witnessing the ongoing famine, had made her reluctant to throw away anything at all edible (Leeder 1989, 59, 1993, 37; Pesotta 1944, 188–190; Wexler 1989, 224).

In 1939, encouraged by Pesotta to move permanently to Canada (rather than to the United States, to which she would be unlikely to be allowed to return although, despite her deportation, she had previously received a visitor's visa one time, in 1934), Emma Goldman embarked on a lecture tour of cities in Canada to collect funds for Spanish civil war victims. Pesotta visited her twice that year in Toronto. When still in that city the next year, Goldman died, and her body, which was apparently viewed as less of a threat by authorities than it had been when she was alive, was returned to the US and interred at Chicago's Waldheim cemetery. Rose attended the funeral ceremony; while she was there, she put flowers on the grave of another female anarchist, Voltairine de Cleyre. A couple of weeks later, she spoke at a memorial at the Town Hall in New York City to commemorate Goldman and her achievements (Leeder 1989, 61, 62; Pesotta 1944, 190, fn 21; Wexler 1989, 241).

Pesotta's lifelong commitment to anarchism is particularly apparent from her work from time to time on behalf of assorted beleaguered anarchists, including Nicola Sacco and Bartolomeo Vanzetti, and Tom Mooney, and her feelings about an earlier group, the Haymarket Martyrs. Sacco and Vanzetti, both immigrants from Italy as well as anarchists themselves, were accused of committing the April 15, 1920 murders of Alessandro Berardelli and Frederick Parmenter, employees of a shoe factory called Slater and Morrill who had been transporting nearly $16,000 in payroll money on a street in South Braintree, Massachusetts. Their convictions and 1927 executions have long been controversial, not least because the judge, Webster Thayer, referred to the defendants as "those anarchistic bastards" (Avrich and Avrich 2012, 342), and many different arguments exist concerning their guilt or innocence, including an impassioned plea that was made at the time by future US Supreme Court justice Felix Frankfurter (1927) for a new trial. In 1922, Rose Pesotta met her future husband, the Spanish anarchist, Frank Lopez, also known as Albert Martin, who had been working to save Sacco and Vanzetti from execution, and she joined him in that effort.[1] In Boston, Pesotta led an eight-mile march in the rain to protest the execution. Along the way, the protesters were goaded by police

---

1   When Robinson (1991, 8) writes that "she never married," she appears to be relying on the situation as of the date 1944, when Rose's first autobiography, *Bread Upon the Waters*, appeared.

in an attempt to push them into breaking a law so that they could be arrested. One of Pesotta's favorite possessions became an ivory penholder that Vanzetti had carved for her while waiting in jail for his fate to be implemented (Leeder 1993, xiii–iv, 43, 138; Marks 1929, 59; Topp 2005, 1–4; Young and Kaiser 1985, 1–9, 23). Both of Pesotta's autobiographies were written with help from a journalist called John Nicholas Beffel. Like Rose, Beffel was involved in assisting Sacco and Vanzetti, and would also, again like her, involve himself in the attempts to free Tom Mooney and Warren Billings from jail, efforts which are described below (Avrich 1996, 277, fn 320; "John Beffel Dead; Aided Sacco Defense" 1973; Leeder 1993, 96).

When the Road to Freedom group was formed in New York City and Stelton, New Jersey in 1924, Pose Pesotta soon became one of its leaders, serving as general secretary of its self-described "Anarchist publication," *The Road to Freedom*, and one that was openly critical of the Russian Revolution and the role of the Communists in distorting its purposes (Leeder 1993, 39–40, 106; Zimmer 2010, 396–397). Its first issue, overseen by Hippolyte Havel, appeared in November of that year; in it, an editorial announced:

> How has history progressed? What has pushed it onward? Energetic, fanatical men, risking everything and ready to sacrifice everything are necessary.
>
> 'Comments' 1924, 4

The arrest of five persons and eventual conviction of two of them, Tom Mooney and Warren Billings, for a July 22, 1916 Preparedness Day rally bombing on Market Street in San Francisco that killed ten people and wounded another forty caused consternation in anarchist ranks. Worried that he might be connected with the crime, Alexander Berkman left the Bay Area, where he had based his periodical, *The Blast*, whose offices had been the subject of police raids following the bombing; Tom Rooney had written an article for the publication. Berkman returned to New York, and then moved *The Blast* there. Interviewed by immigration agents who were seeking to deport him back to Italy, another anarchist, Luigi Galleani, claimed to know who was the real San Francisco bomber as an unsuccessful tactic to avoid being removed from the country, although he never revealed any names (Avrich and Avrich 2012, 257; McCormick 2005, 24–25; Wenzer 1996, 57–59; Zimmer 2010, 291–293).

Rose Pesotta was naturally supportive of Mooney, who had been sentenced to death. In 1934, he was languishing in San Quentin Prison, where she was able to visit him along with Mooney's sister, Anna. Radicals, labor activists, and many others, including President Woodrow Wilson and even the trial judge, were worried that Mooney's conviction was based on false evidence, with a former Pinkerton detective, a Swedish-born former US Marine named Martin Swanson, having in collusion with the police and prosecutor railroaded him and threatened at least one witness not to testify; concerns about the trial, pressure from the White House, and growing evidence that Mooney had been framed caused California Governor William D. Stephens (many sources incorrectly give his last name as "Stevens") to commute Mooney's sentence to life imprisonment, though he did nothing more. Eye witnesses had pinpointed the perpetrators of the bombing as being dark-skinned and probably of Mexican origin, and a police lineup had failed to produce any identification of the five arrested persons (Mooney, Billings, Mooney's wife Rena, Edward Nolan, and Israel Weinberg) as having been there; in fact, Tom and Rena had a photograph showing that they were somewhere else at the time. It was not until 1939 that a new governor, Culbert L. Olson, who was a labor-friendly atheist, would pardon Mooney and commute the sentence of Billings, who would be pardoned eventually in 1961 (Avrich and Avrich 2012, 345; Federal Writers' Project of the Works Progress Administration of Northern California [1940] 2011, 124; Leeder 1993, 119; Pesotta 1944, 57; Stevens 2009, 128).

As noted in previous chapters, on May 4, 1886, there was an attempt by Chicago police to close down a public gathering in Haymarket Square of anarchists who were protesting developments of the previous night, when officers had fired at strikers from the McCormick Reaper Works, causing several deaths. A bomb was thrown – again, as would take place in San Francisco in 1916, there was a situation with an unknown assailant who would never be correctly identified – and the Haymarket bomb killed a policeman, Mathias J. Degan. A similar response ensued, with local anarchist leaders being rounded up and being accused of, and then framed for murder. Pesotta, like many anarchists, including Kropotkin, Voltairine de Cleyre, and the widow of one of executed anarchists, Lucy Parsons, saw the Haymarket Tragedy, to which it is often now referred, as an earth-shattering event, and also, like the trials of Tom Mooney and Warren Billings, a deliberate attempt by the authorities to commit the judicial murder of those of certain beliefs: in the case of the Haymarket trial, Rose identified "a hysterical atmosphere, before a biased judge, and with a jury crookedly chosen to serve anti-labor forces" (Pesotta 1944, 67). In fact, her skepticism even extended to doubting about whether one of the Haymarket martyrs, Louis Lingg, had killed himself in his cell, before he was hanged. However, it seems quite likely that Lingg did commit suicide, seeking to avoid the court-ordered fate, and it is probable that a fellow-anarchist, Dyer D. Lum, smuggled the means of doing so into the Cook County Jail. At the trial, Lingg proclaimed:

> I despise you. I despise your order, your laws, your force-propped authority. Hang me for it!.
>
> LINGG, quoted in AVRICH and AVRICH 2012, 38

Alexander Berkman and Emma Goldman and other radical anarchists saw Lingg as a role model, and when Berkman decided to kill industrialist Henry Frick, he planned to commit suicide in exactly the same way, by biting a dynamite blasting capsule; when he was arrested after attacking but not killing Frick, he was in possession of two such caps. Goldman recalled a conversation in which Berkman declared this intention:

> But I will die by my own hand, like Lingg. Never will I permit our enemies to kill me.
>
> BERKMAN, quoted by GOLDMAN [1931] 1970, 87, 1996, 284–285

One weekend, Pesotta visited Waldheim Cemetery, where the bodies of Lingg and the executed Haymarket Square anarchists lie, and led a ceremony in their memory, along with Arturo Giovannitti, the Italian-born union leader and poet, paying tribute to them and to Illinois Governor Altgeld, who in 1893 had freed the executed men's imprisoned colleagues, Michael Schwab, Oscar Neebe, and Samuel Fielden,[2] citing the obvious intimidation, bias, and fake evidence that characterized their trial (Avrich and Avrich 2012, 22, 70–71, 85–86; De Grazia 2006, 310; DeLamotte 2004, 5; Pesotta 1944, 67). Altgeld ([1893] 1915, 304–305) criticized the Chicago police, whom he said, "deliberately planned to have fictitious conspiracies formed in order that they might get the glory of discovering them." This had led to the November 11, 1887 hanging of Albert Parsons, George Engel, August Spies, and Adolph Fischer. Pesotta saw the Chicago anarchists as being engaged in a similar pursuit to her own, pointing out that they had campaigned for an eight-hour day, while some Wobblies (Industrial Workers of the World) had been "brutally manhandled and lynched because they dared speak out against exploitation" (Pesotta 1944, 149). Earlier in *Bread Upon the Waters*, Pesotta (1944, 93) speaks fondly of the Wobblies and their work on behalf of the disadvantaged, mentioning among others Bill Haywood (who, as discussed in Chapter Eight, invited Margaret Sanger to take care of the malnourished children of textile workers in Lawrence, Massachusetts during the Bread and Roses Strike), and Lucy Parsons, who never gave up trying to remedy the execution of her husband.

---

2   For Fielden's story, see Shone 2013, Chap. 5.

Rose maintained a friendship with Mollie Steimer, the subject of Chapter Nine, who had been deported from the United States in 1921, meeting with her and her partner, Senia Fleshin in Paris, where the couple were now working as photographers. With them, she traveled around France, witnessing the societal changes of the late 1930s. While there, Pesotta beheld the same heavy-handed tactics being used against unions that she had encountered in the US. She notes that a general strike planned by the *Confédération générale du travail* (CGT) in Paris by city and subway employees to try to increase their wages lasted for only a day after the Radical Party premier, Camille Chautemps, who formed two short-lived Popular Front (*Front populaire*) governments in 1937 and 1938, threatened to induct the strikers into the army if they did not abandon the action (Leeder 1989, 59, 1993, 37; Pesotta 1944, 184, 186, 187; Wardhaugh 2009, 203, 205). So, what she witnessed was nothing like what she had hoped for: "The beaten wage-earners walked to and from their jobs with dull expressions on their faces, moving like automatons" (Pesotta 1944, 188). The growth of fascism and Nazism throughout Europe was altering political positions across a range of issues as ever-changing Popular Front coalitions responded to rapid change and crises by nationalizing industries. Back in 1933, Chautemps would have been viewed as someone particularly sympathetic to Jewish people, but by 1938 his government developed a plan (which would be actualized by his successor, Édouard Daladier, who had always wanted to limit the number of refugees) to relocate some of France's undocumented Jewish immigrants away from the cities and into agricultural jobs, offering them legal status as refugees only if they accepted, but otherwise deporting them (Caron 1998, 29, 60–61; Dobbin 1993, 42; Maga 1982, 430–431). For Rose, whose consciousness and cultural identity were affected dramatically by the Holocaust and by her own father's murder in Ukraine, this reevaluation of refugee norms could only have added to her disillusionment.

Pesotta foresaw similar threats against strikers being used to undermine union activity in the United States, with strikers being drafted and, she argued, perhaps being used as soldiers to break work stoppages. For instance, she mentions the Smith-Connally Act of 1943, which allowed the federal government to seize businesses during wartime. Although the law was passed by Congress over President Franklin D. Roosevelt's veto (Roosevelt opposed allowing strikes during the Second World War, but thought the Act would make them more likely), his administration was nevertheless able to utilize it in the Philadelphia transit strike of the next year, threatening to draft employees unless they returned to work (Pesotta 1944, 239; Roosevelt 1943).

While Pesotta was sometimes viewed as having made a choice to dedicate her life to labor activism – editor Marcus Graham (real name, Shmuel Marcus) and his anarchist newspaper, *MAN!*, who, while not hostile to rank-and-file union activism, believed Pesotta had violated some kind of anarchist code by taking a paid position with the ILGWU (Leeder 1989, 53, 1993, 80; Zimmer 2010, 409–410) – putatively abandoning her commitment to anarchist theories and undertakings, it is in fact the case that she remained a firm anarchist, and through her union work she was able to improve the lot of the disadvantaged, which is hardly incompatible with the goals of most anarchists. Bussel (1988, 654) writes of "Pesotta's ... unshakable commitment to rank-and-file participation and her view of the union as an institution encompassing workers' lives in both the factory and the community." This was hardly a perspective unique to Pesotta as Kosak notes:

> [M]ost Jewish women anarchists, while deeply committed to transforming a whole way of life, gave priority to the struggle against oppression by employers, a struggle in which labor organizations played an essential role.
>
> KOSAK 2009

Leeder sees the growth of the radical labor perspective with which Pesotta was actively involved as presenting an opportunity to bring about the goal which most anarchists hold highest, "that revolution ... would occur through an uprising of the workers, hopefully through unionism" (Leeder 1993, 23). She continues:

> It was anarchism – both its philosophy and the members of the movement – that most significantly influenced Rose's labor organizing and political activities. The ideology to which she was drawn early in her education remained an underlying theme of all her later accomplishments. It was her approach to the world. Rose adhered to the ideas of Kropotkin, who believed in the need for revolution and the development of communes and collectives as the basic unit of society. He also believed in people taking from society based on what they needed, not just based on what they earned.
>
> LEEDER 1993, 105

Of course, the story of Rose Pesotta remains for some the chronicle of a pioneering labor activist, with the consequence that Buhle (1988, 15) speaks of "crucial yet hidden elements of the story, such as Pesotta's anarchism (which included the practice of free love)." Some commentators – for example, Peterson (1995, 1316) – appear to be unaware that Rose wrote two autobiographies,

the second of which, *Days of Our Lives*, despite giving much valuable information about her life in the Russian Empire, has not been widely disseminated.
Perhaps that is because, in the opinion of Anne E. Goldman, *Days of Our Lives*
is much more about the Jewish cultural environment in Derazhnya where Pesotta was raised (unlike *Bread Upon the Waters*, which gives us the narrative of
an immigrant labor activist), and is thus a sociological endeavor, rather than
what it appears at first sight to be, a personal one (Boardman 1997, 88, 89;
[Anne E.] Goldman 1996, 167–173; Leeder 1993, 157–158). While she lived in the
Pale, Rose became dismayed that radical dissidence was rewarded mostly by
executions, imprisonment, or banishment to Siberia, and she was already concerned that if she chose to focus on her more explicitly political goals, her life
would probably be a failure (Leeder 1993, 12; Pesotta 1958, 220). In the United
States, as a labor organizer, it turned out she was a great success.

2   Pesotta as an Anarchist Union Activist

When Rose Pesotta became associated with the International Ladies' Garment
Workers' Union, the organization was undergoing a period of expansion beyond the cities of New York and Chicago where it had mainly concentrated its
activities since its founding in 1900. In this era, there were many radically-
oriented women, often born in Eastern Europe, who decided to join her New
York section, Local 25, which had more than 20,000 members, making it the
largest local within the ILGWU; these radical seamstresses were often influenced to some extent by anarchism or by Marxism, or by both (Cornell 2011,
199; Glass 2016, 221). Melech Epstein describes the situation in 1917 in the factories in which the largely female union membership were employed as follows:

> The girls went to work carrying Karl Marx and Kropotkin under their
> arms. From Russia they had brought over their romantic and lofty con-
> ception of a labor organization.
>   EPSTEIN 1969, vol. 2, 130

Along with Pesotta leading the anarchist side of the divide were Russian-born
labor activist Clara Rothberg Larsen, and Anna Sosnovsky, who, like Pesotta
would become a vice-president of the ILGWU; both Larsen and Sosnovsky
would be involved in publishing the pro-anarchist and anti-communist weekly
newspaper, *Der Yunyon Arbeter* (*The Union Worker*) with Rose between 1923
and 1927. The ideological divide would become important for the future of the
industry as anarchists and communists came to fight for control over the

garment unions and wider swaths of organized labor. It is unsurprising that anarchists who had emigrated from the Pale would be skeptical of union activities conducted by communists connected to the Bolsheviks in Russia, and thus this conflict within the ILGWU itself was bound to dilute its power, and eventually, in 1928, some communist members were expelled, while others were tolerated. The non-communist side was championed by Pesotta and also by two other Ukrainian-born leaders of the union, the West Coast director, Louis Levy, a former tailor and fellow admirer of Kropotkin who would eventually try to upstage Rose and take credit for her achievements, and Morris Sigman, who was president of the union from 1923 to 1928 (Avrich 1988, 196; Cornell 2011, 199; Jensen 1984, 186; Stolberg 1944, 116, 334–335; Zimmer 2010, 349–350). Pesotta (1944, 16) blamed the Russian communists for seeking to "take over the labor movement of the whole world" and eventually eliminate its rivals, a strategy resulting in conflict that she also thought accounted for the weakening of the ILGWU, due to its inability to present a unified strategy while communist organizations were offering rival arguments (Jensen 1984, 188). She portrayed the communist union organization that competed with the ILGWU in the United States and Canada, the Needle Trades Workers' Industrial Union, as having the goal of "'ruling or ruining' every labor organization in that field" (Pesotta 1944, 27). She also disliked Levy's sister, Tillie, a communist whom she accused of undermining her own efforts to recruit Hispanic dressmakers in Los Angeles into the ILGWU (Pesotta 1944, 201). In 1924, Pesotta addressed the ILGWU's convention, successfully persuading them to adopt a motion calling on the Soviet Union to release its political prisoners (Leeder 1993, 33). Some of these prisoners were anarchists who had returned to Russia inspired by the rhetoric of the Bolshevik Revolution, and in the years following that event, many radicals in the West, including left-leaning publications, refused to believe that Lenin and Trotsky were setting up a dictatorship, preferring to deny the testimony of Goldman and Berkman who, disillusioned, had left Russia in 1921; Berkman's *The Kronstadt Revolution* (Berkman [1922] 2001), documenting the crushing of dissent by the communist leaders had appeared in 1922.

Not to be ignored is the fact that Pesotta's work as a labor organizer frequently involved advocacy on behalf of ethnic minorities and immigrants. This brought her into contact with many people who spent their lives struggling to survive in a condition of permanent poverty, constantly vulnerable to shifts in the economy, and, in the case of those who were not US citizens, to being suddenly deported, possibly only because they had participated in a strike for higher pay. The extent of this deprivation was particularly apparent to her in the years that Pesotta spent in downtown Los Angeles (in 1933–1934 and 1940–1942), and in Puerto Rico (in 1934). As an anarchist, she was responsive to this need, and committed to letting ordinary workers participate in union decision-making; that goal to some extent framed the way she structured her organizing activities (Laslett 1993, 22; Leeder 1993, 53).

Earlier in 1933, building on her Local 25 experience in New York, Pesotta had worked in the Los Angeles garment industry and was soon blacklisted for forming a labor union, one that had members in a number of different clothing factories; after saying she would return to exact her revenge in the form of a more successful organizing effort, she then went back to the northeast. Soon afterwards, trying to expand its influence in California, the ILGWU dispatched Israel Feinberg to be its West Coast director, along with Pesotta as a general organizer who, after talking with the union's president, David Dubinsky, and pointing out her previous experience out west, arrived in Los Angeles on September 15, 1933 to take charge of a garment industry workforce there comprised mostly of Mexican and Mexican-American women, many of whom had not lived in the United States for very long, a group that numbered up to 7,500 employees depending on the season (Epstein 1969, vol. II, 444; Laslett 1993, 23–24; Pesotta 1944, 8–9; Zimmer 2010, 366).

What she encountered on her return to Los Angeles was again the union-busting tactics of the local Merchants and Manufacturers' Association, which routinely conspired to fire and blacklist dressmaking employees believed to have joined the union, a fate that had already, earlier in the year, befallen Pesotta herself. She discovered that some companies required workers to clock in and out with their timecard so that they would only be paid for the minutes they spent sewing, while other employers forced workers to return some of their pay that nominally they had received in compliance with minimum wage laws (Pesotta 1944, 20). Pesotta responded in creative ways. Since many of the women spoke Spanish and had cultural roots in Mexico, she contracted with a Spanish-language radio station to make announcements each day promoting the union perspective, and she also used leafleting and put out a bilingual newspaper, *The Organizer*, twice a week, while the union's picketers dressed well and sang songs, presenting a favorable image to the public. When the owners of the radio station balked, she found a Tijuana, Mexico station that was willing to continue the broadcasts. She provided meals for picketers, which caused some hungry persons unconnected with the industry to attempt to register as strikers. Rose's own background in the Ukraine and the lack of opportunity for women that it had promised her, pushing her to emigrate to the United States, made it easy to identify with the garment workers who told her that in Mexico, they had been dominated by their husbands and fathers. As poor immigrants, they now encountered a new threat to their liberty, employers who terrorized them by saying they would have them deported if they joined the union. She made it clear to non-citizens that the ILGWU would go to court on behalf of anyone who encountered this type of menacing behavior, which, she felt, actually worked to the advantage to the ILGWU, which strived to treat the Hispanic women as equals, and consequently many of them did exactly what they were threatened not to do, which was to unionize (Glass 2016, 224, 225; Pesotta 1944, 21, 22–23, 25, 31, 32; Sánchez 1993). Robinson writes:

> Pesotta's organizing drives and strike support always took account of ethnic and cultural differences, as expressed in food, music, and entertainment; she made the union hall a place where workers could live their culture, form couples, bring the family, not just the place for work-connected actions that would be as alienated from real life as the work itself.
>
> ROBINSON 1991, 8

Her organizational success led to the Dressmakers' Strike of 1933, and her recently created organization of female dressmakers, Local 96, was able to sign up a thousand members in just three weeks. However, she found out that she had only lukewarm support from the male cloakmakers of Local 65, which had successfully negotiated a union shop contract of their own and were reluctant to strike; their leaders influenced Dubinsky and prompted him to resist a work stoppage. It was obvious that many male IGWU officials had problems relating to or representing the female and largely ethnic minority members of Local 96; meanwhile, those same men expected to be in charge. Kessler-Harris writes:

> In 1933, Pesotta compromised to the extent of abandoning the negotiating process to men and confining her own activities to organizing women.
>
> KESSLER-HARRIS 1976, 21

As a woman leader of the ILGWU, who would in 1934 become one of its vice presidents, Pesotta often encountered bias because of her gender, a factor that eventually, after she went back to Los Angeles on another union assignment, would become the prime cause of her resignation.

In 1933, due to the encouragement she had managed to engineer, Pesotta was able to go ahead with her goal, and the strike began on October 12; during the first few days, some of the cloakmakers honored the picket lines. By November 6, an agreement was reached to respect the codes of the federal National Recovery Administration (NRA), which had been instituted earlier that year under the National Industrial Recovery Act, and which had putatively established improved working conditions, shorter work weeks, and minimum wages for the industry, as well as the right to unionize. However, although the dressmakers returned to work, there were few mechanisms available to ensure that employers would comply with the agreement, which they did not (Glass 2016, 222; Laslett 1993, 26, 30; Sánchez 1993). As Vargas notes:

> Just as ILGWU president Dubinsky forewarned, Los Angeles dress shop owners took advantage of the industry showdown, returned to the low wage scale, and denied work to employees who participated in the strike. Complaints of continued firings, intimidation, and discrimination were turned over to the NRA arbitration board, but it did nothing to remedy these violations.
>
> VARGAS 2005, 88

Sent to organize in El Fanguito, an enormous slum area of San Juan, Puerto Rico, Pesotta arrived on July 16, 1934 to discover employees living in zinc-roofed shacks built on stilts on marshland, who were obliged to walk through foul-smelling mud to reach their homes, a hazard which caused them to remove their shoes, which in turn put them at risk of becoming infected with hookworm, an intestinal parasite. She compared the slum-dwellers' predicament with that of farmworkers she had encountered back home in the Ukraine, who removed their shoes when they walked into town in order to make them last longer (Hewitt 2009, 272; Pesotta 1944, 74). She noted how, ironically, the town of Aguadilla celebrated the fact that Columbus was believed to have replenished ship water supplies there, but Rose found that the only water to which the wife of the school principal had access was a basin of rainwater contaminated by insects. It was not hard for Pesotta to make the connection between the low wages that workers in Puerto Rico made and much of the inability of people there to purchase adequate amounts of food, a situation that led to a high rate of infant mortality. Owners of garment factories were transferring work to contractors who used home-based employees, some of whom had to pay to rent a sewing machine; the effect of this transfer was to reduce costs considerably, and it allowed the owners to avoid restrictions imposed by the federal National Recovery Administration's codes. Later, some of the manufacturers would relocate away from the island, finding more opportunities to exploit workers in China and the Philippines. She saw also the inconsistency between the United States government telling other countries how to organize their economies while many of its own citizens, despite working hard, had basic needs that were not taken care of (Pesotta 1944, 8, 70–71, 80, 83–84, 87). In this respect, her commitment to the ideas of Kropotkin, who advocated provision of everyone's basic needs as a fundamental function of society fit well with her concerns about the condition of many people in Puerto Rico.

Sent to Montréal, where the ILGWU leadership believed that contracts that had been recently obtained quite easily by the cloak cutters in 1934 and the dress cutters in 1936 might bode success for their own union if it was able to sign up the less skilled employees, Pesotta again employed some creative tactics, including setting up a restaurant and a newspaper to facilitate her activities. As in Los Angeles, she saw the need to utilize a language other than English, and created bilingual radio broadcasts, attempting to attract the interest of French-Canadians. In connecting with the latter, and mitigating the argument that the union leaders were outsiders who could not speak the local language, she hired Montréal-born Léa Roback, who would become a lifetime supporter of radical causes, and who spoke French as well as English, Yiddish, and German, and also Claude Jodoin, who would eventually run the ILGWU in Canada and become the president of the Canadian Labour Congress. The other outsider, who would essentially be the one to lead the union activity, was Bernard Shane, who had also been born in Ukraine. Arriving in Québec, Pesotta expressed the view that what the dressmakers needed was a female leader, but in fact she would, as was typical, encounter gender bias in the assignment of the workload. Steedman (1997, 255) notes that, despite her extensive experience working for the ILGWU and the fact that she was one of its vice presidents, it was Shane who spearheaded the negotiations, while Rose was obliged to be "caterer and support worker." This scenario would be a continuing problem for her in her profession, and was continued in Los Angeles in 1941. When the Montréal dressmakers went on strike in April 1937, at least 5,000 of them participated in the action. Although a union contract increasing pay, which applied to contractors as well as to the manufacturers who hired them, was soon agreed to by the Montréal Dress Manufacturers Guild, it lasted for less than a year. Consequently, while *la grève des midinettes*, the latter word coined to describe women who would be seen in downtown Montréal leaving their dress factories at noon to go out for lunch, was one of the most important work stoppages in the history of Québec, it achieved little in the long term beyond the formation of the ILGWU's Local 262. Despite Pesotta's attempts to portray the ILGWU as being a more responsible partner than communist-run unions, and ironically given her own dislike of communism, the manufacturers and local Catholic priests railed against the strike leaders, referring to them as communists, and demanding that Pesotta and Shane be deported (Copp 1982, 850; Cutler 2017; En grève avec Léa et les midinettes 2015; Pesotta 1944, 165; Steedman 1997, 246–248; Tyler 1995).

Though she had become a naturalized citizen, Pesotta was from time to time personally subject to such threats. In March 1935, when Pesotta was organizing dressmakers in Seattle, Washington, she found herself condemned by the press as an outside agitator who should be expelled from the United States. While she was picketing at the factory of Nelly Dwyer, Inc., someone threw a tomato at the proprietor, Nelly Dwyer, who was outside arguing with the strikers; the missile hit her in the face. Rose, who saw the object land but did not hurl it, and who attempted to apologize, was identified by the victim as the assailant. As at Haymarket Square in Chicago and the Preparedness Day rally in San Francisco, violence at protests has often been blamed on any anarchists who happen to be present, and Pesotta was briefly arrested. Local newspapers immediately claimed that she was to be deported for her "crime." Eventually, another striker, named Mary O'Brien, was fined $5 for the incident, but Pesotta believed that the thrower was actually someone else, more distantly connected to the union (Leeder 1993, 66, 68; Pesotta 1944, 104–105; Shepherd 1993, 267). Shepherd comments:

Most immigrant anarchists were, as she [Pesotta] was, followers of Kropotkin and Bakunin, with a vision of a future society based on voluntary and co-operative institutions. Few were capable of the violence that some anarchists believed inevitable if the world was to be changed. But in America all anarchists were believed to be terrorists, and often punished merely for their beliefs.

SHEPHERD 1993, 259

In 1940, after she had also worked on unionization activities in San Francisco; Portland, Oregon; Buffalo, New York; Milwaukee, Wisconsin; Boston; Cleveland and Akron, Ohio; Detroit and Flint, Michigan; and other places, union president Dubinsky pushed her to return to Los Angeles, which she did not really wish to do, but she was told that it was just a temporary assignment as the new Pacific Coast director, Louis Levy, was sick (Pesotta 1944, 198). Once there, she targeted the Malouf family-owned Mode O'Day Company, which had a chain of retail stores as well as the downtown Los Angeles factory where she campaigned; its employees were typically poor and minority, and they were not represented by a labor union. When she arrived, Rose discovered that, to some extent, the dressmaking workforce had changed from what she had encountered there in the early thirties, having become more diverse, including immigrants from many different backgrounds, as well as displaced farmworkers. Among them were some Molokans, spiritual Christians viewed by the Russian Orthodox Church as heretics, who had moved to California (Pesotta 1944, 204).

At Mode O'Day, Rose worked hard to set up a new sportswear affiliate, Local 484, and to enroll the company's workers in it. She used some of the same tactics that had been a success for her earlier: again, she created a newsletter to promote the position of the union, and she held meetings away from the employer's operation so that people would be more willing to participate. One particularly innovative idea was to have picketers appear at the Market Week and Style Show being held at the Biltmore Hotel, arrayed in the latest evening-wear fashions, with the union women ready to identify to the buyers the names of the more exploitative dressmakers. Although the Biltmore complained and a police officer asked the union to leave, the newspapers had already arrived and taken pictures of the event (Pesotta 1944, 201; Stolberg 1944, 338). Despite this and other inventive successes, which led to an agreement with the Maloufs in March 1941, Dubinsky decided to send out another manager to replace Rose as the head of the new grouping. This was one of the specific motivating factors in her choice in June 1942 to resign from the union hierarchy and return to working at a sewing machine in a clothing factory in New York, as was the fact that, once she had unionized the Mode O'Day employees, Levy tried to take over the negotiation process. There were also other concerns, which as Leeder (1993, 83–84) points out, tended to reflect Rose's anarchist philosophy. In a letter to Dubinsky that she sent in November 1939 (Pesotta 1939), she stated her dislike of the ILGWU becoming involved in election campaigns, she found fault with his authoritarian approach, and she suggested there should be more rotation in the union's leadership positions. Her criticism may have prompted her dispatch to Los Angeles not too long afterwards, against her wishes (Leeder 1993, 83), since her comments will not have been what he wanted to hear. In a sense, her forthrightness, imbued as it was with anarchistic perceptions, along with her competence and creativity as a labor leader, worked against her because she was a woman. Parmet comments:

> Culturally, Dubinsky was a vestige of the Eastern European Jewish society ... he had a traditional attitude toward the role of women in society, as Rose Pesotta sadly discovered.
>
> PARMET 2005, 206

Pesotta's main motivation for quitting was the sexism of many the union officials she had been working with; she was never able to convince the union to overturn its formal policy of only having one woman in a leadership position in an organization that now represented 300,000 people, most of whom were female (Buhle 1988, 15; Fields 2007, 246; Laslett 1993, 20, 35–36; Leeder 1993,

82–83, 86, 90–91; Pesotta 1944, 237; Shepherd 1993, 244–245). She was a casualty of institutionalized gender discrimination that Zimmer (2010, 113) notes weakened the organization's effectiveness, since "anarchist women were among the staunchest rank-and-file union militants. They were the first on the picket lines and not afraid to clash with strikebreakers and the authorities." Orleck (1995, 296) states simply that "Pesotta ... resigned ... to protest the union's failure to recognize the talents of women." Of course, what is important to union officials can vary according to their gender. In recalling their own activism, male and female labor leaders may select quite different memories. Reporting on the transactions of an academic conference about historical memory, Kathleen A. Brown and Gigi Peterson summarize Robert Bussel's contribution to the topic as follows:

> Robert Bussel ... found contrasts between the memoirs of male labor leaders and those of International Ladies' Garment Workers' Union organizer Rose Pesotta. While the former focused on union bureaucracy and factional intrigues, Pesotta was extremely sensitive to issues of gender, race, and ethnicity, and highlighted individual workers and what organizing meant to them.
>
> BROWN and PETERSON 1997, 144

Consequently, Rabinowitz's (1995, 182) claim that "Rose Pesotta left the International Ladies Garment Workers Union to make money" seems difficult to substantiate given all the examples of sexism presented by researchers and by Pesotta's own explanation of why she quit her position. Laslett writes:

> Pesotta's frustration with the autocratic and male-dominated character of the ILGWU leadership was expressed in a letter she wrote to President Dubinsky on November 7, 1939.
>
> LASLETT 1993, 32

More cautiously than in her letter, Rose complained:

> Many times across a decade I dared to contradict him [Dubinsky], when I saw that with all his knowledge of governmental, labor, and social problems, he was unaware of the existence of issues confronting me at the moment in some remote part of the country.
>
> PESOTTA 1944, 65

Later, she commented:

Somewhere in the Talmud there is an ancient Hebrew saying: The soldiers fight, the kings are heroes. It comes to mind as I review the rise of the International Ladies' Garment Workers' Union.

PESOTTA 1944, 117

First set up in 1935 as a committee of the American Federation of Labor (AFL), the Committee for Industrial Organization, as it was originally known, arose as an effort to bring lesser-skilled workers, women, immigrants, and minorities under union protection, although traditionally many factions within the AFL had not wished that to occur. The ILGWU's David Dubinsky was one of the participants in setting up this new approach, and the ILGWU provided some funding to help secure its financial independence. The CIO and its constituent unions were soon expelled from the AFL and in 1938, adopting the amended name of Congress of Industrial Organizations, it became a separate federation. Thus, Shepherd (1993, 243; 269 is similar) is technically incorrect when she writes that "[i]n the spring of 1936," Pesotta was "loaned to the Congress of Industrial Organizations (CIO), the rebel wing of the American Federation of Labor (AFL)," since the alliance's name had not yet been changed. In 1955, the organizations remerged, into the American Federation of Labor and Congress of Industrial Organizations (AFL-CIO) (Glass 2016, 249; Leeder 1993, 55; Paulson 2004). While the persons who set up the CIO shared many of the same goals as the older Wobblies, Pesotta viewed the new grouping, on behalf of which she worked in Akron, Ohio at the Goodyear tire factory, as having a superior grasp of tactics. This was partly because, she believed, the CIO was able to learn from the mistakes that the IWW had made, such as the latter's failure to obtain written contracts with employers. Also, she felt, the CIO was fortunate to come into existence during the era of President Roosevelt and his New Deal. The ILGWU, however, prompted by Dubinsky's concerns about communist influence in the new federation, soon left the CIO and returned to the AFL in 1940 (Pesotta 1944, 96, 211; Weir 2013, 371).

Pesotta died in Miami, Florida, in 1965. In her later years, she had become an advocate for the recently created state of Israel, which she visited in 1950. She was horrified by what she saw of the aftermath of the Second World War in Poland, including the Majdanek concentration camp where the atrocities of the Nazi occupation are well-preserved, and to some extent this rekindled her awareness of her own cultural beginnings (Leeder 1993, 155–157; Pesotta 1958, 215–216). Rose embraced liberty not only through her anarchist sensibilities and with the assistance she gave to those of a similar political perspective, but through her long quest to help the unfortunate, regardless of their origin, to live their lives with dignity, and guaranteed their basic needs.

Conclusion: Liberty Lost

Among the thinkers discussed in this book, one of the most important concerns is the *lost liberty of women*, denied the right to be educated, to be an individual, to go out to work each day and receive an equal wage, to find out about contraception or to use it to avoid pregnancy, to end a relationship, to decide whether or not to have a child or more children, to have legal authority over the care of your dependents, to find a partner who respects you rather than someone who was once attracted to you due to the way you looked, to decide whom you wish to marry without being cajoled by your parents to wed someone for reasons of finance or status or family honor, and to be held to the same moral standard as men, rather than to a higher one. Also, not to be regarded as an attachment to a male, bearing the father's or the husband's last name, and not to be stigmatized by illegitimacy, the absence of attachment, an unfairness that haunted Louise Michel throughout her life, and for which Tennie C. Claflin sought a solution.

Mercy Otis Warren was not afforded the opportunity to go to school, and had to educate herself using the books she found in her uncle's library, mixing in this information with what her brother Jemmy told her on visits home about what he was learning at Harvard; later, she worked in the background, having conversations and writing tracts, poems, plays, and letters as her husband involved himself more formally in talk of revolution as a member of the Massachusetts Committee of Correspondence. Today, one of her books, *Observations on the New Constitution and on the Federal and State Conventions. By a Columbian Patriot*, is still, notwithstanding the evidence, listed by some libraries without qualification as having been written by Elbridge Gerry, a male Anti-Federalist, rather than by herself, the female Anti-Federalist.

Although Warren at first criticized what she believed was the injurious intent of the US Constitution, only, like many Jeffersonian and Anti-Federalist demurrers, to be consoled by the Amendments that were swiftly added to that document, her more far-reaching and longlasting excoriation of the new nation is surely her argument that the real Founders, persons like herself, meeting in houses and on farms in local communities, had been railroaded by the avaricious desires of individuals like Alexander Hamilton, John Hancock, and the Massachusetts governor, Thomas Hutchinson. Similarly, the people's liberty was threatened by John Adams, whom she believed as president really wanted to become a king. Thus the United States had quickly become a nation that had a wealthy, greedy elite, along with a mass of poor people betrayed by a hijacked Revolution; the majority were now unable to enjoy the liberty they had been promised and for which they had willingly sacrificed. An aristocracy based on riches had been created in the nation that believed itself to have overthrown distinctions of class, and now there was also a *de facto* monarch. Decades later, Lois Waisbrooker would explain how this acquisitiveness threatened relations between men and women, engendering the sacrifice of love and affection, causing women to accept and tolerate unsuitable marriages, or to engage in prostitution. Elizabeth Cady Stanton would lament the role of wealthy elites in the United States and Ireland whose land and money and jewellery they possessed at the expense and in virtue of the toil of ordinary people who worked for them but could not feed or clothe their children, and Michel would recall the lot of peasants and farm animals in France, their bodies slowly broken by hefty servitude as children starved.

Michel had access to formal education herself only because her "grandparents" chose to treat her as a grandchild, and later they bequeathed money to her mother, Marie-Anne, the family's servant, which meant she was able to help Louise buy a school where she could continue as a teacher. Elizabeth Cady Stanton was powerless to continue her studies by following the boys to Union College, and Margaret Sanger started working and never went to Cornell as she had wished; Victoria C. Woodhull and her sister, Tennie C. Claflin, probably each received only about three years of formal schooling, and Waisbrooker was only able to train to be a teacher after poverty forced her to give up her children for adoption.

Consequently, the writings and lives of the ten women described in this volume evoke also the *lost liberty of the poor*. The Claflin sisters, for example, as teenagers did every kind of work in order to rise above their privation, selling fake medicines and cancer treatments, and probably also working as prostitutes. Victoria was soon saddled with an ill-considered marriage to an unfaithful, drunken husband, and a mentally challenged infant. As Tennie would note, society provides little education on how to pick a mate beyond the urging of parents who may be seeking their own financial advantage and will frequently perpetuate the subservience of their daughters. In their actions and their ideas, all ten of these women fought back. As soon as she started work in a clothing factory in New York City, Rose Pesotta involved herself with the labor union, and started a career campaigning for improved conditions for seamstresses. Mollie Steimer, also slaving in a shirtwaist facility, challenged the authority of the US government because it deployed troops to the Soviet Union to fight the leaders of a new nation with which it was not at war.

Steimer and Pesotta, immigrants from the Ukraine who had experience of hardship before they came to the United States, did not seek or secure the

American Dream, but rather devoted themselves to improving the situation for others. Similarly, Michel, during the existence of the Paris Commune, in the slums of London's Whitechapel area, and while she was living far away in New Caledonia, dedicated her life to bettering the circumstances of poor people, including the local Kanaks and the colonized Algerians who like her had been transported to the South Pacific, as well as the lives of animals. Michel marched with the unemployed in France, and Pesotta described the dismay she witnessed of French transportation workers forced to call off a strike under threat of being drafted if they did not. Claflin could see that being poor often means that you pay the most for what you purchase, and that you buy the goods that are the least well-made. The harm caused by failure to acknowledge the right of all to have their essential needs secured, which Sanger, herself the product of a poor family, encountered when she worked with impoverished children in Massachusetts during the Bread and Roses Strike, the constant, disruptive economic pressure that caused Waisbrooker to say goodbye to her own kids, today forms a basis for considering instituting programs guaranteeing universal basic income (UBI), amid the recognition that no one can function adequately if they lack food, housing, education, or healthcare, and no one should be expected to.

The women also symbolize the *lost liberty of political participation*. Woodhull used sophisticated arguments explaining why women should be able to vote, as did Waisbrooker, who later changed her mind, doubting that such a change would achieve very much improvement. Elizabeth Cady Stanton was skeptical also, fearing that black men, if they could vote, would use the franchise to continue to promote male superiority. Again, many of the women fought back. In terms of the traditional, limited way that participation has been viewed, Woodhull and Claflin personally attempted to vote, but were not allowed to do so. Woodhull became the first woman to compete for president, entering subsequent races several more times and Claflin and Cady Stanton were the first two women to run for Congress. Tactically, Cady Stanton moved away from Susan B. Anthony as the latter remained committed mainly to the issue of voting, but Elizabeth could see that problems like drunken husbands, restrictive clothing, offensive religious teachings, and the inability to obtain a divorce would undermine much of the progress that enfranchisement offered to women. Waisbrooker noted that voting could not possibly work without significant changes to society that advanced the interests of women and lessened their domination by men. For all of these thinkers, therefore, modernity is an unfinished revolution. Sitting by quietly and thinking that because you have a vote, you live in a democracy and everything is fine, is to give up on the problems and fail to appreciate the true potential of humankind. With regard to less ceremonial modes of civic involvement, Michel contributed to the Commune's implicit modernization of Paris society, changing the norms, helping secularize the schools and nourish the poor, resisting the imposition of national government rule. Pesotta fed strikers in many different cities in North America, and used her own print media and radio broadcasts to motivate them to cooperate and resist power as they agitated for a living wage. Sanger found food and clothing for the children of striking Lawrence, Massachusetts workers, and dedicated her life to freeing women worldwide from the oppression of forced pregnancy and childbearing. Having too many children, or having them too close together, Woodhull, Claflin, Sanger, and Waisbrooker pointed out, not only negatively impacts the progeny, and is an instrument for subordinating women, but it also leaves the mothers weary, too tired to live the way they really wish to, as a human being, rather than a species of domestic animal. Sanger emphasized the right to continue to enjoy having sexual relations with your husband without the certainty that unwanted childbirth would result, especially if becoming pregnant again might mean your death.

Thus several of the women whose ideas are presented here address the *lost liberty imposed by the institution of marriage*. Waisbrooker, and Woodhull in her most anarchistic phase, want to eliminate formal legal marriage. For Waisbrooker and Stanton, it is women who make the better romantic choices, and for Waisbrooker, it is females who are naturally prepared to raise children and should be in charge of this function. For Claflin, there needs to be education so that people will choose their partners more reliably. For Itō Noe, love and marriage are two completely separate ideas that need not be linked. Thus, Waisbrooker, Sanger, and Itō all rebel against the wifely role, and Cady Stanton ceased living with her husband. Woodhull argues persuasively for social freedom, including sexual freedom, demanding that it be considered just as important as the freedom of speech or the right to practice religion, yet in her time, of course, this was not tolerated.

Accordingly, there is the *lost liberty of speech*, to say or write what you think, regardless of whether or not other people or the government like it, a right that in the United States is enshrined in the First Amendment, but is ever under attack. This would seem to include permission to criticize and object to financing a war whose legality is at the very least questionable, but Steimer found that she enjoyed no such protection. The absence of social freedom also limits the freedom of speech: Cady Stanton and Sanger note that is difficult to educate your sons to treat women in a more humane way because of taboos and embarrassment concerning talking about sex. Waisbrooker believed it was possible that boys could be educated by their mothers to look at sex in a much less exploitative way. In the eras when they were writing, women were unable to obtain information about sexuality or birth control because it was deemed to be obscene, as Waisbrooker found out when she was prosecuted for writing supportively about an extramarital relationship, and Sanger soon discovered when she tried to open a clinic to dispense contraceptives.

Additionally, there is the *lost liberty of selfhood*. Itō and Cady Stanton believe that there is an area of human existence that is completely private and can only be articulated and understood by the individual in question. Herein lies an epistemological basis for the anarchist conviction that people's behavior should as far as possible be controlled by the person in question. However, as Steimer realized in encountering its abeyance as she attempted to convince the judge who tried her for sedition, a court ought to treat everyone who comes before it equally, and not disparage them because they are female or an anarchist or a pacifist or they criticize war or they consider the government to be dishonest. Every time Pesotta won a victory for worker rights, some of the men she was working with tried to take credit for her achievement, treating her with disrespect because she was female. Thus liberty seems to involve a concern for the right of anarchists, women, prostitutes, people with unusual points of view, etc., to be treated with some deference. This would seem to imply that there is also a *lost liberty of community*. In the early years of the United States, as Otis Warren complained, chance and the pursuit of fortune came to replace the certainty of security and cooperative spirit that had initially propelled the American Revolution and which in France would inspire the Commune. Consequently, for Woodhull, like Stephen Pearl Andrews and Benjamin R. Tucker, anarchists who influenced her, the limits to individual freedom need to be drawn by a governing principle of equality, which occurs at the point at which the community interacts with the person in question.

There is, too, a *lost liberty to work* and be self-supporting, which in turn enables people to pursue their other interests. Waisbrooker argues that females will never be able to have sexual freedom without economic independence. Cady Stanton and Claflin note how some women, unable to support themselves without a man, or even if they have a relationship with someone of meager earnings, might not only be influenced to terminate a pregnancy but also to commit infanticide: as with the overlapping category of the poor, there are societal rules that make it impossible for many women to make the choices they desire, and that even make it impossible for them to survive.

Additionally, we find a *lost liberty of reason*. For Cady Stanton, the use of intelligence is preferable to reliance on faith and religious teachings, and for Sanger, a much more egalitarian and logical future will be brought about through the embrace of science, rather than by the dogmas of Christianity. Religious authority empowers church officials to issue rules that undermine what is naturally right or makes sense, Waisbrooker and Sanger say, while Cady Stanton points out that many Bible teachings contradict natural laws. Using logic, Waisbrooker, Itō, and Claflin question the worth of sexual abstinence, a tool that has been used for millennia to control women's beliefs and actions. Reason should also tell you that, as Waisbrooker and many other anarchists have argued, and Woodhull believed when she was young, crime is social: few individuals are naturally bad. Cogent thinking leads to the recognition that there is also a *lost liberty caused by overpopulation*. For Sanger, it makes sense to limit inhabitants to a number that can be reasonably or optimally accommodated by the resources of the Earth. Fortunately, she points out, if contraception is allowed and promoted and information about it is freely available, there will be much less need for abortion.

Finally, in wishing the twenty-first century to be able to rely upon having a more contemplative citizenry, we can identify the *lost liberty of education*. This is a loss that many of the women discussed here would have appreciated keenly: for instance, Michel, whose status as the illegitimate daughter of a household servant might have rendered her illiterate, and Cady Stanton, who criticized the fact that women who paid property taxes could not, due to their gender, enroll at the colleges those remunerations helped finance. There is need for everyone to read the great literature of the world, as Otis Warren did at her uncle's home and Pesotta did as a teenager in the Ukraine and continued to do so when she arrived in New York City. In an age of great and understandable dissatisfaction with governments, this might well include the lost wisdom of the anarchists, which Pesotta, Steimer, and Itō stumbled upon early in life, but which is often, like the contribution of women to intellectual thought, missing from classes supposedly documenting the history of political theory.

Bibliography

"Abrams, Jacob." 1991. In *Political Trials in History: From Antiquity to the Present*, ed. Ron Christenson. New Brunswick, N.J.: Transaction.

Adams, Charles F., ed. 1856. *The Works of John Adams, Second President of the United States: With a Life of the Author, Notes and Illustrations*. Vol. 10. Boston: Little, Brown.

Adams, Charles F., ed. [1878] 1972. *Correspondence between John Adams and Mercy Warren*. Reprint. New York: Arno.

Adams, John. [1768–1770] 1961. *John Adams Diary 15*. Adams Family Papers: An Electronic Archive. Massachusetts Historical Society. http://www.masshist.org/digitaladams/ (March 13, 2014).

"A Free-Love Heroine." 1871. *Saturday Review of Politics, Literature, Science, and Art*, December 9.

"A Lamp Without Oil." 1872. *New York Times*, February 22.

Alexander, Robert J. 1953. "Splinter Groups in American Radical Politics." *Social Research* 20:282–310.

Altgeld, John. [1893] 1915. *Gov. John Altgeld's Pardon of the Anarchists and his Masterly Review of the Haymarket Riot*. Chicago: Lucy Parsons.

"Anarchists Assassinated by Japanese Government." 1923. *Freedom*, November.

Andrews, Stephen Pearl. [1851] 1895. *The Science of Society*. Boston: Sarah E. Holmes.

Andrews, Stephen Pearl. 1874. "Obituary." *Woodhull & Claflin's Weekly*, May 2.

Anthony, Susan B. 1870. "The 'Working Woman.'" *Revolution*, March 10.

"A Piebald Presidency." 1872. *New York Herald*, May 11.

Armogathe, Daniel. 1985. "Le Sort de la Nouvelle-Calédonie: L'exemple de Louise Michel." *Le Monde*, February 8.

"Attempt to Kill Louise Michel." 1888. *Liberty*, February 11.

Auerbach, Nina. 1998. "Eminent Victoria." *Women's Review of Books* 15:21–22.

Avrich, Paul. 1978. *An American Anarchist: The Life of Voltairine de Cleyre*. Princeton: Princeton University Press.

Avrich, Paul. 1980. *The Modern School Movement: Anarchism and Education in the United States*. Oakland, Cal.: AK.

Avrich, Paul. 1988. *Anarchist Portraits*. Princeton, N.J.: Princeton University Press.

Avrich, Paul. 1996. *Anarchist Voices: An Oral History of Anarchism in America*. Abridged ed. Princeton, N.J.: Princeton University Press.

Avrich, Paul, and Karen Avrich. 2012. *Sasha and Emma: The Anarchist Odyssey of Alexander Berkman and Emma Goldman*. Cambridge, Mass.: Belknap.

Bailyn, Bernard. [1967] 1992. *The Ideological Origins of the American Revolution*. Enlarged ed. Cambridge, Mass.: Harvard University Press.

Baker, Jean H. 2011. *Margaret Sanger: A Life of Passion*. New York: Hill and Wang.

Ballentine, Claire. 2015. "ADPhi Controversy Through the Years." *Duke Chronicle*, September 15.

Banner, Lois. 1980. *Elizabeth Cady Stanton: A Radical for Woman's Rights*. Boston: Little, Brown.

Bantman, Constance. 2006. "Internationalism without an International? Cross-Channel Anarchist Networks, 1880–1914." *Revue belge de philologie et d'histoire* 84:961–981.

Bardsley, Jan. 2007. *The Bluestockings of Japan: New Woman Essays and Fiction from Seitō, 1911–16*. Ann Arbor: Center for Japanese Studies, University of Michigan.

Bardsley, Jan. 2008. "The New Woman of Japan and the Intimate Bonds of Translation." *Review of Japanese Culture and Society* 20:206–225.

Bardsley, Jan. 2012. "The New Woman Meets the Geisha: The Politics of Pleasure in 1910s Japan." *Intersections: Gender and Sexuality in Asia and the Pacific* 29:1–24.

Barkalow, Jordon B. 2009. "Forging American Identity: The Revolutionary Histories of Mercy Warren and David Ramsey." Paper presented at the annual meeting of the Midwest Political Science Association.

Barnes, Paul. 1999. "Elizabeth Cady Who? Why We Chose Elizabeth Cady Stanton and Susan B. Anthony as Subjects for a Film Biography." *Public Historian* 21:21–26.

Barrow, Logie. 1986. *Independent Spirits: Spiritualism and English Plebeians, 1850–1910*. London: Routledge & Kegan Paul.

Barry, Maltman. [1872] 1958. "Report of the Fifth Annual General Congress of the International Working Men's Association, Held at The Hague, Holland, September 2–9, 1872." In *The First International: Minutes of The Hague Congress of 1872 with Related Documents*, ed. Hans Gerth. Madison: University of Wisconsin Press.

Bashford, Alison. 2007. "Nation, Empire, Globe: The Spaces of Population Debate in the Interwar Years." *Comparative Studies in Society and History* 49:170–201.

Baskin, Alex. 1976. *Margaret Sanger, the Woman Rebel, and the Rise of the Birth Control Movement in the United States*. New York: Archives of Social History.

Battan, Jesse F. 2004. "'You Cannot Fix the Scarlet Letter on My Breast!': Women Reading, Writing, and Reshaping the Sexual Culture of Victorian America." *Journal of Social History* 37:601–644.

Baym, Nancy. 1991a. "Between Enlightenment and Victorian: Toward a Narrative of American Women Writers Writing History." *Critical Inquiry* 18:22–41.

Baym, Nancy. 1991b. "Mercy Otis Warren's Gendered Melodrama of Revolution." *South Atlantic Quarterly* 90:531–554.

Beaumont, Gustave de. [1835] 1958. *Marie or Slavery in the United States*. Stanford: Stanford University Press.

Belknap, Michal R. 1989. "Political Justice Personified." *Reviews in American History* 17:248–253.

Bell, John. 1903. "The Story of Louise Michel." *Otago Witness*, July 8.

Berkman, Alexander. [1922] 2001. *The Kronstadt Revolution.* Reprint. Charlestown, Mass.: Acme Bookbinding.

Berkman, Alexander, and Emma Goldman. 1922. "Bolsheviks Shooting Anarchists." *Freedom,* January.

Bernstein, Samuel. 1951. "American Labor and the Paris Commune." *Science & Society* 15:144–162.

Berthoff, Rowland. 1982. "Peasants and Artisans, Puritans and Republicans: Personal Liberty and Communal Equality in American History." *Journal of American History* 69:579–598.

Blacker, Carmen. 2002. "Shizue Kato: Courageous Feminist Campaigner for Birth Control and Women's Rights in Japan." *Guardian,* February 1.

Bloch, Ruth H. 1987a. "The Constitution and Culture." *William and Mary Quarterly,* Third Series 44:550–555.

Bloch, Ruth H. 1987b. "The Gendered Meanings of Virtue in Revolutionary America." *Signs* 13:37–58.

Blondeau, Nicole, and Jean-Paul Feuillebois, with the assistance of Anne-France Dautheville. 1979. *Victoria la Scandaleuse: La vie extraordinaire de Victoria Woodhull 1838–1927.* Paris: Éditions Mengès.

Blustain, Sarah. 2012. Review of *Margaret Sanger: A Life of Passion* by Jean H. Baker. *Women's Review of Books* 29:3–5.

Boardman, Kathleen A. 1997. Review of *Take My Word: Autobiographical Innovations of Ethnic American Working Women* by Anne E. Goldman. *Rocky Mountain Review of Language and Literature* 51:87–89.

"Bolshevist Witness Curbed by Court." 1918. *New York Times,* October 22.

Botting, Eileen Hunt, and Christine Carey. 2004. "Wollstonecraft's Philosophical Impact on Nineteenth-Century American Women's Rights Advocates." *American Journal of Political Science* 48:707–722.

Bradford, Roderick. 2006. *D. M. Bennett: The Truth Seeker.* Amherst, N.Y.: Prometheus.

Braude, Ann. 1989. *Radical Spirits: Spiritualism and Women's Rights in Nineteenth-Century America.* Boston: Beacon.

Breen, T.H. 1998. "Subjecthood and Citizenship: The Context of James Otis's Radical Critique of John Locke." *New England Quarterly* 71:378–403.

Brennan, Ellen Elizabeth. 1939. "James Otis: Recreant and Patriot." *New England Quarterly* 12:691–725.

Brooker, Peter, Sascha Bru, Andrew Thacker, and Christian Weikop, eds. 2013. *The Oxford Critical and Cultural History of Modernist Magazines,* Volume 3. Oxford: Oxford University Press.

Brookhiser, Richard. 1998. "The Happy Medium." *New York Times,* March 29.

Brough, James. 1980. *The Vixens: A Biography of Victoria and Tennessee Claflin.* New York: Simon and Schuster.

Brown, Alice. 1896. *Mercy Warren*. New York: Charles Scribner's Sons.

Brown, Kathleen A., and Gigi Peterson. 1997. "North American Labor History Conference." *International Labor and Working-Class History* 52:143–146.

Buckman, Rilma. 1944. "Social Engineering: A Study of the Birth Control Movement." *Social Forces* 22:420–428.

Buescher, John B. 2002. "More Lurid Than Lucid: The Spiritualist Invention of the Word 'Sexism.'" *Journal of the American Academy of Religion* 70:561–592.

Buhle, Mary Jo. 1988. Review of *Bread Upon the Waters* by Rose Pesotta. *Women's Review of Books* 5:15–16.

Bullard, Alice. 2000. *Exile to Paradise: Savagery and Civilization in Paris and the South Pacific, 1790–1900*. Stanford: Stanford University Press.

Burgan, Michael. 2005. *Elizabeth Cady Stanton: Social Reformer*. Minneapolis: Compass Point.

Bussel, Robert. 1988. Review of *Bread upon the Waters* by Rose Pesotta. *Industrial and Labor Relations Review* 41:653–654.

Bussel, Robert. 1999. *From Harvard to the Ranks of Labor: Powers Hapgood and the American Working Class*. University Park: The Pennsylvania State University Press.

Capello, Lawrence. 2014. "In Harm's Way: The Lawrence Textile Strike Children's Affair." In *The Great Lawrence Textile Strike of 1912: New Scholarship on the Bread & Roses Strike*, eds. Robert Forrant and Jurg K. Siegenthaler. New York: Routledge.

Capo, Beth Widmaier. 2004. "Can This Woman Be Saved? Birth Control and Marriage in Modern American Literature." *Modern Language Studies* 34:28–41.

Caron, Vicki. 1998. "The Antisemitic Revival in France in the 1930s: The Socioeconomic Dimension Reconsidered." *Journal of Modern History* 70:24–73.

Carpenter, Cari M. 2010a. "Introduction." In *Selected Writings of Victoria Woodhull: Suffrage, Free Love, and Eugenics* by Victoria C. Woodhull, ed. Cari M. Carpenter. Lincoln: University of Nebraska Press.

Carpenter, Cari M. 2010b. "Note on the Text." In *Selected Writings of Victoria Woodhull: Suffrage, Free Love, and Eugenics* by Victoria C. Woodhull, ed. Cari M. Carpenter. Lincoln: University of Nebraska Press.

Cayleff, Susan E. 2016. *Nature's Path: A History of Naturopathic Healing in America*. Baltimore: Johns Hopkins University Press.

Chafee, Zachariah, Jr. 1921. "A Contemporary State Trial – The United States *versus* Jacob Abrams *et als.*" *Harvard Law Review* 35:9–14.

Chapman, Mary 1896. *Revolutionary Ancestry: Mercy Warren Chapter*. Springfield, Mass.: N.p.

Chesler, Ellen. [1992] 2007. *Woman of Valor: Margaret Sanger and the Birth Control Movement in America*. New York: Simon & Schuster.

Chevalier, Lucien. [1922] 1925. "Freedom of Thought." In *Letters from Russian Prisons*: consisting of reprints of documents by political prisoners in Soviet prisons, prison camps and exile, and reprints of affidavits concerning political persecution in Soviet Russia, official statements by Soviet authorities, excerpts from Soviet laws pertaining to civil liberties, and other documents, with introductory letters by twenty-two well known European and American authors, ed. International Committee for Political Prisoners. London: C.W. Daniel. https://wdc.contentdm.oclc. org/digital/collection/russian/id/4671 (February 15, 2018).

Chincholle, Charles. 1885. *Les Survivants de la Commune*. Paris: L. Boulanger.

Cima, Gay Gibson. 2000. "Black and Unmarked: Phillis Wheatley, Mercy Otis Warren, and the Limits of Strategic Anonymity." *Theatre Journal* 52:465–495.

Claflin, Tennie C. 1871a. *Constitutional Equality: A Right of Woman*. New York: Woodhull, Claflin & Co.

Claflin, Tennie C. 1871b. "My Word on Abortion, and Other Things." *Woodhull & Claflin's Weekly*, September 23.

Claflin, Tennie C. 1871c. "Virtue: What it is and what it isn't." *Woodhull & Claflin's Weekly*, December 23.

Claflin, Tennie C. 1872a. "Beginning of the Battle." *Woodhull & Claflin's Weekly*, November 2.

Claflin, Tennie C. 1872b. "The Ethics of Sexual Equality." *Woodhull & Claflin's Weekly*, April 6.

Claflin, Tennie C. 1872c. "Seduction: What It Is and What It Is Not." *Woodhull & Claflin's Weekly*, January 6.

Claflin, Tennie C. 1874a. "Pictures from the Dubuque (Iowa) Papers." *Woodhull & Claflin's Weekly*, February 21.

Claflin, Tennie C. 1874b. "Miss Tennie C. Claflin." *Woodhull & Claflin's Weekly*, May 23.

Claflin, Tennie C. 1897. *Talks and Essays*, volume I. Westminster, UK: Roxburghe.

Claflin, Tennie C. 1898a. *Essays on Social Topics*, volumes I and II. Westminster, UK: Roxburghe.

Claflin, Tennie C. 1898b. *Essays on Social Topics*, volume III. Westminster, UK: Roxburghe.

Claflin, Tennie C. 1912. *A Discourse on the True Meaning of the Bible as Applied to Morals and Laws*. London: St. Clements.

Claflin, Tennie C. 1920. *The Need of Revising Morals and Laws: A Lecture Delivered by Lady Cook (née Tennessee Claflin) at the Royal Albert Hall, London, on May 6, 1910*. London: Hayman, Christy & Lilly.

Claflin, Tennie C. 1922. *Illegitimacy*. London: Lady Cook [Tennie C. Claflin].

Clews, Henry. 1886. *Twenty-Eight Years in Wall Street*. New York: Irving.

Cohan, William D. 2014. *The Price of Silence: The Duke Lacrosse Scandal, the Power of the Elite, and the Corruption of Our Great Universities*. New York: Scribner.

Cohen, Lester H. 1980. "Explaining the Revolution: Ideology and Ethics in Mercy Otis Warren's Historical Theory." *William and Mary Quarterly*, Third Series 37:200–218.

Cohen, Lester H. 1983. "Mercy Otis Warren: The Politics of Language and the Aesthetics of Self." *American Quarterly* 35:481–498.

Cohen, Lester H. 1994. "Foreword." In *History of the Rise, Progress, and Termination of the American Revolution* by Mercy Otis Warren, ed. Lester H. Cohen, vol. 1. http://oll .libertyfund.org/title/815 (September 1, 2011).

"Col. Fisk's Successor." 1872. *Woodhull & Claflin's Weekly*, June 1.

Collins, Henry. 1962. "Karl Marx, the International and the British Trade Union Movement." *Science & Society* 26:400–421.

Coman, Martha. 1922. "Girls Who Work Charmed with Bryn Mawr Industrial School." *New York Herald*, June 25.

"Comments." 1924. *Road to Freedom*, November.

"Conditional Pardons for Four Deportees." 1921. *New York Herald*, November 24.

Copp, Terry. 1982. "The Rise of Industrial Unions in Montréal 1935–1945." *Relations Industrielles / Industrial Relations* 37:843–875.

Corn, David. 2016. "The Time Ted Cruz Defended a Ban on Dildos." *Mother Jones*, April 13.

Cornell, Andrew. 2011. "'For a World Without Oppressors': U.S. Anarchism from the Palmer Raids to the Sixties." Ph.D. diss. New York University.

Cornell, Saul. 1999. *The Other Founders: Anti-Federalism & the Dissenting Tradition in America, 1788–1828*. Chapel Hill: University of Carolina Press.

Cortázar, Julio. 1989. *Nicaraguan Sketches – Observations and Reflections on the Revolutionary Struggle of Latin America*. New York: W.W. Norton.

Coutts, Angela. 2006. "Gender and Literary Production in Modern Japan: The Role of Female-Run Journals in Promoting Writing by Women during the Interwar Years." *Signs* 32:167–195.

Coutts, Angela. 2012. "Imagining Radical Women in Interwar Japan: Leftist and Feminist Perspectives." *Signs* 37:325–355.

Crichfield, Grant. 1972. Review of "Louise Michel ou La Velleda de l'anarchie" by Édith Thomas. *Nineteenth-Century French Studies* 1:53–54.

Crockett, Carrie. 2016. "The Great Escape." *Carceral Archipelago*, April 19. http://staff blogs.le.ac.uk/carchipelago/2016/04/19/the-great-escape/ (February 19, 2018).

Crump, John. 1998. "The Anarchist Movement in Japan, 1906–1996." Anarchist Communist Editions, Pamphlet No. 8. http://libcom.org/library/anarchist-movement-japan (April 20, 2018).

Cullen-DuPont, Kathryn. 1999. "Introduction." In *Margaret Sanger: An Autobiography*, by Margaret Sanger. New York: Cooper Square.

Cutler, Sofia. 2017. "The Midinette Spring: How Hemmed-in Garment Workers Burst the Seams of Canadian Labour History." *Briarpatch*, June 30. https://briarpatch magazine.com/articles/view/the-midinette-spring (January 19, 2018).

Danaswamy, Jayacintha. 2006. "Michel, Louise, 1830–1905." https://libcom.org/history/michel-louise-1830–1905 (May 6, 2018).

Darwin, M.F. 1919. *One Moral Standard for All: Extracts from the Lives of Victoria Claflin Woodhull (now Mrs. John Biddulph Martin) and Tennessee Claflin (now Lady Cook)*. New York: Caulon.

Davies, Kate. 2005. *Catharine Macaulay and Mercy Otis Warren: The Revolutionary Atlantic and the Politics of Gender*. Oxford: Oxford University Press.

Davis, Sara deSaussure. 1979. "Feminist Sources in *The Bostonians*." *American Literature* 50:570–587.

Davis, Sue. 2008. *The Political Thought of Elizabeth Cady Stanton: Women's Rights and the American Political Traditions*. New York: New York University Press.

Dawson, Oswald. 1897. *Personal Rights and Sexual Wrongs*. London: William Reeves.

De Grazia, Edward. 2006. "The Haymarket Bomb." *Law and Literature* 18:283–322.

DeLamotte, Eugenia C. 2004. *Gates of Freedom: Voltairine de Cleyre and the Revolution of the Mind*. Ann Arbor: University of Michigan Press.

Deland, Lorin F. 1912. "The Lawrence Strike: A Study." *Atlantic*, May.

Delaney, Ed, and M.T. Rice. 1927. *The Bloodstained Trail: A History of Militant Labor in the United States*. Seattle: Industrial Worker.

DeLeon, David. 1978. *The American as Anarchist: Reflections on Indigenous Radicalism*. Baltimore: The Johns Hopkins University Press.

"Deported Radicals Enter Soviet Russia." 1921. *Richmond* [Va.] *Palladium*, December 17.

DeVoto, Bernard. 1928. "Victoria Woodhull." *Saturday Review of Literature*, December 29.

Dickey, Larry. 1987. "The Pocockian Moment." *Journal of British Studies* 26:96–107.

Diggs, Nancy Brown. 1998. *Steel Butterflies: Japanese Women and the American Experience*. Albany: State University of New York Press.

Dirck, Brian R. 2003. *Waging War on Trial: A Handbook with Cases, Laws, and Documents*. Santa Barbara, Calif.: ABC-CLIO.

Doane, Right Rev. William Croswell. 1896. "Some Later Aspects of Woman Suffrage." *North American Review* 163:537–548.

Dobbin, Frank R. 1993. "The Social Construction of the Great Depression: Industrial Policy during the 1930s in the United States, Britain, and France." *Theory and Society* 22:1–56.

Douglass, Frederick. 1867. "An Appeal to Congress for Impartial Suffrage." *Atlantic*, January.

Doyle, J.E.P. 1875. *Plymouth Church and its Pastor; or Henry Ward Beecher and his Accusers*. St. Louis : Bryan, Brand.

Drinnon, Richard. 1961. *Rebel in Paradise: A Biography of Emma Goldman*. Chicago: University of Chicago Press.

"Dr. Pincus, Developer of Birth-Control Pill, Dies." 1967. *New York Times*, August 23.

DuBois, Ellen Carol. 1975. "Introduction." In "On Labor and Free Love: Two Unpublished Speeches of Elizabeth Cady Stanton." *Signs* 1:257–259.

DuBois, Ellen Carol. 1987. "Outgrowing the Compact of the Fathers: Equal Rights, Woman Suffrage, and the United States Constitution, 1820–1878." *Journal of American History* 74:836–862.

DuBois, Ellen Carol. 1992. "Introduction to Part Three." In T*he Elizabeth Cady Stanton – Susan B. Anthony Reader: Correspondence, Writings, Speeches*, ed. Ellen Carol DuBois. Revised ed. Boston: Northeastern University Press.

DuBois, Ellen Carol, and Richard Cándida Smith, eds. 2007. *Elizabeth Cady Stanton, Feminist as Thinker: A Reader in Documents and Essays*. New York: New York University Press.

Duniway, Abigail Scott. 1872. "Editorial Jottings from the East." *New Northwest*, May 31.

Durham, Martin. 1985. "British Revolutionaries and the Suppression of the Left in Lenin's Russia, 1918–1924." *Journal of Contemporary History* 20:203–219.

Editorial. 1871a. *Evening News* [Indianapolis], September 15.

Editorial. 1871b. *The Enterprise* [Sweetwater, Tenn.], September 7.

Editorial. 1894. *Western Mail* [Cardiff, UK], February 28.

Eichner, Carolyn J. 2004. *Surmounting the Barricades: Women in the Paris Commune.* Bloomington: Indiana University Press.

Eig, Jonathan. 2014. "The Team That Invented the Birth-Control Pill." *Atlantic*, October 9. https://www.theatlantic.com/health/archive/2014/10/the-team-that-invented-the-birth-control-pill/380684/ (December 25, 2017).

Endo, Mika. 2008. "Nation, Education, and the Female Teacher: A Reading of Hirano Fumiko's Record of a Woman Teacher." *U.S.-Japan Women's Journal* 35:80–97.

Engbers, Susanna Kelly. 2007. "With Great Sympathy: Elizabeth Cady Stanton's Innovative Appeals to Emotion." *Rhetoric Society Quarterly* 37:307–332.

Engels, Friedrich. 1884. The Origin of the Family, Private Property, and the State. https://www.marxists.org/archive/marx/works/1884/origin-family/cho2d.htm (February 23, 2016).

En grève avec Léa et les midinettes. 2015. *Journal de Montréal*, November 21. http://www.journaldemontreal.com/2015/11/21/en-greve-avec-lea-et-les-midinettes (January 27, 2018).

Epstein, Melech. 1969. *Jewish Labor in U. S. A.: An Industrial, Political and Cultural History of the Jewish Labor Movement.* 2 vols. Brooklyn, N.Y.: Ktav.

"Facts and Fancies." 1872. *Public Ledger* [Memphis, Tenn.], June 17.

Falk, Candace, ed. 2005a. *Emma Goldman: A Documentary History of the American Years.* 2 vols. Berkeley: University of California Press.

Falk, Candace. 2005b. "Forging Her Place: An Introduction." In *Emma Goldman: A Documentary History of the American Years*, ed. Candace Falk. Vol. 1. Berkeley: University of California Press.

Farrell, James M. 2006. "The Writs of Assistance and Public Memory: John Adams and the Legacy of James Otis." *New England Quarterly* 79:533–556.

Federal Writers' Project of the Works Progress Administration of Northern California. [1940] 2011. *San Francisco in the 1930s: The WPA Guide to the City by the Bay.* Oakland: University of California Press.

Felix, David. 1983. "The Dialectic of the First International and Nationalism." *Review of Politics* 45:20–44.

Ferguson, Adam. 1767. *An Essay on the History of Civil Society.* Indianapolis: Liberty Fund. http://oll.libertyfund.org/?option=com_staticxt&staticfile=show.php%3Ftitle =1428&Itemid=27 (January 7, 2013).

Ferguson, James R. 1979. "Reason in Madness: The Political Thought of James Otis." *William and Mary Quarterly*, Third Series 36:194–214.

Ferretti, Federico. 2016. "Anarchist Geographers and Feminism in Late 19th Century France: the Contributions of Elisée and Elie Reclus." *Historical Geography* 44:68–88.

Fetridge, W. Pembroke. 1871. *The Paris Commune in 1871; with a Full Account of the Bombardment, Capture, and Burning of the City.* New York: Harper & Brothers.

Feuerbach, Ludwig. 1854. *The Essence of Christianity.* Trans. Marian Evans. 2nd ed. London: John Chapman.

Fields, Jill. 2007. *An Intimate Affair: Women, Lingerie, and Sexuality.* Berkeley: University of California Press.

Filler, Stephen. 2009. "Going beyond Individualism: Romance, Personal Growth, and Anarchism in the Autobiographical Writings of Itō Noe." *U.S.-Japan Women's Journal* 37:57–90.

Fleming, Thomas. 2009. *The Intimate Lives of the Founding Fathers.* New York: HarperCollins.

Flexner, Eleanor, and Ellen Fitzpatrick. 1996. *Century of Struggle: The Woman's Rights Movement in the United States.* Enlarged ed. Cambridge, Mass.: Belknap.

Foner, Philip S. 1972. "Two Neglected Interviews with Karl Marx." *Science & Society* 36:3–5.

Fowler, Robert Booth. 1996. Review of *The Woman Who Ran for President: The Many Lives of Victoria Woodhull* by Lois Beachy Underhill. *Journal of American History* 83:634–635.

Frankfurter, Felix. 1927. "The Case of Sacco and Vanzetti." *Atlantic*, March.

Frederick, Sarah. 2017. *Turning Pages: Reading and Writing Women's Magazines in Interwar Japan.* Honolulu: University of Hawaii Press.

"Free Love and Politics: The Multitude that Besieged the Academy Last Night." 1872. *Sun* [New York], March 30.

Frese, Joseph R. 1957. "James Otis and Writs of Assistance." *New England Quarterly* 30:496–508.

Friedman, Lawrence J., and Arthur H. Shaffer. 1975. "Mercy Otis Warren and the Politics of Historical Nationalism." *New England Quarterly* 48:194–215.

Frisken, Amanda 2008. "Obscenity, Free Speech, and "Sporting News" in 1870s America." *Journal of American Studies* 42:537–577.

Frühstück, Sabine. 2003. *Colonizing Sex: Sexology and Social Control in Modern Japan.* Berkeley: University of California Press.

Gabriel, Mary. 1998. *Notorious Victoria: The Life of Victoria Woodhull, Uncensored.* Chapel Hill, N. C.: Algonquin Books of Chapel Hill.

Galpin, W. Freeman. 1935. "Elizabeth Cady Stanton and Gerrit Smith." *New York History* 16:321–328.

Garrison, Dee. 1978. Review of *The Sex Radicals. Free Love in High Victorian America* by Hal D. Sears. *American Historical Review* 83:537.

Gaskell, Tamara. 2008. "A Citizen's, not a Woman's Right: *Carrie Burnham v. the Pennsylvania Supreme Court.*" *Pennsylvania Legacies* 8:20–27.

Gerber, Scott D. 1994. "The Republican Revival in American Constitutional Theory." *Political Research Quarterly* 47:985–997.

"German Communism – Manifesto of the German Communist Party." 1871. *Woodhull & Claflin's Weekly*, December 30.

Gerth, Hans, ed. 1958. *The First International: Minutes of The Hague Congress of 1872 with Related Documents*, trans. Hans Gerth. Madison: University of Wisconsin Press.

Giesberg, Judith. 2011. Review of *Elizabeth Cady Stanton: An American Life* by Lori D. Ginzberg. *Historian* 73:561–563.

Ginzberg, Lori D. 2009. *Elizabeth Cady Stanton: An American Life.* New York: Hill and Wang.

Girault, Ernest. 1906. *La Bonne Louise: Psychologie De Louise Michele.* Paris: Bibliothèque Des Auteurs Modernes.

"Girl Won't Accept Deportation Offer." 1921. *New York Times*, July 15.

Glass, Fred B. 2016. *From Mission to Microchip: A History of the California Labor Movement.* Oakland: University of California Press.

Glickstein, Jonathan A. 1998. Review of Timothy Messer-Kruse, "The Yankee International: Marxism and the American Reform Tradition, 1848–1876." *H-Pol, H-Net Reviews*, September. https://networks.h-net.org/node/9997/reviews/10484/glickstein-messer-kruse-yankee-international-marxism-and-american (March 29, 2017).

"Glimpses of Gotham." 1871. *Charleston Daily News* [S.C.], August 15.

Goldman, Anne E. 1996. *Take My Word: Autobiographical Innovations of Ethnic American Working Women.* Berkeley: University of California Press.

Goldman, Emma [1908] 2005. "Anarchy and What It Really Stands For." In *Emma Goldman: A Documentary History of the American Years*, ed. Candace Falk. Vol. 1. Berkeley: University of California Press.

Goldman, Emma [1910] 1917. *Anarchism and Other Essays.* 3rd ed. New York: Mother Earth Publishing Association.

Goldman, Emma. 1914a. Letter to Margaret Sanger, April 9. http://wyatt.elastic beanstalk.com/mep/MS/xml/ms106565.html (January 3, 2018).

Goldman, Emma. 1914b. Letter to Margaret Sanger, April 14. http://wyatt.elastic beanstalk.com/mep/MS/xml/ms106566.html (January 3, 2018).

Goldman, Emma. 1914c. *The Social Significance of the Modern Drama*. Boston: Richard D. Badger.

Goldman, Emma. 1916. "The Social Aspects of Birth Control." *Mother Earth* 11:468–475.

Goldman, Emma. 1918. "On the Way to Golgatha." *Mother Earth Bulletin*, February.

Goldman, Emma. 1923a. Letter to Dr. Magnus Hirschfeld, undated. Emma Goldman Papers, International Institute of Social History, Amsterdam, Netherlands.

Goldman, Emma. 1923b. "Offener Brief an den Herausgeber der Jahrbücher über Louise Michel." *Jahrbuch für sexuelle Zwischenstufen* 23:70–92.

Goldman, Emma. 1931a. Letter to Mollie Steimer, May 18. Emma Goldman Papers, International Institute of Social History, Amsterdam, Netherlands.

Goldman, Emma. [1931b] 1970. *Living My Life*. 2 vols. New York: Dover.

Goldman, Emma. 1936. Letter to the *Manchester Guardian*, June 17. Emma Goldman Papers, International Institute of Social History, Amsterdam, Netherlands.

Goldman, Emma. 1996. *Red Emma Speaks: An Emma Goldman Reader*. Ed. Alix Kates Shulman. 3rd ed. New York: Humanity.

Goldman, Emma. 2016. *Anarchy and the Sex Question: Essays on Women and Emancipation, 1896–1926*, ed. Shawn P. Wilbur. Oakland, Calif.: PM.

Goldstein, J.J. 1917. "The Birth Control Clinic Cases." *Birth Control Review*, February.

Goldstein, Sanford, and Kazuji Ninomiya. 1993. "Introduction." In *Beauty in Disarray* by Harumi Setouchi. Boston: Tuttle.

Gomel, Elana. 2007. Review of *Altered States: Sex, Nation, Drugs, and Self-Transformation in Victorian Spiritualism* by Marlene Tromp; and *Possessed Victorians: Extra Spheres in Nineteenth-Century Mystical Writings* by Sarah A. Willburn. *Victorian Studies* 49:751–753.

Gopnik, Adam. 2014. "The Fires of Paris: Why Do People Still Fight about the Paris Commune?" *New Yorker*, December 22 and 29.

Gordon, Ann D. 1999. "Who Replaces Stanton, Anthony, and Stone?" *Public Historian* 21:35–40.

Gordon, Linda. 1973. "Voluntary Motherhood; The Beginnings of Feminist Birth Control Ideas in the United States." *Feminist Studies* 1:5–22.

Gordon, Linda. [1974] 2007. *The Moral Property of Women: A History of Birth Control in America*. 3rd. ed. Urbana: University of Illinois Press.

Gordon, Thomas. [1721] 1995. "Character of a good and of an evil Magistrate, quoted from Algernon Sidney, Esq." In *Cato's Letters*, ed. Ronald Hamowy. Vol. 2. Indianapolis: Liberty Fund. http://oll.libertyfund.org/?option=com_staticxt&staticfile=show .php%3Ftitle=1238&chapter=64458&layout=html&Itemid=27 (February 6, 2014).

Gornick, Vivian. 2005. *The Solitude of Self: Thinking About Elizabeth Cady Stanton.* New York: Farrar, Strauss and Giroux.

Gray, Madeline. 1979. *Margaret Sanger: A Biography of the Champion of Birth Control.* New York: Richard Marek.

Greenberg, Wendy. 1999. *Uncanonical Women: Feminine Voice in French Poetry (1830–1871).* Amsterdam: Rodopi.

Griffith, Elisabeth. 1984. *In Her Own Right: The Life of Elizabeth Cady Stanton.* New York: Oxford University Press.

Grossman, Joanna. 2003. "Is the Tort of Wrongful Seduction Still Viable? A North Carolina Court will Get the Chance to Decide." *North Carolina State Bar Journal,* Summer.

Gullickson, Gay L. 1996. *Unruly Women of Paris: Images of the Commune.* Ithaca, N. Y.: Cornell University Press.

Gullickson, Gay L. 2016. "Women and the Paris Commune." http://www.dsausa.org/women_and_the_paris_commune (May 11, 2018).

Gutierrez, Cathy. 2005. "Sex in the City of God: Free Love and the American Millennium." *Religion and American Culture: A Journal of Interpretation* 15:187–208.

Guttmacher, Alan F. 1967. "Margaret Sanger's Two Monuments." *Journal of Sex Research* 3:251–252.

Hagedorn, Ann. 2007. *Savage Peace: Hope and Fear in America, 1919.* New York: Simon & Schuster.

Hane, Mikiso. 2003. *Peasants, Rebels, Women, and Outcastes: The Underside of Modern Japan.* 2nd ed. Lanham, Md.: Rowman & Littlefield.

Harison, Casey. 2007. "The Paris Commune of 1871, the Russian Revolution of 1905, and the Shifting of the Revolutionary Tradition." *History and Memory* 19:5–42.

Harman, Moses. 1897. "Lois Waisbrooker." *Lucifer the Light Bearer,* September 22.

Harman, Moses. 1900. "Lois Waisbrooker." *Lucifer the Light Bearer,* December 22.

Harper, Ida Husted. 1898. *The Life and Work of Susan B. Anthony,* 2 vols. Indianapolis: Hollenbeck.

Harper, Ida Husted. 1915. "Suffrage and a Woman's Centenary." *North American Review* 202:730–735.

Harpham, Edward. 1984. "Liberalism, Civic Humanism, and the Case of Adam Smith." *American Political Science Review* 78:764–774.

Hart, Kathleen. 1999. "Louise Michel's Utopian Cosmogony." In *Corps/ Décors: Femmes, Orgie, Parodie: Hommage à Lucienne Frappier-Mazur,* ed. Catherine Nesci with Gretchen Van Slyke and Gerald Prince. Amsterdam: Rodopi.

Hart, Kathleen. 2001–2002. "Oral Culture and AntiColonialism in Louise Michel's "Mémoires" (1886) and "Légendes et chants de gestes canaques" (1885)." *Nineteenth-Century French Studies* 30:107–120.

Hart, Kathleen. 2004. *Revolution and Women's Autobiography in Nineteenth-Century France*. Amsterdam: Rodopi.

Hasday, Jill Elaine. 2000. "Contest and Consent: A Legal History of Marital Rape." *California Law Review* 88:1373–1505.

Hassell, James E. 1991. "Russian Refugees in France and the United States between the World Wars." *Transactions of the American Philosophical Society*, ns 81:1–96.

Havelin, Kate. 2007. *Victoria Woodhull: Fearless Feminist*. Minneapolis: Twenty-First Century.

Hayden, Wendy. 2010. "(R)Evolutionary Rhetorics: Science and Sexuality in Nineteenth-Century Free-Love Discourse." *Rhetoric Review* 29:111–128.

Hayden, Wendy. 2012. "From 'Mothers of the Nation' to 'Mothers of the Race': Nineteenth-Century Feminists and Eugenic Rhetoric." In *Feminist Rhetorical Resilience*, ed. Elizabeth A. Flynn, Patricia Sotirin, and Ann Brady. Logan: Utah State University Press.

Hayden, Wendy. 2013. *Evolutionary Rhetoric: Sex, Science and Free Love in Nineteenth-Century Feminism*. Carbondale: Southern Illinois University Press.

Hayes, Edmund M. 1976. "Mercy Otis Warren: The Defeat." *New England Quarterly* 49:440–458.

Healy, Thomas. 2013. *The Great Dissent: How Oliver Wendell Holmes Changed His Mind – and Changed the History of Free Speech in America*. New York: Metropolitan.

Hedrick, Joan D. 1997. Review of *Women Without Superstition: "No Gods-No Masters": The Collected Writings of Women Freethinkers of the Nineteenth and Twentieth Centuries* ed. Annie Laurie Gaylor. *Women's Review of Books* 15:12–13.

Henry, Josephine K. 1902. "Tribute to Elizabeth Cady Stanton." *Blue Grass Blade* [Lexington, Ky.], November 9.

Hewitt, Julia Cuervo. 2009. *Voices Out of Africa in Twentieth-Century Spanish Caribbean Literature*. Lewisburg, Penn.: Bucknell University Press.

Hibben, Paxton. 1927. *Henry Ward Beecher: An American Portrait*. New York: George H. Doran.

Hicks, Philip. 2005. "Portia and Marcia: Female Political Identity and the Historical Imagination, 1770–1800." *William and Mary Quarterly*, Third Series 62:265–294.

Higgins, Lynn A. 1982. Review of *The Red Virgin: Memoirs of Louise Michel* by Louise Michel. *Tulsa Studies in Women's Literature* 1:212–216.

Hodgson, Dennis, and Susan Cotts Watkins. 1997. "Feminists and Neo-Malthusians: Past and Present Alliances." *Population and Development Review* 23:469–523.

Hogan, Lisa S., and J. Michael Hogan. 2003. "Feminine Virtue and Practical Wisdom: Elizabeth Cady Stanton's 'Our Boys.'" *Rhetoric and Public Affairs* 6:415–435.

Holton, Sandra Stanley. 1994. "'To Educate Women into Rebellion': Elizabeth Cady Stanton and the Creation of a Transatlantic Network of Radical Suffragists." *American Historical Review* 99:1112–1136.

Horne, Eileen. 2016. "Notorious Victoria: the First Woman to Run for President." *Guardian*, July 20.

Horowitz, Helen Lefkowitz. 1999. "A Victoria Woodhull for the 1990s." *Reviews in American History* 27:87–97.

Horowitz, Helen Lefkowitz. 2000. "Victoria Woodhull, Anthony Comstock, and Conflict over Sex in the United States in the 1870s." *Journal of American History* 87:403–434.

Howe, Daniel Walker 1989. "Why the Scottish Enlightenment Was Useful to the Framers of the American Constitution." *Comparative Studies in History and Society* 31:572–587.

Howe, Rebecca. 1864. "To Whom It May Concern." *Ottawa Free Trader* [Ottawa, Ill.], June 4.

Hoyt, Edwin P. 1962. *The Vanderbilts and Their Fortunes*. Garden City, N. Y.: Doubleday.

Humphreys, Leonard A. 1995. *The Way of the Heavenly Sword: The Japanese Army in the 1920s*. Stanford: Stanford University Press.

Hutcheson, Maud Macdonald. 1953. "Mercy Warren, 1728–1814." *William and Mary Quarterly*, Third Series 10:378–402.

Huxley, Julian. 1928. "Biology of Population." *Birth Control Review*, March.

"In the Ninety-Second Year of the Revolution." 1889. *Lyceum*, May.

Isett, Benjamin. 2010. *From Victoria to Vladivostok: Canada's Siberian Expedition, 1917–1919*. Vancouver: University of British Columbia Press.

Itō, Noe. [1913a] 2003. "Recent Thoughts." In *Peasants, Rebels, Women, and Outcastes: The Underside of Modern Japan* by Mikiso Hane. 2nd ed. Lanham, Md.: Rowman & Littlefield.

Itō, Noe. [1913b] 2003. "The New Woman's Road." In *Peasants, Rebels, Women, and Outcastes: The Underside of Modern Japan* by Mikiso Hane. 2nd ed. Lanham, Md.: Rowman & Littlefield.

Itō, Noe. [1914a] 1996. "On 'The Tragedy of Women's Emancipation.'" In "Ito Noe: Living in Freedom. A Critique of Personal Growth in Japanese Society" by Lori Sue Shube. M.A. thesis. University of Southern California.

Itō, Noe. [1914b] 2003. "To Lady Shimoda Utako." In *Peasants, Rebels, Women, and Outcastes: The Underside of Modern Japan* by Mikiso Hane. 2nd ed. Lanham, Md.: Rowman & Littlefield.

Itō, Noe. [1914c] 2003. "To Mr. Shimoda Jirō." In *Peasants, Rebels, Women, and Outcastes: The Underside of Modern Japan* by Mikiso Hane. 2nd ed. Lanham, Md.: Rowman & Littlefield.

Itō, Noe. [1914d] 2003. "To My Cousin." In *Peasants, Rebels, Women, and Outcastes: The Underside of Modern Japan* by Mikiso Hane. 2nd ed. Lanham, Md.: Rowman & Littlefield.

Itō, Noe. [1915] 2003. "On Chastity." In *Peasants, Rebels, Women, and Outcastes: The Underside of Modern Japan* by Mikiso Hane. 2nd ed. Lanham, Md.: Rowman & Littlefield.

Itō, Noe. [1916a] 2003. "Response to Aoyama Kikue." In Peasants, Rebels, Women, and Outcastes: The Underside of Modern Japan by Mikiso Hane. 2nd ed. Lanham, Md.: Rowman & Littlefield.

Itō, Noe. [1916b] 2003. "To the Readers." In *Peasants, Rebels, Women, and Outcastes: The Underside of Modern Japan* by Mikiso Hane. 2nd ed. Lanham, Md.: Rowman & Littlefield.

Itō, Noe. [1923a] 2003. "A Group of Ambitious People in Pursuit of Power." In *Peasants, Rebels, Women, and Outcastes: The Underside of Modern Japan* by Mikiso Hane. 2nd ed. Lanham, Md.: Rowman & Littlefield.

Itō, Noe. [1923b] 2003. "Opinion on the Cursory Aspect of the Movement for the Prevention of Unemployment – The Need for Thoroughgoing Emphasis on the Right to Life." In *Peasants, Rebels, Women, and Outcastes: The Underside of Modern Japan* by Mikiso Hane. 2nd ed. Lanham, Md.: Rowman & Littlefield.

Itō, Noe. [1923c] 2003. "The Happiness of Personal Development." In *Peasants, Rebels, Women, and Outcastes: The Underside of Modern Japan* by Mikiso Hane. 2nd ed. Lanham, Md.: Rowman & Littlefield.

"Japan's First Feminist Magazine was a 1910s Phenomenon." 2018. *Bust*, February/March.

Jefferson, Thomas. 1816. Letter to Samuel Kercheval, September 5. https://founders.archives.gov/documents/Jefferson/03-10-02-0255 (May 18, 2018).

Jensen, Joan M. 1981. "The Evolution of Margaret Sanger's "Family Limitation" Pamphlet, 1914–1921." *Signs* 6:548–567.

Jensen, Joan M. 1984. "Inside and Outside the Unions: 1920–1980." In *A Needle, a Bobbin, a Strike: Women Needleworkers in America*, ed. Joan M. Jensen and Sue Davidson. Philadelphia: Temple University Press.

"John Beffel Dead; Aided Sacco Defense." 1973. *New York Times*, September 18.

Johnson, Gerald W. 1956. "Dynamic Victoria Woodhull." *American Heritage*, June.

Johnson, R. Christian. 1977. "Feminism, Philanthropy and Science in the Development of the Oral Contraceptive Pill." *Pharmacy in History* 19:63–78.

Johnston, Johanna. 1967. *Mrs. Satan: The Incredible Saga of Victoria C. Woodhull*. New York: G. P. Putnam's Sons.

Jones, Jason. 2009. "Breathing Life into a Public Woman: Victoria Woodhull's Defense of Woman's Suffrage." *Rhetoric Review* 28:352–369.

Katz, Daniel. 2011. *Altogether Different: Yiddish Socialists, Garment Workers, and the Labor Roots of Multiculturalism*. New York: New York University Press.

Katz, Esther. 1994. "The Editor as Public Authority: Interpreting Margaret Sanger." *Public Historian* 17:41–50.

Katz, Philip M. 1994. "The American Clergy Responds to the Paris Commune." *Church History* 63:393–406.

Kaufmann, Dorothy. 2004. *Édith Thomas: A Passion for Resistance*. Ithaca: Cornell University Press.

Kennedy, Kathleen. 1998. "Casting An Evil Eye on the Youth of the Nation: Motherhood and Political Subversion in the Wartime Prosecution of Kate Richards O'Hare, 1917–1924." *American Studies* 39:105–129.

Kennedy, Kathleen. 1999. *Disloyal Mothers and Scurrilous Citizens: Women and Subversion in World War I*. Bloomington: Indiana University Press.

Kent, Austin. 1873. *Mrs. Woodhull and her "Social Freedom."* Clinton, Mass.: Independent Radical Tract Society.

Kerber, Linda K. 1976. "The Republican Mother: Women and the Enlightenment – An American Perspective." *American Quarterly* 28:187–205.

Kerber, Linda K. 1985. "The Republican Ideology of the Revolutionary Generation." *American Quarterly* 37:474–495.

Kerber, Linda K. 1986. *Women of the Republic: Intellect and Ideology in Revolutionary America*. New York: W.W. Norton.

Kerber, Linda K. 1988. "Making Republicanism Useful." *Yale Law Journal* 97:1663–1672.

Kerber, Linda K. 1992. "The Paradox of Women's Citizenship in the Early Republic: The Case of *Martin v. Massachusetts*, 1805." *American Historical Review* 97:349–378.

Kern, Kathi. 2001. *Mrs. Stanton's Bible*. Ithaca, N. Y.: Cornell University Press.

Kern, Kathi. 2007. "'Free Woman is a Divine Being, the Savior of Mankind': Stanton's Exploration of Religion and Gender." In *Elizabeth Cady Stanton, Feminist as Thinker: A Reader in Documents and Essays*, ed. Ellen Carol DuBois and Richard Cándida Smith. New York: New York University Press.

Kesselman, Amy. 1991. "The "Freedom Suit": Feminism and Dress Reform in the United States, 1848–1875." *Gender and Society* 5:495–510.

Kessler-Harris, Alice. 1976. "Organizing the Unorganizable: Three Jewish Women and their Union." *Labor History* 17:5–23.

Kett, Joseph F. 1978. Review of *From Private Vice to Public Virtue. The Birth Control Movement and American Society since 1830* by Joseph Reed. *Science*, New Series 200:645–646.

Kinsman, Gary. 1982. Review of *Louise Michel* by Édith Thomas. *Atlantis* 8:151–155.

Kirk, Eleanor. 1869. "Is Hester Vaughan Guilty?." *Revolution*, January 21.

Koenig, Brigitte. 2004. "Law and Disorder at Home: Free Love, Free Speech, and the Search for an Anarchist Utopia." *Labor History* 45:199–223.

Kohn, Stephen M. 1994. *American Political Prisoners: Prosecutions Under the Espionage and Sedition Acts*. Westport, Conn: Praeger.

Komatsu, Ryūji, and Arnaud Nanta. 2002. "Un Retour sur le parcours du mouvement anarchiste au Japon." *Ebisu* 28:49–60.

Konefsky, Samuel [1956] 1974. *The Legacy of Holmes and Brandeis: A Study in the Influence of Ideas*. Reprint. Boston: Da Capo.

Konishi, Sho. 2007. "Reopening the 'Opening of Japan': A Russian-Japanese Revolutionary Encounter and the Vision of Anarchist Progress." *American Historical Review* 112:101–130.

Konishi, Sho. 2013. "Translingual World Order: Language without Culture in Post-Russo-Japanese War Japan." *Journal of Asian Studies* 72:91–114.

Kosak, Hadassa. 2009. "Anarchists, American Jewish Women." *Jewish Women: A Comprehensive Historical Encyclopedia*, March 1. https://jwa.org/encyclopedia/article/anarchists-american-jewish-women (January 19, 2018).

Kramnick, Isaac. 1982. "Republican Revisionism Revisited." *American Historical Review* 87:628–664.

Kropotkin, Peter. 1904. *Mutual Aid: A Factor of Evolution*. Revised ed. New York: McClure Phillips.

Kropotkin, Peter. [1906] 1990. *The Conquest of Bread*. Montréal: Black Rose.

Kropotkin, Peter. 1909. *The Commune of Paris*. London: Freedom.

Kropotkin, Peter. 1924. *Ethics: Origin and Development*. Trans. Louis S. Friedland and Joseph R. Piroshnikoff. New York: Dial.

Kropotkin, Peter. [1927] 1970. *Kropotkin's Revolutionary Pamphlets: A Collection of Writings by Peter Kropotkin*, ed. Roger N. Baldwin. New York: Dover.

Large, Stephen S. 1977. "The Romance of Revolution in Japanese Anarchism and Communism during the Taishō Period." *Modern Asian Studies* 11:441–467.

Laslett, John H.M. 1993. "Gender, Class, or Ethno-Cultural Struggle? The Problematic Relationship between Rose Pesotta and the Los Angeles ILGWU." *California History* 72:20–39.

Leeder, Elaine. 1989. "The Indomitable Militant Spirits: The Rose Pesotta and Emma Goldman Relationship." *Phoebe* 1:52–65.

Leeder, Elaine. 1993. *The Gentle General: Rose Pesotta, Anarchist, and Labor Organizer*. Albany: State University of New York Press.

Lehfeldt, Hans. 1967. "Margaret Sanger and the Modern Contraceptive Techniques." *Journal of Sex Research* 3:253–255.

Leighton, Marian. 1990. "Anarcho-Feminism and Louise Michel." *Our Generation Journal* 21:22–29.

Lenin, V.I. [1921] 1965. "Preliminary Draft Resolution of the Tenth Congress Of the R.C.P. on The Syndicalist and Anarchist Deviation in our Party" in *The Tenth Congress of the R.C.P. Verbatim Report, March 8–16, 1921*, 1st English Edition. Moscow: Progress Publishers. https://www.marxists.org/archive/lenin/works/1921/10thcong/ch04.htm (February 17, 2018).

Lerner, Gerda. 1971. "Women's Rights and American Feminism." *American Scholar* 40:235–248.

Levinson, Michael R. 2009. "Clear and Present Danger During World War I." *Litigation* 35:47–50, 54.

LeWarne, Charles P. 1972. "The Anarchist Colony at Home, Washington, 1901–1902." *Arizona and the West* 14:155–168.

LeWarne, Charles P. 1975. *Utopias on Puget Sound, 1885–1915*. Seattle: Washington University Press.

Lewis, I.M. [1971] 1989. *Ecstatic Religion: A Study of Shamanism and Spirit Possession.* 2nd. ed. London: Routledge.

Lewis, Jan. 1987. "The Republican Wife: Virtue and Seduction in the Early Republic." *William and Mary Quarterly*, Third Series, 44:689–721.

"Libel – Against British Museum." 1894. *Harvard Law Review* 8:113–114.

"Literary Intelligence." 1893. *British Medical Journal* 1:975.

Livy, Titus [Titus Livinius Patavinus]. 1905. *(Early) History of Rome*, trans. Rev. Canon Roberts. London: J.M. Dent.

"Long Prison Terms for the Bolsheviki." 1918. *New York Times*, October 26.

Lowenthal, Max. 1950. *The Federal Bureau of Investigation*. New York: William Sloane Associates.

Lowry, Bullitt, and Elizabeth Ellington Gunter. 1981a. "Epilogue." In *The Red Virgin: Memoirs of Louise Michel* by Louise Michel, eds. and trans. Bullitt Lowry and Elizabeth Ellington Gunter. Tuscaloosa: University of Alabama Press.

Lowry, Bullitt, and Elizabeth Ellington Gunter. 1981b. "Translators' Introduction." In *The Red Virgin: Memoirs of Louise Michel* by Louise Michel, eds. and trans. Bullitt Lowry and Elizabeth Ellington Gunter. Tuscaloosa: University of Alabama Press.

Lowy, Dina. 2007. *The Japanese "New Woman": Images of Gender and Modernity*. New Brunswick, N.J.: Rutgers University Press.

Lu, Yan. 2004. *Re-understanding Japan: Chinese Perspectives, 1895–1945*. Honolulu: University of Hawai'i Press.

Lutz, Alma. 1940. *Created Equal: A Biography of Elizabeth Cady Stanton, 1815–1902*. New York: John Day.

Mace, Emily R. 2009. "Feminist Forerunners and a Usable Past: A Historiography of Elizabeth Cady Stanton's *The Woman's Bible.*" *Journal of Feminist Studies in Religion* 25:5–23.

MacKinnon, Jan, and Steve MacKinnon. 1977. "Introduction." In "Agnes Smedley's 'Cell Mates,'" ed. Jan MacKinnon and Steve MacKinnon. *Signs* 3:531–533.

Maclean, Marie. 2003. *The Name of the Mother: Writing Illegitimacy*. London: Routledge.

Maclellan, Nic. 2004a. "Introduction." In *Louise Michel*, ed. Nic Maclellan. Melbourne, Victoria: Ocean.

Maclellan, Nic, ed. 2004b. *Louise Michel*. Melbourne, Victoria: Ocean.

MacPherson, Myra. 2014. *The Scarlet Sisters: Sex Suffrage and Scandal in the Gilded Age*. New York: Hachette.

Maga, Timothy P. 1982. "Closing the Door: The French Government and Refugee Policy, 1933–1939." *French Historical Studies* 12:424–442.

Maguire, John Thomas. 2009. "Maintaining the Vitality of a Social Movement: Social Justice Feminism, Class Conflict, and the Bryn Mawr Summer School for Women Workers, 1921–1924." *Pennsylvania History: A Journal of Mid-Atlantic Studies* 76:393–421.

Maier, Pauline. 1991. *From Resistance to Revolution: Colonial Radicals and the Development of American Opposition to Britain, 1765–1776*. New York: W.W. Norton.

Malin, James C. 1964. *A Concern about Humanity: Notes on Reform, 1872–1912 at the National and Kansas Levels of Thought*. Lawrence, Kans.: James C. Malin.

Maloyed, Christie Leann. 2010. "The Religious Foundations of Civic Virtue." Ph.D. diss. Texas A&M University.

Mann, Nora. 1914a. "Louise Michel: The Red Virgin (1830–1905)." *Woman Rebel*, April.

Mann, Nora. 1914b. "Louise Michel (Concluded)." *Woman Rebel*, May.

Marberry, M.M. 1967. *Vicky: A Biography of Victoria C. Woodhull*. New York: Funk & Wagnall's.

Marcus, Marvin. 1993. Review of *The Autobiography of Osugi Sakae* by Ōsugi, Sakae. *Journal of Asian Studies* 52:730–732.

"Margaret Sanger and Edith How-Martyn: An Intimate Correspondence." 1993. *Margaret Sanger Papers Project Newsletter*, Spring.

Marks, Jeannette. 1929. *Thirteen Days*. New York: Albert & Charles Boni.

Marquant, Robert. 1971. Review of *Louise Michel* by Édith Thomas. *Bibliothèque de l'école des chartes* 129:176–179.

Marsh, Margaret S. 1981. *Anarchist Women 1870–1920*. Philadelphia: Temple University Press.

Marshall, Byron K. 1992. "Translator's Introduction." In *The Autobiography of Ōsugi Sakae* by Ōsugi Sakae. Berkeley: University of California Press.

Marshall, H. Snowden. 1916. Letter to Thomas Watt Gregory, July 13. http://wyatt .elasticbeanstalk.com/mep/MS/xml/ms303889.html#ms303889 (January 3, 2018).

Mason, Paul. 2017a. "The Rebel France Could Not Crush: Paul Mason on his Play about the Passion of Louise Michel." *Guardian*, April 25. https://www.theguardian.com/ stage/2017/apr/25/the-rebel-france-could-not-crush-paul-mason-on-his-play-about-the-passion-of-louise-michel (April 30, 2018).

Mason, Paul. 2017b. "Tracing Louise Michel in the Pacific: Researching the Women Communards on New Caledonia." https://medium.com/mosquito-ridge/tracing-louise-michel-in-the-pacific-15d2a53716c3 (May 10, 2018).

Maupassant, Guy de. 1926. "Useless Beauty." In *Original Short Stories*, volume 6. New York: Alfred A. Knopf.

Maurice, Lori Klatt. 2004. "Stamping Out Indecency the Postal Way." http://academic
.evergreen.edu/k/klalor09/Post%20Office%20Censorship%20home.htm (May 25,
2015).

McAllister, Pam. 1985. "Introduction." In *A Sex Revolution* by Lois Waisbrooker. Philadelphia: New Society.

McCormick, Charles H. 2005. *Hopeless Cases: The Hunt for the Red Scare Terrorist Bomb-
ers*. Lanham, Md.: University Press of America.

McCrimmon, Barbara. 1975. "Victoria Woodhull Martin Sues the British Museum for
Libel." *Library Quarterly* 45:355–372.

McCrimmon, Barbara. 1986. "Richard Garnett as Censor." *British Library Journal*
12:64–75.

McCullough, David. 2001. *John Adams*. New York: Simon & Schuster.

McGuinness, Patrick. 2015. *Poetry and Radical Politics in Fin de Siècle France: From Anarchism to* Action française. Oxford: Oxford University Press.

McIlwain, C.H. 1931. Review of *Some Political Writings of James Otis* by Charles F. Mul-
lett. *New England Quarterly* 4:540–543.

McLaren, Angus. 1992. "Sex Radicalism in the Canadian Pacific Northwest, 1890–1920."
Journal of the History of Sexuality 2:527–546.

Meade, Marion. [1976] 2000. *Free Woman: The Life and Times of Victoria Woodhull*. Lincoln, Neb.: iUniverse.com.

Messer-Kruse, Timothy. 1998. *The Yankee International: Marxism and the American Reform Transition, 1848–1876*. Chapel Hill: The University of North Carolina Press.

Meyer, Kathryn. 2014. *Life and Death in the Garden: Sex, Drugs, Cops, and Robbers in
Wartime China*. London: Rowman and Littlefield.

Michel, Louise. [1871] 1986. "To Th. Ferré." In "Louise Michel's Poetry of Existence and
Revolt" by Charles T. Stivale. *Tulsa Studies in Women's Literature* 5:50–51.

Michel, Louise. [1885] 1980. *Légendes et chants de gestes canaques: Avec dessins et vo-
cabulaires*. Paris: Kéva.

Michel, Louise. [1886] 1981. *The Red Virgin: Memoirs of Louise Michel*, eds. and trans.
Bullitt Lowry and Elizabeth Ellington Gunter. Tuscaloosa: University of Alabama
Press.

Michel, Louise. 1890. *Le claque-dents*. Paris: E. Dentu.

Michel, Louise. [1905] 1987. *Avant la Commune*. Alfortville, France: Librairie
Internationaliste.

Michel, Louise. 1912. *Au gré du Vent: Poesies*. Paris: Fontemoing.

Michelman, Frank I. 1986. "Foreword: Traces of Self-Government." *Harvard Law Review*
100:4–77.

Michelman, Frank I. 1988. "Law's Republic." *Yale Law Journal* 97:1493–1537.

Mill, John Stuart. [1859] 1956. *On Liberty*, ed. Currin V. Shields. Indianapolis:
Bobbs-Merrill.

Miller, Lillian B. 1985. Review of *Cincinnatus: George Washington and the Enlightenment* by Garry Wills. *William and Mary Quarterly*, Third Series. 42:527–530.

Milton, John. [1644] 2011. *Areopagitica*. Santa Barbara, Calif.: Bandanna.

Minister, Meredith. 2013. "Religion and (Dis)Ability in Early Feminism." *Journal of Feminist Studies in Religion* 29:5–24.

Mitchell, Annie. 2003. "Character of an Independent Whig – 'Cato' and Bernard Mandeville." *History of European Ideas* 29:291–311.

Mitchell, Richard H. 1992. *Janus-Faced Justice: Political Criminals in Imperial Japan*. Honolulu: University of Hawai'i Press.

"Mollie Steimer Gets Six Months in Workhouse." 1919. *Evening World* [New York], October 30.

"Mollie Steimer is Held." 1919. *New York Tribune*, October 21.

"Mollie Steimer May be Freed to be Deported." 1920. *New York Tribune*, August 4.

"Mollie Steimer Put in Jail as a Radical." 1919. *Sun* [New York], October 19.

Molony, Barbara, Janet Theiss, and Hyaeweol Choi. 2016. *Gender in Modern East Asia: An Integrated History*. Boulder, Colo.: Westview.

Morgan, Murray. 1955. *The Last Wilderness*. Seattle: University of Washington Press.

Morrissey, James W. 1910. *Noted Men and Women: A Profusely Illustrated Book*. New York: Klebold.

Morton, James P., Jr. 1902. "Ruminations." *Lucifer the Light-Bearer*, May 29.

Moss, Jane. 1987. "Women's Theater in France." *Signs* 12:548–567.

Mullaney, Marie Marmo. 1984. "Gender and the Socialist Revolutionary Role, 1871–1921: A General Theory of the Female Revolutionary Personality." *Historical Reflections / Réflexions Historiques* 11:99–151.

Mullaney, Marie Marmo. 1990. "Sexual Politics in the Career and Legend of Louise Michel." *Signs* 15:300–322.

Nelson, Eric. 2004. *The Greek Tradition in Republican Thought*. Cambridge, UK: Cambridge University Press.

"Net for Bolsheviki in East Side Raid." 1918. *American Jewish Chronicle*, August 30.

Neuss, Margret. 1971. "Die Seitōsha: Der Ausgangspunkt der japanischen Frauenbewegung in seinenzeitgeschichtlichen und sozialen Bedingungen," part II. *Oriens Extremus* 18:137–201.

Newman, Louise Michele. 1999. *White Women's Rights: The Racial Origins of Feminism in the United States*. New York: Oxford University Press.

"News from Japan: A Letter from Baroness Ishimoto." 1923. *Birth Control Review*, January.

New York State Senate. 1920. "Revolutionary Radicalism: Its History, Purpose and Tactics with an Exposition and Discussion of the Steps Being Taken and Required to Curb It." Report of the Joint Legislative Committee Investigating Seditious Activities, April 24. Albany, N.Y.: J. B. Lyon.

Norton, Mary Beth. 1984. "The Evolution of White Women's Experience in Early America." *American Historical Review* 89:593–619.

Offen, Karen. 1989. "Reply to DuBois." *Signs* 15:198–202.

Oliver, Leon. 1873. *Great Sensation: A Full, Complete and Reliable History of the Beecher –
Tilton – Woodhull Scandal, with Biographical Sketches of the Principal Characters.*
Chicago: Beverly.

Orleck, Annelise. 1995. *Common Sense and a Little Fire: Women and Working-Class Politics in the United States, 1900–1960.* Chapel Hill: University of North Carolina Press.

Orleck, Annelise. 2001. Review of *"To Do and to Be": Portraits of Four Women Activists,
1893–1986* by Ann Schofield. *Journal of American History* 88:242–243.

O'Shaughnessy, Andrew Jackson. 2013. *The Men Who Lost America: British Leadership,
the American Revolution and the Fate of the Empire.* New Haven: Yale University
Press.

Ōsugi, Sakae. [1923] 2002. "Ma Vie Quotidienne en Prison." In "La Vie en prison d'un
anarchiste: Osugi Sakae" by Gilles Bieux. *Ebisu* 27:119–154.

Ōsugi, Sakae. [1930] 1992. *The Autobiography of Ōsugi Sakae.* Trans. Byron K. Marshall.
Berkeley: University of California Press.

Otis, James, Jr. 1765. *The Rights of the British Colonies Asserted and Proved.* Boston: J.
Almon.

Paglia, Camille. 1991. *Sexual Personae: Art & Decadence from Nefertiti to Emily Dickinson.* New York: Vintage.

Parker, Gail. 1971. "Introduction to the Paperback Edition." In *Eighty Years & More: Reminiscences 1815–1897* by Elizabeth Cady Stanton. New York: Schocken.

Parmet, Robert D. 2005. *The Master of Seventh Avenue: David Dubinsky and the American Labor Movement.* New York: New York University Press.

Parsons, Lucy E. 2004. *Freedom, Equality, & Solidarity: Writings & Speeches, 1878–1937,*
ed. Gale Ahrens. Chicago: Charles H. Kerr.

Passet, Joanne E. 2003. *Sex Radicals and the Quest for Women's Equality.* Urbana: University of Illinois Press.

Passet, Joanne E. 2004. "Yours for Liberty: Women and Freethought in Nineteenth-
Century Iowa." *Annals of Iowa* 63:137–169.

Passet, Joanne E. 2006. "Power through Print: Lois Waisbrooker and Grassroots Feminism." In *Women in Print* ed. James P. Danky and Wayne A. Wiegand. Madison: University of Wisconsin Press.

Paulson, Linda Dailey. 2004. "Committee for Industrial Organization." *St. James Encyclopedia of Labor History Worldwide: Major Events in Labor History and Their Impact.*
http://www.encyclopedia.com/history/encyclopedias-almanacs-transcripts-and-
maps/committee-industrial-organization (January 27, 2018).

Pearce, Fred. 2010. *The Coming Population Crash and Our Planet's Surprising Future.*
Boston: Beacon.

Pelletier, Philippe. 2002. "Ōsugi Sakae, Une Quintessence de l'anarchisme au Japon." *Ebisu* 28:93–118.

Perry, Michael W. 2005. "Introduction to 'Trial as by Fire; or, True and the False, Socially.'" In *Free Lover: Sex, Marriage and Eugenics in the Early Speeches of Victoria Woodhull*, by Victoria C. Woodhull. Seattle: Inkling.

Pesotta, Rose. 1939. Letter to David Dubinsky, November 7. Rose Pesotta Papers, New York Public Library, Rare Books and Manuscripts Division.

Pesotta, Rose. 1944. *Bread Upon the Waters*. https://theanarchistlibrary.org/library/rose-pesotta-bread-upon-the-waters (September 25, 2017).

Pesotta, Rose 1958. *Days of Our Lives*. Boston: Excelsior.

Peterson, Joyce Shaw. 1995. Review of *The Gentle General: Rose Pesotta, Anarchist and Labor Organizer* by Elaine Leeder. *American Historical Review* 100:1316.

Phelan, Craig. 2000. Review of *From Harvard to the Ranks of Labor: Powers Hapgood and the American Working Class* by Robert Bussel. *American Historical Review* 105:1759–1760.

Pirok, Alena R. 2011. "Mrs. Satan's Penance: The New History of Victoria Woodhull." *Legacy* 11:35–50.

Plotkin, Ira L. 1990. *Anarchism in Japan: A Study of the Great Treason Affair, 1910–1911*. Lewiston, N.Y.: Edwin Mellen.

Pocock, J.G.A. 1972. "Virtue and Commerce in the Eighteenth Century." *Journal of Interdisciplinary History* 3:119–134.

Pocock, J.G.A. [1975] 2003. *The Machiavellian Moment: Florentine Political Thought and the Atlantic Republican Tradition*. New Afterword ed. Princeton: Princeton University Press.

Pocock, J.G.A. 1998. "Catharine Macaulay: Patriot Historian." In *Women Writers and the Early Modern British Tradition*, ed. Hilda L. Smith. Cambridge, UK: Cambridge University Press.

Polenberg, Richard. 1985. "Progressivism and Anarchism: Judge Henry D. Clayton and the Abrams Trial." *Law and History Review* 3:397–408.

Polenberg, Richard. 1987. *Fighting Faiths: The Abrams Case, the Supreme Court, and Free Speech*. New York: Penguin.

Political Prisoners Defense and Relief Committee. 1919. *Sentenced to Twenty Years Prison*. New York: Political Prisoners Defense and Relief Committee.

Porter, David. 2006. "Introduction: Emma Goldman's Life and Involvement with Spain." In *Vision on Fire: Emma Goldman on the Spanish Revolution*, ed. David Porter. 2nd ed. Oakland, Calif.: AK.

Rabban, David M. 1997. *Free Speech in Its Forgotten Years*. Cambridge, UK: Cambridge University Press.

Rabinovitch, Eyal. 2001. "Gender and the Public Sphere: Alternative Forms of Integration in Nineteenth-Century America." *Sociological Theory* 19:344–370.

Rabinowitz, Paula. 1995. Review of *Heretics and Hellraisers: Women Contributors to "The Masses," 1911–1917* by Margaret C. Jones; *Rediscovering Forgotten Radicals: British Women Writers, 1889–1939* by Angela Ingram and Daphne Patai; and *A Price below Rubies: Jewish Women as Rebels and Radicals* by Naomi Shepherd. *Signs* 21:180–183.

Ramshorn. 1876. "The International." *Woodhull & Claflin's Weekly*, April 22.

Rasmussen, Cecelia. 2000. "Jewish Feminist Drew Latinas to Garment Union," *Los Angeles Times*, September 24.

Reed, Miriam. 2003. *Margaret Sanger: Her Life in Her Words*. Fort Lee, N.J.: Barricade.

Reekie, Gail. 1998. *Measuring Immorality: Social Inquiry and the Problem of Illegitimacy*. Cambridge, UK: Cambridge University Press.

Reich, Pauline C., and Atsuko Fukuda. 1976. "Japan's Literary Feminists: The 'Seito' Group." *Signs* 2:280–291.

Reif, Harriet. 1960. Review of *First Lady of the Revolution: The Life of Mercy Otis Warren* by Katharine Anthony. *William and Mary Quarterly*, Third Series 17:131–132.

"Remarks." 1872. *Woodhull & Claflin's Weekly*, May 4.

Richards, Jeffrey H. 1995. *Mercy Otis Warren*. New York: Twayne.

Riddle, Albert Gallatin. 1871. *The Right of Women to Exercise the Elective Franchise under the Fourteenth Article of the Constitution: Speech of A. G. Riddle in the Suffrage Convention at Washington*. Washington, D.C.: Judd & Detweiler. https://iiif.lib.harvard.edu/manifests/view/drs:2582325$2i (April 21, 2017).

Riegel, Robert E. 1963. "Women's Clothes and Women's Rights." *American Quarterly* 15:390–401.

Robbins, Mark W. 2012. "Bread, Roses, and Other Possibilities: The 1912 Lawrence Textile Strike in Historical Memory." *Historical Journal of Massachusetts* 40:94–121.

Roberts, Cokie. 2008. *Ladies of Liberty*. New York: HarperCollins.

Robinson, Lillian S. 1991. "Women on the Job: Work Life or Real Life?" *Review of Japanese Culture and Society* 4:1–10.

Robinson, Solveig C. 2010. "Victoria Woodhull-Martin and *The Humanitarian* (1892–1901): Feminism and Eugenics at the Fin de Siècle." *Nineteenth-Century Gender Studies* 6:1–27.

Roche, Anne, and Francoise Chatôt. 1982. *Louise/Emma*. Paris: Éditions Tierce.

Rocker, Rudolf. [1972] 1983. "Two Fighters: Mollie Steimer and Senya Fleshin." In *Fighters for Anarchism: Mollie Steimer & Senya Fleshin*, ed. Abe Bluestein. Minneapolis: Libertarian Publications Group.

Rocker, Rudolf, Augustin Souchy, Emma Goldman, and Alexander Berkman. 1924. "The Persecutions in Russia." *Freedom*, September.

Rodgers, Daniel T. 1992. "Republicanism: The Career of a Concept." *Journal of American History* 79:11–38.

Roosevelt, Franklin D. 1943. "Veto of the Smith-Connally Bill." *The American Presidency Project*, June 25. http://www.presidency.ucsb.edu/ws/?pid=16420 (January 27, 2018).

Ross, Kristin. 1989. "Commune Culture." In *A New History of French Literature* ed. Dennis Hollier. Cambridge, Mass.: Harvard University Press.

Ross, Kristin. 2015. *Communal Luxury: The Political Imaginary of the Paris Commune.* Brooklyn, N.Y.: Verso.

Rossiter, Clinton. 1953. *Seedtime of the Republic: The Origin of the American Tradition of Political Liberty.* New York: Harcourt, Brace & World.

Rupp, Leila J. 2009. *Sapphistries: A Global History of Love Among Women.* New York: New York University Press.

Ryang, Sonia. 2007. "The Tongue That Divided Life and Death. The 1923 Tokyo Earthquake and the Massacre of Koreans." *Asia-Pacific Journal* 5:1–13.

Sachs, Emanie. [1928] 1978. *The Terrible Siren: Victoria Woodhull.* New York: Arno.

Samuelson, Richard A. 1999. "The Constitutional Sanity of James Otis: Resistance Leader and Loyal Subject." *Review of Politics* 61:493–523.

Sánchez, George J. 1993. *Becoming Mexican American: Ethnicity, Culture, and Identity in Chicano Los Angeles, 1900–1945.* New York: Oxford University Press.

Sanger, Margaret. 1914. "Class and Character, Article No. 3." *Woman Rebel*, August.

Sanger, Margaret. 1917. "Woman and War." *Birth Control Review*, June.

Sanger, Margaret. 1918a. "Birth Control or Abortion?" *Birth Control Review*, December.

Sanger, Margaret. 1918b. "Clinics, Courts and Jails." *Birth Control Review*, April.

Sanger, Margaret. 1919a. "Are Birth Control Methods Injurious?" *Birth Control Review*, January.

Sanger, Margaret. 1919b. "Breaking Into the South – A Contrast." *Birth Control Review*, December.

Sanger, Margaret. 1919c. "How Shall We Change the Law[?]" *Birth Control Review*, July.

Sanger, Margaret. 1920a. "A Birth Strike to Avert World Famine" *Birth Control Review*, January.

Sanger, Margaret. 1920b. *Women and the New Race.* New York: Brentano's.

Sanger, Margaret. 1921a. "Birth Control the Key to International Peace and Security." *Birth Control Review*, February.

Sanger, Margaret. [1921b] 2003. "The Limitations of Eugenics." In *Margaret Sanger: Her Life in Her Words* by Miriam Reed. Fort Lee, N.J.: Barricade.

Sanger, Margaret. 1921c. "Woman's Error and Her Debt." *Birth Control Review*, August.

Sanger, Margaret. [1922a] 2003. "Birth Control in China and Japan." In *Margaret Sanger: Her Life in Her Words* by Miriam Reed. Fort Lee, N.J.: Barricade.

Sanger, Margaret. 1922b. "Our Fight in New York." *Birth Control Review*, December.

Sanger, Margaret. 1922c. "The Morality of Birth Control: An Address Delivered at the Park Theatre, New York City, on November 18, 1921." *Birth Control Review*, February.

Sanger, Margaret. 1922d. *The Pivot of Civilization*. New York: Brentano's.

Sanger, Margaret. 1924a. "The Fight Against Birth Control." *Birth Control Review*, September.

Sanger, Margaret. 1924b. "The War Against Birth Control." *American Mercury*, June.

Sanger, Margaret. 1925. "Editorial." *Birth Control Review*, June.

Sanger, Margaret. [1926] 2003. "Girlhood." In *Margaret Sanger: Her Life in Her Words* by Miriam Reed. Fort Lee, N.J.: Barricade.

Sanger, Margaret. 1931. *My Fight for Birth Control*. New York: Farrar & Rinehart.

Sanger, Margaret. [1938] 1999. *Margaret Sanger: An Autobiography*. New York: Cooper Square.

Sanger, Margaret. [1956] 2003. "Asia Discovers Birth Control." In *Margaret Sanger: Her Life in Her Words* by Miriam Reed. Fort Lee, N.J.: Barricade.

Sanger, Margaret. [1960] 2003. "Why I Went to Jail." In *Margaret Sanger: Her Life in Her Words* by Miriam Reed. Fort Lee, N.J.: Barricade.

Sanger, William. 1915. Letter to Margaret Sanger, January 21. http://wyatt.elastic beanstalk.com/mep/MS/xml/b2265654.html#b2265654 (January 3, 2018).

Sartwell, Crispin. 2005. "Priestess of Pity and Vengeance." In *Exquisite Rebel: The Essays of Voltairine de Cleyre – Anarchist, Feminist, Genius* by Voltairine de Cleyre, ed. Sharon Presley and Crispin Sartwell. Albany: State University of New York Press.

Sato, Barbara. 2003. *The New Japanese Woman: Modernity, Media, and Women in Interwar Japan*. Durham, N. C.: Duke University Press.

Saxton, Martha. 2009. Review of *Prodigal Daughters: Susanna Rowson's Early American Women* by Marion Rust and *The Muse of the Revolution: The Secret Pen of Mercy Otis Warren and the Founding of a Nation* by Nancy Rubin Stuart. *Women's Review of Books* 26:23–26.

Scates, Bruce. 1986. "'Millenium or Pandemonium?': Radicalism in the Labour Movement, Sydney, 1889–1899." *Labour History* 50:72–94.

Schauer, Frederick. 2005. "The Wily Agitator and the American Free Speech Tradition." *Stanford Law Review* 57:2157–2170.

"School for Women Workers." 1922. *New York Herald*, May 13.

Sears, Hal D. 1977. *The Sex Radicals. Free Love in High Victorian America*. Lawrence: Regents Press of Kansas.

Setouchi, Harumi. 1993. *Beauty in Disarray*, trans. Sanford Goldstein and Kazuji Ninomiya. Boston: Tuttle.

Setzer, Claudia. 2011. "A Jewish Reading of The Woman's Bible." *Journal of Feminist Studies in Religion* 27:71–84.

Shaffer, Arthur H. 1975. *The Politics of History: Writing the History of the American Revolution 1783–1815*. Chicago: Precedent.

Shalhope, Robert E. 1972. "Toward a Republican Synthesis: The Emergence of an Understanding of Republicanism in American Historiography." *William and Mary Quarterly*, Third Series 29:49–80.

Shalhope, Robert E. 1991. "In Search of the Elusive Republic." *Reviews in American History* 19:468–473.

Shepherd, Naomi. 1993. *A Price Below Rubies: Jewish Women as Rebels and Radicals*. Cambridge, Mass.: Harvard University Press.

Shone, Steve J. 2010. *Lysander Spooner: American Anarchist*. Lanham, Md.: Lexington.

Shone, Steve J. 2013. *American Anarchism*. Leiden, Netherlands: Brill.

Shryock, Richard. 2000. "Anarchism at the Dawn of the Symbolist Movement." *French Forum* 25:291–307.

Shube, Lori Sue. 1996. "Ito Noe: Living in Freedom. A Critique of Personal Growth in Japanese Society." M.A. thesis. University of Southern California.

Sievers, Sharon L. 1983. *Flowers in Salt: The Beginnings of Feminist Consciousness in Modern Japan*. Stanford: Stanford University Press.

Slosson, E.E. 1903. "An Experiment in Anarchy." *Independent* [Thermopolis, Wyo.], April 2.

Smedley, Agnes. 1977. "Cell Mates." In "Agnes Smedley's 'Cell Mates,'" ed. Jan MacKinnon and Steve MacKinnon. *Signs* 3:533–539.

Smith, Arthur D. Howden. 1927. *Commodore Vanderbilt: An Epic of American Achievement*. New York, Robert M. McBride.

Smith, Helena Huntington. 1930. "They Were Eleven." *New Yorker*, July 5.

Smith, Matthew Hale. 1871. *Twenty Years among the Bulls and Bears of Wall Street*. Hartford, Conn.: J.B. Burr.

Smith, Richard Cándida. 2007. "Stanton on Self and Community." In *Elizabeth Cady Stanton, Feminist as Thinker: A Reader in Documents and Essays*, ed. Ellen Carol DuBois and Richard Cándida Smith. New York: New York University Press.

Smith, William Raymond. 1966. *History as Argument: Three Patriot Historians of the American Revolution*. The Hague: Mouton.

Sneider, Allison N. 2010. Review of *Elizabeth Cady Stanton: An American Life* by Lori D. Ginzberg. *Women's Review of Books* 27:15–16.

"Social Freedom." 1871. *Woodhull & Claflin's Weekly*, December 2.

Solomon, Eugene. 2010. *Lies and Deceits*. New York: iUniverse.

Sommers, Christina Hoff. 2000. *The War Against Boys: How Misguided Feminism is Harming our Young Men*. New York: Simon & Schuster.

"Soviet Deports Girl Anarchist." 1922. *Washington Herald*, November 18.

Spivajc, Joseph. 1925. "Los Angeles: Report of Activity of the Libertarian Group." *Road to Freedom*, March.

Squire, Belle. 1911. *The Woman Movement in America: a Short Account of the Struggle for Equal Rights*. Chicago: A.C. McClurg.

Stanley, Thomas A. 1982. *Ōsugi Sakae: Anarchist in Taishō Japan; The Creativity of the Ego*. Cambridge, Mass.: Harvard University Press.

Stansell, Christine. 2007. "Missed Connections: Abolitionist Feminism in the Nineteenth Century." In *Elizabeth Cady Stanton, Feminist as Thinker: A Reader in Documents and Essays*, ed. Ellen Carol DuBois and Richard Cándida Smith. New York: New York University Press.

Stanton, Elizabeth Cady. [1848] 1992. "Address Delivered at Seneca Falls, July 19, 1848." In *The Elizabeth Cady Stanton – Susan B. Anthony Reader: Correspondence, Writings, Speeches*, ed. Ellen Carol DuBois. Revised ed. Boston: Northeastern University Press.

Stanton, Elizabeth Cady. [1851] 1991. "Sewing is a Dead Loss to the One Who Does It." In *The Radical Women's Press of the 1850s*, ed. Ann Russo and Cheris Kramarae. New York: Routledge.

Stanton, Elizabeth Cady. [1853] 1992. Letter to Susan B. Anthony. In *The Elizabeth Cady Stanton – Susan B. Anthony Reader: Correspondence, Writings, Speeches*, ed. Ellen Carol DuBois. Revised ed. Boston: Northeastern University Press.

Stanton, Elizabeth Cady. [1854] 2007. "Address to the Legislature of New York, Albany, February 14, 1854." In *Elizabeth Cady Stanton, Feminist as Thinker: A Reader in Documents and Essays*, ed. Ellen Carol DuBois and Richard Cándida Smith. New York: New York University Press.

Stanton, Elizabeth Cady. [1855] 1991. "Women and Men Are Not So Unlike." In *The Radical Women's Press of the 1850s*, ed. Ann Russo and Cheris Kramarae. New York: Routledge.

Stanton, Elizabeth Cady. [1856] 1991. "Woman Alone Must Be the Judge." In *The Radical Women's Press of the 1850s*, ed. Ann Russo and Cheris Kramarae. New York: Routledge.

Stanton, Elizabeth Cady. [1860a] 2007. "Address to the Legislature on Women's Right of Suffrage, Albany, February 18, 1860." In *Elizabeth Cady Stanton, Feminist as Thinker: A Reader in Documents and Essays*, ed. Ellen Carol DuBois and Richard Cándida Smith. New York: New York University Press.

Stanton, Elizabeth Cady. [1860b] 1994. "The Slave's Appeal." In "Elizabeth Cady Stanton, Reformer to Revolutionary: A Theological Trajectory" by Jeanne Stevenson-Moessner, *Journal of the American Academy of Religion* 62:690–696.

Stanton, Elizabeth Cady. 1868a. "Brick Pomeroy on the Situation." *Revolution*, December 17.

Stanton, Elizabeth Cady. 1868b. "Capital and Labor." *Revolution*, April 30.

Stanton, Elizabeth Cady. 1868c. "Editorial Correspondence." *Revolution*, September 10.

Stanton, Elizabeth Cady. 1868d. "Hester Vaughan." *Revolution*, November 19.

Stanton, Elizabeth Cady. 1868e. "Hester Vaughan." *Revolution*, December 10.

Stanton, Elizabeth Cady. 1868f. "Land for the Landless." *Revolution*, April 2.

Stanton, Elizabeth Cady. 1868g. "Letter from Frances Power Cobbe." *Revolution*, March 5.

Stanton, Elizabeth Cady. [1868h] 1990. Letter to Marvin Bovee. In "Elizabeth Cady Stanton on Capital Punishment" by Louis P. Masur. *Huntington Library Quarterly* 53:240–241.

Stanton, Elizabeth Cady. 1868i. "Manhood Suffrage." *Revolution*, December 24.

Stanton, Elizabeth Cady. 1868j. "Man the Usurper." *Revolution*, March 12.

Stanton, Elizabeth Cady. [1868k] 2000. "Miss Becker on the Difference in Sex." In *The Selected Papers of Elizabeth Cady Stanton and Susan B. Anthony*, volume II, ed. Ann D. Gordon. New Brunswick, N.J. Rutgers University Press.

Stanton, Elizabeth Cady. [1868l] 1975. "On Labor." In "On Labor and Free Love: Two Unpublished Speeches of Elizabeth Cady Stanton" by Ellen DuBois, *Signs* 1:260–263.

Stanton, Elizabeth Cady. 1868m. "Our Jails and Prisons." *Revolution*, July 23.

Stanton, Elizabeth Cady. 1868n. "Sharp Points." *Revolution*, April 9.

Stanton, Elizabeth Cady. 1868o. "The Strong-Minded Women of the Bible." *Revolution*, February 26.

Stanton, Elizabeth Cady. 1869a. "Hester Vaughan Once More." *Revolution*, August 19.

Stanton, Elizabeth Cady. 1869b. "I Have All the Rights I Want." *Revolution*, April 1.

Stanton, Elizabeth Cady. 1869c. "John Stuart Mill." *Revolution*, August 26.

Stanton, Elizabeth Cady. 1869d. "Peter and Paul in the Toledo Convention." *Revolution*, March 25.

Stanton, Elizabeth Cady. 1869e. "Prisons and Punishments." *Revolution*, January 7.

Stanton, Elizabeth Cady. 1869f. "The Clergy and Women." *Revolution*, May 8.

Stanton, Elizabeth Cady. 1869g. "The Women and the State." *Revolution*, August 19.

Stanton, Elizabeth Cady. 1869h. "Woman's Dress." *Revolution*, July 22.

Stanton, Elizabeth Cady. 1870a. "Editorial Correspondence." *Revolution*, May 5.

Stanton, Elizabeth Cady. [1870b] 1975. "On Marriage and Divorce." In "On Labor and Free Love: Two Unpublished Speeches of Elizabeth Cady Stanton" by Ellen DuBois, *Signs* 1:265–268.

Stanton, Elizabeth Cady. 1871. "Dress and Disease." *Revolution*, January 27.

Stanton, Elizabeth Cady. 1872a. Letter to Lucretia Mott. Elizabeth Cady Stanton Papers, Vassar College.

Stanton, Elizabeth Cady. 1872b. "The True Republic." *Woodhull & Claflin's Weekly*, May 18.

Stanton, Elizabeth Cady. 1872c. "Those Who Know Us." *Woodhull & Claflin's Weekly*, March 23.

Stanton, Elizabeth Cady. [1885] 2007. "Has Christianity Benefited Woman?" In *Elizabeth Cady Stanton, Feminist as Thinker: A Reader in Documents and Essays*, ed. Ellen Carol DuBois and Richard Cándida Smith. New York: New York University Press.

Stanton, Elizabeth Cady. [1888] 1992. "Address of Welcome to the International Council of Women, March 25, 1888." In *The Elizabeth Cady Stanton – Susan B. Anthony Reader: Correspondence, Writings, Speeches*, ed. Ellen Carol DuBois. Revised ed. Boston: Northeastern University Press.

Stanton, Elizabeth Cady. 1889. "Be Content in the Sphere where God has Placed You." *Free Thought Magazine*, March.

Stanton, Elizabeth Cady. [1890] 2007. "Divorce versus Domestic Warfare." In *Elizabeth Cady Stanton, Feminist as Thinker: A Reader in Documents and Essays*, ed. Ellen Carol DuBois and Richard Cándida Smith. New York: New York University Press.

Stanton, Elizabeth Cady. [1892] 2001. *Solitude of Self.* Ashfield, Mass.: Paris.

Stanton, Elizabeth Cady. [1895] 1999. *The Woman's Bible*. Amherst, N.Y.: Prometheus.

Stanton, Elizabeth Cady. [1898] 1971. *Eighty Years & More: Reminiscences 1815–1897*. New York: Schocken.

Steedman, Mercedes. 1997. *Angels of the Workplace: Women and the Construction of Gender Relations in the Canadian Clothing Industry, 1890–1940*. Toronto: Oxford University Press.

Steimer, Mollie. 1920a. Letter to Fannie Steimer, August 22. Elizabeth Gurley Flynn Papers, Wisconsin Historical Society, Madison, Wisc.

Steimer, Mollie. 1920b. "Steimer's Letter on Refusal to Sign." In *Attorney General A. Mitchell Palmer on Charges Made Against Department of Justice by Louis F. Post and Others.* Hearings Before the Committee on Rules, House of Representatives, Sixty-Sixth Congress, Second Session, Part 1. Washington, D. C.: Government Printing Office.

Steimer, Mollie. 1923. "Persecution of Anarchists in Russia." *Freedom*, November.

Steimer, Mollie. 1924a. "On Leaving Russia." *Freedom*, January.

Steimer, Mollie. 1924b. "The Communists as Jailers." *Freedom*, May.

Steimer, Mollie. 1925. "Statement by Mollie Steimer." In *Letters from Russian Prisons*: consisting of reprints of documents by political prisoners in Soviet prisons, prison camps and exile, and reprints of affidavits concerning political persecution in Soviet Russia, official statements by Soviet authorities, excerpts from Soviet laws pertaining to civil liberties, and other documents, with introductory letters by twenty-two well known European and American authors, ed. International Committee for Political Prisoners. London: C.W. Daniel. https://wdc.contentdm.oclc.org/digital/collection/russian/id/4671 (February 15, 2018).

Steimer, Mollie. [1930] 1983. "With Jack Abrams: Imprisonment and Deportation, A Memoir." In *Fighters for Anarchism: Mollie Steimer & Senya Fleshin*, ed. Abe Bluestein. Minneapolis, Minn.: Libertarian Publications Group.

Steimer, Mollie. 1931a. Letter to Alexander Berkman, October 19. Alexander Berkman Papers, International Institute of Social History, Amsterdam, Netherlands.

Steimer, Mollie. 1931b. Letter to Emma Goldman, May 12. Emma Goldman Papers, International Institute of Social History, Amsterdam, Netherlands.

Steimer, Mollie. 1931c. Letter to Emma Goldman, June 6. Emma Goldman Papers, International Institute of Social History, Amsterdam, Netherlands.

Steimer, Mollie. 1931d. Letter to Emmy Eckstein, January 22. Emmy Eckstein Papers, International Institute of Social History, Amsterdam, Netherlands.

Steimer, Mollie. 1932. Letter to Emma Goldman, January 12. Emma Goldman Papers, International Institute of Social History, Amsterdam, Netherlands.

Steimer, Mollie. 1936a. "Le cas de Zenzl Muhsam." *Le Réveil*, July 18.

Steimer, Mollie. 1936b. Letter to Emma Goldman, July 31. Emma Goldman Papers, International Institute of Social History, Amsterdam, Netherlands.

Steimer, Mollie. 1936c. Letter to Emma Goldman, June 11. Emma Goldman Papers, International Institute of Social History, Amsterdam, Netherlands.

Steimer, Mollie. [1966] 1983. "Tribute to Alexander Berkman on the Thirtieth Anniversary of His Tragic Death." In *Fighters for Anarchism: Mollie Steimer & Senya Fleshin*, ed. Abe Bluestein. Minneapolis, Minn.: Libertarian Publications Group.

Steimer, Mollie. N.d. Letter to Agnes Smedley, November 7. Elizabeth Gurley Flynn Papers, Wisconsin Historical Society, Madison, Wisc.

Stepniak, Sergei. 1882. *Underground Russia: Revolutionary Profiles and Sketches from Life*. https://theanarchistlibrary.org/library/sergei-stepniak-underground-russia-revolutionary-profiles-and-sketches-from-life (February 19, 2018).

Stern, Madeleine B. 1968. *The Pantarch: A Biography of Stephen Pearl Andrews*. Austin: University of Texas.

Stevens, Errol Wayne. 2009. *Radical L.A.: From Coxey's Army to the Watts Riots, 1894–1965*. Norman: University of Oklahoma Press.

Stevenson-Moessner, Jeanne. 1994. "Elizabeth Cady Stanton, Reformer to Revolutionary: A Theological Trajectory." *Journal of the American Academy of Religion* 62: 673–696.

Stewart, Pamela Joan. 2006. "Invisible Revolutions: Women's Participation in the 1871 Paris Commune." Ph.D. diss. University of Arizona.

Stinchcombe, Owen. 2000. *American Lady of the Manor, Bredon's Norton: The Later Life of Victoria Woodhull Martin, 1901–1927*. Cheltenham, UK: Owen Stinchcombe.

Stirner, Max. [1842] 1967. *The False Principle of Our Education, or Humanism and Realism*. Trans. Robert H. Beebe. Colorado Springs, Colo.: Ralph Myles.

Stirner, Max. [1907] 2005. *The Ego and His Own: The Case of the Individual Against Authority*. Trans. Steven T. Byington. Mineola, N. Y.: Dover.

Stivale, Charles T. 1986. "Louise Michel's Poetry of Existence and Revolt." *Tulsa Studies in Women's Literature* 5:41–61.

Stoehr, Taylor. 1979a. "Anthony Comstock." In *Free Love in America: A Documentary History*, ed. Taylor Stoehr. New York: AMS.

Stoehr, Taylor. 1979b. "Introduction." In *Free Love in America: A Documentary History*, ed. Taylor Stoehr. New York: AMS.

Stoehr, Taylor. 1979c. "Victora [sic] C. Woodhull." In *Free Love in America: A Documentary History*, ed. Taylor Stoehr. New York: AMS.

Stolberg, Benjamin. 1944. *Tailor's Progress: The Story of a Famous Union and the Men Who Made It.* Garden City, N.Y.: Doubleday, Doran.

Stoll, Ira. 2008. *Samuel Adams: A Life.* New York: Free Press.

Stone, Geoffrey R. 2004. *Perilous Times: Free Speech in Wartime From the Sedition Act of 1798 to the War on Terrorism.* New York: W.W. Norton.

Stone, Geoffrey R. 2006. "Constitutions Under Stress: International and Historical Perspectives." *Bulletin of the American Academy of Arts and Sciences* 59:34–36.

Stone, Geoffrey R. 2017. "'Sex and the Constitution': Margaret Sanger and the Birth of the Birth Control Movement." *Washington Post*, March 24.

Stopes, Harry. 2015. Review of Ross, Kristin. *Communal Luxury: The Political Imaginary of the Paris Commune* by Kristin Ross. *Financial Times*, May 1.

Strassel, Annamarie. 2012. "Designing Women: Feminist Methodologies in American Fashion." *Women's Studies Quarterly* 41:35–59.

Stuart, Nancy Rubin. 2008. *The Muse of the Revolution: The Secret Pen of Mercy Otis Warren and the Founding of a Nation.* Boston: Beacon.

Sumner, William Graham. 1914. *The Challenge of Facts and Other Essays.* Ed. Albert Galloway Keller. New Haven: Yale University Press.

Sumner, William Graham. [1940] 1971. *Sumner Today: Selected Essays of William Graham Sumner.* Reprint. Ed. Maurice R. Davie. Westport, Conn.: Greenwood.

Sunstein, Cass R. 1988. "Beyond the Republican Revival." *Yale Law Journal* 97:1539–1590.

Susumu, Yamaizumi. 2013. "The Significance of the Centennial of the High Treason Incident." In *Japan and the High Treason Incident*, eds. Masako Gavin and Ben Middleton. New York: Routledge.

Sutton, Charles. 1874. *The New York Tombs; its Secrets and its Mysteries. Being a History of Noted Criminals, with Narratives of their Crimes*, ed. James B. Mix and Samuel A. Mackeever. San Francisco: A. Roman.

Suzuki, Michiko. 2010. *Becoming Modern Women: Love and Female Identity in Prewar Japanese Literature and Culture.* Stanford: Stanford University Press.

Szajkowski, Zosa. 1971. "Double Jeopardy – The Abrams Case of 1919." *American Jewish Archives*, April.

Szpilman, Christopher W.A. 1998. "Conservatism and its Enemies in Prewar Japan: The Case of Hiranuma Kiichirô and the Kokuhonsha." *Hitotsubashi Journal of Social Studies* 30:101–133.

Taithe, Bertrand. 2001. *Citizenship and Wars: France in Turmoil, 1870–1871.* London: Routledge.

Takeuchi-Demirci, Aiko. 2010. "Birth Control and Socialism: The Frustration of Margaret Sanger and Ishimoto Shizue's Mission." *Journal of American-East Asian Relations* 17:257–280.

Tamboukou, Maria. 2013. "Educating the Seamstress: Studying and Writing the Memory of Work." *History of Education* 42:509–527.

Tanaka, Hikaru. 2013. "The Reaction of Jewish Anarchists to the High Treason Incident." In *Japan and the High Treason Incident*, eds. Masako Gavin and Ben Middleton. New York: Routledge.

Taylor, Barbara. 2003. *Mary Wollstonecraft and the Feminist Imagination*. Cambridge, UK: Cambridge University Press.

"Tennie and the Germans: Bankers and German Citizens Endorsing Claflin." 1871. *Sun* [New York], August 12.

"Tennie C. Claflin." 1874. *Omaha Bee*, April 16.

"Tennie Claflin Wants to be a Joan d'Arc – Asking for the Colonelcy of the Ninth." 1872. *Sun* [New York], May 15.

"Tennie's Tirade." 1872. *New York Herald*, March 30.

"The Allies and Russia." 1918. *Freedom*, August.

"The Allies' Intervention Cant." 1919. *Freedom*, January.

"The Claflin-Woodhull Difficulty." 1872. *New York Herald*, November 3.

"The 'Internationale' Initiative." 1871. *Woodhull & Claflin's Weekly*, December 30.

"The National Woman Suffrage Association at Steinway Hall." 1872. *New York Times*, May 11.

"The People of the State of New York, Respondent, vs. Margaret H. Sanger, Appellant." 1920. *Birth Control Review*, June.

"The Persecutions in Russia." 1924. *Freedom*, July–August.

"The Trial of Louise Michel." 1883. *Liberty*, July 21.

"The Victoria League." 1872. *Woodhull & Claflin's Weekly*, May 25.

"The Week." 1921. *New Republic*, November 16.

"The Woman With Two Husbands and a Newspaper." 1871. *Belmont Chronicle* [St. Clairsville, Ohio], August 31.

Thomas, Édith. 1971. *Louise Michel ou La Velléda de l'anarchie*. Paris: Gallimard.

Thomas, Édith. 1980. *Louise Michel*. Trans. Penelope Williams. Montréal: Black Rose.

Thomas, Tracy A. 2016. *Elizabeth Cady Stanton and the Feminist Foundations of Family Law*. New York: New York University Press.

Tilton, Theodore. 1871. *Victoria C. Woodhull: A Biographical Sketch*. New York: Golden Age.

Tipton, Elise K. 1997. "Ishimoto Shizue: The Margaret Sanger of Japan." *Women's History Review* 6:337–355.

Tobin-Schlesinger, Kathleen. 1997. "The Changing American City: Chicago Catholics as Outsiders in the Birth Control Movement, 1915–1935." *U. S. Catholic Historian* 15:67–85.

"To Get Rid of the Bolsheviks." 1918. *Freedom*, September.

"Tokyo Gov. Skips Eulogy to Koreans Massacred after 1923 Quake." 2017. *Mainichi*, August 25.

Tolstoy, Lev Nikolayevich. 1889. "The Kreutzer Sonata," trans. Louise and Aylmer Maud. Tolstoy Library OnLine. http://lol-russ.umn.edu/hpgary/russ1905/kreutzer%20so nata.htm (May 3, 2017).

Topp, Michael M. 2005. *The Sacco and Vanzetti Case: A Brief History with Documents*. Boston: Bedford/ St. Martin's.

Townley, Wayne C. 1948. *Two Judges of Ottawa*. Ottawa, Ill.: Egypt Book House.

"Tracing *One Package* – The Case that Legalized Birth Control." 2011. *Margaret Sanger Papers Project Newsletter*, Winter.

Train, George Francis. 1902. *My Life in Many States and in Foreign Lands: Dictated in my Seventy-Fourth Year*. New York: D. Appleton.

Tsuzuki, Chushichi. 1966. "Kotoku, Osugi, and Japanese Anarchism." *Hitotsubashi Journal of Social Studies* 3:30–42.

Tucker, Benjamin R. 1874. "An Open Letter to Francis Barry." *Woodhull & Claflin's Weekly*, November 21.

Tucker, Benjamin R. 1888. "Mr. Blodgett's Final Question" *Liberty*, April 28.

Tucker, Benjamin R. [1897] 2005. *Instead of a Book: By a Man Too Busy to Write One*. Reprint. New York: Elibron.

"Two Wonderful Women." 1872. *Woodhull & Claflin's Weekly*, June 1.

Tyler, Gus. 1995. *Look for the Union Label: History of the International Ladies' Garment Workers' Union*. London: Routledge.

Underhill, Lois Beachy. 1995. *The Woman Who Ran for President: The Many Lives of Victoria Woodhull*. Bridgehampton, N.Y.: Bridge Works Publishing.

Untitled News Item. 1872. *Woodhull & Claflin's Weekly*, April 6. [It begins "The legislature of California has presented ..." and is on p. 6.].

US House of Representatives. 1912. *"The Strike at Lawrence, Mass." Hearings before the Committee on Rules of the House of Representatives on House Resolutions 409 and 433, March 2–7, 1912*. Washington: Government Printing Office, April 4.

Valenza, Charles. 1985. "Was Margaret Sanger a Racist?" *Family Planning Perspectives* 17:44–46.

Vargas, Zaragosa. 2005. *Labor Rights are Civil Rights: Mexican American Workers in Twentieth-Century America*. Princeton: Princeton University Press.

Velasquez-Manoff, Moises. 2015. "Should You Bring Your Unborn Baby to Work?" *Atlantic*, March.

Verity, Oliver A. 1902. "News From Home," *Lucifer the Light Bearer*, March 20.

Wadland, Justin. 2014. *Trying Home: The Rise and Fall of an Anarchist Utopia on Puget Sound*. Corvallis: Oregon State University Press.

Waisbrooker, Lois. 1868. *Suffrage for Woman: The Reasons Why*. St. Louis: Clayton & Babington.

Waisbrooker, Lois. 1871. *Mayweed Blossoms*. Boston: William White.

Waisbrooker, Lois. 1875. "Introduction." In *Economic Science; or, The Law of Balance in the Supply of Wealth* by Joel Densmore. Boston: Colby & Rich.

Waisbrooker, Lois. 1890a. *From Generation to Regeneration: The Sex Question and The Money Power and The Tree of Life Between Two Thieves. Three Pamphlets on the Occult Forces of Sex*. New York: Murray Hill.

Waisbrooker, Lois. 1890b. Letter to the editor. *Lucifer the Light Bearer*, March 27.

Waisbrooker, Lois. [1893] 1985. *A Sex Revolution*. Philadelphia: New Society.

Waisbrooker, Lois. 1895. *Anything More, My Lord?* Topeka, Kan.: Independent Publishing Company.

Waisbrooker, Lois. 1896. *My Century Plant*. Topeka, Kan.: Independent Publishing Company.

Waisbrooker, Lois. 1897a. "A Last Word." *Lucifer the Light Bearer*, May 12.

Waisbrooker, Lois. 1897b. "Things as I See Them." *Lucifer the Light Bearer*, December 22.

Waisbrooker, Lois. 1897c. "Woman's Power." *Lucifer the Light Bearer*, April 21.

Waisbrooker, Lois. 1898a. "The Rainstorm Duck." *Lucifer the Light Bearer*, January 26.

Waisbrooker, Lois. 1898b. "Who Protects the Wife?" *Lucifer the Light Bearer*, December 3.

Waisbrooker, Lois. 1898c. "Woman's Source of Power." *Lucifer the Light Bearer*, April 20.

Waisbrooker, Lois. 1900. "Mediumship." *Lucifer the Light Bearer*, August 11.

Waisbrooker, Lois. 1902. "Expenses." *Clothed With the Sun*, April.

Waisbrooker, Lois. 1903. *Woman's Source of Power*. Denver, Colo.: R.A. Southworth.

Waisbrooker, Lois. 1904. "Another Woman's View." *Lucifer the Light Bearer*, August 18.

Waisbrooker, Lois. 1905. "Very Strange." *Lucifer the Light Bearer*, May 25.

Waisbrooker, Lois. 1906. "Eighty Years Young and a Human Dynamo." *To-Morrow*, October.

Waisbrooker, Lois. 1907. *Eugenics: Or, Race Culture Lessons*. Chicago: N.p.

Waisbrooker, Lois. 1910. "The Curse of Christian Morality." *American Journal of Eugenics* 3:25–29.

Wang, Shirley S. 2012. "The Genetic Ripple Effect of Hardship." *Wall Street Journal*, February 28.

Ward, Lucy. 2007. "Mother's Stress Harms Foetus, Research Shows." *Guardian*, May 31.

Wardhaugh, Jessica. 2009. *In Pursuit of the People: Political Culture in France, 1934–39*. London: Palgrave Macmillan.

Warren, Josiah. 1852. *Equitable Commerce: A New Development of Principles as Substitutes for Laws and Governments, for the Harmonious Adjustment and Regulation of the Pecuniary, Intellectual, and Moral Intercourse of Mankind*. Reprint. New York: Burt Franklin.

Warren, Josiah. 2011. *The Practical Anarchist: Writings of Josiah Warren*, ed. Crispin Sartwell. New York: Fordham University Press.

Warren, Mercy Otis. [1766] 1981. "To J. Warren Esq." In "The Private Poems of Mercy Otis Warren," ed. Edmund M. Hayes. *New England Quarterly* 54:206–207.

Warren, Mercy Otis. 1773. *The Adulateur*. Transcribed by Richard Seltzer. Boston: New Printing Office. http:www.samizdat.com/warren.adulateur.html (March 9, 2014).

Warren, Mercy Otis. 1775. *The Group*. Transcribed by Richard Seltzer. Boston: Edes and Gill. http:www.samizdat.com/warren.group.html (March 9, 2014).

Warren, Mercy Otis. [1788] 1888. *Observations on the New Constitution, and on the Federal and State Conventions. By a Columbian Patriot*, ed. Paul Leicester Ford. New York: N.p.

Warren, Mercy Otis. 1790. *Poems: Dramatic and Miscellaneous*. Boston: I. Thomas and E. T. Andrews.

Warren, Mercy Otis. 1805a. *History of the Rise, Progress, and Termination of the American Revolution*, ed. Lester H. Cohen. Vol. 1. http://oll.libertyfund.org/title/815 (January 7, 2013).

Warren, Mercy Otis. 1805b. *History of the Rise, Progress, and Termination of the American Revolution*, ed. Lester H. Cohen. Vol. 2. http://oll.libertyfund.org/title/696 (January 7, 2013).

Warren, Theodore. 1895. *Warren Genealogy*. Alfred, Maine: De Wolfe & Wood.

Waters, John J., Jr. 1975. *The Otis Family: In Provincial and Revolutionary Massachusetts*. New York: Norton.

Watson, D.R. 1978. "Clemenceau and Blanqui: A Reply to M. Paz." *Historical Journal* 21:387–397.

Weinberger, Harry. 1921a. "Repentance and Amnesty." *Freedom*, July.

Weinberger, Harry. 1921b. "Four Russians Need Help." *New Republic*, November 2.

Weir, Robert E. 2013. *Workers in America: A Historical Encyclopedia*. Santa Barbara, Cal.: ABC-CLIO.

Wenzer, Kenneth C. 1996. *Anarchists Adrift: Emma Goldman and Alexander Berkman*. St. James, N.Y.: Brandywine.

West, William. 1871. "The Memorial Demonstration of the International." *Woodhull & Claflin's Weekly*, December 23.

Wexler, Alice. 1989. *Emma Goldman in Exile: From the Russian Revolution to the Spanish Civil War*. Boston: Beacon.

Wilcox, Ben. 2012. "Published by Authority: A Case of Anonymous Authorship in Pre-Revolutionary Rhode Island." *Tempus* 13:1–16.

Willburn, Sarah A. 2006. *Possessed Victorians: Extra Spheres in Nineteenth-Century Mystical Writings*. Aldershot, UK: Ashgate.

Wills, Garry. 1978. *Inventing America: Jefferson's Declaration of Independence*. Garden City, N.J.: Doubleday.

Wills, Garry. 1984. *Cincinnatus: George Washington and the Enlightenment*. Garden City, N.J.: Doubleday.

Wolff, Cynthia Griffin. 1989. "Emily Dickinson, Elizabeth Cady Stanton, and the Task of Discovering a Usable Past." *Massachusetts Review* 30:629–644.

Wollstonecraft, Mary. [1792] 2008. *A Vindication of the Rights of Women*. New York: Cosimo.

Woloch, Nancy. 1996. *Women and the American Experience: A Concise History*. New York: McGraw-Hill.

"Woman's Rights – New Books." 1871. *Newark (N. J.) Register*. Reprinted in *Woodhull & Claflin's Weekly*, August 5 (and again on November 18).

"Woman Suffrage." 1871. *New York Times*, January 31.

"Women at the Polls: Their Experiences at New York." 1871. *Staunton Spectator* [Va.], November 14.

Wood, Gordon S. [1969] 1998. *The Creation of the American Republic, 1776–1789*. Chapel Hill: University of North Carolina Press.

Wood, Gordon S. 1992. *The Radicalism of the American Revolution*. New York: Alfred A. Knopf.

Wood, Janice. 2008. "Prescription for a Periodical: Medicine, Sex, and Obscenity in the Nineteenth Century, As Told in 'Dr. Foote's Health Monthly.'" *American Periodicals* 18: 26–44.

"Woodhull & Claflin." 1876. *Woodhull & Claflin's Weekly*, January 29.

"Woodhull and Claflin in Jail." 1872. *New York Daily Tribune*, November 4.

"Woodhull at Cooper Institute." 1873. *New York Herald*, October 18.

"Woodhull, Claflin & Co.: The Petticoat Financiers in Another Flutter." 1870. *Sun* [New York], March 26.

Woodhull, Victoria C. 1870a. "The Coming Woman." *New York Herald*, April 2.

Woodhull, Victoria C. [1870b] 1919. *The Memorial of Victoria C. Woodhull*. In *One Moral Standard for All: Extracts from the Lives of Victoria Claflin Woodhull (now Mrs. John Biddulph Martin) and Tennessee Claflin (now Lady Cook)*, by M.F. Darwin. New York: Caulon.

Woodhull, Victoria C. 1871a. "Are We a Christian People?" *Woodhull & Claflin's Weekly*, December 9.

Woodhull, Victoria C. 1871b. "Letter from Victoria C. Woodhull." *Woodhull & Claflin's Weekly*, December 2.

Woodhull, Victoria C. [1871c] 2010. "My Dear Mrs. Bladen." In *Selected Writings of Victoria Woodhull: Suffrage, Free Love, and Eugenics* by Victoria C. Woodhull, ed. Cari M. Carpenter. Lincoln: University of Nebraska Press.

Woodhull, Victoria C. 1871d. "Speech of Victoria C. Woodhull on The Great Political Issue of Constitutional Equality." New York: Woodhull, Claflin & Co. https://iiif.lib.harvard.edu/manifests/view/drs:2673042$1i (April 24, 2017).

Woodhull, Victoria C. 1871e. "The Fifteenth Amendment." *Woodhull & Claflin's Weekly*, December 23.

Woodhull, Victoria C. 1871f. *The Origin, Tendencies and Principles of Government*. New York: Woodhull, Claflin & Co. https://iiif.lib.harvard.edu/manifests/view/drs:2573503$2i (April 24, 2017).

Woodhull, Victoria C. 1871g. "The Right of Women to Vote – A Protest from Mrs. Woodhull." Letter. *New York Times*, November 8.

Woodhull, Victoria C. 1871h. "What is the Issue?" *Woodhull & Claflin's Weekly*, December 9.

Woodhull, Victoria C. 1872a. "An Unanswered Letter." *Woodhull & Claflin's Weekly*, January 20.

Woodhull, Victoria C. 1872b. "Journalistic Justice." *Woodhull & Claflin's Weekly*, March 16.

Woodhull, Victoria C. 1872c. "Letter of Acceptance." *Woodhull & Claflin's Weekly*, June 19.

Woodhull, Victoria C. [1872d] 2010. "Speech of Victoria C. Woodhull." In *Selected Writings of Victoria Woodhull: Suffrage, Free Love, and Eugenics* by Victoria C. Woodhull, ed. Cari M. Carpenter. Lincoln: University of Nebraska Press.

Woodhull, Victoria C. 1872e. "The Religion of Humanity." *Woodhull & Claflin's Weekly*, November 2.

Woodhull, Victoria C. 1873a. "Henry Ward Beecher." *Woodhull & Claflin's Weekly*, January 25.

Woodhull, Victoria C. [1873b] 2010. "Reformation or Revolution, Which? Or, Behind the Political Scenes." In *Selected Writings of Victoria Woodhull: Suffrage, Free Love, and Eugenics* by Victoria C. Woodhull, ed. Cari M. Carpenter. Lincoln: University of Nebraska Press.

Woodhull, Victoria C. 1873c. *The Elixir of Life; or, Why Do We Die? An Oration Delivered before the Tenth Annual Convention of the American Association of Spiritualists, at Grow's Opera House, Chicago, Ills.* http://www.iapsop.com/spirithistory/elixir_of_life.html (March 14, 2017).

Woodhull, Victoria C. 1873d. "The Impending Revolution." *Woodhull & Claflin's Weekly*, November 1.

Woodhull, Victoria C. [1873e] 2010. "The Scare-Crows of Sexual Slavery." In *Selected Writings of Victoria Woodhull: Suffrage, Free Love, and Eugenics* by Victoria C. Woodhull, ed. Cari M. Carpenter. Lincoln: University of Nebraska Press.

Woodhull, Victoria C. 1874a. "Mrs. Woodhull on Social Ethics. She Replies to a *Herald* Correspondent – The Real Meaning of Her Views of Free Love" *Woodhull & Claflin's Weekly*, December 12.

Woodhull, Victoria C. 1874b. "To Social Freedomists." *Woodhull & Claflin's Weekly*, December 5.

Woodhull, Victoria C. 1874c. "To Women Who have an Interest in Humanity, Present and Future – Personal Greeting." *Woodhull & Claflin's Weekly*, October 31.

Woodhull, Victoria C. [1874d] 2010. "Trial as by Fire; or, True and the False, Socially." In *Selected Writings of Victoria Woodhull: Suffrage, Free Love, and Eugenics* by Victoria C. Woodhull, ed. Cari M. Carpenter. Lincoln: University of Nebraska Press.

Woodhull, Victoria C. 1875a. "A Fatal Error of the Defense." *Woodhull & Claflin's Weekly*, April 10.

Woodhull, Victoria C. 1875b. "A Vision." *Woodhull & Claflin's Weekly*, August 7.

Woodhull, Victoria C. 1876a. "Journalistic Courtesy and Justice." *Woodhull & Claflin's Weekly*, June 10.

Woodhull, Victoria C. [1876b] 2010. "The Beecher-Tilton Scandal Case." In *Selected Writings of Victoria Woodhull: Suffrage, Free Love, and Eugenics* by Victoria C. Woodhull, ed. Cari M. Carpenter. Lincoln: University of Nebraska Press.

Woodhull, Victoria C. [1876c] 1890. "The Garden of Eden; or. The Paradise Lost and Found." In *The Temple of God; or, The Philosophy of Sociology*, ed. Victoria C. Woodhull and Tennie C. Claflin. London: N.p.

Woodhull, Victoria C. [1876d] 1890. "The Review of a Century; or, the Fruit of Five Thousand Years. A Lecture delivered at Boston, October 22nd, 1876." In *The Temple of God; or, The Philosophy of Sociology*, ed. Victoria C. Woodhull and Tennie C. Claflin. London: N.p.

Woodhull, Victoria C. 1890. *Humanitarian Government*. London: N.p.

Woodhull, Victoria C. 1892a. "A Declaration of In[ter]dependence." *The Humanitarian*, September.

Woodhull, Victoria C. 1892b. "Aristocracy of Blood." *The Humanitarian*, July.

Woodhull, Victoria C. 1892c. "Division of Labor." *The Humanitarian*, July.

Woodhull, Victoria C. 1892d. "Manifesto." *The Humanitarian*, July.

Woodhull, Victoria C. 1893. "Address by Victoria C. Woodhull (Mrs. John Biddulph Martin) at St. James's Hall, Piccadilly, 24th March, 1893" *The Humanitarian*, April.

Woodhull, Victoria C. [1894] 2010. "'And the Truth Shall Make You Free': A Speech on the Principles of Social Freedom." In *Selected Writings of Victoria Woodhull: Suffrage, Free Love, and Eugenics* by Victoria C. Woodhull, ed. Cari M. Carpenter. Lincoln: University of Nebraska Press.

Woodhull, Victoria C., and Tennessee C. Claflin. 1872. "An Open Letter." *Woodhull & Claflin's Weekly*, April 3.

Woodhull, Victoria C., and Tennessee C. Claflin. 1875. "An Appeal." *Woodhull & Claflin's Weekly*, November 13.

Wright, Julian. 2017. *Socialism and the Experience of Time: Idealism and the Present in Modern France.* Oxford: Oxford University Press.

Wu, Peichen. 2002. "Performing Gender along the Lesbian Continuum: The Politics of Sexual Identity in the Seitō Society." *U.S.-Japan Women's Journal. English Supplement* 22:64–86.

Wyman, Margaret. 1952. "Harriet Beecher Stowe's Topical Novel on Woman Suffrage." *New England Quarterly* 25:383–391.

Yelensky, Boris. 1958. *In The Struggle for Equality: The History of the Anarchist Red Cross,* ed. Matthew Hart. Los Angeles: Los Angeles Anarchist Black Cross. www.abcf.net/la/pdfs/layelensky.pdf (September 2, 2017).

"Yokohama Recalls Texts Describing 1923 'Massacre' of Koreans." 2013. *Japan Times,* August 29.

Youmans, Henry. 1899. "An Anarchist Colony." *Lucifer the Light-Bearer*, February 24.

Young, William, and David E. Kaiser. 1985. *Postmortem: New Evidence in the Case of Sacco and Vanzetti.* Amherst: University of Massachusetts Press.

Zagarri, Rosemarie. 1992. "Morals, Manners, and the Republican Mother." *American Quarterly* 445:192–215.

Zagarri, Rosemarie. 1995. *A Woman's Dilemma: Mercy Otis Warren and the American Revolution.* Wheeling, Ill.: Harlan Davidson.

Zimmer, Kenyon. 2010. "'The Whole World is Our Country': Immigration and Anarchism in the United States, 1885–1940." Ph.D. diss. University of Pittsburgh.

Index

Blatch, Harriot Stanton (daughter of
    Elizabeth Cady Stanton)   222
Blood, James (partner of Victoria C.
    Woodhull)   82, 85, 88, 89, 91, 92, 95
Bluestocking Society (Japan). *See Seitō-sha*
Blue Stockings Society (UK)   200, 201–202
Bloomer, Amelia   142
Bloomer costume   219
Bonaparte, Napoleon   101
Bonham's Case. *See Thomas Bonham v.*
    College of Physicians (1610)
Boswell, James   28
Bowers v. Hardwick (1986)   43
Boyesen, Bayard   246
Boyesen, Hjalmar Hjorth   246
Brandeis, Louis   272
Bread and Roses Strike   239, 292
Brest-Litovsk. *See* Treaty of Brest-
    Litovsk (1918)
British Coffee House, Boston   11
British Constitution   12
British Museum   96–97, 242
British Parliament   14, 28, 29, 245
Bryn Mawr College   285–286
Buchanan, Patrick J. "Pat"   257
Buford (ship)   277, 287
Burke, Edmund   28–29
Bush, George W.   90
Butler, Benjamin   100
Byrne, Ethel (sister of Margaret Sanger)   243

Cady, Daniel (father of Elizabeth Cady
    Stanton)   208
Cady, Margaret Livingston (mother of
    Elizabeth Cady Stanton)   208
Canadian Labour Congress   300
capitalism   35, 37–38, 66, 82, 117–119, 171–172,
    254–255, 267
Catholic Church   29, 60, 73, 108, 151, 195n,
    260, 261
Cato's Letters   35, 39–40
cats   49, 73
Chafee, Zachariah, Jr.   272–273
Champseix, Victoire Léodile Béra. *See* Léo,
    André
Chang, M. C. (Min Chueh)   245
chastity   143, 156, 199–200
Chatôt, Françoise   67
Chautemps, Camille   293

Chevalier, Lucien   277
Chicago anarchists. *See* Haymarket Tragedy
Chicago Convention of Spiritualists   105
Cicero, Marcus Tullius   37
Cincinnati, The. *See* Society of the
    Cincinnati
Cincinnatus, Lucius   45–46
civic humanism   35, 36, 37, 39, 42
Civil War, American   82, 120, 212
Claflin, Reuben "Buck" Buckman (father of
    Tennie C. Claflin and Victoria C.
    Woodhull)   80, 135–136
Claflin, Roxanna "Roxy" Hummel (mother of
    Tennie C. Claflin and Victoria C.
    Woodhull)   80, 136
Claflin, Tennessee. *See* Claflin, Tennie C.
Claflin, Tennie C.   79, 81, 82, 83, 85, 87, 88,
    91, 92, 93, 100, 106, 107, 123, 127,
    129, 133–158, 161, 198, 199
Clarke, John H.   272
Claverack College and Hudson River
    Institute   239
Clayton, Bertram Tracy   269
Clayton, Henry DeLamar, Jr.   268–271, 273
Clémenceau, Georges   59
Clews, Henry   95, 138, 140
Clothed with the Sun   161, 164
Coke, Edward   13
Colton, James   288
Columbia University   246
comfort women   198
Comité de Vigilance de Montmartre. See
    Vigilance Committee of Montmartre
Committee on Public Information   268
Committees of Correspondence. *See*
    Correspondence, Committees of
Comstock Act (1873)   163, 164, 181, 241
Comstock, Anthony   83, 113, 116, 146, 163,
    242, 261
Confédération générale du travail (CGT)   68,
    293
Confucius   90
Congress of Industrial Organizations
    (CIO)   304
contraception   178–179, 240–244, 245, 247,
    249, 254–255, 258–259, 261–262
Cook County Jail, Chicago   291
Cook Islands   157
Cook, Lady. *See* Claflin, Tennie C.

www.ingramcontent.com/pod-product-compliance
Lightning Source LLC
Chambersburg PA
CBHW070902030426
42336CB00014BA/2288